Catholics and Contraception

LESLIE WOODCOCK TENTLER

Catholics and Contraception

An American History

CORNELL UNIVERSITY PRESS

Ithaca and London

For my mother, Loula Martin Woodcock

First published 2004 by Cornell University Press

Printed in the United States of America

Library of Congress Cataloging-in-Publication Data
Tentler, Leslie Woodcock.
    Catholics and contraception : an American history / Leslie Woodcock Tentler.
      p. cm. — (Cushwa Center studies of Catholicism in twentieth-century America)
   Includes bibliographical references and index.
   ISBN 0-8014-4003-3 (cloth : alk. paper)
    1. Birth control—United States—Religious aspects—Catholic Church.
   2. Contraception—United States—Religious aspects—Catholic Church.
   3. Catholics—United States—History—20th century.   I. Title.   II. Series.
   HQ766.3.T44 2004
   241′.66—dc22   2004010278

Cloth printing   10 9 8 7 6 5 4 3 2 1

Contents

Acknowledgments

I owe debts of gratitude to a great many people. The largest is to Scott Appleby and the Cushwa Center for the Study of American Catholicism at Notre Dame, which Scott until recently directed. Cushwa (through the Lilly Foundation) provided the money that made a full year of sabbatical research possible and by means of its "twentieth-century Catholicism" project provided essential intellectual companionship. Special thanks go to the members of my Cushwa working group: Joseph Chinnici, O.F.M., Paula Kane, Maggie McGuinness, and Jim O'Toole. But thanks are owed to all participants in those lively Cushwa sessions.

Archivists and librarians are the patron saints of the historical profession. My heartfelt gratitude, then, for the various intercessions of Tim Cary (Archives, Archdiocese of Milwaukee), Joseph Casino (Archives, Archdiocese of Philadelphia), Kevin Cawley (Archives of the University of Notre Dame), Michael Connolly (formerly at the Paulist Archives, St. Paul's College, Washington, D.C.), Roman Godzak (Archives, Archdiocese of Detroit), Bro. Michael Grace, S.J. (Archives, Loyola University of Chicago), Barbara Henry and Brian Cardell (Rare Books and Special Collections, Mullen Library, Catholic University), Rev. Carl W. Hoegerl, C.SS.R. (Redemptorist Archives, Baltimore Province, Brooklyn, N.Y.), Robert Johnson Lally (Archives, Archdiocese of Boston), Tim Meagher (American Catholic History Research Center and University Archives, Catholic University), Rev. George Michalek (Archives, Diocese of Lansing), Rev. Roger Mercurio, C.P. (Passionist Provincial Archives: Holy Cross Province), Rev. Paul Nelligan, S.J. and Rachel Segaloff (Archives, New England Province of the Society of Jesus), Nicholas Sheetz (Special Collections Division, Georgetown University Library), Rev. Paul Thomas (Archives, Archdiocese of Baltimore), Jack Treanor (Archives, Archdiocese of Chicago), and the helpful if mostly invisible staff of the library at the Sacred Heart Seminary in Detroit.

Various friends and colleagues provided tips on archival resources and interview subjects, not to mention hospitality on sometimes lonesome research trips. Thanks especially to Patty Crowley for permission to use the Crowley papers at Notre Dame, for generous hospitality, and good conversation. Thanks as well to Rev. Steven Avella for helping me to negotiate Milwaukee, Rev. Robert Sullivan for providing interview contacts in Boston, and Rev. Rob Carbonneau, C.P. for providing information on his order's archival holdings. Peter Quint and Chris and Helen Kauffman were good companions in Baltimore; Rev. John O'Malley, S.J. provided hospitality in Boston; Bob and Helen Tentler did the honors in Chicago, as Kate Tentler did in New York. Ellen Skerrett, Steve Rosswurm, and Rev. Stanislaus Hajkowski generously shared archival and other sources with me. My colleagues at Catholic University and especially the members of the "Clio" working group on American Catholic history have been good intellectual companions, always willing to listen to just "one more thing" about Catholics and contraception.

The last-mentioned debts are those closest to my heart. I owe more than can be reckoned to the priests who agreed to be interviewed for this project. They brought a special grace to the research, as I hope the following pages will show. Thomas Tentler, for his part, has not only patiently borne the burden of a research-obsessed spouse but has lightened many of her own burdens. Cooking dinner, correcting my Latin, saving me from horrendous theological gaffes— Tom has been a rock. Our children—Sarah, Gregory, and Daniel—lightened my burdens, too, simply by growing, seemingly overnight, into exemplary young adults. They give me hope for the future, without which the writing of history would seem to have little purpose.

Abbreviations

AAB	Archives of the Archdiocese of Baltimore
AABo	Archives of the Archdiocese of Boston
AAC	Archives of the Archdiocese of Chicago
AAD	Archives of the Archdiocese of Detroit
AAM	Archives of the Archdiocese of Milwaukee
AAPhi	Archives of the Archdiocese of Philadelphia
ACUA	American Catholic History Research Center and University Archives, the Catholic University of America
ADL	Archives of the Diocese of Lansing MI
AFAP	Archives of the Franciscans of the Assumption Province, Pulaski, WI
APF	Archives of the Paulist Fathers
AUND	Archives of the University of Notre Dame
GULSC	Georgetown University Library Special Collections
Loyola	Loyola University of Chicago Archives
NCWC	National Catholic Welfare Conference
NESJ	Archives of the New England Province of the Society of Jesus
PPA	Passionist Provincial Archives: Holy Cross Province, Chicago
RAB	Redemptorist Archives: Baltimore Province

Glossary

Augustinian. A member of the Order of Hermits of St. Augustine, a men's religious order established in 1256 by Pope Alexander IV. Dedicated mainly to education and missionary work, the order is best known in the United States for founding Villanova University.

Benedictine. A monk or nun of one of the congregations following the rule of St. Benedict and devoted especially to scholarship and liturgical worship.

Capuchin. A member of the Order of Friars Minor Capuchin, which broke away from the Franciscans in 1525 to live a more austere life. The Capuchins have historically been one of the Church's largest missionary societies.

Carmelite. A member of the Order of Our Lady of Mount Carmel, founded in 1155.

Cistercian. A member of a monastic order founded by St. Robert of Molesme in France in 1098, to follow a more strict observance of the Benedictine rule.

Dominican. A member of the Order of Preachers, founded by St. Dominic in 1215. Dominicans have long been noted for scholarship—St. Thomas Aquinas was a Dominican—but the order is particularly dedicated to preaching.

Franciscan. A member of the Order of Friars Minor, founded by St. Francis of Assisi in 1205, or the Order of Friars Minor Conventual, which broke away from the parent body in 1415.

Holy Cross Father. A member of the Congregation of the Holy Cross, a religious congregation of men, established in France in 1837 and dedicated to missionary work and education. The order is best known in the United States for founding the University of Notre Dame.

Jesuit. A member of the Society of Jesus, a men's religious order founded by St. Ignatius Loyola in 1534. The order is especially known for missionary and educational work. Founders of numerous colleges and high schools in the United States, the Jesuits also publish the influential Catholic weekly *America*.

Judgment, General and Particular. The General Judgment, often called Last Judgment, takes place at the end of time, when Christ will return to earth to judge all humans who have ever lived. The Particular Judgment refers to God's judgment of the individual soul immediately after death. Separate mission sermons were usually devoted to the two forms of judgment, perhaps because of the different emotional responses that each evoked.

Novena. A prayer or prayer-service that extends over a period of nine days, usually said for a particular intention.

Oblate. A member of one of several Roman Catholic communities of men or women. In the United States, the term usually refers to a member of the Oblates of Mary Immaculate or the Oblates of St. Francis de Sales.

Passionist. A member of the Congregation of the Passion, founded in Italy by St. Paul of the Cross in 1721. The order is devoted chiefly to missionary work and the preaching of missions and retreats.

Pastoral letter. Written by a bishop to the laity and/or clergy of his diocese, a pastoral letter can address any issue that affects the spiritual life of Catholics. Pastoral letters directed to the laity are read at all Masses on a particular Sunday and usually published in the diocesan newspaper.

Paulist. A member of the Society of Missionary Priests of St. Paul, a men's religious order founded in 1858 by the American priest-convert Isaac Hecker. The order specialized in the preaching of missions from its inception; by the late nineteenth century it had embarked on mission preaching to non-Catholics as an innovative means of reducing ignorance of and hostility to Catholicism in the United States.

Precious Blood priest. A member of the Congregation of the Most Precious Blood, an association of secular priests living in community. Founded in Italy in1814, its principal purpose is the preaching of missions and retreats.

Redemptorist. A member of the Congregation of the Most Holy Redeemer, founded in Italy in 1732 by St. Alphonsus Liguori. The order is especially devoted to preaching, particularly the preaching of missions.

Sulpician. A member of the Society of Priests of St. Sulpice, a society of secular priests founded in France in 1642 by Jean Jacques Olier. The Sulpicians are dedicated to the training of men for the priesthood, and have served in this capacity in the United States since 1791.

Ursuline. A member of the Order of St. Ursula, the first community of women dedicated to the education of girls. Founded in Italy in 1535, the first Ursulines arrived in North America in 1639.

Vincentian. A member of the Congregation of the Mission, founded in France in 1625 by St. Vincent de Paul. The order is primarily devoted to missionary work and education. The first Vincentians arrived in the United States in 1867.

Catholics and Contraception

Introduction

It was after the birth of our fourth child that we seriously considered using a contraceptive. We had had no success with the rhythm method, nor had basal temperature readings given any marked indication of the time of ovulation. We found the idea of artificial contraception repugnant, and the resultant breach with the Church untenable. So we limited our relations severely during the following year, and our marriage suffered because of it. It was a period of fear and reluctance and we were not drawn closer for sharing it. During my last pregnancy I decided that I had no other choice but to use a contraceptive after the baby was born. I knew the consequences: that I would no longer be able to receive Communion, that I would no longer have Him to sustain me and that my own children would be the victims. Again, for me there was no longer a choice, no alternative, except abstinence, and that for me is unthinkable. Through it all I felt that I was disobeying the Church rather than God, but since God and the Church are synonymous to me, I felt that the Church could rightly deny me God. But I never truly believed that God would condemn me forever for my decision.

Mother of five to Pat and Patty Crowley, undated but 1965[1]

I have never resorted to artificial contraception. I know of Catholics who have; however, most of my friends have relied unsuccessfully on the usual so called 'natural' methods. We have, at last, been forced to twin beds. One priest suggested separate bedrooms which was absurd as I didn't have enough bedrooms for the children at the time, let alone one apiece for us. I have been frustrated beyond comprehension—at least twice on the brink of suicide. I am no longer the person I once was. I am torn most of the time. My conscience not allowing me to be disobedient to my authorities—my better judgment telling me it is not natural for married couples to live the way we have had to.

Mother of eight, West Virginia, to the editor, *Jubilee* magazine, undated but early 1964[2]

The present situation is an intolerable one. Confusion reigns among our people on this question, and it seems that confusion reigns among our priests. The more I read on this controversy, the more confused I become. In fact I find it increasingly difficult to give direction in the confessional, when the only solution I can propose is one I do not completely accept myself. If the present situation continues, I fear that I may face a time when my conscience will not allow me to give the only direction the Church allows.

Young priest, Baltimore, to Cardinal Lawrence Shehan, June 1966[3]

In the Seminary one of the arguments used against artificial Birth Prevention was reference to a list of physical and psychological ailments said to afflict those given to the practice, both in the mental and physical area, from nervous breakdown to horrible bodily disease, especially of the female. Truthfully in my observation of the last twenty-eight years I have not observed such results: rather, those seem to be more physically and psychologically affected who try to deal with the dilemma conscientiously in contrast to those who engage in the practice.

Pastor, Baltimore, to Cardinal Lawrence Shehan, May 1966[4]

These voices spoke, in the mid-1960s, for a majority of American Catholics. Probably half of all Catholic wives of childbearing age were by then making use of contraceptives, many with an apparently easy conscience.[5] But others were burdened by guilt, some of it intense; a few were so troubled by their behavior that they used contraceptives only intermittently. A substantial number of couples, moreover, were still unwilling to ignore Church teaching, which forbade all modes of regulating fertility but abstinence and the so-called rhythm method. The most conscientious in this regard, as well as those most prone to guilt, were typically devout.[6] Their difficulties in the realm of birth control were thus well known to parish priests, for whom the teaching on contraception posed increasingly onerous pastoral burdens. "This issue ranks number one in the problem category of confessional work," a Baltimore priest reported in 1966, "and as of late, thanks to the openness of our people, in conversations on the street and in the office."[7] The problem was obviously not new for confessors: the occasional priest reported trouble on this score even prior to the First World War. What was new in the mid-1960s was precisely "the openness of our people"—their willingness to testify publicly to their suffering, question the grounds on which the teaching rested, and plead, even argue, for change. For growing numbers of priests, this new lay assertiveness posed a radical challenge to pastoral confidence. "Our pious platitudes do not solve any problems," as a rueful Benedictine observed in 1965. "Couples are in agony."[8]

By the mid-1960s, then, the teaching on contraception had generated what can only be called a major crisis among American Catholics. Though the Second Vatican Council, which closed in 1965, had promulgated a startling array of reforms, it had spoken to the issue of family limitation in only the most peripheral way. But for most of the laity, no reform was more important than a change in the teaching on contraception.[9] An increasing number of priests agreed: "To my mind the future of the church as a great power for good is in the balance," as one pastor put it. "The laity must be taken 'off the hook' and if this is done, the confessor will be taken 'off the hook' also."[10] A papal commission, charged with review of Church teaching in the realm of family planning, continued to sit after the Council's close, which kept alive hopes for an eventual change in Church teaching—as well as fears in this regard. A sizeable minority among the clergy and a smaller but still significant portion of the laity opposed reform: the credibility of the Church's teaching authority was at stake, they believed, as was firm grounding for a genuinely Christian sexual ethic. But the tide of opinion by the mid-1960s ran powerfully toward reform. When Pope Paul VI reaffirmed the traditional teaching in the summer of 1968, he spoke to an American Church whose values and practice with regard to sex were in the first stages of something close to revolution.

A crisis of such magnitude was bound to affect more than the teaching on birth control, which for most Catholics after 1968 was simply a dead letter.[11] As conservatives had warned, the question of authority was centrally at issue. "To claim that Catholic teachings, even those contained in such official documents as an encyclical, can be flatly denied when circumstances warrant," in the prescient words of Franciscan father Aidan Carr, "is to tend toward vitiating the force of the Church's ordinary doctrinal function."[12] Many observers at the time failed to see, or perhaps to acknowledge, the degree to which these developments imperiled core beliefs. The effects in the realm of morality were evident to nearly everyone. If Catholics had in practice rejected a procreative norm for sex, then who—in the context of a vitiated teaching authority—was to guide the faithful when it came to such contentious issues as premarital sex, divorce and remarriage, homosexuality, and even abortion? And on what grounds might that vitiated authority speak to the moral dilemmas increasingly posed by medical science? Like their Protestant confreres before them, American Catholics after 1968 were more and more forced to confront modernity on the strength of their own internal resources. In the end it was individual authority that reigned supreme.

For many lay Catholics, this sea change in authority relations was fundamentally liberating. Those who lived through the 1960s often spoke of the laity's coming of age—of their having achieved adult status in the church. The metaphor is problematic, given its implications for earlier generations. But it points nonetheless to an important emotional truth. It was precisely in the context of birth control, an issue that intimately affected nearly all adult Catholics, that a remarkable generation—better educated and perhaps more devout than any before it—came to a sense of moral autonomy.

Circumstances were otherwise for the clergy: the birth control crisis and its protean aftermath meant for them a diminution of confidence and moral authority. It was lay experience, after all, that ultimately set the moral agenda with regard to birth control. A celibate clergy seemed more and more irrelevant to the debate, not only in the eyes of the liberal laity but of many priests themselves. Growing numbers of priests, indeed, found it hard to square their celibacy with the positive theology of marital sex that increasingly framed the debate. Did the celibate's moral witness not suffer by comparison to the other-centeredness of married love? Was the very ideal of celibacy not premised on a truncated, even damaging, view of the psyche? Young priests especially were more and more troubled by such doubts. The problem of birth control, moreover, was a principal factor in the declining frequency of confession, a trend that was evident by 1966. Most priests found deep satisfaction in their work as confessors, many regarding it as the most rewarding of their pastoral roles.[13] The near-collapse of that role—for such was the state of affairs by 1969—held potentially devastating consequences for clerical morale.

Nothing that happened in the 1960s was more decisive for the Church's future than this radical erosion of clerical confidence. Priests were resigning in unprecedented numbers by 1967, while seminary enrollments had already begun their precipitous plunge. The resulting shortage of clergy—something that has worsened steadily—led of necessity to the creation of numerous lay ministries and contributed to a general enhancement of lay authority in the Church. This authority was—and is—especially pronounced with regard to sexual morality. "Lay Catholics receive very little clear guidance on sexual matters from the clergy, who seem to be uncertain and indecisive and usually end by telling the laity to 'follow their own conscience,'" as the Jesuit Avery Dulles noted in 1993—an assessment encountered in recent years across the Church's political spectrum.[14] Things had been exactly the opposite prior to Vatican II: for the great majority of Catholics then, it was in the realm of sex that clerical authority was most pervasive and wielded with the most evident certainty.

The recent history of American Catholicism, then, can only be understood by taking birth control into account. That is a major reason for this book. But the story does not begin with the 1960s. Birth control has been a divisive issue in American Catholicism since at least the 1920s, when the teaching—itself of antique origin—began to assume a dominant role in American Catholic life. The story as it evolved in these years entailed great suffering, most of it unrecorded. (It was rare before the 1960s for lay Catholics to speak or write publicly about their experience of sex.) Many Catholics were spurred to complete or partial compliance with Church teaching by a literal fear of hell. At the same time, the story was one of pride and solidarity. Many laity admired their Church's increasingly lonely defense of a procreative sexual ethic. Many shared their clergy's anxieties when it came to emancipated views of sex. And a great many Catholics responded with a visceral surge of tribal loyalty when public proponents of birth control attacked the Catholic Church. The story was one of idealism, too, especially after the Second World War, when the teaching was increasingly presented in personalist terms and in a context of national prosperity. Young Catholics then, especially the best educated, were among the teaching's most fervent proponents, with birthrates exceeding the burgeoning national average. Aspiring to domestic sanctity, these young idealists won the admiration of numerous priests, who were thereby confirmed in their own commitment to a near-heroic sexual discipline. Undergirding it all was a devotional ethos that was at once hostile to sex and almost opulently sensual.

Thus this book takes for its purview the whole of the twentieth century. It assumes the centrality of birth control to a full understanding of Catholic culture in that century. It likewise assumes the complexity of that culture and the consequent complexity of the Catholic struggle with contraception and sexual modernity. The narrative, in short, goes well beyond a saga of oppression and ultimate emancipation. The book also assumes that this Catholic struggle had meaning not simply for Catholics but for the nation in which they constitute the single largest religious minority. Since this last assertion is apt to engender at least mild surprise, let me briefly explain the reasons why.

Earlier in the century, Catholics had allies in their resistance to a contraceptive ethic. No Protestant denomination in the United States gave a formal blessing to birth control prior to 1930; a conservative few failed to do so until the 1950s.[15] Catholics, however, were unique in the extent and duration of their prohibition, and in their cultural visibility. Few Americans knew, in the 1950s, that Missouri Synod Lutherans were still formally committed to a ban on contraception.[16] Nearly everyone knew about Catholic opposition. In the circumstances, Catholics enjoyed an odd sort of cultural authority in the realm of sex. This authority was most prominently exercised for essentially negative ends: by dint of its hierarchical organization and numbers, the Church could retard moves toward sexual liberalization, whether in the realm of popular entertainment or state and national law. It was exercised, moreover, at increasingly heavy cost. By the 1940s if not before, elite opinion was hostile to—and generally contemptuous of—Catholic assumptions about the role of sex in human life. But it is nonetheless important that these assumptions were part of an evolving national conversation with regard to the meaning of sex, which was simultaneously a conversation about gender and the parameters of selfhood. Catholic participation shaped that discourse in manifold ways, which in turn shaped private behavior and public policy. When Catholics ceased to speak with a single and distinctive public voice, as had already happened by the mid-1960s, the national conversation about sex was decisively altered. This too had consequences for public policy and private behavior.

So this book is not about Catholics alone, but about the American experience of rethinking sex in the twentieth century. To be sure, its contents deal mainly with Catholic realities: with the evolving rhetoric and logic attached to the prohibition on contraception, with the means by which the teaching was enforced, with the factors that made for incremental and eventually wholesale change. But the Catholics who lived this history were also Americans. As voters, consumers, and creators of voluntary organizations, they helped to shape an evolving national culture. So did their example as founders of families and the anchors of urban neighborhoods, a sentimentalized version of which was a staple of popular culture. Their Church's leaders, moreover, aspired to national influence: not even the most parochial wished the Church to be anything less than a force in the cultural mainstream. This meant of necessity a progressive engagement in the nation's emerging sexual politics. When it came to rethinking sex, in short, neither Catholics nor other Americans could proceed in isolation.

Appropriately, then, the narrative opens on a more or less ecumenical note. In the earliest years of the twentieth century, nearly all religious leaders were united in their formal opposition to contraception. Some certainly gave private sanction to contraceptive use in marriage, which a steadily falling birthrate suggests was already widespread in the American middle and upper classes. But no mainstream Protestant clergy openly endorsed the practice, frank discussion of which breached the canons of polite public discourse. A substantial if diminishing number, moreover, were vigorous opponents of what Catholic propagandists often dubbed a contraceptive mentality. Many Protestant clergy were uneasy, in some cases deeply alarmed, at the prospect of sex without reproductive consequences. Most Catholic leaders doubted the efficacy of the Protestant clergy's opposition and even, at times, its authenticity. Prior to the First World War, however, they nearly all assumed that opposition to contraception was a broadly Christian stance.

Catholic pastoral practice in these years reflected this fundamental confidence. Mission preachers, it is true, were worried even in the nineteenth century about what they saw as a disturbing increase in contraceptive behavior as well as abortion among Catholics.[17] As we shall see in chapter one, such preachers—Catholic versions of the itinerant Protestant revivalist—sometimes denounced these "detestable crimes" in appropriately graphic terms.[18] But even mission preachers were subject to cultural convention. Though they usually addressed congregations that were segregated by sex, they seldom spoke frankly about sexual sin when such congregations included both married and unmarried persons. (Such "mixed" congregations were generally the norm; only the Redemptorist Fathers, the best known and probably the largest of the mission-preaching orders, made routine provision in their missions for separate "state in life" instruction to the married and the single.) As for the parochial clergy, they almost never preached against contraception or abortion prior to the First World War. They were cautious in the confessional, too, seldom if ever questioning penitents about the sin of "onanism." Their reticence, like that of the missioners, was largely of cultural origin; the Catholic clergy were eminently Victorian in their codes of public speech and conduct. But the parish clergy, if not their missionary counterparts, apparently also believed that prevailing values would do the job of enforcement for them. It was not only Catholics, after all, who regarded contraception as "unspeakable."

Maintaining this posture of trust was increasingly hard in the wake of the First World War. The public silence on birth control had by then been decisively broken, and various factors pointed to an imminent cultural shift on the question. True, public championing of contraception was confined to the political margins, where it would mostly remain throughout the 1920s. But erstwhile Protestant allies were increasingly reluctant to do public battle against the pro-birth control forces. Such developments called for change in Catholic pastoral practice, or so it seemed to a relative handful of clerical reformers. Their efforts, which bore fruit unevenly, are the principal subject of chapter two. By the late 1920s, most American Catholics lived in an altered climate with regard to contraception. Reformers had by then produced a vigorous pamphlet literature on the subject, whose contents were more and more reflected in the Catholic press. Mission preachers were addressing the topic with unprecedented frequency and frankness. A portion of the laity had been mobilized for the first of many legislative battles over legal reform with regard to contraception. Still, many priests clung to older habits of reticence, and a good many Catholics apparently remained in what a gentle confessor might call "good faith" ignorance of the teaching.

The situation was fundamentally altered in 1930, as chapter three explains. The global depression which began in that year prompted change in a number of Protestant denominations, where tolerant silence on birth control gave way to cautious public endorsement of marital contraception. Partly in response to the Anglicans' "defection"—for so the matter appeared to Catholic leaders—Pope Pius XI issued *Casti Connubii,* his encyclical on Christian marriage, in the waning days of 1930. That document provided a comprehensive synthesis of Catholic teaching against contraception and directed the clergy to enunciate that teaching in clear and uncompromising terms, especially in the confessional. (It was widely regarded by Catholic authorities as an infallible statement, and so taught—prior to the 1960s—in Catholic schools and seminaries.[19]) The publicity attendant on the encyclical made it harder than ever for Catholics to plead ignorance of Church teaching. So did the increasingly heated secular politics of birth control, which were covered by an increasingly respectful press. Growing numbers of Catholics, moreover, faced confessors and preachers who felt obliged in conscience to enforce Church teaching, even at the risk of uncomfortable frankness. Younger Catholics by 1930 had for the most part been habituated to a regular reception of the sacraments; they were apt to have recourse to confession more frequently than their parents had done—as often as once a month and sometimes even weekly.[20] As such, they were arguably more vulnerable to clerical discipline and perhaps to increased scrupulosity, especially with regard to sexual sin.

American Catholics in the 1930s were a mostly working-class population, on whom the Depression bore with particular ferocity. Not surprisingly, their birthrate declined precipitously in the early years of the 1930s, as did the birthrate nationally. One can hardly imagine more difficult circumstances in which to enforce a ban on contraception. Many laity simply ignored the ban, at least according to their priests. But the psychological costs of so doing could be terribly high, especially for women. Many priests suffered, too, though they were not—like some laity—disposed to doubt the teaching itself. Still, they were often torn between their obligation to enforce Church teaching and compassion for the sufferings of a hard-pressed laity.[21] Some priests even worried that the teaching on birth control was generating the kind of anti-clericalism among American Catholics that had hitherto been characteristic only of Europe.[22]

It was in this crisis-ridden context that news of the so-called rhythm method was first promulgated. The theory of a monthly sterile period in the female was not new in the early 1930s—various nineteenth-century physicians had argued that such a period existed. But nineteenth-century theories were based on erroneous assumptions: most identified as the "safe period" precisely that time in the menstrual cycle when a woman is most likely to conceive. Thus few priests by the 1920s were commending "periodic continence" to their most troubled penitents, although it was licit for them to do so. Late in that decade, however, researchers achieved an accurate understanding of the human ovulatory cycle, which raised new hopes for the effectiveness of rhythm as a mode of family limitation. These discoveries—initially known only in scientific circles—were introduced to a broad American audience in 1932. That some priests publicly attributed these developments to a beneficent Providence suggests the extent of the pastoral problems by then attendant on the birth control question.

The secular politics of birth control were such by the 1930s that the nation's bishops were almost immediately made uneasy by public discussion of rhythm among Catholics. Many took steps to frustrate this, as chapter three explains. But if rhythm went "underground" in the mid-1930s, it did not cease thereby to play a role in Catholic pastoral practice. Indeed, it became increasingly central to that practice in the 1940s and 1950s, as we will see in chapters four and five. Not every priest gave an unreserved blessing to the practice of rhythm: as late as the early 1960s, there were those who regarded the method as permissible only in extreme marital circumstances. Most priests, however, welcomed rhythm as at least a potential solution to a pressing pastoral problem. Men like these ensured that Catholics would be widely familiar with the method, if less sure of its efficacy than many of the clergy, regardless of the hierarchy's strictures. Many of these same priests were freed, by virtue of their faith in rhythm, to embrace a positive view of marital sex—a subject on which a significant theological discourse was initiated in the 1930s. This initiative bore major fruit after World War II in such efforts as Cana Conference and the Christian Family Movement, and ultimately helped to pave the way for a wholesale assault on the Church's teaching with regard to contraception.

Chapters four and five deal with the 1940s and '50s. The pastoral burden with regard to birth control seems to have been lightened then, at least to a degree. A recovered economy and a rising birthrate made it easier, certainly in the psychological order, for priests to insist on the teaching. Still, birth control continued to be a major problem for confessors and a source of worry for those good pastors who knew that it kept a portion of the laity from regular reception of the sacraments. At the same time, the social disruptions attendant on the Second World War gave the teaching on contraception an enhanced legitimacy for nearly all priests and many of the more devout laity. It was not just the nation's bishops who were alarmed by increased divorce and the growing dominance of what looked to be a purely instrumental approach to the values that ought to govern sex. Catholics, moreover, were by the 1940s acutely conscious of standing alone in most of the nation's battles over law and sexual morality. (Those conservative Protestant leaders who agreed with Catholics on such questions were seldom disposed to cooperate publicly with a church that some still regarded as the Whore of Babylon.) In the circumstances, the teaching on birth control came for growing numbers of Catholics to stand for their Church's unyielding defense of Christian morals in an increasingly pagan world. It had also emerged by this time as a kind of tribal marker—a proud if onerous badge of Catholic identity.

Developments like these were reinforced in the late 1940s by a culture-wide romance with domesticity and a concurrent revival of religiosity across the confessional spectrum. They were also reinforced by a surge in enrollments at Catholic colleges, which was fueled in probably equal parts by the G.I. Bill and a rising tide of Catholic piety. In this altered national climate, young Catholics—especially the well educated—embarked with unprecedented enthusiasm on family founding, marrying earlier than their parents had done and typically bearing more children. They also bore more children than other Americans of their generation, with the college educated—in flat contradiction of demographic precedent—producing on average the largest families of all. This Catholic version of postwar domesticity was suffused with religious meaning and intensity. Young Catholics in this generation were sometimes more ardent than their priests when it came to defending the Church's ban on contraception. Their example alone lent legitimacy to that ban and boosted morale among the clergy, for whom its enforcement was still burdensome. Devout young parents, presiding over their growing broods with apparent joy and serenity, preached more eloquently to the community that watched them than the most accomplished sermonizer could do.

Under the tranquil surface of postwar domesticity, however, tensions persisted with regard to contraception and eventually began to intensify. By marrying so early, young Catholics of this generation virtually insured themselves maximal fertility. Even the most idealistic couples generally experienced financial and emotional strain after the birth of a fourth or fifth child, sometimes in as many years. College educated themselves in many cases, these parents expected no less for their children—and at a time when the cost of college was escalating rapidly. Nor were these couples immune to the vastly enhanced cultural authority of a mostly Freudian psychology. Catholics might proudly cling to their own high standards with regard to marriage, but when those standards required the exercise of essentially celibate virtues—as they sooner or later did—it was harder and harder to square those standards with the culture's assumptions about sexuality and marital health.

Still, the more overtly devout seem seldom or never to have had recourse to contraception: only 30 percent of Catholic wives admitted to such in a national study conducted in 1955.[23] Many of the "dissenters," moreover, appear to have had troubled consciences. Birth control figured prominently in confessions heard at Christmas and especially Easter, according to priests. This suggests that most Catholics making regular or intermittent use of contraceptives tried nonetheless to remain in at least nominal communion with their Church. Such confessions were often difficult for priests, who worried at length about recidivism with regard to birth control and were frequently vexed by hard cases. They were even more difficult for the laity. The shame attendant on confessing to sexual sin should not be underestimated, especially for penitents raised on preternaturally high standards with regard to purity. Questions of honesty entered in, too: Could a penitent claim in good conscience to have a firm purpose of amendment—necessary for receiving sacramental absolution—when she knew how likely she was to resume the practice of contraception? Could a penitent profess genuine sorrow for something that he might not regard as intrinsically wrong? Issues like these, addressed from a lay perspective, were seldom aired publicly prior to 1963. But they simmered beneath the deceptively bright surface of postwar Catholic life, and do much to explain the anger that increasingly characterized the debate over birth control in the mid-to-late 1960s.

That debate, and the anger which swirled around it, is the principal subject of chapter six. Catholic practice changed dramatically in this time of reform. But no change was greater, or more consequential, than the altered perspectives that Catholics increasingly brought to questions of sex and authority. In the process, as has already been noted, many laity came to a new sense of moral autonomy—a development that most, though not all, of them regarded as unambiguously positive. The clergy, however, had staked their lives on the certainties of the old moral order. Its collapse called into question not only their claims to moral authority but their competence as judges of the human condition. Even priests of long and successful tenure suffered painful bouts of self-doubt. "The question seems to be the difficulty in determining whether the current principles of thought are realistic and reasonable for human beings in today's world," as a Baltimore priest noted with particular reference to birth control. "One gets the feeling that the layman more and more regards the priest/confessor as an ogre—chained to traditional principles of theology with little regard for life in its raw reality."[24] The erosion of certainty in the moral order, moreover, was accompanied by—and often causally related to—widespread questioning of core religious precepts, especially by younger and more educated Catholics. The effect on many clergy was nothing less than devastating. By the mid-1960s, growing numbers were doubting the meaning, and not simply the efficacy, of their lives as priests.

Such developments among priests, as previously noted, were immensely consequential for the life of the Church. That is why priests' experience looms so large in a book whose subject might plausibly seem to be of significance mainly for the laity. "You cannot run an organization of a half billion people with a more than decimated and near-devastated work force," as Martin Marty pointed out in 1973. "The romantics say that the Church can make it without a clergy; this is the age of the laity. But how few all-lay entities in the Church survive!"[25] Priests figure prominently too because of their critical roles as apologists for, and enforcers of, the teaching on contraception. Their work as confessors was especially important; it alone does much to explain why the Catholic encounter with contraception differed so markedly in the twentieth century from that of even conservative Protestants. Priests are also the authors of, and often the audience for, probably a majority of the sources on which this book is based. Unlike the laity, who for decades maintained a public near-silence on the subject of contraception, priests as early as the First World War were approaching the issue with keen professional interest. To this end, they produced and consumed an increasingly vast pastoral literature. That literature, prior to the 1960s, is the single best means we possess for reconstructing the lay experience of coming to terms with birth control and sexual modernity.

Not that my sources are confined to pastoral literature—far from it. A surprising number of archival documents speak to the question of birth control, as does a printed literature aimed at a broad Catholic audience. Many of the archival sources address issues of pastoral practice. Others bear on the shaping of Catholic opinion with regard to contraception and related questions of sexual morality. Still others speak to the secular politics of birth control. This last-mentioned topic is not a central focus of the present narrative, but politics cannot be wholly ignored. Catholic political activity around the question of birth control reveals much about the mentality of a mostly clerical elite; it was also a means by which Church teaching was reinforced for a sometimes-wavering laity. In certain circumstances, moreover, such activity clearly worked to intensify Catholic tribal loyalties and exacerbate a sense of beleaguered Catholic separatism. This is nowhere more true than the 1948 Massachusetts referendum on liberalization of the state's Draconian law against medical prescription of contraceptives, which is discussed in chapter four.

Once we reach the 1960s, the available sources increase dramatically both in number and diversity. Lay voices come to the fore; the clergy speak with unprecedented frankness about their own difficulties with the teaching. These wonderfully rich sources do more than document an era of change; they speak—in sometimes heartrending accents—to the complexities of Catholic life and culture in the years just prior to the Second Vatican Council. Oral sources can do this, too, when used with appropriate care. Accordingly, I have spoken at length—and nearly always on tape—with fifty-six priests, who discussed with me their training in moral theology and their pastoral experience with regard to birth control. These men vary considerably in age—the oldest was ordained in 1938, the youngest in 1963—and in locale, though the majority come from the upper Midwest. Nearly all spent their careers in one of the following archdioceses: Baltimore, Boston, Chicago, Detroit, Milwaukee, or Washington, D.C. Most spent their careers primarily in parish work; some are veterans of family life ministry; several were, or are, professors of moral theology; two are bishops. In terms of ethnic origins, the group is diverse: the largest number identify themselves as Irish Americans, but nearly as many are of German or Polish ancestry while others claim French, Belgian, Italian, or Hungarian roots. Notwithstanding this variety, these priests described a training and practice that was, on the whole, remarkably similar. Ethnicity is obviously a critical variable in the history of American Catholicism. But it can be an elusive one, as the experience of my priest interviewees suggests and as we will have further occasion to explore.

I do not pretend that these priests are "representative" of any experience but their own. The group does not constitute anything remotely like a scientific sample; I typically located interviewees by asking priest colleagues or interviewees themselves for the names of likely prospects. Priests willing to talk to a laywoman about so delicate a subject were highly self-selected and generally liberal in orientation. Only a few were firm supporters of the doctrine enunciated in *Humanae Vitae,* the encyclical on birth control issued by Pope Paul VI in 1968. Even fewer, however, held radical views: many were troubled—some deeply so—by the current climate with regard to sexual morality. Still, the group was sufficiently liberal that I quickly decided against interviewing men who had left the active priesthood. (I hoped in this crude way to redress the political balance somewhat and permit moderate voices to be heard more clearly.) The usual distortions attached to memory, moreover, are probably exacerbated when the subject has to do with sex, not least because so much has changed in the realm of sexual values and practice. Most of my interviewees told a story of personal liberalization with regard to birth control; where I could compare that story to relevant documentary evidence, I nearly always found that the remembered process of liberalization had been accelerated—sometimes quite significantly. I suspect that this not surprising pattern is characteristic of many, perhaps most, of the thoughtful narratives I heard.

I have, accordingly, used my oral evidence with caution. But this book is much the richer for it. Thanks to my interviewees, I brought a more nuanced understanding to the documentary evidence, particularly with regard to questions of pastoral practice. As priests of long experience, they helped me to think more deeply about clerical self-understanding and supports for priestly morale and authority. Their most important contribution, however, was simply themselves: my informants were, to a man, gracious and intelligent; nearly all were widely read; most were psychologically acute. They had splendid senses of humor, too, usually of the dry variety. Any church that could draw such admirable souls to the celibate ranks of its priesthood was obviously doing something right. So my interviewees served to remind me—and there were many occasions when I needed this—that Catholic religious culture in its "unreformed" state was dense and supremely complicated: psychically rewarding as well as punitive, nourishing to the mind and senses as well as restrictive of the body, consoling as well as alienating. The Catholic encounter with birth control can only be understood in the context of this complex world we have lost—of the transcendent moments it afforded, the fears it generated, the bonds of human solidarity that it underwrote. This was a world simultaneously oriented to the Four Last Things—death, judgment, heaven, hell—and to the sustaining of a vibrant communal life.

Given the extent to which their collective spirit infuses this book, it seems right to give the final word to one of my priest informants. Monsignor William Sherzer was ordained in 1945 for the Archdiocese of Detroit. His first assignment brought him to St. Theresa's parish—then mostly lower middle class and, with about 3500 families, one of Detroit's largest. "It was a great place," as Sherzer recalls. "I have affection for it still."

For example, I remember an occasion when the young people came to me and they asked me if I would get up and say Mass for them at 5 o'clock New Year's morning [a holy day of obligation]. . . . They knew they were going to be up all night and they wanted to go to Mass. You know the size of St. Theresa's church—it seats about 1200 people, and I'd say that there were 1200 people at that Mass. All teens and twenties in their gowns and tuxes. . . . Nobody went to Holy Communion because you had to fast and they'd all broken their fast but I remember it as a dramatic example of the intensity of faith and Catholic esprit de corps, the loyalty at that time in history—that would have been around 1948 probably.

Monsignor Sherzer is not a man given to sentimentality or undue romanticization of the past. He spoke frankly in the course of our interview about the heavy psychological costs attached to the teaching on contraception. He rightly saw that those ardent young Mass-goers were integral to the story. As he himself explained: "You're dealing with a cultural phenomenon [that] you have to understand to understand the birth control thing."[26]

1

"The Abominable Crime of Onan"

Catholic Pastoral Practice and
Family Limitation, 1873–1919

Father Gaudentius Rossi (1817–1891) was a widely admired member of the Passionists—a men's religious order dating from 1721—and a veteran mission preacher. Presumably because of his reputation and thirty years' missionary experience, he was asked in 1875 to compile a set of teaching notes for a neophyte instructor of "Sacred Eloquence" at his order's Midwestern seminary. (That document, prosaically titled "Some Instructions about the Sermons, Meditations, and Catechisms Delivered by Our Fathers, in Our Missions," was still being used for teaching purposes at the turn of the twentieth century.) Father Rossi described in detail the course of a typical Passionist mission—a weeklong series of sermons and religious instruction. Tuesday evenings, as he explained at one point, ought normally to feature "a well prepared and powerful sermon on Mortal sin." This should be followed on Wednesday by a sermon devoted to its commoner, and hence most dangerous, manifestations.

Predictably, the Wednesday sermon dwelt extensively on sins of the flesh. "Lust the seven-headed monster, is producing terrible havoc amongst souls," Fr. Rossi informed the students, who faced the unenviable task of combating this monster from the pulpit. "Great prudence must be used in treating this delicate subject," Rossi cautioned, "but the demon of lust should be strongly attacked in all its manifold forms." That these should include the "private abuses of youth, which destroy body and soul" is hardly startling, still less so an "unwarranted freedom in company-keeping." Given the date, however, not to mention the heavily immigrant cast to the Catholic population, it is more than a little surprising to learn that Rossi was also concerned about family limitation. "The abominable crime of Onan (Gen. 3) in the marriage state, more common than many suspect, should be HINTED AT PRUDENTLY, and reprobated severely. There is need of this; but aged Missioners should be the ones to look after this matter."[1]

Religious leaders of every denomination in the last decades of the nineteenth century, and indeed in the first years of the twentieth, maintained a near-total public silence on the subject of contraception.[2] So Rossi's "instructions" provide rare and valuable access to a mostly hidden world of pastoral practice. But the document raises more questions than it answers. How well grounded were Rossi's fears? How widely were they shared among the Catholic clergy? Were there differences in this regard between diocesan priests and members of religious orders? Under what circumstances might the clergy preach against contraception, and how frankly? How aggressively might they question about so "delicate" a subject in confession? Did the sex of the penitent make a difference? Rossi's "instructions" do convey the deep suspicion of sexuality that underlay nearly all Catholic thinking and pastoral practice prior to the 1930s, and in many quarters for some years thereafter. But here too an unanswered question remains: How could so relentlessly negative an approach even to marital sex be remotely plausible to the laity?

It is the purpose of this chapter to probe these and related questions. We look first at what little is known, for the late nineteenth and early twentieth centuries, about fertility control and fertility values among the American Catholic laity. We look next at the range of clerical views with regard to sex and marriage. We then turn to the strategies used by the clergy to convey and enforce Church teaching on marital sex, looking successively at confession, the various forms of preaching, and premarital instruction. In terms of chronological time, the chapter covers nearly half a century: from the passage of the Comstock Act in 1873, which banned contraceptive devices and information from the U.S. mails, to the 1919 publication of an omnibus pastoral letter by the American bishops, in the course of which they made their first public statement in opposition to birth control. For practically the whole of this period, contraception remained an unmentionable topic in polite public discourse. Beneath the veneer of silence, however, important changes were occurring, not least among lay Catholics and the priests who served them.

Fertility Control: Lay Practice and Values

So little is known about this topic that we must operate mostly in the realm of informed speculation. Not much hard evidence bears on the subject, and even less comes from a lay point of view. The clergy who spoke to the issue—typically in literature meant for priests and seminarians alone—sometimes argued, especially prior to the First World War, that Catholics in the United States were significantly less likely than their European counterparts to know about, much less practice, family limitation. "Among us (in America) this plague does not have such ancient and universal roots as it does in other places," according to Father William Stang in 1897.[3] Father Stang, who taught at the American College in Louvain, obviously knew that birthrates were falling in much of Europe, including many of its Catholic regions—a phenomenon that typically dated from the 1870s.[4] Historically Catholic France led the way: declining fertility was evident there at the end of the eighteenth century and fell in the course of the nineteenth century even faster than in the United States. As early as 1872, when hardly any religious leaders were willing to speak publicly about such matters, a celebrated French Dominican was preaching against "sinfully restricted families" in his annual Lenten conferences at Notre Dame in Paris.[5] Even the most triumphalist Catholic could hardly attribute the French decline to that country's Protestants. But in the United States, where birthrates fell first and fastest among the more affluent sectors of the population, this was not difficult to do. "It [contraception] will be found among our Protestant fellow citizens," as the *Michigan Catholic* opined with typical optimism in 1893; "it will not be found among our Catholic fellow citizens."[6]

Even in the 1890s, however, it is clear that growing numbers of American Catholics were limiting their families. In terms of fertility, there were two distinct Catholic populations in the United States. The first was composed of recent immigrants, nearly all of them poor, and characterized not only by high rates of birth but also of infant and child mortality. The second, whose numbers were growing rapidly by the late nineteenth century, was native born and more or less assimilated. Particularly among the more affluent reaches of this second population, birthrates by the end of the century were in steady decline, as were deaths among the very young.[7] "In many cities the number of children per family among Catholics of the middle and comfortable classes is little more than half the average that obtained in the families of their parents," as Father John A. Ryan acknowledged in 1916.[8] A priest colleague some ten years later made telling use of successive federal religious censuses to document the declining Catholic birthrate and especially the impact on said rate of immigration restriction.[9]

We cannot assume that all, or even most, of these smaller families were the products of contraceptive practice. Late marriage was a means of family limitation for some Catholics—a pattern identified in an Iowa study as late as the 1920s.[10] And many seem to have endured at least periodic bouts of abstinence in the course of their marriages, prompted not only by the teaching of their Church but also by the shame that most Americans in these years attached to contraceptive devices. Some of these abstinent Catholics were probably attempting to achieve smaller families by means of "rhythm," but it is doubtful that many persisted for long. Their clergy, after all, were uniformly schooled in a physiological theory that identified the middle of the menstrual cycle as the time when conception was least likely to occur.[11]

In the circumstances and without late marriage, it was no mean feat to limit a family to four children—much less the two or three children increasingly found in middle-class households. A greatly reduced frequency of intercourse would have helped in this regard, particularly if a couple had abandoned all faith in the putative safe period. But it is hard to imagine that at least some couples were not at least on occasion driven to forbidden modes of family limitation. Contraceptive devices could not be openly advertised after the passage of the Comstock Act, which probably had the effect for a time of enhancing the shame that surrounded them. Such devices were not, however, hard to obtain, nor was information about them difficult to come by—at least for those who lived outside the immigrant ghettoes. Many Catholic couples would have had access not only to pessaries and douches but condoms as well.[12] And couples at every level of income and education could practice coitus interruptus. Priests who wrote on the subject of family limitation in the late nineteenth and early twentieth centuries appear to assume that this last-mentioned mode was fairly widespread. Their near-universal use of the term "onanism" alluded not only to the putative scriptural basis for the prohibition on contraception but to its equation, in the words of Father William Stang, with "voluntary pollution."[13]

A word is in order at this juncture about abortion, which in the middle decades of the nineteenth century was apparently quite widely employed as a supplementary means of family limitation.[14] Most contemporary critics of the practice associated it mainly with Protestants. But priests in the last decades of the century increasingly spoke of abortion as a Catholic practice, too, despite its status by then as a felony in nearly every American jurisdiction. Apparently at least some Catholics believed, in company with most medieval theologians, that ensoulment occurred only after two or three months' gestation—a notion supported by the then-popular assumption that a fetus in its initial stages was nothing more than inert matter. An early abortion, by such logic, was not necessarily gravely sinful, although few Catholics would have denied that some degree of moral wrong was involved. Many period priests believed that they faced an urgent task of re-education in this regard. "Let it be understood that the child has life and a soul from the first moment of its existence in its mother's womb," as the Redemptorist Joseph Wissel instructed his order's mission preachers in 1885.[15]

We do not know how frequently Catholics had recourse to abortion in the late nineteenth and early twentieth centuries, or which Catholics were most likely to do so. In the first decades of the twentieth century, the early proponents of birth control claimed that poor immigrant women sought abortions in disproportionate numbers. This seems probable, but it was perhaps less true in the mid-to-late nineteenth century, when better-off Catholics may have been more ignorant or fearful of contraceptive practice than those in later generations. In an abortion-permissive climate, even assimilated Catholic women may have turned to abortion as a remedy for family-planning lapses. Preaching a mission in Kalamazoo, Michigan, in 1885, a Redemptorist priest evinced no surprise at having heard forty-nine confessions of actual or attempted abortion—this in a "universe" of 1,303 confessions, probably close to half of them men's, and in a community with a large assimilated Catholic population.[16] But his experience also suggests that Catholics regarded abortion as matter for confession, as they did not invariably do with other modes of family limitation. Indeed, priests as late as the 1940s evinced deep frustration at the stubborn conviction of certain Catholics "that there is no sin in what they do before life begins," in the words of an anonymous Passionist, who was clearly referring to birth control. He had evidently met in the confessional with the argument that while abortion was surely sinful, marital contraception was not.[17]

Fertility and the values surrounding it are affected by economic status. Even the more affluent members of the Catholic population had, for the most part, only recently arrived at security. Many who inhabited the lower-middle class were by no means secure economically: a prolonged recession or loss of the principal breadwinner could easily result in poverty. This largely explains why so many Catholics remained deeply committed to an understanding of family that valued obligation over autonomy or individual expression. For adolescent sons and daughters, the ethic might prescribe early wage earning—with said wages belonging in whole or part to the family. For parents, it meant fidelity even to desperately unhappy marriages and an approach to marital sex that ultimately had little room for romance or sensuality. Most religiously engaged Catholics, in short, were in these years members of what Simon Szreter has aptly called a "culture of abstinence."[18] If those same Catholics sometimes defied the teaching of their Church with respect to family limitation and sometimes doubted the gravity of this behavior as a sin, they were still in fundamental agreement with their priests when it came to weighing the balance between individual desire and the common welfare. Almost none were prepared to argue for sensual gratification per se as a moral good.

The values enforced by this culture of abstinence did much to enhance the authority of the clergy when it came to sex. A priest's life clearly entailed a degree of sexual discipline that few lay Catholics would willingly embrace. Working-class males in particular were prone to regard the clergy as a kind of "third sex"—even as subversive of masculinity.[19] But working-class males were taught in the family the same hard lesson that they learned from their Church: in the world of the family economy, as on the road to salvation, the senses were always at war with the imperatives of security. As for women, the seeming harshness of the Catholic sexual ethic was probably mitigated, or at least rendered more comprehensible, by the evident protections it promised to family integrity. The woman "must be secure in her position, as wife and as mother," in the typical words of a Passionist sermon decrying divorce. "She must be queen in her own little home."[20] The laity and especially the males among them might resent their priests' teaching in the realm of sex; they might grumble against a celibate clergy's presuming to police the marriage bed. But the teaching had resonance, too, and precisely because it was not wholly alien.

Priests' Views on Marriage and Marital Sex

In the most general sense, Catholic priests were schooled to a positive view of marriage. As a sacrament, marriage was a continual means of grace for both partners, who were morally obliged to love one another and work for each other's earthly and eternal happiness. "Therefore one should not embitter the life of the other," as a Redemptorist artlessly wrote at the turn of the century. "On the contrary they should make it pleasant." Marriage, in an oft-invoked scriptural reference, was analogous to Christ's union with His Church. Spouses were thus bound to an ethic of self-sacrificing mutuality. "Therefore as you love yourself," in the words of the just-quoted Redemptorist with regard to husbands, "so love your wife. What you grant yourself—grant also to her. . . . Work—frugality—liberality—no avarice—[no] locking up the money bag as though the wife must beg her support from the husband."[21] As for marital sex, it was the means that God had chosen to people the earth and swell the hosts of heaven; the married couple, as moralists never tired of pointing out, were "co-creators" with God when their sexual union resulted in pregnancy. This fact alone endowed marital sex with an aura of holiness, presuming that the couple was willing to accept perhaps numerous children. And since frequent sex in marriage was believed to deter spouses from the grave sins of masturbation and adultery, willing payment of the "marital debt" was a moral obligation of both parties.

At the same time, priests were trained to regard sexuality as external to the moral self and powerfully subversive of it. Sexuality, in other words, was not integral to identity in any remotely positive way but evidence of our nature's fallenness. Thus the most perfect mode of existence was consecrated virginity. The great majority of people were not called to this state, and for them marriage was necessarily the better part. Marital sex, after all, was redeemed by its intimate connection to procreation—either actually or, in the case of the old or infertile, by analogy. But literature written by and for priests still invoked the ideal of "conjugal chastity." Father Thomas J. Gerrard was typical in his commendation of "conjugal restraint" as "one of the chief means to happiness proposed by the Church. . . . It would be very strange if in all the other animal tendencies she counseled moderation, and in this allowed unlimited indulgence."[22] It was not unusual for Catholic moralists even at the turn of the twentieth century to advise, though not to require, marital continence during Advent and Lent and at major Church feasts. Gerrard did so, as did the Redemptorist quoted above, who commended continence as well prior to receiving communion.

The Catholic clergy were not nearly as isolated in their views on sex as we might today imagine. Few Protestant clergy, and those typically of a radical stripe, were willing prior to the First World War to give public blessing to deliberately non-procreative sex. Most were silent on the subject, some for reasons of propriety but others presumably as a way of endorsing their parishioners' right to decide for themselves on this most intimate of questions. A growing minority of Protestant leaders, however, was sufficiently troubled by falling birthrates in the early years of the twentieth century to denounce contraception publicly. The Anglicans' Lambeth Conference in 1908 provides the period's most famous example—one which, though not canonically binding, had powerful moral import for Episcopalians in the United States. Despite evident dissent in the ranks of the lower clergy, the Conference expressed its alarm at "the growing practice of the artificial restriction of the family"—a practice denounced by the assembled bishops "as demoralizing to character and hostile to national welfare." Contraception, they asserted, was by its nature un-Christian—nothing more, indeed, than "preventive abortion." Its advocates ought to be prosecuted at law.[23]

But what of clerical celibacy? However troubled non-Catholic clergy might be at the prospect of widespread contraceptive use, few of them were celibates. Their own experience of marriage and parenting was likely to nuance their private views on marital sex and presumably their pastoral practice as well. Men like these could not look with equanimity on the probable consequences of endorsing birth control—many, perhaps most, were persuaded that such a step would weaken marriage and erode an essential ethic of self-discipline. Many had probably endured periods of abstinence in their own marriages, or employed contraceptives with distinct feelings of shame. Marie Stopes's correspondence with Anglican clergy in the early 1920s suggests that this was true in England.[24] Some were doubtless tormented by guilt over unruly sexual impulses. Conflicts like these might sometimes make for a less-than-empathetic pastoral posture when it came to birth control. But non-celibates were apt to know in their bones that the reality of marriage was more complex than theological dicta typically allowed. Marriage, in short, probably provided most Protestant clergy with an existential opening to other-than-absolutist views on marital contraception.

Even a celibate clergy possesses an intimate knowledge of family life. Priests are sons, siblings, and uncles, not to mention confessors. But a celibate clergy, particularly when its training begins in adolescence, is almost bound to experience sexuality as an unusually troubling and disruptive force. There is not much room for nuanced views when one's sexual impulses appear to threaten one's moral core and vocational identity. (Such distress would not be unknown among non-Catholic clergy, but apt for obvious reasons to be far less common.) For many priests, then, the anti-sexual elements in the Christian tradition, which were arguably strongest in its Tridentine Catholic incarnation, had particular resonance. Even licit marital intercourse was hard for at least some priests to envision as genuinely expressive of love and personality. The married "experience a feeling of shame when discharging their conjugal duties," as Father Joseph Frassinetti assured the readers of his popular manual for parish priests, though he was for his time a relative liberal on questions of sexual sin.[25]

As for non-licit marital intercourse, this provoked language among priests that was frequently—though not invariably—more redolent of shame and disgust than that employed by their Protestant counterparts. (Conservative Lutherans produced in these decades some remarkably vigorous invective on the subject of family limitation.[26]) Contraception "strikes at the very root and sacredness of life, and transforms the home into a mere brothel," in the typical phrasing of an Augustinian priest in 1918. "So-called good and devout Christians spend most of their lives in the commission of that most heinous of sins"—for which, in his view, the Great War was God's retribution.[27] That contraceptive marital intercourse was analogous to prostitution seems to have been an especially popular argument, not peculiar to Catholics but enduring longer among them. A Passionist sermon on the Last Judgment warned those guilty of this sin that their "scandalous immoralities" would be "dragged out of the dark, and thrust glaring into the view of the universe"—that "their long career of race suicide, or rather, marriage prostitution, [will be] boldly staged before the gaze of heaven and earth."[28] Indeed, this sin was worse than prostitution, according to a later Passionist sermon, and worse perhaps than incest or murder. God killed Onan, as that preacher pointed out, but not Lot or Noah or even Cain.[29]

The more extreme language in this vein was typically produced by priests in religious orders. It was they, as previously mentioned, who were principally charged with preaching frankly on sexual sin. Given the certainty of eternal punishment, it was clearly one's duty to preach on this subject as arrestingly as possible. But differing modes of priestly life probably played a role as well. Though some religious order priests were stationed in parishes, others lived at far greater remove from the laity. Chief among them were seminary-based moralists and mission preachers. Both groups typically resided in quasi-monastic settings; both were shielded, by the very nature of their work, from sustained contact with lay Catholics. Mission preachers, indeed, were regularly cautioned against any sort of fraternizing with the laity in the many parishes they visited. Their very remoteness was thought to enhance their reputation as confessors.[30] The parish-based clergy, by contrast, lived in close proximity to the people they served. And no matter how gentlemanly his self-conception and demeanor, the model pastor was still expected to know his people well.

In the circumstances, it seems likely that most parish priests possessed a more intimate knowledge than many religious of the human complexities surrounding the sin of contraception. This is emphatically not to say that they took the sin itself lightly; too much in their own formation militated against this. But they had ample cause to be grateful for conventions that kept them from preaching on marital contraception or even from close questioning on the subject in confession. Unable or unwilling to be proactive in this regard, those same clergy were almost forced to assume "good faith" on the part of most laity who employed forbidden modes of family limitation. (Such persons, most of whom probably assumed that Church prohibitions in this regard were less than absolute, would be "materially" guilty of a serious sin, but not "formally" so. This meant in the practical order that their souls were not in immediate danger.) "We prefer to think that they are obstinately unconvinced rather than that they sin grievously and repeatedly with their eyes open," as John A. Ryan put it in 1916—a position, interestingly, that seems to have been widespread among the French clergy in the nineteenth century.[31] It was precisely "our acquaintance with many of these families" that had brought Ryan to this conclusion.[32]

There was a clear division of labor, then, when it came to the teaching and enforcement of Church doctrine on family limitation. Mission preachers, nearly all of them members of religious orders, took the leading role—though it was of necessity an episodic one in any given parish. Few parishes had missions more than once every two or three years; in some they occurred at five or occasionally ten-year intervals.[33] Parish priests in theory played a supporting role, but most were quite passive in this regard prior to the 1920s. Many persisted in a passive mode even for some years thereafter. Such passivity was, to be sure, increasingly hard to defend: evidence of Catholic contraceptive use mounted steadily in the early years of the twentieth century, as of a growing if still-unacknowledged cultural acceptance of the practice. Still, customary ways were hard to abandon, perhaps especially for older men, whose roots were deep in a culture of sexual reticence. Parish priests, moreover, had reason to fear estrangement from many of their people should they opt for a more aggressive stance. Such estrangement was likely to undermine, even to reverse, the progress made by American priests in bringing substantial numbers of the laity to a more disciplined religious practice. This achievement was not so secure or of such long standing as to be casually tested.

Confession

Every confessor at the turn of the twentieth century was heir to a prudential ethic when it came to sexual sin. One had to avoid scandalizing penitents; one had above all to avoid inadvertently instructing them in sins about which they were ignorant. "There is a subject in which the confessor's caution can hardly be excessive, and that is impurity," as one widely read moralist put it. "Better to fail in the material integrity of the confession than in prudence."[34] Authorities certainly existed who advised a more vigorous stance; mission preachers were especially apt to be schooled by them. But most priests were taught to opt for caution, and nowhere more so than with regard to marital sex. Detroit's Bishop Caspar Borgess, for example, simply followed a ruling of the Sacred Penitentiary in Rome when he warned his clergy in 1882 against close questioning in the confessional about contraception.[35] Beyond the welfare of the penitent was that of the confessor himself: imprudent questions about impurity might stimulate sinful desires of his own, especially when put to women.[36] And such questions were widely believed to keep Catholics from receiving the sacrament of penance, at least on anything approaching a regular basis. "Parish priests who dislike the milder opinions almost invariably find their confessionals deserted," as Father Frassinetti warned.[37]

Catholics are required by canon law to confess at least once a year, something that was customarily done during the season of Easter. Most priests by the late nineteenth century were urging a more frequent regime on their people: the ordinarily observant ought to confess at least four times a year, while the pious were encouraged to monthly confession.[38] There is evidence as early as the 1890s of success in this regard: growing numbers of parish societies, for example, were by then requiring of their members a minimum of four confessions annually. By the second decade of the twentieth century, Catholic schools nationally were instructing a whole generation in the practice of monthly confession.[39] But many Catholics even then continued to confess at Easter only. This was particularly true of recent immigrants and especially the males among them. There were, in addition, unknown numbers who failed for many years to confess at all. Persons in this situation had, according to Church law, ceased to be Catholics. They remained nonetheless a concern for priests and a factor in thinking about pastoral practice.

What amounted to a nascent crusade for more frequent confession, then, seems to have strengthened a tradition of pastoral prudence, at least among the parish clergy. But if priests were mostly disposed to discretion, they clearly believed that more frequent confession would lead to a greater scrupulosity about sexual sin. The penitent who confessed only annually was typically depicted as ignorant of even the basic requirements of religion. "Very many have no idea of the manner in which they should examine their consciences," according to the Passionist Gaudentius Rossi, "and consequently their confessions are very imperfectly made."[40] Reports from the grassroots sometimes bear him out. Preaching a mission "in the slums of New York" in 1884, Rossi's confrere Xavier Sutton found "the work in the box . . . very hard. The last night for the men two of them began to fight in front of my box, because one went ahead of the other."[41]

Some of those who confessed once a year doubtless prepared conscientiously; perhaps there were those for whom the very infrequency of confession prompted deeper-than-usual introspection and prolonged searching of the heart. Priests themselves, accustomed to confessing weekly, naturally found it hard to allow that virtue could bloom in such thin sacramental soil. But annual confession may in fact have encouraged a certain independence when it came to clerical authority. A Detroit priest, ordained in 1938, remembers from his early years of ministry a stubborn male remnant who continued the practice of annual confession. Some of "those old Belgians and Italians"—in the words of my informant—presented a year's worth of sins with remarkable dispatch: "Same as last year, Father."[42] Perhaps they were largely indifferent to the sacrament and ignorant of the moral law; perhaps they were motivated by fear or shame. In either event, these penitents did their manful best to avoid self-disclosure and clerical judgment.

Indeed, it makes sense to assume that more frequent recourse to confession generally resulted in enhanced authority for priests and the moral code they embodied. No matter how gentle the confessor, the ritual still entailed its own brand of humiliation. A confessor judged as well as absolved. And because many—probably most—confessions centered on sexual sin, the status of one's judge as a presumably inviolate celibate lent a particular asymmetry to the encounter. "Confession is certainly a medicine," as John Montgomery Cooper conceded in a 1916 sermon, "it may be looked on with anything from stern repugnance to mild dislike."[43] Frequent confession, moreover, presumably disposed the penitent to a closer internal monitoring of thought and behavior. Those who confessed only once a year could hardly have lived in constant fear of mortal sin and the dangers of sudden death and hell. Their God had of necessity to be One for whom the intent to confess at the traditional season would be sufficient for salvation. Those who confessed more frequently—and the norm for the most pious Catholics would eventually be weekly—had the psychic space for a more acute anxiety and a more exacting God as well. So late-nineteenth-century priests were probably right: more frequent confession, even in a context of clerical reticence when it came to certain matters, was apt to result in a heightened consciousness of sin and greater deference to a clerically defined morality. The outcome has obvious relevance for the problem of marital contraception.

The clerical reticence just invoked was apparently characteristic of the entire period under discussion—as apt to be found among parish priests in 1915 as in 1885. It simply reflected the substance of most priests' training as confessors. (The situation among mission preachers was different, as we shall shortly see.) We cannot be certain that every priest acted as he was taught. But it seems unlikely that significant numbers chose to ignore the counsels of their elders or the authority of the moralists whose texts they absorbed in seminary. Their formation placed so high a value on obedience that improvisation was hardly an option, especially with regard to sexual teaching. We can thus look with reasonable confidence to the most widely read manuals of pastoral theology for standard practice in confession, at least when it comes to the parish clergy. Read in seminary and consulted thereafter, such manuals summarized the reigning approach to moral theology and embodied the seasoned wisdom of admired older priests.

Given the advice of the manualists, it would have required something close to an oppositional personality for a parish priest to have routinely questioned penitents about family limitation.[44] "In the matter of vile sin, it is better to be deficient in questioning than to scandalize the penitent," warned the influential Father Stang. "With married people one must never even mention the conjugal debt unless there is grave reason."[45] Father Stang's manual did address the problem of contraception, though like virtually all his contemporaries he veiled his brief remarks in the decency of Latin.[46] Moralists writing even twenty years earlier sometimes failed to mention the subject at all. Father Aloysius Roeggl, whose manual dates from the mid-1870s, advised his priest readers to "admonish" married penitents with regard to their state in life. But nowhere in the script he provided was fertility restriction even obliquely addressed.[47] His single invoking of Onan's punishment had reference to masturbation rather than contraception, a subject Roeggl did not discuss. Joseph Frassinetti's mid-century manual was equally silent on the topic.

By the early years of the twentieth century, some manualists were making room for confessors' suspicions about contraception and for penitents who might seek advice on the matter. But here, too, the counsel of prudence prevailed. "He can, perhaps, in quite a general way, ask a wife if she has been obedient to her husband in all her duties, or if they have lived their married lives in a truly Christian manner," as Caspar Schieler quite typically advised. "If anything *in conjugali debito* has really taken place, opportunity is given to the penitent of saying so himself, and then it is for the confessor either to investigate further, or to instruct, which should, however, be generally done in only a few words."[48] (That the wife was evidently the marital partner to whom such questions might be put is a subject to be taken up shortly.) Should a penitent ask directly about matters relating to marital sex, the confessor ought to respond but without "saying more than is necessary. . . . To explain in greater detail what things are licit or illicit to the married partners may be equally dangerous for the confessor as for them."[49] Father Frederick Schulze agreed. If married penitents asked about the conjugal debt or "other questions dealing particularly in base matters," he wrote in 1906, the confessor should answer "briefly and with the maximum caution, and only to that which was asked, never anything more."[50] A penitent whose language the confessor spoke imperfectly—and such were not uncommon in this period—presented particular problems; the subtleties necessary to any discussion of marital sex would be for all practical purposes impossible. The Paulist Joseph McSorley assumed that penitents like these required utmost pastoral caution. His 1916 bilingual guide to the hearing of Italian confessions contains no questions at all about marital sex. The appended glossary does include the Italian word for "abortion" and the verb "to withdraw"—the latter a term with possible contraceptive reference. But it does not otherwise equip the priest to respond to a penitent's questions about family limitation.[51]

In the circumstances, one can readily see how even quite devout laity might remain in "good faith" ignorance when it came to the teaching on contraception. "Some Catholics have been able to persuade themselves that contraceptive practices are not necessarily sinful, at least in certain extreme cases," as John A. Ryan acknowledged in 1916. Ryan blamed the problem in part on "the wrong notions prevalent among their non-Catholic neighbors" and in part on "the inherent moral difficulties of the situation."[52] But he blamed confessors, too: their reticence simply encouraged Catholics in erroneous thought and behavior. (Interestingly, Ryan's own teaching notes for his courses in moral theology at St. Paul's Seminary in Minnesota paid scant attention to contraception, though he taught at that institution until 1915.[53]) Ryan was ready by 1916 to endorse a more proactive stance, and not only in the confessional. He ultimately played an important role in what would be a significant reform of pastoral practice with regard to family limitation. But this took years. A more typical voice of the period belonged to the moralist Antony Koch. A confessor was obligated to instruct all his penitents in "the truths necessary for salvation and the more important duties of life," Koch acknowledged. Not every penitent, however, was in practice a candidate for such instruction. "When a penitent is invincibly ignorant in regard to some of these duties, the confessor should not instruct him unless he has good reason to think that his advice will be heeded, lest what was purely a material sin should become a formal sin. The same rule holds good whenever there is reason to apprehend that instruction of the penitent would result in quarrels, enmity, scandal, or other serious evil."[54] Father Koch most surely did not intend to excuse or encourage what he would have called the sinful abuse of marriage. But he hewed so tenaciously to a prudential ethic that the effect may have been just that.

Presumably conscious of the strictures under which the parish clergy labored, the various mission-preaching orders took a harder line. This seems to have been especially true of the Redemptorists, one of the largest of these orders in the United States. "The confessor . . . is very frequently required to inquire into this thing," as Joseph Wissel noted with regard to the sin of what he invariably called onanism, "for out of one hundred married people scarcely five or six are immune." Wissel, who wrote in the mid-1880s, was paraphrasing an Italian moralist. But he did not doubt that these observations applied equally to the American scene. It was true, he conceded, that penitents often claimed to believe that marital onanism—by which Wissel probably meant coitus interruptus—was not gravely sinful. The confessor, however, was to have none of it. "If the confessor examines the condition of his onanistic penitents he will easily perceive and understand that the ignorance in which they are enmeshed is vincible and culpable, because they always have at least some confused grasp of the evil of onanism. Therefore, as often as they assert that they are ignorant of the evil of so great a sin, they are not to be listened to, for they deceive themselves."[55] Redemptorist confessors were also expected to question penitents about abortion, at least when there were plausible grounds for so doing.[56] But given the order's deep distrust of human nature, the simple fact of a penitent's being married might be so construed.

Whether confessors from other mission-preaching orders were equally proactive is difficult to say, although most would surely have been so by the 1920s. The Jesuit F. X. Weninger, who preached hundreds of German-language missions in the United States, recommended to his confreres so forthright a sermon on marriage in 1885 that one can hardly imagine his being delicate in the confessional.[57] But Weninger, who like Wissel produced an authoritative mission handbook, did not in his handbook urge Jesuit confessors to interrogate penitents with regard to family limitation. He seemed to assume, however, that the subject would surface in confession—presumably at the initiative of the penitent who, responding to a hard-hitting mission sermon, would all too often, pace Wissel, justify his conduct by a specious claim to "good faith ignorance." Again, the confessor was to have none of it. "Is that a serious sin, you ask? That I certainly did not know. Friend, that does not excuse you—that is a foolish evasion. That which one never sees an animal do, and for which one would feel shame if others knew about it—that you didn't recognize as evil?"[58] Was Weninger endorsing a regime in confession that was notably less intrusive than what Wissel prescribed for the Redemptorists? One could presumably make such a case, but the dangers of overstatement are obvious.

If the Redemptorists were in fact distinctive, it was only a matter of degree. Every order that preached missions addressed the problem of sexual sin more explicitly than the parish clergy and regarded the willingness to do so as a principal raison d'être of the missioner's calling. So the mission confession took place in a markedly different atmosphere than its parochial counterpart—one that generated different expectations for both confessor and penitent. The anonymous mission preacher whose late-nineteenth-century prayer book included an examination of conscience for a general confession—the kind that a lapsed or indifferent Catholic would be encouraged to make at a mission—asked directly about both contraception and abortion.[59] (I have found only one other printed "examen" prior to the 1920s where either question is addressed.[60]) The priests of his unidentified order were presumably accustomed to ask the same in at least some confessions. And in the early 1920s, the Paulist Walter Elliott included "birth control" among the sins which justified a confessor's taking additional time with a penitent, even in the busy context of a mission.[61] The Paulists were for many years notably more circumspect than the Redemptorists when it came to preaching on family limitation. But Elliott's counsel, taken from his missioners' manual, suggests that as confessors the Paulists were both direct and frank. Since Elliott was reflecting on long-standing practice in his order, the Paulists' frankness in confession presumably predated the 1920s.

Mission confessors do not appear to have made distinctions based on the sex of the penitent. Women were apparently to be questioned as directly as men, even with regard to sexual sin. The parish clergy, by contrast, were encouraged by several weighty authorities to a practice inflected by gender. It was true, these authorities conceded, that the hearing of women's confessions was hazardous to a priest—"the most dangerous and fatal rock which the minister of God has to encounter in the stormy sea of this world," as Father Frassinetti put it.[62] But women were more dependably devout than men, and far more likely to come regularly to confession. "In church men are shy and timid; they feel more comfortable in the rear than in front; they come in last and leave first," in the words of the authoritative Father Stang. "Women, on the contrary, push themselves forward in church as if they owned it." Precisely because of this, priests should strive to make men's confessions as non-alienating as possible. Have a separate confessional exclusively for men, Stang recommended, and on crowded occasions hear their confessions first. "Make them feel that you consider it a privilege and pleasure to hear the confessions of men."[63] So despite the dangers attendant on speaking of sex to female penitents, it made sense to address to them any hard counsels on marital sex that circumstances might require. Hence Father Schieler's advice to confessors: should it be necessary to question or admonish with regard to "marital chastity," do so to wives rather than husbands.[64]

Nineteenth-century authorities evidently did not regard women as the more culpable sex when it came to family limitation, perhaps in part because coitus interruptus was so widely assumed to be the principal method. When Covington's Bishop Camillus Maes issued a pastoral letter in 1890 that dealt in part with the evils of contraception, his warning against the practice was addressed solely to men.[65] (Maes was the only American bishop, to my knowledge, to have spoken publicly on the subject in the nineteenth century.[66]) But by the early years of the twentieth century, Catholic leaders and moralists increasingly spoke of women as the primary instigators of contraceptive practice. "No doubt many women thoughtlessly discuss this subject among each other," Baltimore's Cardinal Gibbons told the New York *World* in a remarkably frank

1907 interview. "It is not unusual, in all probability, for older women to advise their younger sisters, who are about to assume the relations of wifehood, not to bring children into the world for a few years, but to 'have a good time and travel.' This instruction that has been given the young wife is probably without the knowledge of the husband."[67] Gibbons nowhere indicated that he had Catholic women specifically in mind; like many of his Catholic contemporaries, he liked to associate birth control with presumably Protestant "society women." Period sermons, however, suggest that growing numbers of priests saw Catholic women as tainted, too. "The modern up-to-date girl or woman pride themselves [*sic*] on knowing all the different tricks and expedients whereby they may escape the results of conjugal intercourse and shirk the burden of child bearing," according to a Passionist mission sermon probably dating from 1915.[68] A 1913 clerical journal commended to its readers a sermon on marriage that seems to hold women largely responsible even for male-controlled modes of family limitation. (The context makes clear that this is indeed the author's reference.) "Sometimes, in order to please his wife, a man allows himself to violate the commandments of God or of the Church. No one can serve two masters, and he ought to offend his wife rather than sin against God."[69]

Views like these reflect a growing clerical anxiety, broadly evident in the early years of the twentieth century, over women's autonomy and the increasing sexualization of popular culture. "Why do wives rebel against the rule of husbands as the natural heads of families?" a Jesuit asked in 1917 in the telling context of a speech that deplored the falling birthrate.[70] Not every priest would have put the sentiment so bluntly, but it was widely shared. So too was distress at the contemporary dance craze, the content of popular music and fiction, and especially the movies. An Ursuline sister summed matters up neatly in 1919 with particular reference to this last-mentioned innovation. "Do you know that your daughters, taught by the exciting school of the picture-screen, are half-convinced already that 'love' justifies anything?" she asked a putative audience of Catholic mothers. "That 'a woman has the right to live her own life' as she pleases?"[71] Women's dress was also cause of increasingly frequent clerical complaint, some of it extreme. "The outrageously immodest dress of modern women has broken down the line of demarcation between the pure Christian lady and the harlot," according to a Holy Ghost father in 1913—sentiments that contrasted sharply with the 1896 musings of Father William Stang: "Americans have little to complain of on the score of modesty in dress. Nowhere in the world is Christian decorum better observed in this respect than in America, especially with ladies."[72] A western Michigan priest in 1907 even found ominous import in the popularity of the teddy bear. "The very instincts of motherhood in a growing girl are blunted and oftentimes destroyed if the child is allowed to lavish upon an unnatural toy of this character the loving care which is so beautiful when bestowed upon a doll representing a helpless infant," he informed his congregation.[73]

Reinforcing such anxieties was the prominence of women as leaders in the nascent movement to legalize contraceptives. The flamboyant Margaret Sanger, who emerged as a national figure in 1914, was for Catholics a particular bête noire. Any woman who selfishly refused to bear numerous children, in the typical view of a Detroit Jesuit, "places Mrs. Sanger on a pedestal and makes that woman's diabolical doctrine an article of her own profession of faith."[74] Gender tensions are palpable here. For many Catholics, including priests, class tensions were at work as well. Women active in the pro-contraception cause were often portrayed by Catholic spokesmen as hostile to working-class folkways and values. "Hysterical club-women," according to a Passionist sermon, "are daily committing in secret against God detestable and heinous deeds, and then they try to sop their uneasy consciences by excessive display of public zeal against the petty vices of the laborer and the poor, zeal against those who drink beer, smoke cigarettes, or play ball on Sunday."[75] The result in at least some clerical cases was a near-virulent misogyny, particularly apt to surface in mission sermons. Even those many priests who kept their emotional balance were increasingly distressed, as the young century progressed, by what they saw as betrayal by the hitherto more docile sex. These emotions infected preaching, especially of the mission or "occasional" variety.

Preaching

Parish priests prior to the 1920s almost never preached on abortion or contraception, though the likelihood of their so doing increased somewhat during the period under study. (The earliest non-mission sermon text I have found that addresses family limitation dates from 1896.[76]) When they did make reference to these highly charged topics from the pulpit, it was only in oblique and euphemistic terms. The typical Sunday congregation included both sexes, all ages, the married and the single. Given period conventions, a priest could not in such a setting speak frankly about sexual sin; there was also the danger of instructing less-worldly members of the congregation in sins hitherto unknown to them. "Especially dangerous . . . are those subjects which are apt to draw the will of man into sin, for instance graphic descriptions of various vices, too plain a description of secret sins and of the excuses and means which sinners adopt," according to Father Frederick Schulze in 1906.[77] The Sunday sermon, moreover, was often a hurried affair; many priests at low Masses dispensed with the sermon entirely. And since no dioceses in this period prescribed a standard course of sermons, most priests would have no cause to speak even once a year on a subject like marriage.[78] "Many Sunday sermons are on the Gospel of the day, and are prepared in ten minutes, if prepared at all," acknowledged

Bishop Francis C. Kelley, reflecting on the doleful state of Catholic preaching even in 1929. "Dogmatic instructions are not sufficiently insisted upon."[79]

The occasional parish sermon on marriage would certainly have denounced divorce in clear and uncompromising terms, as well as the hazards of mixed marriage.[80] It would probably—though not invariably—have emphasized the blessings attendant on numerous offspring, by which period preachers often meant at least eight children.[81] Less frequent were references to marital chastity, since this skated close to the sexual edge. "Bring to the marriage a pure and holy intention," advised an unusually direct 1908 sermon text. "Come to it with passions under control and evil habits aside. 'Unhappy those,' says Pope Gregory XVI, 'who enter upon the married state from merely earthly motives, or for sensual gratification, and do not think of the graces and mysteries which this Sacrament confers and represents.'"[82] Very few priests ventured further. Only one text from the principal homiletics journal of the period came close to addressing birth control in unmistakable terms: "People have a very mistaken idea of marriage who complain of having children," according to this 1913 sermon, "and still worse are those who are ready to enjoy the privileges of married life but not its burdens."[83] Words like onanism, contraception, and birth control, however, did not appear in the journal prior to 1924.[84] Father John Montgomery Cooper, author in 1923 of one of the earliest Catholic pamphlets against contraception, was sufficiently worried by 1916 that he drafted a Sunday sermon on "Race Suicide." The notes for this sermon are remarkably frank for the time. Cooper denounced both abortion and contraception in straightforward language and addressed the arguments most commonly offered in support of the latter. Neither poverty nor ill health on the part of the mother, he asserted, could justify contraception; marital continence was difficult but not impossible; justice required a family wage rather than a weakening of the laws against birth control. Penciled at the top of the manuscript, however, are the words "not preached."[85]

Priests who preached missions were notably freer than their parish counterparts. They typically addressed same-sex congregations: most orders allotted a mission's first week to women and the second to men. A very large parish might merit a mission of four-week's duration, with congregations segregated not only by sex but also by marital status. Mission preachers, moreover, were transients in the parish; they did not have to live with whatever resentment their hard counsels might prompt, or worry about the consequences. Indeed, dispensing hard counsel was for them a principal source of identity. "They are powerful preachers," wrote the Paulist Walter Elliott of his missionary confreres, "confessors as indefatigable as they are kindly; priests full of energetic zeal, moving in disciplined accord against vice. The call they address to the people is the peremptory one: 'Do penance, for the kingdom of heaven is at hand.'"[86] A Dominican contemporary seconded him: "In the mission sermon there is place for the fiery denunciation of sin, for the exposure of its enormity; there is opportunity to drive home in a practical way the rugged truths of Christ."[87]

For all their greater freedom, many mission preachers were surprisingly reluctant to speak frankly about contraception, at least before the early years of the twentieth century. This was sometimes even true of abortion. (The Redemptorist Order, as we shall see, was an exception on both counts, as was Jesuit Father F. X. Weninger.) Father Gaudentius Rossi may have summoned his fellow Passionists, or at least the "aged" among them, to rail against "the abominable crime of Onan" as early as 1875. But I have found no Passionist sermon texts on this topic from before 1900. Among the Paulist Fathers, a preaching order established in the mid-nineteenth-century United States, no extant sermons of this sort predate the early 1920s.[88] Many Paulist missions were apparently preached to congregations of both sexes, which doubtless explains at least part of that order's reticence. But Paulists early in the century steered clear of birth control even when speaking to same-sex groups. Father James Gillis, for example, thundered mightily against fornication in a mission sermon preached to men, probably in 1907. He spoke with particular frankness about prostitution: "Who worries about the eternal destiny of the one he has chosen as a partner to help him shatter the commandment of God? All that a man knows is that his passions were rising; he could not or would not exercise self-restraint; he sought and found a poor creature whose body and soul were to be had for hire—he satiated his lust, he went his way." Gillis said not a word, however, about abortion or contraception.[89]

Every religious order has an ethos of its own—a distinctive rhetoric and sense of purpose. So it is hardly surprising that the various mission-preaching orders should differ in their approaches to so controversial a topic. The Paulists, proud of their native roots and relatively liberal on social questions, envisioned their work in terms of Americanization. They strove to make Catholics into good Americans and, equally important, to persuade the nation's Protestant majority that the two allegiances were fully compatible. Perhaps their relative restraint as preachers deferred to what they assumed were mainstream sensibilities. The Redemptorists, by contrast, saw their work in terms that were intensely eschatological: their primary mission was to preach the terrible reality of eternal punishment. (Not that the Paulists would in these decades have disputed this terrible reality; the issue is one of preacherly style rather than theological substance.) The Redemptorists, moreover, had inherited from their founder the practice of giving "state in life" instruction to the married and the single, though St. Alphonsus Liguori had provided such only to women. But by the late nineteenth century, the order routinely gave instruction of this sort to men as well. A typical Redemptorist mission had time set aside—Tuesday evenings were usual—for separate preaching to married women, single women, married men, and single men. "These instructions are to be given to each class alone," as Father Joseph Wissel explained, "that the preacher may have more freedom in expressing himself on matters which those not belonging to that state of life need not or should not hear."[90]

Prominent among these "matters," at least for the married, were abortion and the various modes of contraception. (Redemptorist "state in life" instructions to the single do not mention birth control prior to the 1930s.[91]) "It is well known how modern society regards matrimony," according to Father Wissel in 1885, "and what horrible abuses are made of it, to the great detriment of souls and the ruin of society itself. These false notions have taken possession of the minds of all classes of people. It may be safely said that the abuse of marriage is the chief cause of the other kinds of immorality deluging the world at present."[92] Not even Father Wissel, however, thought that such preaching would be easy. "The missionary who gives these instructions should be a man of mature age, great experience and gravity of deportment." He should choose his words with utmost care: speaking "superficially" about sinful means of fertility control "is tantamount to saying nothing; saying too much gives scandal."[93] But the risks attendant on such preaching were as nothing compared to the gains. Countless souls were at stake, and the nation's future, too. Children born despite their parents' efforts at contraception were apt, in Wissel's view, to be sickly and prone "to most unnatural excesses of lust even in their infancy."[94] Then there were the "thousands" of infants rescued from spiritual as well as physical death in abortion, which Wissel evidently believed was widespread even among Catholics. Those "who, in consequence of the words of the missionary, are allowed to live long enough to receive baptism, will forever bless him who deterred their parents from murdering them before birth."[95]

Wissel's manual for Redemptorist preachers included model texts for "state in life" instructions, as did an 1885 mission handbook published in German by the Jesuit F. X. Weninger. Neither Wissel nor Weninger's sermons were particularly graphic, at least by the standards of later mission fare, but they were for the period remarkably straightforward. "Married people begin to live in a bad state as soon as they begin to wish to have no more offspring, or not so soon, or not in so rapid succession; and yet continue to live as usual in regard to their marriage privileges," in the words of Father Wissel. "A shocking crime in this respect is the direct exclusion of offspring, or the limiting of its number, by positive means. . . . But a worse crime is the willful murder of the poor child before it is born, by procuring an abortion—or by bringing on a miscarriage."[96] Both Wissel and Weninger knew the predictable justifications for family limitation: "We cannot support a numerous family. . . . The woman is sickly. . . . We do not want to be burdened with many children." Their rejoinders were equally predictable: God will provide; this life is short and a time of probation; virtue yields a reward that lasts for all eternity.[97] As Father Weninger noted, moreover, sins against nature were often punished in this life as well as the next. "Perhaps your wife will die earlier because of it, or God will send you a sickness—or a misfortune, like your business failing, or the death of a child who would otherwise have been a support in your old age."[98]

Wissel's Redemptorist contemporaries seem to have taken his counsels to heart. (I have found too few Jesuit sermon texts from the nineteenth century to comment on Weninger's confreres.) At least some Redemptorists preached "state in life" instructions to the married that were considerably more vigorous than the model text Wissel provided. Father Michael Burke, who died in 1891, was firm in his insistence that the primary end of marriage was procreation, the frustration of which "brings ruin and desolation upon society and [a] fearful curse upon the married man or woman in life and the torments of an eternal hell on the other side of the trace." To prevent one's wife from conceiving was "a detestable crime," according to Burke's text, which had evidently been drafted with a male audience in mind. "The brute, why did he marry, if he did not wish to take upon himself the consequences of married life?" Procuring an abortion was still worse, "even in the first moment of conception."[99]

A few Redemptorists were prepared, even in the nineteenth century, to condemn abortion in sermons addressed to the single as well as the married. A usual venue was the standard mission sermon on the Last Judgment. Father W. M. Brick preached such a sermon in the mid-1880s, presumably many times over. Among the condemned, Father Brick told an audience that surely included both the married and single, were "those who destroyed infants even before birth . . . they are guilty of the sin of murder before God, who sees even all that is most hidden." Other sins against impurity also figured prominently in Brick's version of the final reckoning, as did sins of anger and economic injustice. "There also will be many a liquor-seller who has made money by causing the damnation of other men." But he spoke not even an indirect word against contraception, which was evidently in 1887 too delicate—and doubtless too dangerous—a subject for an audience with unmarried members.[100]

By the early years of the twentieth century, however, growing numbers of mission preachers were opting for greater frankness, and outside the context of "state in life" instruction. A Passionist sermon on the Last Judgment, probably dated shortly after 1900, made explicit if passing reference to birth control before unleashing a wave of invective against abortionists—"those criminal operators, who for a handful of bloodmoney [*sic*] slay millions of the unborn, who with their murderous wrenches crush like eggshells the tender souls of innocent generations." The Judgment sermon, standard to nearly all missions, was a popular vehicle for inveighing against sins of the marriage bed precisely because such sins were so private. Even secret sins would be revealed at the final Judgment for all the world to see. (A sermon on the Last Judgment, in the view of the Paulist Walter Elliott, was especially apt "for the women's week, as it strongly develops the motive of shame."[101]) Where will abortionists hide on that day? asked the Passionist quoted above. What of "their clients and accomplices"—many of whom have passed their lives as ostensibly respectable women and men? "How they shall hang, pilloreed [*sic*] before the universe, and branded with the Herods and Neros, while that long line of their sickening, surgical butcheries shall be paraded before the wide-staring eyes of all the nations."[102]

A subsequent generation of mission preachers would routinely apply rhetoric of this sort not only to those who procured abortions but also to those who practiced contraception. But if prewar sermons were typically more restrained when it came to birth control, their emotional logic was much the same. Mission preachers played skillfully—if somewhat heavy-handedly—on shame, guilt, and fear, typically in equal measure. The all-seeing God was a favorite trope: "eyes that have never slept, they burn like coals of fire into the very soul of the sinner," in the words of the Paulist James Gillis.[103] One's most secret sins could not be concealed from eyes like these. Those who had recourse to abortion were menaced by the wraithlike spirits of their murdered children, which swam into view as the sinner was dying or appeared as their parents'— more commonly, their mothers'—accusers at the last Judgment. "On the whole she was looked upon as an ordinarily good woman," as a Redemptorist sermon on death began. But now she is haunted by her sins. "She recalls the many crimes committed under the sacred veils of matrimony; how she refused to bear the burden of married life, though she always enjoyed its privileges. Yea, perhaps as she lies there she becomes conscious of having sent a child into eternity before the waters of Baptism flowed over its head. She never confessed it, and now, there it is before her dying gaze."[104] A Passionist sermon from 1910 used similar language with regard to couples who engaged in contraception. "The house of the guilty couple is a haunted house. . . . It is haunted by the spirits of children that might have been, but were not allowed to be. These spirits will stand before the guilty couple on the dreadful day [of] Judgment. These spirits will accuse them before their Maker and their Judge."[105] Death was always the subtext—the grim reality that gave special point to sermons on sexual sin. "There now lies prostrate on the couch that lump of flesh—that instrument of sin, already fast decaying," in the words of a Redemptorist text. "Behold the worms are fast eating away every particle of rotten flesh, that yet sticks to the bones. You can hardly discover of that body the shape and form that it once had of which it was so proud."[106]

Sermons like these were clearly meant to generate fear—of death itself and certainly death in mortal sin, of public shaming, of judgment and hell. But missions were also designed to alleviate fear; they invariably climaxed in a tenderly evocative sermon on the mercy of God. And if mission confessions were reputed to be more searching than the usual variety, mission confessors were also determined to leave no sinner unforgiven. "Confessors should seldom or never fail to give absolution," as Father Wissel told his Redemptorist brethren. "A penitent's coming to confession in the context of a mission is powerful presumption in his favor."[107] Absolution, however, required a firm purpose of amendment on the part of the penitent—a sincere determination to avoid a particular sin and its occasions. This was often hard to achieve in the realm of marital sex. An unidentified Passionist betrayed the frustration that many of his confreres clearly experienced with what the manuals called "recidivists." "Therefore I say to all married people, keep yourselves clean from a heathen generation in order that you may not perish with it," as he told a mission congregation, probably in 1915. "Don't profane your holy matrimony with practices which fill heaven with disgust and hell with chuckling grin[s]. . . . But if you will not do that, if you will persist in your nefarious onanism, then for heaven's sake don't come up to this altar seeking communion, or make any more sham promises in confession. Better to go to hell with the instruments of your perdition than try to drag down Christ's all holy body with you."[108] Anger like this left little room for the mercy of God, no matter how eloquent a mission's closing sermon. It was an early signal, too, of how cruelly divisive an issue contraception would ultimately be for Catholics.

The newly public politics of birth control probably account in part for a sermon like the one just quoted. That a topic which "common decency should prevent people even from mentioning," in the words of one Detroit priest, was suddenly being debated in public shocked many Catholic clergy and caused them great anxiety.[109] "In Philadelphia last week," as the *Michigan Catholic* noted uneasily in 1916, "a speaker was almost crushed by an ignorant mob, in their desperation to get Birth-Control literature, which was freely circulated."[110] Given the altered circumstances, at least the occasional parish-based priest was willing to speak to the issue with unprecedented frankness, usually in the context of sermons delivered outside of Sunday Mass. A Lenten lecture at Detroit's Jesuit parish in 1919 excoriated contraception and, typically for the period, directed much of its fire at women. The "modern Herodias," in the words of Father John McClory, "pleads health and the fear of death as an argument against the creation of new lives; arrogates to herself God's exclusive right of birth-control; imagines that quality and numbers in the matter of offspring are irreconcilable; [and] says that income is not adequate to the needs of a large family." Nor did he hesitate to denounce Margaret Sanger by name, clearly assuming that all in his audience were familiar with her work.[111] That the audience was mixed in terms of sex and marital status makes his plain speaking all the more remarkable.

A particularly arresting example of such "occasional" sermonizing dates from 1916. Father Reynold Kuehnel, a diocesan priest from Michigan, had by then embarked on nationwide preaching to the men of the Holy Name Society. (The Society, which was at the time enjoying rapid growth in the United States, brought men to communion on a monthly basis and encouraged them to witness publicly to their faith and especially against blasphemy.) Among the talks that Kuehnel regularly delivered to Holy Name gatherings was "The Right to Life." It begins with an unusually direct attack on what later generations of Catholics would call a contraceptive mentality: "Most decent men take pride in having large families. Still there are those who have been brought in contact with worldly people, men who think they are privileged to dictate how many children, or rather, how few children, they will want to have." Only God has the right to decide the size of a family, Kuehnel reminded his hearers: "It never can be a question for a husband and wife to decide, nor for neighborhood clubs to discuss." He then condemned women who "fear to lose their charm and youthfulness if they give birth to children" and men who worry about the costs of supporting them. Men like these "prefer murder to being fathers." Although the talk has up until this point clearly had reference to family limitation in a general sense, the rest is given over to a diatribe against abortion.[112] Did Kuehnel believe abortion to be the principal means by which period Catholics were limiting their families? That seems unlikely. I suspect, rather, that like most priests of his generation he found it far more difficult to speak about contraception than abortion. The sense of shame associated with contraceptive devices and behaviors was for such men so intense that straightforward talk about their employment was probably in many cases psychologically impossible. And unlike most of their Protestant counterparts, these men had no personal experience of marital sex to give the problem of contraception a genuinely human dimension.

The effect in Father Kuehnel's case was, rhetorically speaking, a near-conflation of contraception and abortion. There may well have been those in his audience who understood him to say that contraception was murder. Certain preachers in the 1920s would in fact make this claim, and in unambiguous terms. That contraception is tantamount to murder is a position with venerable roots in Christian theology.[113] But since at least the mid-eighteenth century, it had rarely featured in Catholic sermonizing and virtually never as a determinant of penitential practice.[114] Caught in a rising panic over what appeared to be growing cultural tolerance of birth control, priests like Father Kuehnel so upped the rhetorical ante that they fell prey—however briefly—to a true theological radicalism.

Premarital Instruction

Every couple who married in the Church had of necessity to confer with a priest prior to the wedding. The canonical fitness of the parties to marry had to be ascertained and arrangements made for the banns to be called. Priests were also encouraged on this occasion to examine the parties in their knowledge of Christian doctrine, though it is by no means clear how exacting or even how common the practice actually was. There were still parishes, after all, where the non-Catholic party to a mixed marriage was not provided with catechetical instruction prior to the ceremony. Still, it seemed to at least some clerical authorities by the early twentieth century that the premarital interview provided a useful venue for instructing the soon-to-be married on the sinfulness of contraception and abortion. These would-be reformers, however, appear to have often been frustrated by the reluctance of nearly all parish priests to speak frankly about such matters to the laity.

This more expansive view of premarital instruction does seem to have been a product of the early years of the twentieth century, at least in the United States. Father Stang's manual for American priests, first published in 1896, makes no mention of premarital warnings against sinful modes of family limitation. But Father Frederick Schulze's manual, published for the same constituency in 1906, advised a proactive stance: "Caution them against the widespread crime of onanism, and the monstrous crime of abortion."[115] The Redemptorist Richard Donohoe, whose teaching notes on the subject date from about the same time, was in fundamental agreement. Couples should be warned against contraceptive behaviors such as coitus interruptus and the even "more terrible" sin of artificial contraception; they should certainly be made aware that abortion was "the greatest crime of all." Donohoe addressed this last-mentioned topic in straightforward language. He spoke of contraception, however, in such convoluted and euphemistic terms that his acute discomfort is palpable. If speaking thus to his fellow Redemptorists was so evidently painful, one wonders about the emotions attendant on counseling the betrothed. Especially with regard to contraceptive behaviors, as Donohoe himself conceded, "how much or how clearly one may speak on the points just mentioned depends . . . on the quality of the persons to be instructed."[116] Any evidence of refined sensibilities on the part of the bridal couple, or indeed any embarrassment, might be grounds for abbreviating or even omitting an instruction that was already couched in language that can only be called opaque.

It was apparently just such conflicted emotions that kept the great majority of priests from speaking frankly about birth control in the context of premarriage instruction, not just in the early twentieth century but for several decades thereafter. Nor were those who eventually opted for plainer speaking necessarily persuaded that in the circumstances it did much good. "What could you expect from a half-hour's instruction given on the eve of the wedding to a young couple when they are dizzy with love and distracted with the thousand and one thoughts about temporal and secular affairs!" as one disgruntled priest put it in the late 1920s. "You may speak with the voice of a prophet, and the young man and woman may be hearing your every word, but they fail to grasp what you are saying." Couples, moreover, were increasingly apt to arrive with wholly secular views on marriage and sex. "The girl has been misinformed perhaps by her own mother, and the instruction now given in the rectory is worse than useless in that it lets the pastor feel that he has done his duty, when his advice actually comes too late to change the minds of those who have formed their own opinions in the matter long ago."[117] There is greater frustration evident here than is normally found in texts from earlier in the century. The manifest inadequacies of premarital instruction were plainly more glaring in the context of the late 1920s, by which time contraception enjoyed widespread popular acceptance if not in most places the blessing of law.

Toward Reform:
John A. Ryan and the 1919 Bishops' Pastoral

A reform of pastoral strategies with regard to family limitation was most influentially urged by John A. Ryan in 1916. Writing in the *Ecclesiastical Review,* Ryan addressed the problem with unusual directness. Contraceptive practice, he asserted, is more widespread among American Catholics than we clergy like to admit. Our people, moreover, seem sometimes not to grasp that such behavior is gravely sinful—even as their marriages and society itself suffer debilitating consequences. "[Contraceptive] devices are debasing to those who employ them, inasmuch as they lead inevitably to loss of reverence for the marital relation, loss of respect for the conjugal partner, and loss of faith in the sacredness of the nuptial bond." The problem, as Ryan saw it, was caused in good part by the increasingly secular ethos of American society: growing numbers of Americans had no moral grounding other than a self-interested utilitarianism. But the Catholic clergy were also to blame. Our people need straight talk on the matter, Ryan reminded them; they need explication of the moral law in clear and uncompromising terms.[118] It no longer sufficed to leave such tasks to the occasional ministrations of the mission preachers.

Ryan was not the only Catholic to make such arguments. Margaret Sanger's emergence as a national figure in 1914 prompted other Catholic spokesmen to defend Church teaching and urge its more vigorous enforcement.[119] But Ryan was by far the best known and connected of these would-be reformers. A prolific writer on social ethics and prominently seated in Washington at the Catholic University, he would soon become head of the Social Action Department of the newly formed National Catholic Welfare Conference. In this latter position, he exerted great influence over the more liberal American bishops and especially their public pronouncements on social welfare policy. It was Ryan who was responsible for drafting the "Program of Social Reconstruction," issued early in 1919 by the Administrative Committee of the National Catholic War Council, immediate predecessor to the Welfare Conference. That document championed a wide array of social welfare programs, remarkably so for the period's growing conservatism. His hand is discernible too in the bishops' omnibus pastoral letter of 1919, which included the American episcopate's first collective public statement condemning contraception.

That Ryan and others like him should simultaneously promote the welfare state and a harder pastoral line on birth control reflects a distinctively Catholic set of assumptions. Individual autonomy, so important a value for the advocates of contraception, was an alien good to men like these, especially where women were concerned. Humans were irreducibly social; their welfare depended on strong bonds of solidarity not only in the family but society, too.[120] As Ryan saw it, contraceptive practice abetted materialism and a crass instrumentalism in social relations and politics. A society that had made its peace with contraception, he believed, would not scruple to exploit the weak in the name of enlightened policy. Employers would be under no obligation to pay a living wage, nor would the state necessarily be willing to assist the dependent poor, especially if they had large families. And ultimately, Ryan feared, acceptance of contraception would lead to tolerance of abortion, even its endorsement for purposes of eugenic control. A just society, as far as Ryan was concerned, had of necessity to be grounded in an objective morality, which for him could only mean the Catholic natural law tradition. Such a society also depended on a broadly internalized ethic of self-discipline and sacrifice—a willingness, as he wrote in 1904, to place "duty" before "self-indulgence."[121] Catholic teaching on contraception was thus for men like Ryan intimately related to a range of social welfare and social justice concerns.

Ryan's views on birth control were obviously rooted in more than concerns about social justice, genuine as these were. His was a celibate's understanding of marital sex, tinctured with a strong dose of Victorian prudery. "It is doubtful whether any normal man or woman ever began such practices," as he wrote of contraceptive intercourse in 1915, "without suffering a severe moral shock, or continued them without serious moral degeneration."[122] He worried too about the Church's authority, given what he saw as widespread doubt among the laity about the teaching on contraception. "In this as in many other matters of doctrine and discipline, the priest is often called upon to vindicate the Church's attitude, to justify the ways of God to men."[123] All the more reason, then, for priests, and indeed the bishops, to reform their reticent ways with regard to the problem of birth control. Their 1919 pastoral suggests that most bishops agreed, very likely spurred on by recent wartime developments. Sex-education programs in the military, as a Knights of Columbus activist reminded War Council chairman Father John Burke, had done harm as well as good. "There is no man, practically, among the four millions called to the colors who does not know that there are diseases attendant on illicit sex relations;

there is none among them who does not know also that there are methods of preventing the infection of these diseases and that the government has provided convenient facilities for prophylaxis."[124]

Thus the stage was set by 1919 for a new chapter in the Catholic encounter with birth control. Reform was to be that chapter's dominant theme, but reform in a limited and frequently frustrated key. It was one thing for Ryan or even a bishop to endorse a more proactive practice when it came to combating sinful modes of family limitation. Men like these, after all, had limited pastoral contact with the laity. It was quite another thing for priests to implement such a reform in the parishes that were their lives. So the 1920s unfold as a kind of transitional decade. Church teaching on birth control was communicated then more broadly and clearly than ever before, and Catholics were increasingly conscious of their standing in this matter as a peculiar people. Pastoral practice changed, too. But it changed more slowly and unevenly than the Church's public pronouncements on birth control would lead one to suppose.

2
A Certain Indocility
Obstacles to Reform, 1919–1930

Late in 1928, the Sulpician priest Joseph Nevins, who taught at the Catholic University of America, published for his clerical brethren what proved to be an influential article. "Birth control is now a practice with Catholics," he bluntly informed his confreres, "and it is on the increase." Father Nevins did not hazard a guess at how widespread the practice was. But the signs of the times were ominous, especially among the young. The culture no longer supported an ethic of duty and self-sacrifice, Nevins asserted, while recent prosperity had created exaggerated expectations with regard to living standards. The altered climate had given rise to "a certain indocile and even hostile spirit among the laity, revealed in the sort of talk that goes on among them about the size of a family or about having a family for a time or at all." Women were especially apt to be affected, as Nevins saw it: having worked before marriage, they were wholly unskilled as young wives in the arts of thrifty living and loathe to give up the extra income their jobs afforded. Nevins's views in this regard were conventional: most priests by the 1920s saw wives as primarily responsible for contraceptive practice. Still, Nevins had sympathy for women in a culture that, by his lights, failed to honor domesticity and motherhood. How distressing it was to hear, as one so frequently did, an otherwise "fine and wholesome-minded" Catholic girl express regret at being female. "They view their future as a prospect of indignity and drudgery."[1]

Father Nevins's article commanded such respectful attention because it spoke, in unusually direct terms, to the dominant fears of the nation's Catholic leaders in the 1920s. Few of these leaders, whether clerical or lay, doubted that contraceptive practice was gaining ground among Catholics. Nearly all were alarmed at recent trends in the nation's popular culture and what looked to be its prevailing values. All were aware that the status of women had undergone swift, dramatic, and probably irrevocable change—change that could hardly fail to affect marriage and family life, perhaps in fundamental ways. Most of these leaders, moreover, shared Nevins's sense that reform was urgently needed. "The Church is challenged," as Nevins said with explicit reference to contraception, "and only a clear trumpet voice calling every Catholic worthy of the name to a crusade will be of much avail." But how, precisely, should such a crusade be mounted? Bold action was presumably required to counter what Nevins called "a new onslaught of paganism."[2] Given the times, however, and especially the nature of the problem, it was no easy matter for leaders to agree on a plan of battle.

The 1920s were thus for Catholics a time of limited reform initiatives when it came to the problem of birth control. The average lay Catholic by 1928 was certainly more conversant with Church teaching on family limitation than he had been prior to the First World War, although substantial numbers apparently remained in something like "good faith" ignorance. But even among the better instructed, confusion seems to have been endemic with regard to the teaching's logic. "The laity are of the mind that contraception is forbidden only by the law of the Church," according to Father Nevins, and hence that the teaching could easily be changed—and perhaps ignored in the interim.[3] Too many "indocile" laity, in short, knew nothing of Catholic natural law doctrine, which forbade contraception as intrinsically immoral, or, indeed, the obligation to obey their pastors. In the circumstances, the limited reform initiatives of the era were bound to seem ineffectual, even scandalously so, to men like Nevins and his increasingly numerous allies. But limited though those initiatives were, they changed the world for a good many Catholics and paved the way for what even Father Nevins would have called a genuine Catholic crusade against birth control.

The Setting: Sexual Politics and Cultural Change

From a Catholic perspective, the 1920s were at once the best and worst of times. The decade saw a resurgence of virulent anti-Catholicism, most dramatically embodied in the Ku Klux Klan, which partly explained a Congressional decision to radically limit foreign immigration—something that worked with particular severity against those portions of Catholic Europe still sending large numbers of immigrants to the United States. But the decade also saw important gains for Catholics in terms of politics. Both leading contenders for the Democratic nomination to the presidency in 1928 were Catholics, while Catholic big-city mayors enjoyed the prominence—and sometimes the notoriety—that came with the rise of the city to a central place in the national life and consciousness. Of even greater significance for Catholics was the decade's economic prosperity. Still mostly working class, Catholics acquired a greater abundance of creature comforts than ever before, although a majority still lived in a state of fundamental insecurity. (Consumer debt in many families took the place of savings.) Their greater prosperity caused most Catholics to feel more genuinely American, regardless of the Ku Klux Klan, and stoked their ambitions for the rising generation, whose levels of formal schooling far outstripped that of their parents. The near-cessation of immigration intensified these trends: deprived of a steady stream of new arrivals from abroad, countless immigrant neighborhoods moved with hastening speed toward at least a surface Americanization.

The 1920s were famously a decade of cultural change, which Catholic leaders predictably deplored but about which most laity probably had mixed emotions. Feminine dress and deportment had undergone something akin to a revolution by mid-decade, when short-skirted flappers with cigarettes were blossoming on city streets. The now-ubiquitous movies did much to encourage this: youngsters in the most remote locations were exposed to a national standard for fashion and speech, and imbibed a romantic ethic of self-expression and pleasure seeking. The movies also encouraged a greater openness when it came to sex. The climate in this regard was such that even Margaret Sanger acquired a limited aura of respectability, as did the cause she so flamboyantly embodied. Two purportedly national organizations emerged in the early 1920s to promote freer access to contraceptives, albeit only for the married. (Sanger's American Birth Control League, the larger and more important, was organized in 1921.) Neither group succeeded in the 1920s with regard to its legislative agenda: repeated efforts to repeal or modify the federal Comstock Act went down to defeat, as did efforts to amend various state laws that prohibited access to contraceptive devices and information. But these same groups made substantial inroads when it came to public opinion. Contraception was more freely discussed in public, and presumably in private, than ever before; contraceptive devices, most notably condoms and the Mensinga-type diaphragm, both manufactured in quantity in the United States for the first time in the 1920s, were more readily available.[4] A rapidly falling birthrate, moreover, suggests that many Americans, and not just the affluent, were making at least episodic use of the various means of birth control.

Nearly every Protestant denomination in the 1920s was still on record as opposing marital contraception. But their pronouncements in this regard were notably fewer as the decade progressed and couched in increasingly mild and general language.[5] Catholic leaders, for their part, no longer assumed that the Protestant clergy were even nominal allies in the fight against birth control; nor did they necessarily assume that Protestant leaders kept public silence solely for fear of offending their people. Most Protestants held to a different standard of morality than good Catholics did, in the not-atypical view of an anonymous priest convert. "In nothing is this fact more evident than in the way in which non-Catholics regard this matter of contraceptive practices, both in the case of the married and the single. To many of them the teaching of the Catholic Church on the subject is nothing more than an incomprehensible piece of old-fashioned and out-of-date rigorism." Protestant morality was essentially situational, according to this anonymous source; even abortion was acceptable under certain hard circumstances. "It has even been known that ministers have advised a criminal operation in the case of young women in their flock who have 'got in trouble.'"[6]

It is true that certain liberal clergy by the mid-1920s were lending public support to Margaret Sanger and her cause. Most Protestant leaders, however, clung throughout the decade to deeply conservative views on sexual expression and marriage. But unlike Catholic moralists, they were less and less apt to think about contraception in terms of an "act-centered" morality. Their focus in the 1920s was increasingly on the general health of marriage, an institution that seemed to a great many ministers to be suddenly and alarmingly fragile. Few endorsed a marital ethic based on happiness or pleasure seeking; duty and self-sacrifice were obviously necessary to sustain a lifelong union. At the same time, Protestant leaders evinced a new concern for emotional growth and fulfillment in marriage and the ability of parents to educate children for self-sufficiency and mature Christian adulthood. Might the spouses' emotional needs and the proper education of their children not in at least some cases mandate a relatively small family? Such a conclusion seemed inevitable. The door was thus left ajar for eventual Protestant endorsement of marital contraception.[7]

The widening gulf between Catholic and Protestant perspectives on marriage is suggested by an unlikely political encounter. Anne Kennedy, then executive secretary of the American Birth Control League, in 1926 paid what seems to have been a courtesy call on Patrick Ward, a layman employed by the National Catholic Welfare Conference. (Ward at the time was point man for the bishops on public matters concerning birth control.) "She holds that aside from the propagation of children, the sexual act has of itself a spiritual and uplifting(!) value which it was intended to have by the Creator," an incredulous Ward reported to his superior. "I told Mrs. Kennedy [that] the so called spiritual value she was putting on the sexual act was a purely emotional and sensual one. The spirituality of the act lay *solely* in the knowledge and in the disposition at the moment of conception that a human being was being brought into existence endowed with a soul in God's image and likeness, and which it was God's intention should one day return to Him to enjoy eternal bliss."[8] Mrs. Kennedy's views on marital sex would even in 1926 have qualified in Protestant circles as more or less "advanced." But she was only a few years ahead of a great many Protestant leaders.

Would-be Catholic reformers in the 1920s were well aware that the cultural tide was running against them. "The most devastating influence in modern sex morality is the clamorously conducted birth-control propaganda," in the words of Father Charles Bruehl, who regularly wrote for clerical publications. "It has completely upset the traditional ideas of sex ethics, and brought about in the minds of many an incredible confusion."[9] If large numbers of Americans were "no longer able to see straight" when it came to the purpose of marital sex, Catholics would inevitably be corrupted, too—as they had, indeed, already been to a still-unknown extent. Father Bruehl, like Father Nevins, saw the need for a veritable crusade against birth control, to which his own writings were meant to contribute. Given the speed and direction of cultural change, however, nearly all reformers saw their task as beset by daunting odds. Not only were the laity vulnerable to the heightened seductions of popular culture; many priests were unprepared to play the crusader's role. "We older men," according to the Jesuit Henry Woods, were raised in a world where contraception was neither discussed nor debated; we stand aghast today "at the blindness of men and women not only apologizing for the practice, but also stoutly defending it." Priests of his generation, according to Woods, were seldom ready emotionally or even intellectually to preach or otherwise speak publicly against birth control. Real reform, in Woods's view, would have to target many priests as well as nearly all the laity. And time was of the essence.[10]

First Steps toward Reform

Men like Nevins and Bruehl were not exactly crying in the wilderness. In the 1920s, however, the Catholic forces for reform with regard to contraception were almost certainly less confident and effectively organized than their pro-birth control adversaries. (If it disconcerts present-day sensibilities to call such men reformers, this is how they saw themselves and what, from an institutional perspective, they most certainly were.) It is true that the Catholic bishops now had a national organization. But the National Catholic Welfare Conference (NCWC), as it was known, was obliged to tread carefully lest it seem to encroach on the power of bishops in their individual dioceses. It suffered in addition from a chronic shortage of money. The bishops were also sensitive to the period's resurgent anti-Catholicism, which clearly affected their collective approach to the politics of birth control. Nor were the bishops, or American Catholics generally, accustomed to national action. Catholic interests had in the past been defended mostly locally. And then there was the problem of a two-front war. Catholic reformers had, on the one hand, to shore up the teaching on birth control among their own people. They had, on the other hand, to engage the external enemy in secular political combat over proposed liberalization of state and national laws.

The reforming forces did have the advantage of a vigorous Catholic press, and they turned immediately to the production of pamphlet literature on the subject of contraception. John Ryan's essay on "Family Limitation," published in 1916 for his brother priests, was circulating in pamphlet form by the early 1920s. The National Catholic Welfare Conference promoted its distribution, and also sponsored the 1923 publication of John Montgomery Cooper's near-book-length pamphlet that bore the stark and even daring title of "Birth Control."[11] (The term, of course, was Margaret Sanger's.) The Conference produced its own series of one-page leaflets attacking contraception in 1925 and oversaw their nationwide distribution. The various religious orders contributed to the genre, too, especially the Paulists and the Jesuits. Many fewer pamphlets on birth control were circulating in the 1920s than would be the case a decade later. But the very existence of such a literature meant that the public near-silence that had hitherto surrounded the subject in Catholic circles was now definitively broken. Catholic periodicals aimed at adults were also increasingly likely to address the topic. This was even true of diocesan newspapers.

The contents of the various pamphlets circulating in the 1920s differed in important ways from what was typical in the 1930s or '40s. Nineteen-twenties' pamphlets were almost invariably densely printed and argued. Devoid of illustrations and breezy anecdotes, they made no concessions to the less-than-well-educated reader. Nor were they heavily "Catholic" in their rhetoric and logic. Various writers might invoke the natural law in their explanation of the teaching, although seldom with explicit reference to Catholic moral theorists. The principal emphasis, however, was almost always both ecumenical and pragmatic. Contraception was offensive to all true Christians, the usual argument ran; it also had dreadful effects in the purely natural order. Artificial birth control coarsened the marital relationship and especially degraded women, who were reduced by its use to the status of sexual objects. Even persons who endorsed the practice, in the typical view of the Paulist Bertrand Contway, were aware that this was true. "There is unquestionably a widespread—almost universal—sense of sin and shame in men and women who practice birth control."[12] Contraceptive devices were said to be injurious to health, particularly women's, with the testimony of non-Catholic physicians often cited as evidence. Contracepting couples were threatened with a lonely, regretful, and perhaps impoverished old age and, more occasionally and cruelly, by loss of the "one or two children they are willing to bear."[13] "The Almighty has infinite resources at His command to defeat those who rise up against Him," in the chilling words of a Jesuit.[14]

The pamphlet writers also argued that children reared in small families were less self-reliant than children from large ones and certainly more selfish. Birth control thus led inevitably to corrosion of the social order. This societal selfishness was already evident in the birth control movement itself: the rich, and especially employers, preferred promoting birth control among the poor to a redistribution of income or the payment of adequate wages.[15] Father John Burke, executive secretary of the National Catholic Welfare Conference, confessed in 1927 to a private belief that the principal reason for pro-birth control agitation was economic: "what I think is really back of it is . . . those who do not wish to pay a living wage.[16] Those same selfish employers were unpatriotic: nearly every 1920s pamphlet writer saw underpopulation as a serious threat to the United States, both economically and militarily. Approximately four children per family were required simply to maintain the nation's population, according to John Montgomery Cooper. "Birth control families average closer to two than to four."[17]

Catholic writers had to address certain hard and eminently practical questions raised by the advocates of contraception. It was all very well to endorse social justice and especially a living wage. How were unskilled working men to support their large families in the meantime? Who doubted, moreover, that multiple pregnancies could in some instances be hazardous to a woman's health—even potentially fatal? Catholic pamphleteers did not deny that such were serious problems, although they never conceded that dangerous pregnancies were nearly as frequent as their adversaries claimed. The Church, as they hastened to assure their readers, "does not require couples to have as many children as they can."[18] But the only licit means of family limitation was abstinence, either episodic or permanent. "It is the program dictated alike by right reason and Divine Revelation."[19] These writers almost never talked the language of the "safe period," which by the 1920s was presumably so discredited as to be almost a dead letter among Catholics. They spoke instead of the ennobling effects of continence in marriage. Continence might be hard at first, the various authors conceded, but with prayer and frequent reception of the Sacraments it grew steadily easier. Eventually the spouses and their marriage would be transformed by this heroic exercise in self-discipline—rendered finer, more spiritual, more open to the love of God. "The union of the spirits and minds in true friendship and love," in the helpful words of a Franciscan, "is much dearer and more satisfying than the union of the bodies."[20]

Such logic is bound today to seem supremely naïve, if not cruelly repressive. Certainly it was deeply rooted in a celibate clergy's view of sexuality as a powerful engine of sin. It was intimately linked as well to an intense eschatological consciousness: the sufferings of this life, especially when borne out of faithfulness to God, were a means of personal purification and assists on the path to heaven—the attainment of which was the purpose of earthly existence. The authority of the Church was also at issue. For the Church to abandon her teaching on "divorce or abortion or artificial birth control," in the words of an anonymous pamphlet writer, "would mean that the Holy Ghost had been derelict in His care for her, that her inerrancy and infallibility in matters of faith and morals were mere figments."[21] Concern for the Church's authority and indeed for the public moral health ruled out concessions in Church teaching to even the hardest cases. "There is no socially safe middle ground between complete prohibition of birth prevention and such general addiction to the practice as will inevitably bring about a declining population and a profound deterioration of social and individual character and competence," in the words of John A. Ryan. "Because of these indirect results the practice is forbidden by the moral law in every case."[22]

Ryan was building a case, in this last-quoted passage, for an "argument from consequences" against birth control. The standard natural law argument, by which contraception was condemned as the perversion of a natural faculty, was in his view too arcane to persuade large numbers of the laity. John Montgomery Cooper, Ryan's colleague at the Catholic University, was himself not wholly persuaded by the natural law argument, at least as a proof that contraception was mortally sinful. "Just precisely how are we going to formulate such a definition of the natural function of the reproductive faculty as will permit relations in pregnancy and sterility and yet bar contraceptive practices?" he wanted to know. "And after we have succeeded—if we succeed—in so formulating this function, just precisely what concrete objective evidence are we going to muster to show that our formulation, and no other, represents the true function?"[23] This is presumably why Cooper's 1923 pamphlet, far and away the most sophisticated Catholic production of the decade, argued not in terms of the natural law but a social ethic of love. Monogamous marriage and parenthood, as the priest anthropologist explained, constituted humanity's—and especially male humanity's—great school of altruism. To "isolate sex passion from love and parenthood," as contraceptive practice did, was to "dethrone love and parenthood and enshrine physical self-regarding pleasures in the central and dominating place of personality." The inevitable consequences included an erosion of marital fidelity, the undermining of women's status, and dangerous vulnerability for the young. Society as a whole would suffer irreparably. The Catholic teaching on contraception, then, "is the one position that can adequately and in practice safeguard individual and collective welfare."[24]

Cooper's *Birth Control* was, for its time, humane and engagingly argued. One can readily imagine its appeal to an idealistic reader. The same might be said of the social justice theme that figured so prominently in Catholic writing on the subject of contraception. There was, after all, a fundamental generosity to the Catholic insistence on workingmen's rights to a living wage and the pleasures of an abundant family life—a generosity that was almost countercultural in the conservative political context of the 1920s. This is true as well of Catholic opposition to state-mandated programs for the involuntary sterilization of the "unfit." Twenty-three states had such laws by 1927, as John A. Ryan noted in a pamphlet on the subject, many of which were "vaguely worded and would seem to target for sterilization a potentially broad swath of the population."[25] (A number of prominent leaders in the pro-contraception ranks were

Figure 1. Rev. John Montgomery Cooper, author of an influential tract opposing contraception and longtime professor of anthropology at the Catholic University of America. Photo courtesy of the American Catholic History Research Center and University Archives of the Catholic University of America (ACUA).

enthusiastic partisans in these years of the eugenics movement.) Ryan and other Catholic commentators were not immune to the seductions of social engineering—habitual criminals, the mentally retarded, and the incurably insane might properly, in their view, be confined to sex-segregated institutions during the reproductive years. But Catholics still defended the right of even the most marginal to bodily integrity and at least symbolic membership in the human community.[26]

So, the 1920s saw a certain development in American Catholic writing on the subject of contraception, which emerged on occasion as notably thoughtful and socially engaged. A man like John Montgomery Cooper did not simply invoke the authority of the Church or the self-evident repulsiveness of contraceptive sex, still less the retribution of an angry God. Perhaps most important, he spoke of marriage in emphatically positive terms: "marriage undertaken with its full responsibilities of home-making, child-begetting, and childrearing," as he wrote in 1928, is "the fundamental divine project for the development and increase of unselfishness in humankind."[27] Such changes in tone and logic were significant. "We are confronted by an increasingly large class of educated Catholics," in the words of an anonymous priest, who want and need a broader and less dogmatic defense of Church teaching on birth control than we clergy have previously offered. "There is nothing to be gained by the assumption of the attitude that they are obedient children of the Church and must obey blindly."[28]

The sophistication and idealism evident in Cooper's writing was eventually incorporated into the best Catholic college teaching on marriage and family life. Cooper himself emphasized marriage in his religion courses at the Catholic University and adjacent Trinity College. "In a four-year course in religion from twenty-five to fifty per cent of the discussions center around this topic in a great many of its phases," he wrote to a professional colleague in 1930. "The problems are discussed with the utmost frankness."[29] Courses like these—which would soon be standard in Catholic colleges across the nation— produced an elite among Catholic leaders, both clerical and lay, for whom the teaching on contraception was grounded in a nuanced and socially progressive logic. Such men and women were central actors in the Catholic story as it evolved in subsequent decades.

Whatever their level of sophistication, Catholic apologists in the 1920s almost certainly failed to reach a mass audience. Even the most "popular" of their pamphlets and occasional pieces were obviously aimed at an educated reader: the prose was complex, even turgid at times, and the publications lacked visual appeal. What might the various authors have had in mind as they targeted so limited a Catholic audience? Most probably assumed that contraceptive practice among Catholics was still largely confined to the more affluent and better educated. Certainly they would not wish, however inadvertently, to instruct the ignorant in sinful conduct. The pamphlet and occasional literature of the 1920s may also have been written, at least in part, for the clergy. The anonymous priest reviewer of an English Jesuit's 1927 pamphlet commended the publication to his confreres as a source of persuasive arguments against birth control for their work "in the confessional or elsewhere."[30] The great majority of priests had received in the seminary only the most formal and probably cursory instruction on the sinfulness of contraception—and that in Latin. With birth control emerging so suddenly into the public forum, there were doubtless large numbers of priests in need of the help that a learned Jesuit could offer. Finally, most Catholic writing on contraception in the 1920s was produced with an educated Protestant audience never far from the author's consciousness. The nation was still committed to a regime that more or less criminalized birth control. It was imperative, from a Catholic perspective, that Protestants be reminded of the reasons their forebears had passed such laws in the first place. Thus the various "fact-sheets" produced by the National Catholic Welfare Conference in 1925 quoted non-Catholic authorities almost exclusively in their arguments against contraception.[31]

We can probably safely assume that the average Catholic in the 1920s never read an anti-birth control pamphlet. Certainly he—or more accurately, she—

did not have access to periodicals like *Commonweal* or *America,* both of which carried a handful of articles on the topic. (These generally made up in acerbity for their small numbers: If a couple "intend to seek sterile venereal satisfaction with the help of chemical or mechanical appliances," the English Dominican Vincent McNabb informed *Commonweal*'s readers in 1925, "this is not marriage. It is a form of harlotry, which keeps the old Christian name of marriage."[32]) Such "average" Catholics—many of whom were immigrants or the children of immigrants—probably had limited access even to the diocesan press, which now carried the occasional screed against birth control. This does not mean, however, that the generality of Catholics in the 1920s heard no more about Church teaching on contraception than their parents had done. Most had at least a limited awareness of the secular politics of birth control, in which Catholic opposition played a prominent role. And changing trends in pastoral practice increased the likelihood that ordinary Catholics would in the normal round of parish life be exposed to straightforward presentations of Catholic teaching on marriage.

The Secular Politics of Birth Control

The birth control politics of the 1920s were decisively shaped by Margaret Sanger. Her charismatic personality and flair for publicity were critical in this regard; so was her astute reading of American popular prejudice. In the wake of her storied arrest at New York's Town Hall in 1921—an arrest Sanger publicly blamed on the political clout of New York's Archbishop Patrick Hayes—the activist turned to a sometimes strident rhetoric that identified virtually all opposition to contraception with Roman Catholic despotism. "All who resent this sinister Church Control of life and conduct," as she editorialized in a 1921 issue of the *Birth Control Review,* "this interference of the Roman Church in attempting to dictate the conduct and behavior of non-Catholics, must now choose between Church Control or Birth Control. You can no longer remain neutral." Given the anti-Catholic climate of the times and Sanger's capacity to elicit press coverage, the strategy was remarkably effective. The public debate over birth control was increasingly cast in the press as one between Catholics and other Americans—an impression inadvertently reinforced by Archbishop Hayes when he twice in the early 1920s debated Sanger in the New York *Times.* The growing tendency for Protestants to maintain public silence on the subject of contraception reinforced the impression, too, and may have been prompted in part by it. The more conservative Protestant churches, those most likely to oppose contraception, were also apt to be the most anti-Catholic. Few of their leaders were eager to make public cause with what Sanger liked to call "a dictatorship of celibates."[33]

Sanger's successful framing of the birth control debate created serious prob-

lems for would-be Catholic activists. How to effectively oppose the liberalization of laws affecting birth control without intensifying anti-Catholicism or
even promoting support for the pro-contraception cause? How to grant the
bishops their rightful leadership role without raising the specter of a celibates'
dictatorship? A resource as valuable as the National Catholic Welfare Conference quite suddenly seemed a potential liability. Catholic leaders, nearly all of
them clerical, attempted to deal with these problems in two principal ways.
They insisted throughout the decade that opposition to contraception was characteristic of "all genuine Christians and . . . all other persons who cherish the
elementary principles and sentiments of morality," to borrow from a 1922
statement of the NCWC's Administrative Committee.[34] They quoted non-
Catholics in their literature, and recruited the same to testify against proposed
changes in the nation's laws. They also tried to enlist the Catholic laity, particularly women, as public actors in the fight against birth control. "Better the
bishops should not figure," as Bishop Edmond Gibbons, who headed the
NCWC's department on laws and legislation, noted in 1925 with regard to anti-
birth control strategy, "or the charges that *Rome* was interfering might be
raised."[35]

Despite the bishops' determination to keep a collective low profile, the most
sustained Catholic politicking in the anti-contraception cause took place at the
National Catholic Welfare Conference—chiefly through the office of its general secretary, the Paulist John Burke. Burke monitored the progress of his adversaries until the mid-1920s through Sara Laughlin, a Philadelphia social
worker who kept in close touch with the work of Margaret Sanger and her allies. Laughlin was also "eyes and ears" for Philadelphia's Cardinal Dennis
Dougherty: "They were selling the copy of the *Birth Control Review* in which
they answer, or attempt to, Dr. Ryan's article," as she wrote to Burke of a 1921
Sanger lecture, delivered before an overflow crowd in Philadelphia. "His
Grace has my copy."[36] It was highly unusual for a churchman like Burke—let
alone a cardinal—to rely so closely on a woman for information and advice;
that this was necessary suggests the extent to which the early birth control
movement was regarded, certainly by Catholic leaders, as a near-Amazonian
female preserve. Laughlin herself may have fed these perceptions, given her
clear fascination with the movement's most prominent women. "I am convinced," as she told Burke in 1921, "that Mrs. Dennett thinks she is doing a
service to womankind and she has the concentration and endurance of a
zealot."[37] Laughlin had referred in this instance to Mary Ware Dennett of the
Voluntary Parenthood League, who led the effort in the mid-1920s to amend
the federal Comstock Act. She was equally intrigued by Margaret Sanger: "She
has an unusual amount of poise. . . . She is certainly a very good-looking
scoundrel."[38] Burke seems to have ended his regular correspondence with
Laughlin late in 1925, at about the time he hired Patrick Ward, a layman who

for some years thereafter worked closely with Burke on birth control-related matters. The birth control movement was apparently by then a more familiar entity, and its opponents had had sufficient success in the legislative arena to feel a modicum of confidence.

The Dennett wing of the birth control movement lobbied hard in the 1920s to remove all references to contraception from the 1873 Comstock Act. The Sanger forces worked mainly to secure an expanded authority for doctors when it came to prescribing contraceptives or counseling patients in this regard. This would have required change in the laws of some twenty-two states, each of which limited access to contraceptive information and devices—some in Draconian fashion.[39] Contraceptives and information about them were in fact more widely available in the 1920s than ever before. Such laws, however, were powerful symbols of a moral order about whose demise many Americans were ambivalent. In the circumstances, it was not difficult to dissuade politicians—including non-Catholic politicians—from supporting reform nor hard to find other-than-Catholic authorities to raise their voices against it. "Father Burke related the history of the fight against Federal legislation to authorize the dissemination of birth control propaganda," as the minutes of the NCWC's Administrative Committee explained in 1926.

> At the beginning, the NCWC was the only organization to protest against such legislation, but through its efforts many non-Catholic bodies have been enlisted in the fight to prevent Federal legislation favoring such propaganda. Father Burke wrote to 181 such organizations and received replies from 84, nearly all of which were favorable to our position. At present, no Senator nor Representative will introduce such a measure into Congress, and those who formerly favored such measures have now completely reversed their position.[40]

Burke certainly did his share of behind-the-scenes lobbying, and prominent Catholics like John A. Ryan testified periodically before Congressional committees. But although it had become a more difficult enterprise by the late 1920s, Burke managed to preserve throughout the decade at least the semblance of an ecumenical opposition to contraception.

Catholic leaders were often less chary of overt Catholic involvement when it came to local squabbles. This was particularly true where a large Catholic population had accustomed the group to an influential role in politics. New York's Archbishop—soon to be Cardinal—Hayes did not scruple to issue a pastoral letter in direct response to Margaret Sanger in 1921, nor did Chicago's George Mundelein—also soon to be cardinal—doubt the propriety of attempting to intervene personally in a 1924 case that involved the denial of a city license to a local birth control clinic.[41] It was far easier locally than at the national level to mobilize lay opposition, which helped to mute—if not to silence—charges of celibate authoritarianism. Such mobilizations of the laity occurred episodically throughout the 1920s: local Catholic organizations, almost invariably at clerical behest, obligingly passed resolutions opposing birth control when local events required it; they might on occasion engage in letter-writing campaigns. A birth control conference held in Syracuse in 1924 even prompted a mobilization of the city's Catholic Boy Scouts, who distributed copies of John Montgomery Cooper's *Birth Control* "not only to the Catholic aldermen," as a local Chancery official explained, "but the leading physicians, lawyers and prominent businessmen, Catholic Club leaders and judiciously even to some influential non-Catholics."[42]

It is hard to assess the extent of lay mobilization in the birth control skirmishes of the 1920s, given widely scattered evidence, and even harder to determine its pedagogic impact. Endorsing a resolution against birth control would at the very least have communicated to those involved the particulars of Catholic teaching on the subject; it would presumably have had a similar effect on those who read or heard about it. But a great many Catholic laity were remote, for reasons of language and class, from the world of extra-parochial organizations and the diocesan press—as indeed were those numerous Catholics whose institutional involvement was confined to irregular Sunday observance. Few of these, in all likelihood, were totally ignorant of the local politics of birth control; the secular and even the ethnic press would have covered such events. In the circumstances, however, there was probably ample room for misapprehension of Church teaching, perhaps especially the absolute nature of the Catholic ban on contraception.

Even among the active laity, it is worth noting, the politics of birth control seem not to have been a high priority. A handful of women did indeed play significant roles on the Catholic side in the 1920s; their numbers include the aforementioned Sara Laughlin, Agnes Regan of the National Council of Catholic Women, and York, Pennsylvania, clubwoman Anna Dill Gamble. Male leaders from several national bodies were also episodically active. But from the perspective of the National Catholic Welfare Conference, lay organizations were uncertain allies. "Catholic organized evidence and opposition against these measures seemed to me weak and inefficient," as Patrick Ward complained in 1927 with regard to pro-birth control initiatives in Pennsylvania, New York, and Connecticut—all states with substantial Catholic populations. Catholic organizations in those states had neither communicated news of the proposed legislation to the NCWC nor taken steps to oppose it once asked by the Conference to do so.[43]

It was newly enfranchised laywomen that the NCWC especially wished to see active, given the widespread assumption that birth control was an issue that particularly affected their sex. But Catholic women had hardly been prepared for such a role. Many clerical leaders had until recently been vocal opponents of women's suffrage; all associated the truly feminine with modesty, domesticity, and a want of intellectualism. John A. Ryan, to choose a typical example, not only wrote the statement by which the National Council of Catholic Women condemned birth control at its 1921 convention but did not hesitate to use a text he had already published.[44] "It is very difficult to secure a married woman who is willing to engage in such a task," Father John Burke conceded with a telling complacency in 1928, referring to public testimony against birth control. "They are not, as a rule, technically informed and all that I have asked shrink from the distasteful course of discussing publicly what is so sacred to them."[45] Doubts about Church teaching may have made for silence, too. Sara Laughlin, for one, believed this to be the case, at least in Philadelphia. "The list of patronesses for this lecture . . . gives me a few surprises," she wrote to Burke with regard to an upcoming visit by Margaret Sanger, "but no more than I have gotten from my Catholic women friends in this past few weeks. The difference being only that my Catholic friends are not active propagandists."[46]

As with the decade's pamphlet literature, the ultimate significance for Catholics of the secular politics of birth control was simply the breaking of silence. One might plausibly argue that Margaret Sanger did more than the bishops when it came to informing American Catholics about their Church's opposition to contraception. Her influence was felt by priests as well, the most reserved of whom could hardly escape the birth control debate. Materials pertaining to proposed amendment of the Comstock Act were "to be widely distributed this summer at priests' retreats," according to John Burke in 1925.[47] Those same priests were expected, at least as Burke saw it, "to interest [their] people in protesting against the proposed infamous Birth Control legislation."[48] To do so meant speaking plainly about a subject that only a few years before had been too offensive for public discussion. The new frankness was meant to extend to pastoral practice as well. "It is not sufficient to bring up the subject in mission sermons, or the Lenten course of conferences," as a Capuchin argued in the late 1920s. "These means have been tried and have not proved adequate."[49] So priests were under increasing pressure to move toward a proactive stance on the difficult question of contraception. How they responded, and with what effects, is the subject to which we now turn.

Pastoral Practice in a Time of Transition

The priest reformers of the 1920s regarded many of their colleagues as unwittingly lax when it came to birth control. "Some assert that we have been unaware of the magnitude of this baleful influence and tardy in dealing with it," as Father Joseph Nevins rather tactfully had it, reminding his colleagues that "this evil practice needs to be handled severely and strongly, in the pulpit and in the confessional." It was axiomatic for Nevins that a confessor's failure to interrogate the married was "a clear and serious default" of his duty, and that absolution should not be granted to contracepting penitents "who do not give moral assurance of their purpose of amendment."[50] Priests, by his lights, were also obliged to preach with firmness and clarity on the subject of marriage, even before their "mixed" Sunday congregations. "To bring home to all, especially those about to marry, that wedlock has no other independent justification than a family, that the having and rearing of children is the life they now choose, that they must from now on think of themselves as mother and father if they are to become husband and wife and live as such, is to give them the mind of Christ in respect to marriage." Such preaching would go a long way, in Nevins's view, to make up for the inevitably cursory nature of premarital instruction.[51]

To follow the counsels of a man like Nevins would obviously mean for most parish priests a radical break with the reticent practice to which they had long been accustomed. And though evidence on the subject is extremely limited, that evidence nearly always suggests that a great many failed to do so. "I do not recall ever having a priest even ask me if I were married," a New Mexico woman remarked with regard to confession in 1927. "My sister's experience and that of several friends has been the same."[52] She was echoed by a disgruntled layman, who remembered his own premarital confessor as reticent in the extreme. "I wanted and I expected instruction," as he explained. "This is the instruction I got: 'Now try and live a good married life, do not quarrel with your wife and God bless you.'" Like the New Mexico woman, this anonymous layman blamed just such confessors for widespread ignorance among the laity when it came to birth control. "They readily admit that abortion is not only sinful, but that it is murder; but they are very hazy about contraceptives and evasive methods often resorted to in married relations."[53]

Notwithstanding such haziness, we must assume that penitents themselves either asked about birth control on occasion or—perhaps more frequently—confessed to its use. Presumably the numbers of such penitents grew as the subject was more and more debated publicly. But even a forthcoming penitent did not invariably solve the problem of priestly reticence. At least some confessors were apparently so terse or euphemistic in their response to such questions that ample room remained for misunderstanding on a motivated penitent's part. Father Nevins, for one, was troubled by tales of penitents who claimed to have gotten a dispensation in confession to make use of contraceptives.[54] A Chicago laywoman had heard these, too: "One is often startled at the different points of view which women offer, who insist they obtained their instruction in the confessional."[55]

Parish priests in the 1920s struggled with more than a deeply ingrained prudentialism. The clergy had had such success at preaching the gospel of frequent confession and communion that confessionals were now more crowded than ever before. "The best work can never be done in a rush," as Father

Charles Bruehl pointed out in 1924. "When the confessor must continually think of the unending line of penitents, pressed for time and eager for their turn, waiting in the church with growing impatience and increasing suspense, he cannot give to the individual case that calm, careful and circumspect consideration which he would bestow under more favorable circumstances."[56] Those long lines, featured especially at Christmas and Easter but characteristic of Saturdays, too, in many of the larger parishes, were a source of pride for the clergy and also of consolation. One was never more a priest than when hearing confessions, or so it was regularly said. But in the new circumstances, as Bishop J. F. Noll observed, "the priest has no time to give advice. . . . He is likely to make himself believe that he has no time to argue with the penitent relative to the avoidance of the occasion of his serious falls, and the absolute need of a determined fight against a predominant weakness."[57]

Might not penitents heard in such "slot-machine" fashion, in the phrasing of Father Stanislaus Woywod, at least sometimes persuade themselves that their sins were not terribly serious?[58] Bishop Noll thought it likely. Certainly the situation was conducive to a motivated penitent's remaining, with regard to birth control, in a kind of good faith ignorance. It may in addition have caused some priests to be brusque in their dealings with penitents who were honestly struggling with the problem. Such insensitivity, no matter how inadvertent, could have decidedly unhappy consequences. "No other class of penitents is so likely to remain away from the Sacraments if dealt with in an inept and cursory manner," as a thoughtful priest psychologist remarked in 1926.[59] The situation may also have kept the well-intentioned from requesting information. It was exceedingly hard for women to ask their confessors about marital sex, the aforementioned Chicago laywoman pointed out, "even if one felt it fair to take up the time of confessors in large parishes on a matter which needs careful elucidation."[60] She had read the situation correctly, according to one anonymous priest: the clergy encounter many occasions where penitents require counsel with regard to family limitation, he noted, but this "cannot be given fully in the confessional on account of the numbers waiting to approach the tribunal."[61]

If habit and circumstance caused at least some priests to be less-than-proactive confessors when it came to contraception, growing numbers among them seem to have had uneasy consciences in this regard. Confessors' queries about birth control began to appear in the principal clerical journals in the mid-to-late 1920s. The questions suggest both a greater readiness on the part of penitents to speak of the subject in confession and a fair degree of anxious uncertainty on the confessor's part. How long after intercourse must a woman wait before she may licitly douche?[62] Can a confessor absolve a woman who has had herself sterilized for contraceptive purposes, or is this reserved to a bishop? What penance ought to be imposed in such a case?[63] How should a confessor respond "when mothers claim their doctor advised them that, if they have any more children, they will ruin their health, or when they say that they cannot support a large family for want of means?"[64] A Capuchin who in the late 1920s asked five hundred pastors for suggestions in training "our young people" for Catholic marriage tapped a vein of concern about confession. Of the 460 who replied—the response rate alone, as the priest author noted, "indicates that priests are widely interested in the problem"—fully 310 recommended that married penitents be regularly questioned "about fulfillment of family obligations." (Whether these priest respondents followed their own advice in this regard the study does not say; its author appears to assume, however, that the practice was not common.) The survey also confirmed what was by now a near-universal tendency among priests to hold women especially responsible for the spread of contraception. Church authorities, according to 296 respondents, should take immediate steps to halt the "propaganda of Catholic women in favor of birth control." Since observant Catholic women were nowhere engaged in public support of the practice, these priests presumably had in mind the private conversations of the female laity.[65]

As had been the case prior to the First World War, confessions heard in the context of a mission were typically more grueling—from a lay point of view— than those heard in the parish. Confessors from virtually every mission-preaching order by the 1920s were apparently expected to question the married about contraception. Mission sermons might even warn the prospective penitent in this regard. "I know many of you are guilty of this crime," as the Redemptorist Joseph Turner told innumerable congregations of married women. "Before you come to confession, talk it over with your husband. Come to some definite decision. Then come to confession, acknowledge your terrible sins and be ready to promise God to give them up forever. . . . If you are not willing to make that promise, then don't come to confession at all."[66] Redemptorist preachers still tended to be the bluntest of the lot, but preachers from other orders made the point as well. "It is . . . useless and idle to approach the priest in the confessional for the purpose of sacramental absolution," a Franciscan routinely told his married hearers in the 1920s, "if you are not minded to quit this sin once and forever, let your circumstances be what they may." Do not plead with the priest for absolution, he warned. "Rather, do not come to confession at all than try to tempt the minister of God to such baseness and treachery."[67]

There was still in the 1920s a clear division of labor when it came to enforcing Church teaching on birth control, with the principal burden assigned to mission preachers and confessors. But it was not as easy now as it had been prior to the First World War for a conscientious parish priest to feel that this arrangement absolved him of responsibility in the matter. Mission preaching was harder-hitting than ever before, at least when it came to sins against marriage. And yet contraception continued to make headway among Catholics.

"At a time when the hideous specter of birth control stalks over the land, we should do everything possible to fortify our people against so horrible a monster," in the words of an influential pastoral theologian.[68] Young priests may have been especially vulnerable to feelings of guilt, being products themselves of a less reticent culture: the younger clergy, in the view of one Jesuit, had "even from seminary days" seen the menace of birth control "drawing daily nearer and growing more urgent."[69]

Thus increasing numbers of the parish clergy embraced the logic of reform, recognizing the need for a more proactive style of pastoral practice when it came to family limitation. But not every man in this state of mind was able to realize his aspirations. Many things worked against it—from the reticent example of one's senior colleagues to penitents with ill-formed consciences, who neglected to confess their lapses into contraception or, at once more brazen and more fearful, badgered the confessor for absolution though they lacked any real intent of reforming their marital ways. Then there were the inevitable hard cases that confronted nearly every confessor, to which he seldom had an answer save that of conjugal abstinence. "These people need help, intelligent help, help calculated, by the best psychological knowledge and practice, to lead them out of the difficulties in which they are plunged," as an admirably pastoral priest explained.[70] In practice, however, such masterful care of souls was almost impossible to accomplish.

Sunday preaching was not, to all appearances, much affected by reforming currents. Clerical writers did call periodically for a greater frankness when it came to preaching on marriage. The laity "read and hear much about birth-control," as a Missouri priest pointed out in 1928. "It is hard to see why they should be barred from the practice, when all the world takes it for granted, unless the motive comes from and goes to the beyond. Preaching must afford the motive."[71] But formidable obstacles stood in the way. Even young priests had little in the way of homiletic training, nor did they conceive of their ministry in terms of the preached word.[72] More fundamental were lingering worries about propriety: "It may not be advisable to discuss this subject before a mixed congregation," a would-be reformer conceded.[73] It is true that the principal homiletics journal of the day carried occasional sermon texts where birth control, as well as abortion, was unmistakably addressed. "Woe to you parents who interfere with the designs of God in the procreation of children," in the words of a 1920 offering for the fourth Sunday in Lent. "The laws of nature cannot be violated with impunity. The married state is but an instrument in the hand of God to create souls for His kingdom."[74] Such texts never featured prior to the First World War. But it seems unlikely that models like these affected most Sunday preaching, rather little of which was explicitly doctrinal in content. "The sermons I have not preached as a Priest are the same as those I did not hear as a layman," confessed one Father Simeon in 1930. Birth control was high on his list of proscribed topics, despite an evident need for its being addressed. "It must take considerable courage, in this day and generation, to lay down the law to a Catholic congregation, especially when it cuts across their inclinations or their vices, or where the following of the right way will lay them open to criticism by their neighbors."[75]

The secular politics of birth control did occasionally make for unusually frank sermons. New York's Archbishop Patrick Hayes, to invoke the most famous example, issued a pastoral letter in December 1921 in direct response to Margaret Sanger's Town Hall arrest, which was also preached at St. Patrick's Cathedral and read at parishes throughout the archdiocese. Hayes was direct and forceful in his condemnation of birth control: "children troop down from Heaven because God wills it. He alone has the right to stay their coming." His rhetoric seemed to deny the morality even of family limitation by means of sexual abstinence, which he nowhere mentioned. Indeed, he proposed the novel and possibly heterodox argument that birth control was actually a graver sin than abortion:

> To take life after its inception is a horrible crime; but to prevent life that the Creator is about to bring into being is satanic. In the first instance the body is killed, while the soul lives on; in the latter not only a body but an immortal soul is denied existence in time and eternity. It has been reserved to our day to see advocated shamelessly the legalizing of such a diabolical thing.[76]

Did Archbishop Hayes really believe that human will could play no moral role at all in procreative matters? That prudence was never a virtue when it came to decisions about marital sex? Almost certainly not. His pastoral letter was a deeply emotional defense of procreation as a good, in the course of which the Archbishop was less than theologically precise—one might say shockingly so. This was a letter written in the heat of political battle; it was meant as much to convert the heart—that of the tribal Catholic, at least—as to persuade the mind. We cannot know the extent to which the Archbishop achieved his goals. But Hayes's letter certainly helped to reinforce the religious dimension of the birth control struggle in New York and by extension, given that city's visibility, in the nation as a whole. With Catholics now clearly identified as the chief opponents of birth control, at least a few clergy—and not only in New York—were probably moved on occasion to speak of the subject from their own Sunday pulpits, though fleetingly, in all likelihood, and in appropriately veiled terms. A young Chicago priest, for example, reproved the above-mentioned Father Simeon for his failure to champion the cause, even while conceding that parish sermons against contraception were still rare. He himself had dared to preach on the topic "and I am only a curate in a big diocese."[77]

Notwithstanding the occasional zealous curate, the vast majority of birth control sermons in the 1920s were still preached in the context of parish missions. A significantly smaller number were preached as Lenten discourses or special addresses to same-sex groups like the Holy Name Society. In this sense not much had changed since the earliest days of the century. But two important developments were evident by the 1920s. Birth control had emerged by then as a staple subject of mission preaching, no matter the order to which the presiding missionaries belonged. And nearly all preachers spoke of the subject in plain and unmistakable terms. "The sin I have reference to goes by divers names," a Franciscan explained in typically direct parlance. "It is called birth-control, race suicide, contraception, the sin of prevention, of being careful, of improper marital relations, of withdrawal, of mutual self-abuse, of wasting nature, of spilling the seed, and the like."[78] Growing numbers of preachers, indeed, were applying to contraception the kind of extravagant language they had previously reserved for abortion.

As had been the case in previous decades, the different mission-preaching orders featured markedly different rhetorical styles. The Paulists, for example, continued to be known for their relative restraint, and nowhere more so than with regard to putative sins against marriage. "You need not go more than half-way toward plain speech," Walter Elliott advised his confreres with reference to contraception. "Nowadays you will easily be understood. Be on your guard in all such matters against words in the least degree unbecoming your holy office, and the holy place in which you are preaching. Repress every least sign of ill temper."[79] The more numerous Passionists, by contrast, and especially the Redemptorists enjoyed deserved reputations for emotionality—for rhetorical performances that were skillfully aimed at evoking guilt, shame, and fear. As for the Jesuits, reputedly more intellectual, they directed their sometimes florid oratory toward precisely the same ends. Whatever the rhetorical style employed, the fundamental message was always the same: contraception was by its nature gravely sinful, no temporal circumstances could justify its use or mitigate the guilt attached to it, unrepentant birth controllers ran the possibly imminent risk of eternal damnation.

Mission preachers nearly always addressed the justifications most commonly offered in defense of birth control. "Let no one dare to excuse his awful, his dastardly guilt on the plea, that he cannot support children," as Father Alfred Menth put the matter with typical Redemptorist bluntness. "Where is that man's faith. Does he not believe, that God can provide for the child WHOM GOD WANTS TO LIVE?"[80] (Menth, like many of his contemporaries, was partial to language that blurred the line between contraception and abortion.) Nor was a wife's ill health a mitigating circumstance, for no earthly concern could ever justify the deliberate commission of serious sin. "I would rather see your body in the coffin, and your soul—the soul of a martyr to duty, in heaven, than to see your soul and body under the curse of an angry God," in the stern words of Father Joseph Turner, who preached more than six hundred missions and conferences during his long career. Here too, the proper response was trust in God. "I have never known a case to go under where both had devotion to St. Gerard," Turner's text notes parenthetically. "Boost medals."[81] And there was always a remedy in sexual abstinence—far safer, in truly life-threatening circumstances, than relying on any known means of birth control. Abstinence brought spiritual benefits, too. "It provides the husband with the best chance to display his true love for his wife in the most eloquent and substantial manner," as a Franciscan explained, "by heroically and cheerfully denying himself, where it hurts or costs most, for the love of her. . . . Every profession in life imposes certain hardships and severe trials that try our mettle and test our love for God, and our worthiness to be received in His kingdom."[82] But no matter how fluent his responses, the missionary still met again and again with the same litany of objections, or so certain irritable passages in the sermon texts suggest. Who stands at the left hand of Christ on the Day of Judgment? asked the Passionist Theophane Gescavitz. "The married man practicing birth-control is there—he is *still* justifying his conduct—'The wife insisted that I do it—I wasn't getting enuf money for more'—*Others* were doing it'—'The doctor advised us not to.'"[83]

Mission preachers had for decades been countering just such arguments. But in the 1920s, they addressed these arguments more insistently and often at greater length. There was a new emphasis as well on refuting the notion that the growing social acceptance of birth control had any effect on its intrinsic immorality. Mission preachers in the 1920s also played on the theme, popular even in the nineteenth century, that contraceptive intercourse was degrading to women, reducing a "beloved wife" to the status of a prostitute. But here too a new extravagance was sometimes evident. "If you are living this life of sin in matrimony," Joseph Turner informed a Knights of Columbus gathering, "you have made of your own wife a creature 10,000 times worse and more execrable than the common woman there in the street. Her sin is greater even though she hides it from the world by the fair externals of honorable marriage."[84] Such arguments did not prevent the very same preachers from regarding women as especially responsible when it came to contraceptive practice—a theme that had been evident even prior to the First World War. "A word about mothers who tell their young married daughters how to do it," Turner prompted himself in his standard sermon text on marriage. "Another word to those women who ridicule a neighbor for having children."[85]

As they had done for decades previously, mission preachers continued to invoke the Day of Judgment, when supposedly hidden sins would be revealed to a watching world. "All appear before Christ the Judge, who is all-seeing and perfectly just," in the words of Father William Thumel. "He was a witness to all your secret abominations in and out of marriage, and the secret devices and artifices you have as husband or wife made use of to limit the number of your children, or to prevent your becoming a father or mother."[86] They stressed the unknown hour of death—closer, perhaps, than the sinner imagines—and the certainty of eternal punishment for those who failed to amend their lives. "Who knows but you, hardened in sin, may return home tonight jesting over this sermon, lie down in full health to rest, and awake in the flames of hell," as Father Thumel summed things up.[87] And for these preachers wholly innocent of modern Scripture scholarship, the fate of Onan was an irresistible theme. "The words of God on this subject are clear in Holy Scripture," according to the Paulist David Kennedy. "Onan and his wife suffered immediate death because they did this thing 'which was an abomination in the sight of God.'"[88] Father Kennedy, in this instance, took certain liberties with the text, presumably in the cause of relevance. According to the book of Genesis, Onan alone was slain.

The inflated rhetoric of period sermons was especially significant in two as yet unmentioned respects. Mission preachers in the 1920s placed more emphasis than ever before on the problem of bad confessions. Too many penitents, they asserted, confessed to the sin of birth control without intending to abandon it, or failed to confess the sin at all. Absolution secured in such circumstances was clearly invalid, and communions subsequently received were almost bound to be sacrilegious.[89] "They knew they were doing wrong as they began to violate nature," as a Franciscan explained, "but they used all kinds of fleshly soporifics to dull their conscience and lull it to sleep. They either made no mention at all of these mortal sins in the confessional, and lied to the Holy Ghost; or, if they mentioned them, it was without genuine sorrow and a firm purpose of amendment."[90] The road once taken, he concluded, led almost invariably to apostasy. Father Alfred Menth was especially inventive with respect to this subject when he preached a mission renewal sermon on the "Particular Judgment"—one that managed to play as well on the theme of the duplicitous woman. The devil is speaking:

> This soul is the soul of a married woman. I gave her to understand that she was more enlightened. I plied [her] with arguments from the scatter-brained magazines, I made her mind receptive to race suicide. And I appointed her a school mistress of birth control—to go out and teach and suggest to other women what fools they were. I suggested what a cinch it was to make a promise to make an effort—a false promise to try to do better in the future. I told her it would avoid trouble. The Priest would never know. On *that* testimony she belongs to me.[91]

Of even greater significance was the new popularity of certain conceits, theologically problematic, that seemed to conflate the sins of abortion and contraception. "I say nothing of the danger to the commonwealth from birth control and abortion," a Jesuit thundered in a Lenten sermon, "but let those who dare provoke God's wrath by their abominable vices remember that He will have His day. . . . Their unborn babes will rise up in judgment against their selfishness and their pride and their lust."[92] Did Father Lonergan mean to say that the unconceived, as well the aborted, would be present at the Day of Judgment? That obviously makes no logical sense. But his text is, to say the least, ambiguous on this point. Some Redemptorist texts on the Judgment featured an angry God who demanded of the contraceptionist, "Where are the others?"—by which was meant the additional children that God had intended the guilty one to have.[93] What if my own parents had decided to have only two children? Father Turner liked to ask, being himself the eighth child born. "When my father and mother stood before God to be judged, He would say, I intended that your eighth child be my priest. Give an account of this. . . . Think this over—you who are practicing birth control—what answer are you going to make?"[94] The effect of such rhetoric, presumably intended, was to blur the boundary between abortion and contraception. The occasional mission preacher, indeed, went so far as to call the latter murder. "How many children have you not murdered by the secret artifices you made use of to limit the number of your children," demanded Father William Thumel, "or deprived them in one way of the other of their life before they were ever born[?]"[95] The Passionist Theophane Gescavitz evoked a guilt-stricken father on the day of judgment, ruing the sons and daughters who had never been conceived: "They clamored at the door of existence and I killed them as they came there!"[96]

What were the probable causes of such rhetoric, which seems to have reached a peak in the late teens and twenties? Visceral emotion was clearly a factor, especially for men whose formation predated the First World War. Few of them could contemplate the subject of contraception without feeling shame and disgust. Most were also convinced, on what they regarded as wholly rational grounds, that contraceptive intercourse represented a denial of life—a veritable attack on the sources of being. "Purity is such a supreme virtue," as the Paulist John Burke explained in an affecting Christmas sermon, "precisely because it borders the very springs of creation."[97] Seen in this light, contraceptive behavior had strong affinities to abortion, which many priests believed was fostered by popular acceptance of birth control. On a more practical level, many missionary preachers in the 1920s were both shocked and frustrated by the apparent pervasiveness of contraceptive practice among Catholics and their refusal to acknowledge the gravity of the sin. "Far too many of our Catholics, wilfully [sic] or otherwise, have the wrong mental attitude toward this question," as a Missouri layman sized up the situation in 1924. "They draw the line at abortion, but anything this side of it they feel is within the law."[98] In the circumstances, it made strategic sense to link the two—to associate contraception with denying life to children already existing in the mind of God. But the rhetoric that resulted raised certain difficulties. No moralist doubted that continence, whether episodic or long-term, was a licit means of family limitation. The emotional logic of some mission preachers suggested otherwise.

Abortion itself remained an important topic for preachers, especially in the mission context. Blunt talk prevailed here. "From the first moment of conception, that being is a human being, enlivened by an immortal soul," as Father William Thumel pointed out. "You are a double murderer, for you murder both soul and body. . . . You are a worse murderer by far than even if you killed a baptized infant. Those innocent victims will cry out on Judgment Day against you."[99] These same themes were regularly echoed by mission preachers of every order, who apparently assumed that the incidence of abortion—outlawed by now in every American jurisdiction—was not insignificant, even among Catholics. Murder and suicide were rare, as the Franciscan Fulgence Meyer noted in 1927, but "the murder of unborn children is appalling [*sic*] frequent."[100] When it came to abortion, however, mission preachers did not anticipate argument from the pews. Likening contraception to abortion was an increasingly popular tactic precisely because both law and popular sentiment branded the latter as a crime. "Will a mother, who in Holy Communion receives the Divine Lover of Children, be able to destroy the life of her own child, in whose mysterious creation she becomes the co-worker of the Almighty?" asked a Franciscan, whose 1929 sermon text moved seamlessly from birth control to "crimes against the nascent life." "Is not in this case the Most Holy Eucharist the best protection of the unborn child?"[101]

We cannot know the actual frequency of abortion in the 1920s. It was almost certainly less common than it had been fifty years earlier, when abortion had for all intents and purposes not yet been criminalized. But illegal abortions were not rare occurrences, especially among the poor. A sober period estimate put the number of abortions annually at roughly 700,000, of which only a relative handful were legally obtained.[102] Proponents of birth control often argued their case by invoking such numbers, which they firmly believed could be reduced by freer access to contraception. "Birth Control is carried on in the tenements all the time," according to Dr. Alice Hamilton, "but it is not prevention of conception, *that* the women do not understand. It is in the form of abortion, which every woman can learn about if she wishes."[103] The urban poor in the 1920s were disproportionately Catholic, at least outside the South—something that Hamilton did not fail to note.

> Not long ago I invited a group of women to spend a Sunday afternoon with me at Hull-House, all of them married women with large families. The conversation turned very soon on abortions and the best method of producing them, and I was

in consternation to listen to the experiences of these women, who had themselves undergone frightful risks and much suffering rather than add another child to the house too full already. These women were all Catholics, but when I spoke of that, they simply shrugged their shoulders. What could a priest know about a woman's life?[104]

Most, perhaps all, of these Hull House visitors were probably Italian—a group with an unusually distant relationship to the institutional Church. Their seemingly easy dismissal of clerical authority was presumably not typical. Italians figured disproportionately as well among the Catholic clients of Margaret Sanger's birth control clinic in New York, which opened in 1924. These Catholic clients, contra Hamilton, were much less likely to have had an abortion than their Jewish or Protestant counterparts. Still, almost 29 percent of them admitted to such, with many reporting the termination of more than one pregnancy.[105] And period sermons do seem to hint at a kind of informal "abortion culture" among women of precisely the sort that Hamilton described, if only by invoking its colloquialisms. "The teaching of the Church is that the soul is present in the first instant of conception," Father Joseph Turner routinely warned in his "state instruction" to married women. "Therefore, if you do anything to 'bring yourself around'—whether by pills, by violent exercise, or in any other way, you are guilty of abortion." Father Turner, of course, had no doubts at all when it came to his knowledge of women's lives—what mattered were moral absolutes and not the vagaries of personal experience. "Know you then," he concluded his *ferverino* on abortion, "that if you have destroyed your unborn child, whether it was one week or one day, or one hour in your womb, your hands are red with the blood of a human being; you are branded with the brand of Cain—you stand before God and man as a murderess; and all you can do now is to spend the rest of your life in penance."[106]

Father Turner's confidence notwithstanding, there were obviously tensions around questions of family limitation between women and the celibate clergy. These surface periodically in sermons and clerical writing, mostly in the form of irritable asides but sometimes in direct attacks on female selfishness and sensuality. Rarely, however, do we hear the question addressed from the other side, for the relevant lay-authored sources are simply not there. So we have particular reason to be grateful that *America* magazine in 1926 and 1927 ran two brief articles by laywomen on the subject of marital sex, and several letters in reply. This was a most unusual venture for the time—one Michigan pastor was so unnerved by the exchange that he accused *America*'s Jesuit editors of doing the work of the devil. "In several parish assignments and in eight years of fairly wide mission and retreat activity I have had a chance to encourage many good fathers and mothers. I would never want the responsibility of precluding God's greater glory or of jeopardizing their salvation by a Birth Control Review, either the Sangerian publication or its Catholic counterpart

'America.'"[107] But editor Wilfrid Parsons did not doubt the propriety, indeed the necessity, of his decision—which, as it happened, had everything to do with gender. "You are probably aware," he reminded his enraged Michigan correspondent, "of how much harm is done to the Catholic faith by an imprudent one-sided preaching of Catholic doctrine as if all rights in marital matters resided in the man and none whatever in the woman."[108] On this score, his lay female authors clearly bore him out.

Neither of the women questioned even indirectly the substance of Church teaching on contraception. What they did object to was the dominant Catholic understanding of the "marital debt"—the obligation, in other words, to consent to sexual relations at the request of one's spouse—something both women regarded as oppressive to their sex. They also resented the anti-female tenor of Catholic preaching on birth control. "Often I have listened while men high in our religious and social scheme of things talked, learnedly and well (and sometimes ranted and raved) on birth control," as Mary Gordon put it. (Otherwise unidentified, Gordon was thirty years old and had borne five children; she and her husband were still unable to afford a home of their own.) "Always it was the woman to whom they directed their remarks, if remarks they might be termed. I wonder at this, when a little self-restraint or self-sacrifice on the part of the men would make so much difference in the home life of so many, many thousands of our middle-class people." Gordon's resentments were deep and palpable. Her evidently phlegmatic husband seemed incapable of "look[ing] up the road of time and looking think a wee bit about his nice family and their many needs and a few of my ambitions for them." Nor had she much patience with males, presumably mostly clergy, who celebrated frequent childbearing: "They do not have to have them; to be so acutely miserable in mind and body, so all drained out; so unfit to do their daily work; so very, very physically unfit to give a baby life."[109]

The Australian woman who read Gordon's essay "with almost incredulous delight and appreciation" made ambition for her children the principal focus of the feature-length letter she wrote in rejoinder. She and her husband were raising four children on a very limited income, though they planned to send at least their sons to college. "We don't want to have just children. We want strong, healthy, happy children, as nearly perfect as possible, in mind and body." Until and unless their circumstances changed, Margaret Hughes was determined to have no more—apparently by means of complete conjugal abstinence: "What I would do if I had a husband who insisted on his rights, and sheltered himself behind pious platitudes, I don't know. Fortunately for me I happen to have a husband whose sensibilities are fine enough to sympathize with me, and who shares my ideals for the children."[110]

The handful of letters that *America* printed in response to the Hughes and Gordon essays were all but two of them hostile. Their mostly female authors accused Gordon and Hughes of materialism and an unladylike want of propriety.[111] But there is other evidence to suggest that these articles spoke to a troubling increase in gender tensions around the problem of family limitation. Certain clerical reformers, for example, coupled their pleas for more vigorous enforcement of Church teaching with a call for more judicious language when it came to the marital debt. Father Joseph Nevins was chief among them. Most of us emphasize the debt too heavily in our premarital instructions, he cautioned his fellows in 1928.

> Women complain bitterly of their burden and it cannot but be that there is much misunderstanding on their part and not the less on the husband's. Like any duty, the *debitum* has a rational basis and reasonable limitations. Reason forbids intercourse at times, just as reason allows refusal of it. Were this better understood by husbands, wives would be spared much distress and the duties of marriage would be better secured. That it is often not sufficiently inculcated has this consequence that women yield rather than risk displeasure, harsh treatment or desertion, but do so grudgingly and with a mind to save themselves all further possible burden, to the prejudice of the ends of marriage. . . . And the trouble is with the man; he needs a liberal education in marriage. His duty should be told him when his inconsiderateness provokes his wife to the practice of birth control.[112]

Nevins's views were orthodox, but they were hardly mainstream.[113] Most of his confreres, in all likelihood, believed—as they had been taught in seminary—that the marital debt might be refused only when a spouse was abusively drunk or adulterous or when intercourse represented an immediate threat to one's life. A physician's warning that another pregnancy might prove fatal, however, was not generally seen as grounds for refusal. Should a husband insist on his rights, as the Franciscan Fulgence Meyer explained, his afflicted wife "will fare best if she yields virtuously and throws herself completely on the sweet and fatherly providence of God."[114] Nevins did not specify what "reasonable limitations" he had in mind when it came to rendering the debt, though it makes sense to assume that these included concern for the mother's health due to excessive childbearing and perhaps economic worries about a too-large family. (Nevins spoke at one point of a spouse's "duty to refuse.") More remarkably, he analyzed the problem in thoroughly gendered terms. Given the changing roles and status of American women, he correctly saw, priests ran the risk of an angry backlash should they continue to preach an unmitigated gospel of female submission.

Summing Up: The State of the Question on the Eve of the Depression

In November of 1929, the American bishops gathered in Washington for their annual meeting, at which—according to the anonymous recorder's notes—

"an extended discussion" was held about birth control. Would it be advisable to attempt "a survey of its prevalence among our Catholic people?" the assembled prelates were asked. What suggestions did they have for effectively countering the pervasive "propaganda" in favor of contraception? Sioux City's Bishop Edmond Heelan proposed that the assembled bishops issue a joint pastoral letter "dealing with this and kindred subjects"—a suggestion that elicited the enthusiastic support of Spokane's Bishop Charles D. White. But "the motion was not favored." In the end, the assembled bishops declined to do more than commission a new generation of anti-birth control pamphlets.[115]

Since the bishops clearly regarded their people as vulnerable to birth control propaganda, their reluctance to act boldly seems something of a puzzle. Like most of the clergy, however, they were constrained by a number of already-discussed considerations. Every bishop in 1929 was of an age to have been schooled to reticence in matters of sexual sin. The prospect of drafting a pastoral letter devoted exclusively to marital morality may have been genuinely alarming to some. (The 1919 bishops' pastoral had dealt with birth control relatively briefly and in highly euphemistic terms.) The bishops as a group were also deeply invested in sustaining the public fiction that opposition to contraception was broadly Christian. Issuing a pastoral letter on contraception would, among other things, have lent powerful support to the increasingly popular notion that Catholics stood more or less alone in this regard. And perhaps the bishops were secretly a bit afraid of the not always docile laity. "One hears constantly from dutiful mothers that for their faithfulness to their marital obligation they are regarded by others as fools," in the words of the influential Father Nevins, "and are told to their faces that they ought to be ashamed, that a large family is vulgar, that they are doing an injustice to their other children, that they are throwing away their lives, and all the rest of the outrageous rot."[116] If churchgoing wives and mothers were really capable of such logic— and numerous clerical writers in the 1920s assured their colleagues that they were—then the problem faced by pastors was formidable indeed. It was no easy matter to determine the most effective response.

So the American bishops, like the great majority of clergy, emerged in the 1920s as exceedingly cautious reformers. Clearly troubled by growing popular acceptance of contraception, even among Catholics, neither bishops nor clergy were yet inclined to say much about the matter publicly. Nor do they seem, for the most part, to have been proactive confessors when it came to married penitents. It would not be hard, in circumstances such as these, for at least some Catholics to remain in more or less honest ignorance of Church teaching. Only the most isolated could have been wholly unaware that the Catholic Church was opposed to birth control. But probably a not insignificant number failed to comprehend the absolute nature of the prohibition and the status of every contraceptive act as mortally sinful. A good many Catholics, after all, had reason to cling to illusions like these. "Now, My Dear Women, you might as well face this thing honestly," as Father Joseph Turner liked to tell his mission congregations. "Sometimes, when a priest denounces this crime, a woman will say to herself—Oh, he doesn't mean me and what I am doing. Yes, I mean you."[117] Still, it was possible to avoid mission preaching or at least those sermons that everyone knew were going to dwell on birth control. One could take comfort too in the knowledge that many evidently good people—even regularly observant Catholics—were limiting their families by artificial means. One might be reassured as well by the public silence of most bishops and a great many parish priests. If something as commonly practiced as marital contraception was always and everywhere gravely sinful, surely one's spiritual leaders would be obliged in conscience to address it.

The situation changed fundamentally, however, at the close of 1930, when Pope Pius XI issued *Casti Connubii,* his encyclical on Christian marriage. The pope clearly and vigorously reaffirmed what he held to be the constant teaching of the Church against contraception: "Any use whatsoever of marriage, in the exercise of which the act by human effort is deprived of its natural power of procreating life, violates the law of God and nature, and those who do such a thing are stained by a grave and mortal flaw." The pope especially warned confessors against "conniving in the false opinion of the faithful" by failing to question married penitents or giving evasive answers to their queries about birth control.[118] The encyclical, moreover, received wide and remarkably respectful publicity in Europe and North America, in the secular as well as the religious press. Its issuance brought new pressure to bear on bishops and their priests with regard to reforming pastoral practice. And it made it much more difficult for lay Catholics to make a credible claim of good faith ignorance when it came to Church teaching on contraception.

That this momentous encyclical coincided with a global depression of unprecedented severity was a piece of historical bad luck. These were hardly ideal circumstances in which to move toward vigorous enforcement of the prohibition on birth control. The early 1930s, especially, were difficult for priests and their often hard-pressed penitents, and nowhere more so than around the vexing question of family limitation. But other developments in the 1930s, not yet widely visible at the issuance of *Casti Connubii,* caused the drama to unfold in unexpected ways. We turn now to this sometimes surprising and immensely important chapter.

3

"No Longer a Time for Reticence"

A Pivotal Decade: 1930–1941

The year 1930 saw dramatically increased polarization in the religious debate over birth control. Four liberal denominational bodies in the United States—the Universalist General Convention, the American Unitarian Association, the New York East Conference of the Methodist Episcopal Church, and the Central Conference of American Rabbis—had by June of that year given public endorsement to marital contraception.[1] They were followed in August by the Anglicans' Lambeth Conference, which reversed its previous stance against birth control for a guarded blessing of its use in difficult marital circumstances.[2] Partly in response to this latter development, Pope Pius XI issued *Casti Connubii* on the last day of December. As noted above, this encyclical affirmed the absolute nature of the Catholic ban on contraceptive practice and summoned confessors to do battle against lingering pockets of good faith ignorance among the laity. The moral law is eternal and unchanging, asserted the pope; those who would alter or modify its claims—and here he had direct reference to the Anglican bishops—"have openly withdrawn from the Christian doctrine as it has been transmitted from the beginning and always faithfully kept."[3] Like the Anglicans' Lambeth declaration, *Casti Connubii* was the stuff of worldwide news. No previous papal encyclical had received anything approaching the publicity accorded it.

Apart from avowedly left-wing publications, *Casti Connubii* was for the most part received with respect and even sympathy. Catholic periodicals accorded it a near-rhapsodic welcome. "Not since the issuance of Leo XIII's encyclical on the subject has the world listened to a more powerful statement on the relation between economic injustice and moral problems," in the view of *Commonweal*'s lay editor, for whom the teaching on contraception "is simply what every Pope has said, and must say, and will continue to say when or if the need arises for the restatement of the unchangeable, irreformable laws of morality."[4] Many secular publications also greeted the encyclical warmly.[5] It was not necessarily that their editors agreed with Catholic teaching on marital sex in every particular; in a great many cases they probably did not. But most

older Americans at this juncture were sexual conservatives and deeply ambivalent as such about the contraceptive revolution. What lay ahead for marital fidelity and chastity among the young? In such a climate, Catholic doctrine
on marriage—for *Casti Connubii* inveighed against divorce as well as birth
control—might plausibly be read as idealistic rather than repressive. And it
was comforting to hear a full-throated vindication of objective moral standards, even if these were rather stricter than those informing one's own private
life.

The wide publicity afforded the encyclical, coupled with its respectful reception, greatly enhanced its ability to effect change among Catholics. Those
who claimed good faith ignorance of Church teaching on contraception would
henceforth have a far more difficult case to make in their own defense. "This
restatement of marital covenants, this courageous 'that shalt not' to all eu-
genists [*sic*] and companionates without any modifying *if*, leaves Catholics no
excuse for further questionings about their ancient duties," in the stern words
of the magazine *Ave Maria*.[6] As John T. Noonan has noted, moreover, this was
an encyclical with a program.[7] Every priest was charged with active enforcement of the teaching, especially but by no means exclusively in the confessional. Since *Casti Connubii* was near-universally regarded as conveying an
infallible teaching, it seems unlikely that many priests took the instruction
lightly.[8] (Doubts about the encyclical's infallible status were not publicly aired
until the early 1960s.) "It will be necessary to use extreme remedies and correct the false notions that have begun to obscure the light," a Franciscan quite
typically warned his clerical brethren in 1931. "It is no longer a time for reticence."[9]

So *Casti Connubii* ushered in an era of increasingly anguished Catholic consciences. This was true for priests as well as the laity. A good many priests were
still loathe to speak publicly about matters that seemed both shocking and inherently indecent. "And the discussions about birth control and having intercourse without having children," in the agitated words of the Paulist John J.
Burke, "these are the common talk of the day and they almost take our feet
from under us, so that we wonder if we are strangers in a strange land."[10] Of
even more ominous import was a deepening economic depression. How to
convey the Church's necessarily hard teaching to laity increasingly ravaged by
long-term unemployment? Might a more proactive posture in this regard not
risk alienating significant numbers from the Church? As for the laity themselves, and especially the impoverished among them, the conjuncture of *Casti
Connubii* and a global depression meant deep and widespread suffering, albeit
a suffering about which we learn only at secondhand. There are almost no lay-
authored sources for this period that address the personal experience of marriage or sex. It does not take a novelist's imagination, however, to realize that

many of them suffered profoundly in this time of tightening Church discipline, even many of those who chose to ignore Church teaching. Guilt, shame, and the fear of hell can be burdens quite as heavy to shoulder as worries about the rent.

Birthrates and Contraceptive Practice in a Depression Context

In the early years of the Depression, birthrates in the United States fell for the first time in the nation's history to below replacement levels. Even at the end of the decade, despite a modest increase in births, American women were on average producing only slightly more than two children each. Postponed marriages played a role in this regard, especially in the early 1930s, but so to all indications did contraception. Despite laws in most states restricting or even prohibiting access to the various means of birth control, contraceptive devices and information were readily available throughout the decade—energetically promoted by an industry that ostensibly trafficked in disease protection and personal hygiene. "Today contraceptive devices are advertised in magazines of national circulation," as an indignant priest summed up the situation in 1934; "they are sold in drug stores, grocery stores, confectionery stores, garages, shoe shining parlors, taverns, dance halls, and in one hundred and thirty other kinds of establishments, and are even hawked from door to door."[11]

No national data on family planning is available for the period in question. But various local and regional studies indicate a growing use by American couples of condoms, antiseptic douches, and vaginal jellies. Affluent and highly educated women were most likely to employ a diaphragm; coitus interruptus, while diminishing markedly in popularity over the course of the decade, was most apt to be favored by those with the least formal schooling.[12] (Catholics were still, at this juncture, a population with a low average level of educational attainment.) Contraceptive use of any variety was positively correlated with education and income, though religious differences mattered as well. A study of middle- and upper-middle-class married women, published in 1940, found its Catholic respondents less likely than Jews and Protestants to engage in contraceptive practice and less likely, when they did, to use either condoms or diaphragms.[13]

Few fertility studies in the 1930s analyzed their sample populations according to religion. Most researchers apparently believed that social class was a more critical variable. So we have almost no systematic evidence as to the extent or nature of Catholic contraceptive practice. The 1940 study of middle-class wives found "that as many as 43 percent of the Catholics interviewed used methods other than safe period, plain douche, or coitus interruptus."[14] (The last-mentioned would have been gravely sinful for Catholics, as would

douching immediately after intercourse.) These findings are certainly sugges-
tive, but the study in question, given its relatively affluent sample population,
hardly speaks to the generality of Catholic experience.

Still, it was widely assumed by Catholic authorities that a good many Catholics in these years made at least intermittent use of forbidden means of family limitation. They based their conclusions in part on demographic data. A
Wisconsin study, for example, concluded that Catholic birthrates there had declined more rapidly than those of non-Catholics between 1919 and 1933—a
pattern that evidently prevailed among every Catholic ethnic group in the state.
More tentative data suggested that this was generally true of cities outside the
South.[15] Equally troubling were numbers deployed by sundry birth control advocates: from one quarter to one half of the patients seen in urban birth control clinics were routinely said to have identified themselves as Catholics, and
sometimes as Catholics who had previously turned to abortion as a desperate
means of family limitation.[16] ("She could not remember how many miscarriages she had induced by taking drugs in huge quantities," a crusading physician noted of a twenty-nine-year old mother, probably the daughter of Eastern
European immigrants, in a Pennsylvania coal town.)[17] The clergy could also
look to their own experience as counselors and confessors. "It is not well to
sneer at the claims of medical advocates of birth-control that good Catholic
women practice it," a worried priest reminded his confreres in 1931. "Many
apparently good Catholic women not only do so but instruct some about to be
married in its technique. . . . As far as men are concerned it [church teaching
on contraception] is generally dismissed without a thought."[18]

Worried priests like the one just quoted were often given to hyperbole. But
their testimony, so ubiquitous in the 1930s, coupled with falling birthrates and
a growing public acceptance of contraception, does indeed suggest that a significant minority of Catholics—some of them devout—had made a kind of
personal peace with contraceptive practice. "If their conscience disturbs them
at all they lull it with the argument that they have a valid reason to resort to
this unnatural practice, just as they are free to absent themselves from mass on
Sunday, when they have sufficient cause," as a Redemptorist based in St. Louis
explained. "In other words they place the natural law in the same category as
the positive legislation of the church and have never learned to distinguish the
one from the other."[19] An indignant Connecticut layman agreed. His convert
wife, herself a staunch defender of the Church's stand on contraception, had
had many debates on the subject with her Catholic female friends. "She tells
me that she has yet to meet the Catholic woman who does not believe in the
hellish practice in one way or another!"[20]

Notwithstanding such testimony, it is likely that a great many Catholics in
the 1930s did not employ contraception on anything like a regular basis, or indeed at all. Some apparently failed to do so out of ignorance. A study of fam-

ily planning in the early 1930s, about 40 percent of whose sample population was Catholic, found fewer than half of its subjects reporting any form of contraceptive practice. Contraceptive use was strongly correlated in this study with income and education; Catholics were the least-educated group in the sample population.[21] Physicians at birth control clinics made similar claims, though perhaps without full understanding of their clients' discursive habits and worldview. Many Catholics in the 1930s were still inclined to associate "birth control"—the term if not the concept—with the practice of abortion, and apt as well to regard coitus interruptus as morally distinct from the various modes of artificial contraception. Even sensitive questioning, whether by doctor or survey researcher, might not succeed in bridging this cultural divide. Some Catholic women, after years of marriage, had simply lost interest in sex. "They do not want to adopt a new and safe method of contraception," as a Pennsylvania doctor explained, "because they want to keep the failure of previous contraceptive practices and the fear of pregnancy as a barrier between them and their husbands."[22] Religious scruples were also a factor, and one that probably grew in significance over the course of the 1930s. The average Catholic almost certainly lacked complete understanding of the natural law argument against contraception. But that same Catholic clearly knew that his Church regarded contraception as a grave moral evil. The message was conveyed, after *Casti Connubii,* with ever-greater frequency and intensity. To imagine that religiously engaged Catholics could simply ignore the message is to deny the power of a religious culture marked in these years by enormous vitality and a remarkably high degree of institutional separatism.

Even in the absence of *Casti Connubii,* the Depression years would have meant new pressures for Catholic priests and their bishops. With immigration no longer augmenting the Catholic population, falling birthrates among Catholics were no longer masked and could in the practical order no longer be ignored. Marriages and baptisms fell sharply in the early 1930s in many urban parishes. Enrollments in many parochial schools were either static or in decline.[23] Uneasy pastors, already experiencing acute financial anxieties, looked to progressively leaner futures. Who would support the vast parish plants erected at such cost for a rapidly growing immigrant church? Would two- or even three-child families produce adequate vocations to the priesthood and religious life? Certain Catholic leaders went further, predicting an eventual decline in the nation's Catholic population and indeed of the nation itself—the latter fear shared by many non-Catholics. (Fears of population decline played as major a role in the birth control politics of the 1930s, especially in Europe but also in the United States, as fears of overpopulation did in the 1960s.)[24] "The trend of our Catholic population is toward extinction," as Msgr. John A. Ryan pronounced early in 1934. "Our people are showing that they have not the capacity, the courage and the endurance necessary to marry and bring into the world sufficiently large families to ensure group survival."[25] Other equally sober authorities deployed equally daunting—and, as it happens, improbable—statistics. "If the present declining rate of births is not checked or offset in some way," a Franciscan asserted in 1940, "by 1961 . . . in the city of New York no child will be born, and a hundred years after that the city will have but one survivor."[26]

Added to these quite genuine fears was the unprecedented respectability now being accorded to birth control. An influential committee of the Federal Council of Churches endorsed marital contraception in 1931, followed by a growing array of denominational bodies. Their actions reflected, as they helped to legitimate, a profound cultural shift with regard to sex and its purposes. Catholics were still a subcultural population in the United States, but not so removed from the larger culture as to be unaffected by its seismic tremors. Most Catholics, fewer and fewer of whom were foreign-born, read mass-circulation magazines and newspapers, listened to national radio programs, and—despite the best efforts of the Legion of Decency—patronized popular movies. Such media typically preached the closely related gospels of personal autonomy and self-expression; romantic love and a couple-centered view of marriage; consumer choice and a gently conventional hedonism. These were not new themes in the 1930s. But they were publicized then more widely, insistently, and skillfully than ever before by national industries of mass information and entertainment.

By the 1930s, moreover, the advocates of birth control had been public actors for sufficiently long to have mostly lost their radical aura. (Mainstream women's magazines were endorsing the cause by the mid-1930s.) Experience had made them adroit publicists, too. The terrible suffering of the early 1930s made highly effective grist for the pro-birth control mills; what could be crueler—or more unfair to taxpayers—than denying the necessary means of fertility control to the long-term unemployed? Even committed Catholics were not unmoved by this logic. "The fact that some 11,000,000 workers are unemployed in America today cannot be pondered without pondering the question of unregulated births," as layman Frank Smothers pointed out in *Commonweal* in 1933.[27]

Many priests in the 1920s, and some lay leaders, too, had been deeply alarmed by inroads among Catholics of contraceptive values and behavior. Circumstances in the early 1930s greatly intensified these fears. So the ranks of "reformers" among the clergy—those who wished their confreres to inveigh against contraception as confessors, counselors, and preachers—would surely have grown then, even in the absence of a papal encyclical on marriage. But it is much less certain, given the context of widespread economic collapse, that such reformers could have mustered a mass clerical following, at least for the duration of the Depression. Would the Catholic teaching on contraception have survived, in any practical sense, had a reforming movement of this sort been delayed until after the Second World War? One could plausibly argue that it would not. In any event, the pope did issue an encyclical—one that summoned all priests to frontline stations in a veritable war against birth control. Catholic pastoral practice, and thus the experience of being a Catholic, was fundamentally altered as a result.

Confession

Casti Connubii had spoken to priests specifically in their role as confessors. "Let not confessors permit the faithful to err about this most serious law," the encyclical cautioned, whether by failing to interrogate penitents when circumstances would warrant it, maintaining silence when penitents voiced mistaken views of the teaching, or neglecting to admonish penitents who confessed to the sin of birth control.[28] There were certainly many American priests who already behaved as the pope commanded. But many others—perhaps even a majority—did not. Most priests, as we have seen, had been trained to a prudential reticence in confession. For older priests, this might easily mean an avoidance of all questions relating to marital sex. Most younger priests had been taught to question, but only in certain circumstances and only in circumspect language. "If a confessor suspects the abuse of matrimony," in the words of a moral theology textbook published in 1930 and written by two Dominicans, "he ought to inquire about it, though prudently, so as not to scandalize the penitent by indiscreet words." In the absence of well-founded suspicion, a confessor should never attempt to interrogate, "lest the penitent become impatient at having his good will called into question." And even this quite conservative volume left room for good faith ignorance on the part of at least the occasional penitent. While the confessor should normally reprove offending penitents "severely" and require that they manifest convincing signs of contrition, "if it should happen that invincible ignorance renders an admonition futile, the penitent may be let go in good faith."[29] Such invincible ignorance might be present, the Dominican authors noted, "when married persons are poor or the woman sickly."[30] Issued just prior to *Casti Connubii,* this widely admired textbook embodied the deeply conflicted mentality of the 1920s. Contraception might rank next to murder "in enormity," as its authors asserted.[31] Priests should nonetheless do battle against it with utmost tact, and be willing to recognize that certain persons were simply incapable of comprehending the intrinsic sinfulness of contraceptive behavior.

Confessors were also handicapped, in a good many cases, by very large numbers of penitents—a problem that generally worsened in the 1930s. The Depression decade saw in most parishes a continuation of the previously discussed trend toward more frequent reception of the sacraments. Growing numbers of Catholics were confessing monthly or even weekly, which placed taxing demands on their priests and had consequences for penitents as well. "The increased number of confessions due to frequent Communion, special devotions, etc, has developed a tendency to incomplete, inaccurate and often mechanical accusation of sins," in the view of New York's Monsignor John Belford. "On the confessors' part, there is a disinclination, for lack of time, to search hearts for underlying dangers in modes of living and association."[32] Others echoed Belford's assessment, some mostly blaming the laity for evasive behavior as penitents but many more placing the principal onus on numbers. We overburdened priests spend too much time hearing "confessions of devotion," the latter argument ran, by which was meant the confessions of persons who were conscious of nothing but venial—that is to say, minor—sins. "Another source of irritation to the priest [is the person] who just has to go to confession every time she (usually) hears a cassock rustle," according to one palpably irritated voice from this camp. "Even if a person goes to Communion every day he is not obliged to go to confession each week."[33] Being thus unprofitably occupied, priests had too little time for adequate treatment of troubled or hardened sinners, who usually compounded the problem by making their infrequent confessions at the busiest times of the year.[34]

The results of such pressures were predictable and with obvious import for a sin like birth control. Few confessors could function as educators with regard to morality, or respond to the particulars of difficult personal circumstances. "I had hardly time enough to get down on my knees before the Father started giving me absolution," a startled laywoman reported in 1934, having just returned from a long stay in Europe. European confessors, in her telling, were patient and courteous with penitents; in the United States, speed was apparently of the essence.[35] Whatever the accuracy of her European memories, this woman's version of her American experience was echoed on all sides, and generally unhappily. "Nothing good but much harm comes from absolutions given at the rate of forty, fifty or more an hour," in the view of a disgruntled priest, who worried especially about the effect on "willfully ignorant and not seldom stubborn people who come to confession once a year."[36] Monsignor Reynold Hillenbrand, rector in the mid-1930s of Chicago's influential archdiocesan seminary, found it necessary in his preaching to apologize for—even to defend—brusque and hurried confessors. "Forget it—overlook it," Hillenbrand advised his hearers. The "abrupt" priest who so offended you "probably had lots of confessions to hear; he probably got up with a headache that day."[37]

For all the burdens created by excessive numbers of penitents, however, only a relative handful of priests were ultimately prepared to argue for a less demanding regime. Pious old women might properly be discouraged from confessing too frequently, but the great majority of Catholics—as their priests saw it—were in urgent need of regular confession. Hillenbrand probably spoke for most of his confreres when he urged weekly confession as the norm for good Catholics in his standard talk on the sacrament. You need not be conscious of serious sin, he told his hearers; "the very fact that we go to confession means we increase the grace in the soul—we are holier in God's sight and our Heaven will be happier."[38] Frequent confession, it was hoped, would dispose even morally sluggish penitents to be more conscientious. No matter how hurried or mechanical their penitents' current confessions might seem, most priests assumed that the process itself would gradually create in them a heightened consciousness of sin and an increased awareness of its dangers. The disciplinary potential of the sacrament, in other words, was simply too great for most priests to regard as ideal anything but its frequent reception.

In the circumstances, *Casti Connubii* posed something of a conundrum for a good many priests and their bishops. All the American bishops endorsed the encyclical publicly; some ordered their clergy to read it from the pulpit on successive Sundays or to preach a series of sermons on its principal themes. But I have found only a single instance of a bishop's responding to the encyclical by directing his priests to alter their practice as confessors. Chicago's Cardinal George Mundelein instructed confessors in 1931 to question married female penitents about the sin of birth control "when a family is small or apparently spaced," which would almost inevitably require a priest to ask every adult woman penitent about her marital status and the number and age of her children.[39] He broadened the instruction to include male penitents in 1932. "In some cases they are the real offenders," he told his priests at their annual clergy conference. Questioning men would be more difficult than questioning women, the cardinal warned. "The man will answer back, will try to argue. . . . A man is not quite so religious as a woman, he will not so likely be frightened by danger of sudden death in sin."[40] But whatever the difficulties, confessors were obliged to question; nor could they absolve a penitent of this sin "until the promise to abstain in the future is given. . . . There can be no such excuse as ignorance or good faith." Mundelein also ordered change with regard to premarital instruction. "There is a long interrogatory to be answered, filled out and sworn to by both parties, with express mention of avoidance of birth control practices," as he explained. When the marriage involved a non-Catholic partner, both parties were required to sign a set of promises that included abstaining "from the practices [*sic*] of birth control."[41]

Though I have found no records to this effect, it is certainly possible that other American bishops behaved as Mundelein did. The cardinal himself, however, seemed to think that his was a brave but lonely stance. "There is of course no intention of criticizing other dioceses or sections," as he put it in 1932, explaining the measures referred to above. "I am responsible only for my own."[42] He commended his example to his episcopal confreres in 1934, implying as he did so that none had yet had the foresight or indeed the courage to embrace it.[43] That Chicago was anomalous in this regard is also suggested by my own interviews with priests. All but the youngest of my Chicago informants—those ordained in the early 1960s—recalled being taught in seminary to question penitents about birth control. But except for some with Roman training, no other priests remembered such instruction. One typically waited for the penitent to confess this sin, or at the very least to provide an obvious opening for a confessor's probing. "The confessor must remember that his own role in the tribunal is not that of Sherlock Holmes on the trail of Professor Moriarity, not that of a District Attorney or County Prosecutor out to secure a conviction," in the words of a popular period manual for confessors.[44]

What, then, was the practical effect of *Casti Connubii* on confessors' practice? Things do seem to have changed in Chicago, or so the available evidence suggests. Mundelein claimed that he ordered the questioning of male as well as female penitents on the advice of certain of his priests, whose obedient questioning of women had implicated husbands.[45] Evidently these same priests had not previously been in the habit of interrogating even their female penitents when it came to birth control. A Jesuit stationed in Chicago offered heartrending testimony to the costs of that archdiocese's new regime. "Every priest who is close to the people admits that contraception is the hardest problem of the confessional today," according to Father Joseph Reiner. "I have spoken to our own missionaries and to many pastors on the subject. Just a few days ago I asked a pastor whether he believed that the statement made to me by a graduate nurse that more than one half our married people use contraceptives is correct. 'I do not think so,' he said, 'I know so.'" Many such Catholics, according to Reiner, had persuaded themselves that birth control was not invariably wrong. For this reason, they were not accustomed to mention their contraceptive lapses in confession. More scrupulous penitents avoided confession, eventually "find[ing] themselves outside the Church." Chicago's now-proactive confessors presumably came into repeated conflict with those in the former group, at least some of whom would have responded by staying away from confession. As for those in the latter group, the new regime might arguably work to drive even more from the Church. Father Reiner, for one, feared "that Catholics are leaving the Church in 'droves' because of her stand in regard to contraception."[46]

Even in Mundelein's Chicago, however, priests could hardly have questioned every married penitent about birth control. The lines outside the confessional were often too long to permit this kind of interrogation. The late Monsignor John Egan, ordained in 1943, recalled being taught at Chicago's major seminary to question only those married penitents who had been away from confession for at least six months—a practice that would catch many but certainly not all of those who employed forbidden means of family limitation.[47] Other Chicago priests whom I interviewed have similar memories, which suggests that seminary teaching in Chicago, by the 1940s if not before, had quietly accommodated the overburdened confessor.[48] Chicago's priests, like those elsewhere, had ultimately to rely on penitents themselves to admit to the sin of contraception. They had ultimately to rely, in other words, on the cumulative educational impact of sermons decrying birth control, pamphlets and periodical articles to this effect, and the by-now highly public drama of Catholic opposition to the easy availability of contraceptive information and devices.

The extent to which such propagandizing affected confession is impossible to measure. We are dealing, lest we forget, with an intensely private encounter. But period sources do suggest this was an era of change, even in venues less strictly policed than Chicago. Consider the well-informed musings of a Redemptorist priest in 1937, who wrote—not insignificantly—to encourage discussion among parish priests about the most effective modes of questioning penitents with regard to contraception. Father H. A. Seifert conceded the existence of apparently numerous Catholics whose consciences were untroubled by this sin because—so they claimed—"the confessor never asks them about it, or the confessor absolves them regularly without further comment." Such testimony appears to implicate priests as well as the laity: Perhaps goodly numbers in both camps were in practice mostly untouched by *Casti Connubii*? But the picture drawn by this Redemptorist was more complicated. "Frequently one hears of penitents changing confessors because this or that priest asks too many personal questions. Or it happens that they say they do not accuse themselves (even when theologically guilty) of the sin, arguing that not they but their partner in marriage is at fault."[49] Observations like these suggest something other than good faith ignorance on the part of many allegedly untroubled penitents; those who shopped around for confessors or blamed a spouse clearly knew the substance of Church teaching on contraception. And many of these allegedly untroubled penitents had evidently encountered confessors who not only asked hard questions but were unwilling to grant absolution without the penitent's promising to amend her marital ways.

Father Seifert also made reference to "those who offer specious arguments, the commonest of which are that they are acting on the advice of a physician or that their financial condition makes the observance of this law impossible."[50] This too suggests conflict in the confessional, or perhaps on occasion in the rectory parlor. (Seifert's was not an isolated observation; the self-justifying penitent featured regularly in the clerical literature of the 1930s.) Conflict of this sort might be sparked by a confessor's questions. It might also result from a penitent's mentioning of a sin which he then proceeded to justify. Both behaviors seem in the 1930s to have become more common. Priests in the wake of *Casti Connubii* were to all appearances increasingly unyielding when it came to the problem of birth control, although some moved in this direction with evident reluctance and uncertainty. The laity, for their part, were increasingly apt to confess to the sin, or at least to leave openings for clerical questions in this regard. This was true, evidently, even in those many cases where penitents themselves were not wholly convinced that their conduct was genuinely sinful. Perhaps the new regime in confession fueled gossip among the laity—gossip that prompted at least some Catholics to a greater, if sometimes confused, scrupulosity about family limitation. "Does the Church order that Catholic married women should have a child every year?" a Brooklyn woman wondered in 1934. "I was told that a Catholic woman was not allowed to go to confession because in her seven years of married life she had given birth to only two children."[51]

Clerical journals in the 1930s strongly suggest that birth control was an increasingly frequent problem in confession. These journals devoted far more space to the contracepting penitent than they had previously done, and carried many more queries on the topic from beleaguered confessors. The latter are especially revealing. Some evoke stubborn or willfully ignorant penitents. Can a woman who "totally disagrees" with Church teaching and plans to practice birth control in her upcoming marriage receive absolution?[52] How should one deal with a man whose wife insists that her own confessor has, on the grounds of the wife's precarious health, given her "special permission" to use contraceptives?[53] Hard cases loom especially large. Can the wife of an alcoholic, the two youngest of whose six children have been born with congenital deformities, protect herself contraceptively when her drunken husband forces her to have sex? "Unfortunately cases of the kind related here by our correspondent are frequent enough to add considerably to the worries of the confessor who wants to do what God commands in the guidance of souls," according to the response by a Franciscan moralist.[54] What guilt is incurred by a priest who fails to admonish penitents who defend their contraceptive practice by invoking "really grave physical or economical circumstances"?[55] May a woman douche immediately after being raped?[56]

Writers sought help too with more mundane difficulties. How should one judge the guilt of the spouse whose partner insists on using contraceptives? Under what circumstances might he or she licitly consent to intercourse?[57] What about fornication—was greater guilt attached to it when a couple took contraceptive precautions?[58] And then there was the vexing problem of recidivism. Was a penitent's mere presence in the confessional a persuasive sign of his sorrow for a sin like birth control? How many lapses on a penitent's part should be tolerated?[59] "Confessors delude themselves if they think they can evade the responsibility of their office by using the mere cliché 'Do the best you can' and then giving absolution," warned an Oblate priest in response to such questions.[60] His stern counsel, however, conflicted directly with a principal tenet of every confessor's training. The model confessor hardly ever refused a penitent absolution.

Very likely the authors of questions like these were recent recruits to the war against birth control. Their queries betray confusion over fairly obvious points of moral theology and a want of long experience. But these authors were probably not unusual. The priest editors of the clerical journals in which their questions appeared evidently assumed that their readers included many such men. They assumed as well that *Casti Connubii* had made the life of confessors more difficult. "It is everywhere conceded that we may not leave our people in good faith on this subject," as the aforementioned Father Seifert noted, hastening to acknowledge the difficulties thereby created.[61] No one doubted that many of the laity failed to grasp the natural law argument on which Church teaching rested, much less to be persuaded by it. No one doubted their puzzlement, and frequently their bitter resentment, at a teaching whose absolute nature made no allowance for even the most extreme cases. Nor did anyone doubt that Catholics heard, and were often influenced by, a Protestant discourse that increasingly spoke of marital contraception as a moral good. The Catholic priest, by contrast, was heir to a moral theology that required a wife to resist the sexual advances of her condom-using husband: "a wife may not consent even under duress," as John A. Ryan explained a 1916 ruling by the Sacred Penitentiary in Rome, "but is obliged to offer the same resistance that a virgin would offer to rape."[62]

To make matters worse, the confessor confronted these problems alone. Priests seldom or never discussed hard cases with their rectory brethren or even their closest clerical friends. Such talk, it was feared, might violate the seal of confession, no matter how general the terms in which a discussion was couched. But priests did hear occasional rumors, sometimes through their unhappy penitents, about allegedly permissive priests. The previously mentioned wife whose drunken husband insisted on sex had apparently been told by her regular confessor that she might legitimately protect herself against another pregnancy. ("The wife got the notion that she has as much right to protect herself against pregnancy as an unmarried woman who is attacked and forced to sexual intercourse by an aggressor."[63]) Many such rumors could be dismissed as the products of lay ignorance or self-deception. Others, however, had the ring of truth—and with potentially demoralizing consequences. If certain of one's confreres could find ways to accommodate hard cases, was it right oneself to take a harder line? The redoubtable Cardinal Mundelein anticipated such qualms of conscience when he addressed his priests at their annual conference in 1932, and provided what he regarded as an irrefutable response. "Many a good priest's heart bleeds when he comes out of the confessional after having insisted on the law of God to some harassed poor father or mother," the cardinal acknowledged. "But that was his duty."[64]

Painful encounters of this sort did not occur in a vacuum. Behavior changed in confession—that of the laity as well as their priests—because changes occurred in the broader context of Catholic life. Chief among these were preaching and the stance of the Catholic media with regard to birth control. It is to these closely linked topics that we now turn.

Preaching in Various Guises

The Catholic laity in the 1930s were more likely than ever before to hear sermons opposing birth control and abortion. Some of these sermons were preached from the regular Sunday pulpit—something that hardly ever occurred prior to *Casti Connubii*. Many more were encountered at missions, retreats, and novenas. These were not new venues in the 1930s for preaching on putative sins against marriage. But that decade saw a substantial increase in attendance at such services, with missions reaching probably the zenith of their popularity and retreats attracting unprecedented numbers of the more affluent laity. The message, moreover, was augmented in ways that were new to the 1930s. Blunt sermons decrying birth control now featured on the radio, and not only in the major archdioceses. Catholic periodicals, including those aimed at a general lay audience, carried regular features on the subject and a seemingly ceaseless stream of editorial invective. Pamphlets on birth control proliferated throughout the decade, nearly all of them aimed at a mass audience and couched for the most part in remarkably forthright terms. Plain speaking was increasingly the order of the day, even at times in the Sunday pulpit: "In these days of moral aberration the advocates of sin have said too much on platform, in press and even handbill thrust impudently at one, for Christian reticence to be any longer a virtue," in the words of a Brooklyn pastor, many of whose sermons—including several on birth control—were reprinted in the Brooklyn *Daily Eagle*.[65]

For a good many parish priests, *Casti Connubii* was the immediate cause of their first pulpit venture in speaking on birth control. Bishops in a number of dioceses directed their priests to read the encyclical from the pulpit and sometimes to preach on it, most typically during the Lenten season of 1931.[66] In some dioceses, the practice was apparently made a regular feature of the Church preaching year. "Many bishops prescribe a yearly series of Lenten instructions on the nature, purpose and right use of matrimony," according to a Precious Blood priest in 1933.[67] That birth control was suddenly mentionable in an ordinary Sunday sermon is a significant development, at least as much for the preacher as his congregation. But the Latinate periods of *Casti Connubii* afforded a certain protection to both. Cardinal Mundelein, for all his promotion of questioning in the confessional, was simultaneously uneasy about frank Sunday preaching on contraception "because of the mixed audiences before us."[68] The diction of *Casti Connubii*, however, evidently seemed safe to the cardinal: when he ordered his priests to preach extensively on marriage during the Church year beginning in Advent of 1935, the prescribed sermons on birth control and abortion consisted almost entirely of passages from the encyclical.[69] Presumably its mildly arcane language and baroque sentences would fall, in the case of the young and unmarried, on uncomprehending ears. This might, of course, be true as well for certain highly motivated members of the married laity.

Mundelein's doubts about frank Sunday preaching were widely shared by his brother bishops and many moral theologians. "Be prudent," Chicago's Reynold Hillenbrand quite typically warned his homiletics students in the later 1930s. "People dislike too much frankness, particularly from their parish priests [and] young priests[;] they will take more from a missionary [or] occasional preacher." But men like these no longer believed that Sunday preachers should avoid the subject altogether. It would be "good," as Hillenbrand told his students, "if pastors preached more on birth control." A pastor's age and station would presumably lend him the requisite authority for this delicate task. Even the pastor, however, should keep his remarks to a minimum, at least as Hillenbrand saw it. He ought to remind his hearers that birth control was a mortal sin, that the term signified more than abortion, and that children brought joy into even objectively difficult circumstances. The message could easily be conveyed in "two or three sentences."[70]

Sunday preaching, then, was in the best of circumstances a difficult balancing act. One could easily say too much, or otherwise give inadvertent offense. "We should give no room, if we can possibly avoid it," as one experienced priest advised, "for knowing smirks or indignant looks amongst our hearers."[71] But what with the pope having spoken and the secular politics of birth control having reached so fierce a pitch, some priests may have felt that at least occasional preaching on "the right use of marriage" was close to a moral imperative. The decade's clerical journals would have encouraged them to think so: these carried far more model sermons on birth control than ever before, as well as articles endorsing such preaching. The model texts were typically brief, though certainly longer than the two or three sentences envisioned by Monsignor Hillenbrand. Nor were they particularly graphic. But the trend was unmistakably toward greater directness and more concrete language. It might suffice to note, in 1932, that "the Church is the only institution in the world which is checking the general drift of human ethics to a purely pagan level. She alone dares to assert that all present-day practices which undermine the sanctity of marriage and family life are directly contrary to the law of God."[72] It was standard just a few years later to name the sin in question. "Birth control is practically always motivated by selfishness," according to a 1937 offering for the Feast of the Holy Family, "and the selfish parent cannot be a good father or mother. The Catholic Church condemns birth-control and the enemies of the Church approve of it—and both for the same reason: birth control is fatal to the existence of family life as God has planned it."[73]

We obviously do not know how many priests based their own sermons on such models, or indeed how many were regular readers of the journals in question. Probably only a minority did so, and a relatively small minority at that. The sermon was still a hurried affair at most Sunday masses. Many big-city pastors, according to Father John A. O'Brien, prided themselves "on getting the congregation out in 38 minutes. The parish announcements consume most of the time allotted for the pulpit, scarcely five minutes being rescued for the sermon." Nor, quite apart from the inevitable inattentiveness, did all present necessarily hear those sermons that did manage to get preached. "In many of our large churches the acoustics are so poor that the preacher cannot be heard by half the congregation."[74] Circumstances like these would hardly encourage elaborate sermon preparation. Priests also worried, though they seldom said so, about alienating a significant portion of the congregation, as sermons on birth control were almost bound to do. "There is a widespread feeling on the part of non-Catholics, shared by many of our own laity, that we of the clergy because of our celibacy do not realize the moral impossibility of continued restraint," Father O'Brien warned in 1933. "This is class legislation, they allege, and is not based upon the stark realities of the case."[75] A Paulist put the problem bluntly, based on his own many years of frank preaching in the course of parish missions. "In certain types of male audiences especially, a preacher can sense the Leftist leaven working, the creeping paralysis of skepticism about the very idea of religion, and it rather tends to unnerve him. . . . Not only will they not give up sin (v.g., contraception), but they are reluctant to accept that it is a sin."[76]

There were other obstacles, too, partly in the psychological order. Young priests, whatever their zeal or idealism, may have shrunk from preaching about marital sex to men and women who were in some cases old enough to be their parents. Even hearing about birth control in the confessional was a cause of profound embarrassment in the early years of his priesthood, as a Polish American priest from Milwaukee confided in the course of our interview, especially when his penitent was obviously a middle-aged woman or man. (Though this priest was ordained in 1956, he had been raised in a working-class world with near-Victorian norms when it came to talk about sex.[77]) Many older priests, never adequately prepared for the preaching ministry nor particularly successful in its performance, may have doubted the utility of Sunday preaching on any but the most basic points of doctrine. A difficult subject like birth control, quite apart from its delicate nature, was best left to men with extensive training in homiletics. Mission preachers were by far the most numerous members of this select population, as every pastor knew. "Missionaries are willing to take the odium of explaining this matter very clearly and can speak impersonally," as a Redemptorist reassured them. "The pastor can feel at ease that at least those of his flock who have attended this sermon (and the rest quickly hear about it), are now very clearly reminded of their serious duty."[78]

If the typical Sunday pulpit was still mostly silent when it came to the problem of family limitation, important changes were nonetheless occurring. Some priests did take the aforementioned model texts seriously, and at least on occasion put them to use. The *Acolyte,* a popular journal for priests, surveyed its readers in 1937 to determine their views on the sermon texts that featured monthly. A substantial majority of those responding endorsed their utility. "As a young, unsophisticated, yet busy assistant," ran a typical reply, this one from Florida, "I consider your sermon suggestions a real port in the storm, after a busy night in a boiling confession box."[79] Texts like these reminded priests of their obligation to make known and enforce Church teaching on birth control. They provided a language for speaking publicly about a subject hitherto addressed in private venues only. Perhaps most important, these model texts provided priests with answers to questions that many felt unprepared to address. How, for example, could parents rear large families in a time of seemingly chronic high levels of unemployment? Couples like these, according to a 1939 text, should approach the sacraments regularly to "draw sufficient strength to do God's will and save their souls." ("Though it is obvious that some of her children do not so regard her, the Church is a good mother and she is in full and heartfelt sympathy with every father and mother who are groaning under the burden of parenthood today."[80]) God would also provide in the material order. "Our lives, our health, our employment are in God's hands," in the words of a 1936 offering, "and since He will never ask the impossible, He will provide the things needed when parents are scrupulous about obeying His laws."[81] The same hard question presented an opening for preaching on social justice. Profiteering landlords and employers who refused to pay a living wage were perhaps more guilty of grave sin than the parents they drove to contraceptive practice, according to a Sunday sermon text by the Jesuit C. C. Martindale. "I feel that for every one denunciation of contraception that we utter, we should proclaim *at least two* against social sin, individual or collective."[82]

Texts like these helped to alter the climate in which most parish priests lived. The gentleman priest of the late nineteenth century—the man for whom "Christian reticence" was a supreme virtue—was no longer a compelling ideal, even for many older clergy. In his stead stood the priest who looked unblinkingly at sin, and spoke to a fallen world in language it could understand. Model sermons were a natural symbol of such an ideal, particularly when they addressed hard problems like birth control. "An element in the sermons which gives me much joy," as an admiring priest wrote of one such series in the *Acolyte,* "is the fact that they not merely recognize the problem of sin, but that the writer is also cognizant of the pyramid of crystallized sin which has incrusted itself on western civilization so thoroughly that it is rapidly stifling its life's breath."[83] Not every priest could live the ideal, especially as a Sunday preacher. But the ideal was still a force for change in probably a good many cases. It eroded the habit of reticence in the confessional. It may well have prompted the occasional frank parish sermon to same-sex groups like the Holy Name Society. And it probably encouraged at least some pastors to make generous provision for various forms of special preaching. A conscientious pastor could import the occasional "straight talker" for a Lenten series aimed at adults. He could promote attendance at retreats. Most important, he could arrange to have regular missions preached in his parish, perhaps as frequently as at two-year intervals. Chicago's Cardinal Mundelein provided a model in 1933. That year saw the silver anniversary of his episcopate, which he ordered commemorated by the holding of a mission in every parish of his vast archdiocese.[84]

Mundelein's directive, in all likelihood, had everything to do with birth control. Mission preachers, as we have seen, had long been known for their frank and sometimes graphic sermons on the subject. Mundelein was deeply concerned about birth control at precisely this juncture in his career. The cardinal chose well: mission preachers in the 1930s invariably spoke against contraception, generally at length and with omnipresent reference to an angry God who punished sin. "Men and women will not admit that what they are doing in secret in their family relations is wrong," as a Paulist told a Minneapolis mission in 1934—one apparently preached to a congregation of both sexes and hence rhetorically muted. "They do not want to hear a priest talk about it. They do not want to be reminded that Almighty God struck a man dead for doing what they are doing. . . . They do not stop to realize that Almighty God has already condemned them."[85] The Redemptorist Alfred Menth made the point more starkly in a sermon on the "General [Last] Judgment." A "faithless" wife—an unrepentant contraceptor—is brought before the Just Judge: "Stand before this tribunal. You outraged your God. You laughed at His laws, thought you knew better, thought you would escape, thought it was all so unreasonable, none of God's business." This sermon was nearly always followed by one on the torments of hell.[86]

As the above-quoted examples indicate, mission preaching in the 1930s did not differ fundamentally from that of the previous decade. It employed many of the same tropes and was informed by the same intense consciousness of death, judgment, and the very real danger of eternal damnation. A highly successful Carmelite preacher quite typically commended meditation on death as an antidote to sexual desire.[87] The general tone with regard to marital sex was still markedly negative. Mission preachers hardly ever spoke of sex as a means of enhancing marital affection, although this was recognized in Church teaching as a legitimate "secondary end" of marital intercourse. Sex in marriage, as these preachers told it, was intended for procreation only; sexual attraction between the spouses was otherwise dangerous—a source of constant temptation to the "shaming and degrading," indeed "vicious," sin of contraception.[88] "Make clear what the essence of marriage is: the mutual conferring of rights to procreation," in the words of a Redemptorist guide to preaching, and an updated guide at that.[89]

Changing circumstances, however, did call for subtle shifts in emphasis. Mission preachers in the 1930s took greater pains than ever before to distinguish contraception from abortion. They placed greater stress on the immutability of Church teaching with regard to birth control, and sometimes spoke to the question—tangentially related—of whether non-Catholics who used birth control would, in the absence of due repentance, go to hell. They assigned to men a greater responsibility for contraceptive practice than they had previously done, although women were still held ultimately accountable for the moral tone of their marriages. And at least some mission preachers broke with past practice and began to denounce birth control before congregations of the young and unmarried.

The distinguishing of contraception from abortion was necessitated by a persistent habit among some laity of assuming that "birth control" meant the actual taking of fetal life. "The nature of birth control is not known by many married people," as an experienced Redemptorist explained in 1940. "They confuse it with abortion. So long as there was not life, so long as life was not taken away, they do not think they are practising [*sic*] birth control."[90] Perhaps mission preachers themselves were partly to blame for the confusion: in the decade after the First World War, as we have seen, many tended in their sermons to conflate the sins of abortion and contraception. Such talk was much less common in the 1930s, in part because of priests' growing worries about seeming lay confusion. But even in the 1930s, talk of this sort had not disappeared.

The alleged confusion, however, resulted from more than ambiguous clerical rhetoric. Equating "birth control" with abortion was, for many of the laity in question, an imprecise way of articulating a kind of dissenting morality with regard to marital sex. This dissenting moral orientation assumed that abortion was gravely wrong, despite the conviction of many priests that lukewarm Catholics were often tolerant of abortion in the earliest stages of pregnancy. Couples unpleasantly surprised by a pregnancy could presumably not turn to it, no matter what their circumstances, without being guilty of serious sin. But the use of coitus interruptus or even artificial contraceptives in marriage fell into a different moral category. The rightness or wrongness of acts like these could not be determined apart from the circumstances in which they occurred. It was not that such "dissenting" Catholics rejected the premise of a natural law. They would probably have explained their opposition to abortion in terms consonant with the natural law tradition. But they clearly rejected the notion that contraception was sinful per se. "The intrinsic deordination of contraceptive practices they cannot regard as morally evil," as John A. Ryan summed up the thinking of "many" Catholic laity, "since it does not necessarily produce bad effects and sometimes has obviously good effects."[91]

Mission preachers in the 1930s did their manful best to dispel the apparently widespread confusion between contraception and abortion. They addressed it routinely in sermons on marriage and in generally forthright terms.[92] "Sometimes people confuse [abortion] and birth control," acknowledged Chicago's Reynold Hillenbrand, first head of that archdiocese's own corps of mission preachers. "So from the outset, that our ideas may be clear, let's see what those words we hear so often, the words 'birth control' mean. . . . It means the kind of control that is had by preventing the conception of the child, it means doing anything to prevent a mother from becoming pregnant[;] that is a sin, a mortal sin, no matter how it's done."[93] Explanations like this do seem to have had an effect. I found few references in the later 1940s to the misapprehension just described, and almost none in the 1950s. The culture's increased openness with regard to contraception presumably made a difference, too. Even working-class Catholics by the 1950s would have been familiar—in theory if not in practice—with the principal means of contraception and its terminology. They would also have been less likely than Catholics in the 1930s to limit their families by coitus interruptus.

Mission preachers had for years been contending against the notion that the Church would one day modify, or even abandon, its opposition to contraception. But in the 1930s, with the public endorsement of birth control by so many Protestant bodies, the question assumed a greater urgency. Mission preachers responded accordingly. The prohibition on contraception was an aspect of the natural law, they argued again and again. The Church was powerless to change it. Should the Church ever try to do so, as Reynold Hillenbrand liked to tell his mission congregations, "she will be acting against God, & is no longer God's church." The pope himself had made this clear in his recent encyclical: "God gave us the Pope to tell us—& because he knew that some people were saying that/ he told us, once and for all, that this [is] a law of God & nature, not a law of the church, & the Church could never change it." As Hillenbrand and his confreres knew, the debate was as much about authority as it was about birth control. "Why[,] if the Church up until now could have made the mistake of teaching that b[irth] c[ontrol] was a sin & it really isn't," as Hillenbrand put it, "then for 1900 [years] she made a grievous error—she had fooled people & she couldn't be the true, infallible church to which we would belong." Catholics who claimed to believe that the Church was wrong in this regard, or that she would eventually repudiate the teaching, were sinfully self-deluding.[94] A Passionist preacher concurred. "Some Catholics can't see why the

Church teaches as she does about marriage," he acknowledged. Such doubts, however, were no excuse for ignoring the teaching. "If you deny just one point of the church's teaching you might just as well deny everything. You are a heretic. You are out of the Church. Should you die in this condition your soul will be eternally lost."[95]

But if Catholics were morally accountable for their self-delusion, what about those many non-Catholics who practiced birth control in apparent good conscience? Since the natural law is by definition accessible to all reasonable people, non-Catholics as well as Catholics could presumably be expected to know that contraception was wrong. The natural law, as a sermon text noted in 1930, "binds every human being on earth."[96] Catholic apologists, however, were reluctant to press the case against non-Catholics, preferring for the most part to ignore the problem but increasingly willing to concede "good faith" on the part of non-Catholics who regarded marital contraception as a moral good.[97] "It is all very well for people who do not believe in God, nor in the soul, nor in heaven to practice birth control, to abuse the power God gave them solely to produce other immortal souls," as the Carmelite Albert Dolan explained. "They do not speak our language and cannot therefore be entirely condemned if they enjoy the privileges of marriage and evade its obligations."[98] Dolan would certainly have included Protestants in this seeming catalogue of unbelievers. The Protestant "sects"—such was period Catholic usage—lacked any principle of authority beyond the individual, a man like Dolan would have argued. They had long since lost any semblance of doctrinal integrity and were hardly more than way stations on the road to agnosticism. An anonymous priest writer put the matter politely in 1940. "We meet many non-Catholic friends every week who have very little religious training. They consider certain acts lawful which we Catholics condemn as sin. Are they all in bad faith? It is hard to say that. Many are in good faith. They think because of their family tradition that Catholics are too strict and wrong on divorce, birth-control, the unity of the faith, the necessity of confession and on dozens of other questions."[99]

Such grudging concessions to "good faith ignorance" were rare indeed prior to the late 1930s. In the most immediate sense, they mark the widespread public acceptance that contraception by then enjoyed. The origins of these concessions, however, lie deep in American Catholic history. Catholics have always been a minority population in the United States, both numerically and—until very recently—psychologically. Despite a longtime commitment to Catholic institutional separatism, few of their leaders have ever evinced much enthusiasm for the public consigning of non-Catholics to hell. Whatever his want of graciousness, Father Dolan's was the prudent logic of American public Catholicism. But these same concessions to good faith ignorance raised a basic problem of fairness, at least in the view of certain lay Catholics. Why should Catholics alone be expected to observe a law that God had allegedly intended for all humankind? Mission preachers, in fact preachers of every variety, addressed the question with increasing frequency in the 1930s and nearly always in the same way. Catholics, they pointed out, belonged to a spiritually privileged class, from whom more was quite properly expected. "Catholics, and only Catholics," in the words of a Lenten text from 1940, "have the benefit of a dependable pilot to guide them safely to the port of Heaven. Catholics and only Catholics, may enjoy union with God throughout their entire life here. Catholics, and only Catholics, can be restored to that union if it should become severed. Evidently because of the greater favor shown to them by God their responsibility is greater, their sins are more heinous, their indifference towards spiritual things is less pardonable."[100]

So the Catholic advantage with regard to salvation came at a heavy price. No Catholic, it seemed, could enjoy the earthly benefits of birth control and still expect to get to heaven. There was always the danger of sudden death in a state of mortal sin. "Take no chances that you will be able to get to confession before death overtakes you," in the standard words of a mission sermon.[101] Every Catholic at the moment of judgment, moreover, would have to account for his stewardship of "the great gift of Faith, the true Faith," as a Paulist preacher reminded his hearers. "Have we always been faithful to it, and given a wholehearted, one hundred percent allegiance to it, or have we attempted to whittle it down to suit ourselves? Have we accepted and lived all its precepts and commandments, or have we deleted the hard sayings, and ignored those commands with which we did not agree or which we found it difficult to keep?"[102] But the Protestant who practiced birth control in the honest belief that it was not sinful would evidently be judged by a more lenient standard. His ignorance of the moral law might even be imputed to some negligent Catholic who, despite the supernatural help to which he had access, failed to set a good example.[103]

The fairness issue just described persisted beyond the 1930s, and ultimately played a significant role in undermining lay support for the Catholic teaching on contraception. A more venerable problem with fairness, however, began in that same decade to be mildly redressed. Preachers in the 1930s did not cease to hold women especially accountable for marital contraception. But the younger among them were increasingly likely to blame men, too, and at least on occasion to sympathize with wives who were, in the words of *Casti Connubii,* more sinned against than sinning. A recently ordained Passionist, probably preaching at a women's retreat, gave voice to this seemingly altered perspective in 1932: "We find even Catholic wives shirking the responsibilities of motherhood; they are frequently influenced, even perhaps forced by, thoughtless and selfish husbands."[104] Preachers like these were obviously influenced by *Casti Connubii.* Pius XI had pointedly commiserated with the unwilling partner to contraceptive intercourse, by which he evidently meant wives whose husbands practiced coitus interruptus. (Such women, unlike those whose spouses used condoms, would not be obliged to resist intercourse, since the act was begun "according to nature.") Priests' fears of a female backlash doubtless entered in, too, for the makings of such were evident even in the 1920s. The defensive tone of period preaching when it comes to gender roles suggests that this was the case. And as Cardinal Mundelein had discovered, it sometimes happened that men were the "real offenders" when it came to birth control—or, as seems not to have occurred to the cardinal, that the practice was the result of a decision jointly made by the spouses. It hardly made sense to address an issue so integral to a couple's life by speaking primarily to women. A more concerted enforcement of the teaching, in other words, led with a certain inevitability to a greater gender equity.

Catholic men may also have been a more accessible population by the 1930s. Their attendance at missions and novenas was widely reported to have increased then, while men's retreats enjoyed an unprecedented popularity, especially among the more affluent. "In this godly movement our Catholic married men are setting an admirable and inspiring example," as the Franciscan Fulgence Meyer wrote at mid-decade. "The number of annual retreatants among them is greater from year to year." Like virtually all of his confreres, Meyer used the many retreats he preached to inveigh against contraception. There is "a certain man in the retreat who is in a bad spiritual way," as he liked to introduce the subject. This man uses "the sacred institution of marriage for mere lust and sensuous delight." He "lasciviously" refuses the gift of fatherhood. "God alone knows how much eternal glory I thereby defraud Him of, and how many possible beings will be forever deprived of existence through my marital depravity." To make matters worse, the man's conscience has "grown callous and unresponsive to this terrible unnatural sin." He seldom confesses it, or does so without genuine sorrow and a firm purpose of amendment. The man in question, Meyer conceded, might initially have been led into sin by his wife. But this did not lessen his guilt. "Instead of ever allowing the woman to drag him and herself down to unworthy self-indulgence and dishonorable self-gratification in marriage, say, through her weak and unjustifiable fear and refusal of sacred motherhood, he should insist, sweetly, graciously, and winningly . . . that their 'marriage be honorable in all, and be undefiled.'"[105] Meyer, in this interesting passage, simultaneously affirmed the "natural" family headship of the husband and assigned him a role as moral exemplar that nearly all Catholics would have regarded as feminine.

But if males were a more frequently targeted population in the 1930s, women remained—in the eyes of most priests—the more blameworthy sex when it came to family limitation. Many priests still regarded women as the principal promulgators of the contraceptive gospel. They had partly in mind those many non-Catholic women who were prominent public advocates of birth control—"a lot of pagan women," as Chicago's Cardinal Mundelein had it, "just like their predecessors of ancient Rome, restless neurotic busybodies [who] are clamoring before the Legislatures of this land for the right to decimate the population of the nation, to weaken in every way our national defense, to raise their hands to stop the procession of little souls that come from the creative hand of God."[106] But Catholic women were also suspect, including some who looked to be devout. "A woman who never misses Mass or First Friday Communion, and at other times is a frequent communicant," as Father Ambrose Adams evoked this specter of the enemy within, "visits a young married woman neighbor, the mother of two children, tells her she should avoid having more for various reasons of economy, health and social life. To the conscientious protests of the younger, the older woman replies that such matters are none of the priests' business, they do not understand, and there is no need to mention the matter in confession."[107] Women like these were principally motivated by selfishness, in the view of a good many priests, and a prideful refusal to accept the submission that was their natural lot. "I accuse birth control of making women selfish," in the words of the Jesuit Daniel Lord. "I accuse them of disparaging the home as a career, of belittling motherhood."[108] The essence of truly Catholic womanhood, as Lord and his confreres regularly pointed out, was the hidden life of self-forgetting. "A woman is a servant-girl—not a slave," as an elderly Passionist artlessly put it. "Be the handmaid of the Lord with Mary!"[109]

Women were also singled out when it came to mission preaching on abortion. Missioners certainly addressed men too with regard to this gravest of moral offenses. They preached on the subject with sufficient heat and frequency to indicate deep-seated worries about its prevalence among Catholics. (The incidence of illegal abortion appears to have risen sharply in the early years of the Depression.) It would hardly do, in the circumstances, to spare the men who were sometimes—even frequently—active parties to the sin. "The *means* used to destroy this life do not lessen the guilt," in the typical words of a Redemptorist instruction to the married, preached separately to women and men, "be it by medicine, or criminal operation, or any other means. Nor is the guilt changed whether that life is destroyed at conception (and life is present at the very instant of conception), or when that life is more developed and matured."[110] But the fiercest of the missioner's rhetoric was typically saved for women, not only because they were of necessity direct participants in an abortion but because the act so egregiously flouted the cardinal female virtues. "In birth control, many go from bad to worse, & commit murder," according to the sermon notes of a Passionist. "Mothers are com[mitting] that terrible murder, putting unborn, unb[aptized] ch[ildren] to death, making slaughter houses of their bodies—mothers are com[mitting] a murder worse than the murder

com[mitted] by Herod when he slaughtered the in[nocent] ch[ildren] of Beth-
lehem."[111]

Most parish-based priests never engaged in blatantly anti-female diatribes,
at least not in public. It would hardly have made pastoral sense to do so. But
nearly all priests were convinced that women bore particular responsibility for
the moral climate of the home. "We ordinarily call women the weaker sex," as
the Passionist Gilbert Kroger put it, "yet unconsciously, most people look to
women to be heroes of love and of self-sacrifice in sufferings."[112] The long-
suffering woman, by force of example, was to elevate those around her—
weaning her man from sensuality, her children from selfishness. "In practically
all cases, her spiritual insight will be deeper than that of her husband," as a
Paulist mission preacher explained. "She will interpret God and the will of God
to her husband who will, in most cases, be slower to see it than she is. Most of
all . . . she holds the power to make something holy of their marriage. . . . It is
the woman who must subdue the coarser nature of man, and keep their relations on a high level."[113]

The good wife, in musings like these, is made in the celibate's romanticized
image of his own good mother. She is a stranger to sexual longing, though not
to suffering. Gracefully subordinate to men, she nonetheless disciplines—gently but unremittingly—when it comes to male desire. Her favor rests, in short,
on her celibate son rather than her appetitive husband. Women who failed to
conform to the model, whatever their other claims to virtue, were profoundly
dangerous—to men, the family, even the nation. The desirous woman un-
leashed the beast in man, undermined the bonds of marriage and the ethic of
duty. Women like these were "selfish and vain," in the words of the just-quoted
Paulist. "Their vain selfishness is the cause of birth control and other evils."[114]
The very prevalence of birth control, not to mention "other evils," proved that
female selfishness was on the rise. "The sex mania of today present to us priests
both a challenge and an opportunity," as a Capuchin summed up the situation.
"If we priests do not rise to this opportunity, Catholic women will continue in
even larger numbers to consult the birth control clinics instead of heeding the
advice of their confessors."[115]

The failure of wives in this regard, if we look to the logic of period preaching, was matched or even exceeded by that of young unmarried women. The
decade's sermons were filled with attacks on young women's provocative
dress, resistance to authority, and thirst for sensate adventure. None of this was
new. But the growing acceptability of contraception and its increasing visibility prompted at least the occasional priest to even more lurid imaginings. That
unmarried Catholics not uncommonly practiced "complete fornication" was
the frankly expressed conviction of a widely published Vincentian, who
seemed to hold females chiefly responsible. "It is now the practice of many
young women to come provided with protective devices, which can easily be

procured in drugstores and filling stations, where they are sold by means of slot-machines, just the same as candy and chewing gum."[116] Few priests in the 1930s were willing to speak so boldly. But fears like these were not confined to an alarmist fringe. "Many Catholic daughters are not living up to their high duties," as a Paulist quite typically saw it. "They are the cause of many young men falling into sin."[117]

Presumably for this reason, mission preachers in the 1930s began for the first time to speak against birth control before congregations of the unmarried. The Carmelite Albert Dolan did so as early as 1931 at the novenas he regularly preached in Chicago.[118] Reynold Hillenbrand, preaching missions in that same city in the mid-1930s, raised the subject in talks to young adults and perhaps even high-school students. (Hillenbrand's discussion of birth control in a sermon evidently prepared for high schoolers bears the marginal note "leave out."[119]) The Redemptorists, for their part, were by then routinely including the topic in their "state in life" instructions to the single. None of these men addressed the subject at length or in particularly graphic terms. The Redemptorist Alfred Menth, who preached to the married with blunt forthrightness, fell into an evasive formality when speaking to those who had not yet tied the knot. "A marriage in which sacred *duties* are *violated,* and sacred obligations *desecrated* and responsibilities *not fulfilled,* in which the law of God or nature is broken, cannot have and never will have His blessing."[120] Few of his confreres went further, though the Carmelite Albert Dolan crowned his closing novena sermon—repeatedly preached—with a brief but memorable condemnation of "Birthless Indulgence, or Mutual Masturbation." Even Dolan, however, mostly hewed to a circumspect line. Though they clearly believed that sexual sin was rapidly gaining among the young, preachers also assumed that congregations of the single invariably included those who were strangers to sexual knowledge. No preacher would willingly disturb so happy a state. "I have used the most general terms," as Albert Dolan liked to say. "The innocent will learn nothing from what I have said whereas to the others all will be perfectly clear."[121]

Dolan's confidence in this regard was probably not unwarranted. Public talk about birth control in the 1930s was sufficiently ubiquitous that even the young were apt to pick up on fairly oblique references. (The "innocent" are rather harder to account for.) The secular media was full of such talk. But so, increasingly, was its Catholic counterpart. A remarkable development on this latter front was the advent of radio sermons addressing the problem of contraception, some of which were subsequently published in Catholic newspapers or as pamphlets. Such were familiar to many Catholics even in the early 1930s. Sermons like these were probably heard mostly by fairly observant laity. Who else would be devotees of programs like the *Catholic Hour,* where Father Fulton Sheen—then a rising rhetorical star—denounced contraception on several occasions in 1932, once in the context of a sermon on "The Crucifixion"?[122] Even regularly observant Catholics, however, struggled hard with the teaching on birth control and sometimes failed to obey it. Hence the importance of the radio sermon's immediacy. Many ordinarily observant Catholics put psychic distance between themselves and those venues where clerical authority held absolute sway—between themselves and the confessional, for example, or the fearsome thunderings of the mission pulpit. But the radio sermon was heard in the intimacy of the home, precisely the place where "sins against marriage" were usually committed. The reproving priest might, however fleetingly, be in the marital bedroom itself.

Most radio sermons were skillfully preached—diocesan authorities wanted only the best for this new medium—and typically couched in forthright language. As a Boston Jesuit warned his hearers in 1931: "A high-powered campaign is being launched with pamphlets, counter displays and advertisements, to spread through the country these nauseating, disgusting and hideous contraceptives. . . . I know of eight women's colleges into which they sent saleswomen disguised as nurses to spread the detestable practices."[123] Like this Boston Jesuit, whose argument turned on sexual license among the unmarried, radio preachers typically spoke the language of real-world consequences, making only brief reference to the natural law and usually none to eternal punishment. Contraception, as various preachers argued, was dangerous to women's health, destructive of marital fidelity, a threat to national security, and a principal weapon in the war against the poor. "The birth control movement is the strongest ally of economic imperialism," in the words of the Jesuit Ignatius Cox, a veteran of the preaching airwaves. "When economic Caesars wanted children for the factories and for the fields they got them. Now machines have taken their place and there is not the same need of children."[124]

By speaking the language of consequences, rather than that of ecclesial authority, the radio preachers were obviously trying to make a larger-than-Catholic case against contraception, and particularly its legalization. But they also hoped to reach those many Catholics for whom the natural law argument was unconvincing or even incomprehensible. In this important sense, the radio sermon provided assistance to overburdened confessors. And though men like Ignatius Cox spoke the language of class, they simultaneously rallied the Catholic tribe. Few Catholics who heard sermons like his would have doubted that the "economic imperialists" were Protestants while the poor they oppressed were mostly Catholic. "What we demand is *wealth control,* not *birth control!*" Father Cox liked to thunder.[125] In the heat of the rhetorical moment, even a hard-pressed married Catholic might cheer him on.

That radio preaching reached surprisingly large numbers of Catholics, including many immigrants, is suggested by the career of Father Justin Figas, whose weekly *Rosary Hour* was broadcast mainly in Polish.[126] Father Justin, though virtually unknown to present-day historians of Catholicism, was vastly popular in the 1930s among Polish Americans. A regular feature of his broadcasts was the "Question Box," when the priest responded to listeners' letters. Substantial numbers of these apparently had to do with birth control—he had received "several thousand" queries on this most delicate subject, Father Justin acknowledged in 1935. But despite evident listener interest, the priest was reluctant to address the issue in the context of a family-oriented program. Young people would inevitably be listening, he explained; he was worried as well about the sensibilities of his married female listeners. (His concern was lost on at least one Cleveland woman, who wondered in 1936 "why Father Justin says nothing about birth control. Everybody writes about it."[127]) Father Justin did eventually devote three programs to the subject of abortion, despite his anticipating negative audience response. "Some will be scandalized, the others will get angry; particularly a certain group of progressive women and modern girls will be indignant with me."[128] But apart from a handful of remarks, he never in the 1930s spoke against contraception—a task that he doubtless regarded as appropriate only to mission preachers. Many in his audience clearly disagreed—a measure of how much had changed for the laity, both in terms of their awareness of Church teaching and their willingness to engage the question publicly. "I have already written three times asking Father Justin to speak up on birth control," as a Detroit correspondent noted in 1935. "I am sure that every woman is interested in it."[129]

Radio sermons provided just a fraction of the many Catholic voices now making a public case against contraception. The laity in the 1930s encountered those voices in the secular press, where the politics of birth control was a staple of domestic news. They found them as well in the Catholic press, and in a ubiquitous pamphlet literature. The Catholic print media was franker than ever before in its approach to birth control, and marked in many instances by a new sophistication. The turgid pamphlets of the 1920s, to pick but one example, were supplemented by numbers couched in colloquial language and featuring efforts at engaging story lines. (Such stories were typically "Catholic" in their diction and content, another important contrast with earlier productions and their seemingly ecumenical thrust.) Some of these pamphlets were almost embarrassing in their naivete. "Frequent contact with the Virginal Flesh of Christ in the Eucharist is just the thing to help kill the lusts of the flesh," according to a Franciscan pamphlet, whose priest protagonist encourages a contracepting penitent, out of work for almost a year, "to live as brother and sister with your wife, as long as it is necessary." This will not be easy, the priest concedes, but "with a little good will on your part, and correspondence with the grace of God, you should be able to persevere—the months will eventually stretch into a year or more of continence."[130] Others, however, deployed their arguments with a fair degree of rhetorical sophistication and psychological acuity. The Jesuit Daniel Lord, probably the best-selling Catholic pamphleteer in the whole of American history, provides the most notable examples.

Obviously worried about the problem, Father Lord published four pamphlets on birth control between 1930 and 1947, and another seven on marriage more generally. Each went into multiple editions. Like many of Lord's pamphlets, these were mostly set in conspicuously upper-middle-class surroundings. Lord's favorite protagonist was one Father Hall, "writer of distinguished novels" and counselor to the Bradley twins, who were among his augmented congregation during their summers at a lakeside "vacation colony." The twins, Dick and Sue, were students at unnamed Catholic colleges and obviously privileged. Dick drives a roadster, while Sue enjoys the social whirl "at parties, bridges, and luncheons." They regularly turn to Father Hall—wise, sympathetic, and evidently leisured—for answers to their most intimate questions. The "girls" at her college, Sue confides in a pamphlet originally published in 1930, talk about birth control "an awful lot." Some are openly scornful of Church teaching on the matter, even planning to use contraceptives once they marry. Sue is troubled by her inability to counter their arguments, some of which make sense to her. Father Hall then proceeds to explain Church teach-

Figure 2. Evoking the fictional world of Fr. Lord's "Bradley twins," members of the 1936 Orange Bowl team at Catholic University pose with their dates. Catholic colleges were a principal venue for inculcating Catholic views on marriage to upwardly mobile members of the laity. Photo courtesy of the American Catholic History Research Center and University Archives, Catholic University.

ing and demolish each of the justifications that Sue's rebellious contemporaries have served up.[131]

The genteel surroundings of this and other of Lord's Depression-era pamphlets seem on first reading to make no sense at all. Not every Catholic was working class, but a clear majority were. Lord perhaps assumed that affluent Catholics were the most likely to practice birth control and targeted his pamphlets accordingly. He may even have thought that the female reader, at whom his pamphlets were certainly aimed, would enjoy a vicarious journey through society's upper reaches. But given Lord's talents as a propagandist, more was probably at issue. His pamphlets succeed in linking the Catholic position on birth control with the politesse of genteel culture—with the decorous serenity of the Bradley's summer lives. Obedient Catholics, as Lord's Father Hall suggests, have learned through long training to master their passions. They move through even sordid environments with the calm self-possession of natural aristocrats. They look with confidence to God, who never fails to provide for their needs, and thus enjoy a faith in the future that even the rich do not possess. Their homes, no matter how cramped or mean, are ordered and joyous places—not much different, emotionally speaking, from the leafy veranda where Father Hall holds forth. So Lord offers his less-than-affluent readers an avenue to spiritual upward mobility. One can readily imagine the attraction of so evocative an appeal, and not only for the affluent reader. He also manages to insinuate that less-than-obedient Catholics have brought on themselves the disappointments and anxieties that constrict their lives.

Lord's pamphlets retailed nearly all of the standard Catholic arguments against contraception. He spoke only briefly of the natural law, conceding that even college students might have difficulty grasping the logic. "You'll both get the argument again in your Catholic ethics [classes]," as Father Hall tells the twins. He dwelt instead on the deleterious social consequences of birth control. Its use encouraged marital infidelity—among women as well as men. It promoted divorce, both because of infidelity and because childless couples soon grew bored with their marriages. The ready availability of contraceptives ensured immorality among the unmarried, even the very young. It made for selfishness and materialism, not only in parents who preferred a new car to a baby but in their pampered one or two children. Borrowing from the eugenics movement, Lord even invoked the specter of racial decline: "Rightly or wrongly, we regard European civilization as superior to Asiatic and African civilization. Yet while France and England see their birthrate rapidly shrinking, China and the oriental nations grow continuously larger and more powerful."[132] This last was not an argument widely deployed by Catholic apologists, given the negative racial stereotypes quite recently affixed to Catholics from southern and eastern Europe. But the argument had its uses for political purposes, as Lord was surely aware. And many assimilated Catholics were hardly discomfited by this sort of casual racism. Chicago's Cardinal Mundelein was apparently among them. "Unless there is a special miracle of God's grace," as he told his priests with regard to the plummeting birthrate in 1932, "the Americans [will] be a slave people subjugated to the yellow races of the Orient."[133]

Lord best reflected his clerical confreres, however, in the highly gendered nature of his anti-birth control logic. He did not exactly hold women accountable for the widespread use of contraception, though intimations to this effect occur in various pamphlets. Sue's female classmates, for example, talk about birth control far more than Dick's male friends. "My gang at college," as Dick says, "are too busy with interesting things." But Lord, like most of his contemporaries, regarded women as the moral guardians of the race. Those who practiced birth control, whether freely or through coercion, abandoned that high calling and furthered a destructive ethic of selfish hedonism. Women, according to Lord's Father Hall, had always belonged to one of two great classes. "To the madonna class sex was associated with the beautiful fact of motherhood; to the 'daughters of joy' it meant self-gratification or gratification of the man." A wife who used contraceptives, no matter how briefly, belonged irrevocably to the latter class. "She is using her physical attraction solely to gratify a man and herself," as Father Hall explained. "Perhaps it is just to keep a roof over her head and food upon her table. This is sad. But don't you see that it is essentially the same attitude toward sex that the prostitute takes?" Many such women, as Lord saw it, were the unwitting victims of a near-diabolical movement to legitimize birth control. The changes that birth control brought in its wake—increased adultery, divorce, and fornication—had, as he argued, particularly negative effects on their sex. For all his attempts at chivalry, however, Lord was finally as one with those of his colleagues who openly blamed women for the period's moral decline. All demanded that female sexuality be subsumed in motherhood—that the woman regard her body, in Lord's words, as a "chalice of life, pure, noble, deeply purposeful."[134]

Daniel Lord's pamphlets circulated widely. His influence was especially great on the idealistic young, who encountered his writings in Catholic college courses on marriage and various Catholic youth movements. Even the prolific Lord, however, could not reach anything like a majority of Catholic Americans. But by the end of the 1930s, the climate for Catholics had changed so profoundly with regard to birth control that Lord and his allies might almost be said to have reached nearly every Catholic adult. Only the most marginal Catholic by then could have been ignorant of the Church's teaching. One might disagree with that teaching—might, indeed, misinterpret it as a covert way of voicing dissent. This latter strategy, nicely exemplified by those who "confused" birth control with abortion, could perhaps be regarded as a form of good faith ignorance. It seems more historically sensitive, however, to see such covert dissent as something new—a first halting step toward a view of authority that made generous room for conscience. Change in the 1930s forced almost all American Catholics to contend with the problem of authority when it came to contraception—many for the first time. For better or worse, the prohibition on birth control had moved to the center of Catholic life. "We do not dodge the issue; we do not straddle the question; most of all, we do not betray our moral principles," as Bishop Robert Lucey articulated this now highly public marker of Catholic identity. "We mean what we say and we say what we mean: artificial birth control is vicious in itself."[135]

But if the thirties was a decade of increased publicity and discipline when it came to the teaching on contraception, it also saw developments that ultimately worked to undermine that teaching. These had to do with the advent of a scientifically plausible method of fertility control by means of periodic abstention from intercourse, or rhythm, as the method quickly came to be known. Though we do not know the extent to which Catholics in the 1930s actually practiced rhythm, much less with what degree of efficacy, the method had enormous impact on the internal Catholic politics of birth control. Its initial effects seemed to strengthen the hand of those who supported the teaching. This was especially true for priests, many of whom found rhythm to be an "enormous help" in the confessional. (The words are those of the Jesuit Joseph Reiner.[136]) Rhythm also made possible the embrace by many younger clergy of a genuinely positive view of marital sex—a development that bore especially rich fruit in the years immediately following the Second World War. In the end, however, these seemingly beneficent "products" of rhythm served to seriously weaken the Church's credibility with regard to contraception—initially for large numbers of the laity and then for a good many priests as well. Rhythm's more prescient critics in the 1930s had predicted precisely this outcome.

The Strange Career of the Rhythm Method

As we have previously seen, Catholic seminarians since the mid-nineteenth century had been taught about the existence of an "agenesic" or "safe" period—that time in a woman's menstrual cycle when she was unable or at least unlikely to conceive. We have also seen that this putative safe period was reckoned according to erroneous physiological assumptions. Catholic authorities clung for a very long time to this particular medical error. A respected textbook of moral theology, published as late as 1929, offered typical counsel in this regard—gravely inaccurate and no longer in accord with dominant medical opinion. (Most physicians believed at this juncture that pregnancy might occur at any stage of the menstrual cycle.)[137] The infertile days of the cycle, according to the textbook's Dominican authors, occurred "between the fifteenth day after the beginning of one menstruation and the fifth day before the beginning of another."[138] Most Catholic moralists assumed that couples might licitly confine their intercourse to the putative safe period, provided that both spouses freely agreed to the practice. If intercourse between permanently sterile spouses was permissible, on what logical grounds could intercourse in times of temporary sterility be regarded as sinful?[139] "As long as they do the act properly when they do it," as a Franciscan told dozens of mission congregations in the 1920s, "married people do not sin by restricting themselves by mutual consent to whatsoever days they choose, even if in this choice they are led mainly or exclusively by their desire not to have any more children."[140] The putative safe period, however, was rightly regarded by most of the laity with near-derisive skepticism. So the issue was seldom discussed at length by moral or pastoral theologians, for whom it had little practical import. "No wonder the assumed 'safe' period raised no serious moral questions," as John A. Ryan mused in 1933, by which time the manifest hazards of that assumed period had been widely publicized. "Typical is the conclusion reached by a certain lady who had unsuccessfully followed the old rule: 'that middle-of-the-month-business is the bunk.'"[141]

The erroneous assumptions of the moralists and those of the doctors as well were radically challenged at the close of the 1920s by two researchers working independently—one in Austria, the other in Japan. Hermann Knaus and Kyusaku Ogino each concluded that ovulation normally occurred from twelve to sixteen days before the anticipated first day of the next menstrual period. Each also concluded, based partly on the research of others, that an unfertilized ovum had a brief life—probably less than a day's duration. The work of Knaus and Ogino, then, both vindicated the existence of a sterile period and purported to make its location a relatively simple matter. Assuming that a woman enjoyed a regular menstrual cycle, she need only abstain from intercourse for a period of eight days at that cycle's midpoint if she did not wish to conceive—the five days during which ovulation was possible, preceded by three days to ensure that no vital sperm remained in the uterus. A woman with an irregular cycle would have to observe a longer period of continence, since the midpoint of her cycle could not be certainly known. The length of the abstinent period corresponded to the degree of menstrual irregularity. A woman whose cycle varied from twenty-six to thirty days in duration, for example, would need to abstain for twelve days; one with a significantly greater variation might have a "safe" period of less than a week. The sterile period could not be reliably calculated during times of extreme menstrual disruption, most notably in the wake of childbirth or, in a great many cases, at the onset of menopause.[142]

Though Ogino had published his research in Japan in 1924, his findings were barely known in the West until Knaus published his own research in 1929. Presumably because Knaus published in German, the "Ogino-Knaus" method of fertility control was initially publicized among Catholics in Dutch and German periodicals. Information about the new method was apparently circulating widely in northern Europe by 1931.[143] The news took somewhat longer to reach American Catholics. It did so first through one Leo Latz, a Chicago physician who late in 1932 self-published a slim volume called *The Rhythm of Sterility and Fertility in Women.* Latz's book was quickly followed by *The Sterile Period in Family Life,* coauthored by Valère J. Coucke, a Belgian moral theologian, and American physician James J. Walsh. Father John A. O'Brien's *Legitimate Birth Control* appeared early in 1934. Each of these publications was approved by an American bishop. The Coucke and Walsh volume bore the imprimatur of New York's Cardinal Patrick Hayes, while O'Brien's brief offering—really no more than a lengthy pamphlet—carried that of Fort Wayne's John Francis Noll. Chicago's Cardinal George Mundelein had initially granted an imprimatur to Leo Latz's *The Rhythm.* (This was the title, incidentally, that gave periodic continence its new American name.) But certain Jesuit members of the medical faculty at Chicago's Loyola University apparently objected, arguing that the Ogino-Knaus method rested on tenuous medical grounds. Mundelein subsequently withdrew his imprimatur, though he did permit Latz to advertise his book as having been published "with ecclesiastical approbation."[144] Latz had the additional consolation of a glowing introduction by Father Joseph Reiner, a Jesuit widely known in Chicago for his leadership work in various social action ministries.

The Coucke and Walsh volume was guarded when it came to rhythm's efficacy. The exact duration of the sterile period was not yet known, as the authors asserted, mildly dissenting from the conclusions of Doctors Knaus and Ogino. Nor were scientists altogether certain of the ovum's life span or that of the sperm. Confessors should therefore "make use of the greatest prudence and circumspection in suggesting anything to their penitents about this time of agenesis," lest unwanted pregnancies follow and unhappy parents-to-be seek abortions.[145] Neither Latz nor O'Brien betrayed such doubts. Their books, clearly written for a broader audience than that intended by Coucke and Walsh, exuded a joyful confidence. Correctly followed, according to both authors, the Ogino-Knaus method was at least as effective as any known contraceptive. "These findings of modern science disclose a rational, natural and ethical means to space births and to regulate intelligently the number of offspring," in O'Brien's near-magisterial formulation.[146] Ideally, each author hastened to note, a prospective user of the method would consult a knowledgeable physician; Latz urged in addition that she chart her menstrual intervals for at least a year. But both offered quite detailed instruction for calculating the safe period on one's own. "A complete explanation of the newly discovered methods by which the periods of sterility and fertility in family life are determined," as an advertisement for the O'Brien book promised. "Tables which show at a glance when these periods occur."[147] Those authoritative tables were probably the most confidence-inducing feature of the two books, at least for those who had not yet put "rhythm" to the test.

The Latz and O'Brien volumes were notable too for their markedly positive views on the role of sex in marriage. Married couples, as Latz saw it, had a veritable right to regular, fear-free intercourse. The "physical, psychic and moral" blessings of such were clearly designed by God as a fundamental good of marriage.[148] Father O'Brien, for his part, spoke almost lyrically of "the many benefits that physicians and psychiatrists picture as flowing from the conjugal relationship in the way of emotional tranquility, mental serenity and the zest to achieve."[149] Both men, significantly, were familiar with the work of the German layman Dietrich von Hildebrand, whose 1928 *In Defense of Purity* went beyond the logic of sex as a procreative function to speak of the marital act in terms of love, interpersonal communion, and the couple's spiritual development. "To overlook the union between physical sex and love or its significance," as von Hildebrand argued, "and to recognise only the purely utilitarian bond between sex and the propagation of the race is to degrade man and to be blind to the meaning and value of this mysterious domain."[150] Von Hildebrand's book, which appeared in an English translation in 1931, represented something genuinely new in Catholic moral theology. "For the first time," as John T. Noonan has noted, "a Catholic writer taught that love was a requirement of lawful, marital coition."[151] Supplemented by the subsequent work of Father Hubert Doms, von Hildebrand's vision would ultimately have a profound effect on Catholic thinking about marriage. So Latz and O'Brien were true pioneers, giving popular voice to ideas that had not yet penetrated American seminaries, much less the thinking of the average mission preacher.

Given their assumptions about marital sex, both Latz and O'Brien necessarily favored a generous publicizing of the rhythm method. Each wrote with a lay audience in mind, and initially advertised his book in publications read by the laity. O'Brien's, indeed, first appeared—though discreetly minus the "how-to" section—in a November 1933 edition of the family-oriented *Our Sunday Visitor.* In this regard too they were true pioneers. Some moralists even in the early 1930s regarded as binding an 1880 instruction from the Sacred Penitentiary in Rome—a tribunal that dealt with various cases of conscience—wherein confessors were told to observe extreme caution when commending the putative safe period to persistent "onanists."[152] This instruction had its liberal side, since it obliquely acknowledged that a couple might restrict intercourse to allegedly infertile times without committing a serious sin, no matter what their motives. But it clearly precluded publicity of the sort that the Latz and O'Brien books represented. Because both were published with a bishop's approval, there were obviously many churchmen who thought the 1880 ruling inadequate to present-day circumstances. Contraceptives had not been widely available in 1880, as John A. Ryan pointed out. Nor was contraception then a subject of general public discussion. The safe period itself had been sufficiently publicized by 1933, in Ryan's view, "that it is idle to discuss ways and means of keeping the publicity at a minimum."[153] Ryan's position made eminent sense and was endorsed by a number of Catholic leaders in the early 1930s. More was at issue, however, than a practical bowing to present-day realities. Widespread publicizing of the rhythm method meant vesting the laity with an unprecedented moral autonomy. Armed with allegedly foolproof instructions, they alone would decide for what reasons to employ them.

How many Catholics by the mid-1930s had heard about the Ogino-Knaus method of family limitation? We simply do not know, although the news was clearly communicated widely. Both the Latz and O'Brien books sold well, each evidently in excess of 75,000 copies by 1935.[154] Priests almost certainly bought many of these, both for their own edification and to give to certain troubled penitents. Latz's private foundation, presumably responding to clerical demand, was offering confessors a free pamphlet on rhythm by 1933; "hundreds of pastors and missionaries," according to the foundation, were already distributing the pamphlet to their married penitents.[155] Mission preachers were apparently among Latz's biggest customers. He had heard of cases where Latz's book had "been ordered as mission literature," a disgruntled Jesuit reported early in 1934, "as well as of cases where the missioner has spoken approvingly on the subject from the pulpit."[156] There were evidently pastors too who distributed pamphlets on rhythm quite widely. An Indiana publisher, advertising in a leading clerical journal, promoted his rhythm pamphlet in 1933 as suitable for public display. "It is being used for bookrack distribution by pastors, with much satisfaction."[157] "Hundreds of priests," according to a clerical observer late in 1934, routinely stocked their pamphlet racks with publications on rhythm.[158] As for John A. O'Brien's small book, an edited version of which appeared in *Our Sunday Visitor*, it was initially urged upon priests as appropriate not only for the desperate married—"order a supply to give to offending penitents"—but for "those about to enter into matrimony."[159]

Catholic periodicals aimed at the laity also advertised the various publications on rhythm, at least prior to 1935, and sometimes referred to the method in their columns. A *Michigan Catholic* editorial on the subject late in 1932 elicited numerous reader inquiries, in response to which the paper provided ordering instructions for Latz's "remarkable book."[160] Such interest also sustained brisk sales in "rhythm calendars" and "calculating wheels," devices marketed by private firms and alleged to result in near-perfect success with what their manufacturers generally called the "natural" method of birth control. ("Not 1 failure in 30,000 cases!" was the slogan prominently borne by one company's product. "Give Mother Nature a chance," urged another. "She never makes a mistake."[161]) The secular press ran stories, too, like the full-page spread in the Chicago *Sunday Tribune* that assured its readers in 1934 that the Catholic Church "sanctioned" this highly reliable means of family limitation.[162] Nor should we discount the gossip that multiplied the publicizing effects of each of the above-mentioned sources. The Jesuit John Ford made passing reference at the end of the decade to Latz's book being given as prizes at unnamed parish bingo games.[163] The story may have been apocryphal—a clerical urban legend. But it spoke to the sense among many priests that talk about rhythm was everywhere.

The Catholic laity had obvious reasons for interest in news about rhythm. "The method is so natural and so safe and best of all it can be accomplished with an easy conscience," as an ecstatic mother of four assured fellow readers of a Catholic devotional magazine in 1935. "I was told about it by a missionary and I thank God for it."[164] Spurred on by such glowing endorsements, a fair number of Catholics presumably gave the method a try. But things were rarely as simple as rhythm's most ardent advocates wanted to believe. (Most of rhythm's early advocates had themselves had relatively brief experience with the method, which generally worked in support of their optimistic assessments.) The Ogino-Knaus method was sufficiently complicated that the poorest and least-educated Catholics—precisely those for whom unregulated fertility would have posed the greatest problem—may often have found its practice beyond them. It required a high degree of discipline on the part of both spouses and essentially gave the wife control of a couple's sexual schedule. Most working-class marriages, according to period observers, were anything but egalitarian. Presumably a good many husbands were unwilling—perhaps in some cases quite literally unable—to surrender power to their wives in so psychically charged an area of marital life.

Even when conscientiously practiced, moreover, the Ogino-Knaus method was hardly foolproof. Couples employing rhythm might indeed succeed in extending the intervals between births, if only because of a much-reduced frequency of sexual intercourse. But sooner or later, save in the most exceptional cases, a pregnancy ensued. It was the rare woman, after all, whose menstrual cycle never varied, and the rare couple who could endure the prolonged sexual drought required by the method in the aftermath of childbirth. As a means of spacing between children, however, the method produced enough satisfied customers to sustain its credibility, at least among the devout and better educated. A Baltimore woman was typical. She had been introduced to the method, as she later recalled, by a mission preacher in 1932. "I had two children then. I later had three more, happily spaced. God truly answered my prayers." Her Baltimore church evidently featured literature on rhythm in its pamphlet rack, which this particular satisfied customer "was happy to distribute." She was many years later an advocate of Church-sponsored rhythm clinics.[165]

Priests too had reason to be eager for news about rhythm, and reason as well to persuade themselves that the method was wholly reliable. There were certainly priests so hostile to sex, or so afflicted by sexual anxiety, that they took an almost perverse delight in prescribing abstinence to anguished penitents. There were others who seemed genuinely puzzled by the purported sexual needs of the married, perhaps because they themselves were possessed of an unnaturally low sex drive. But probably the great majority of priests felt compassion for their married penitents, especially those who were poor or troubled by ill health. He had received "thousands of letters" in response to his championing of rhythm in *Our Sunday Visitor,* Father John A. O'Brien reported, many of them from priests. "Pastors rejoice in the happy solution of a problem that was growing in perplexity, causing disaffection among many, and occasioning latent rebellion and estrangement among more than we like to admit."[166] Both O'Brien and the Jesuit Joseph Reiner referred in print to the "providential" discovery of the Ogino-Knaus method, as did Father Daniel Lord, whose pamphlet on rhythm appeared in 1935. "Well, it's my honest conviction that at this point Divine Providence entered into the whole situation," as Lord's fictitious Father Hall explains to the ubiquitous Bradley twins. "The world collapsed economically. Catholic families, even more in some instances than non-Catholic families, felt the terrible privations of unemployment and want."[167] That the method seemed literally heaven-sent to men not overly given to sentimentality in matters of faith and morals, suggests how heavy a pastoral burden contraception had become. Rhythm provided a welcome way out. "I may be over-enthusiastic about the matter," Joseph Reiner conceded in a private letter defending Dr. Leo Latz, "because of the enormous help that the theory has given me in the confessional and because of the happy results that I have observed in cases where it was and is being applied."[168]

Reiner's serene confidence in rhythm's efficacy was apparently shared by large numbers of priests, especially but not exclusively those who were partisans of the method. Unlike the laity, priests could not test the method personally. Presumably they heard at least on occasion from persons for whom the method had failed. (This would have happened most frequently in confession, since the laity almost never in the 1930s gave public voice to their discontents with rhythm.) But it was quite easy to attribute such failures to a penitent's deficiencies—to a woman's inexact calculation of her safe period or a couple's failing to abstain for the requisite number of days. A physician had told him that rhythm worked in 70 percent of cases, a Holy Cross priest not atypically reported in 1939—a safety record which he quite reasonably regarded as better than that of many contraceptives. Should large numbers of Catholic couples be thoroughly trained in the method, his doctor informant had maintained, the margin of safety could be significantly improved. Hence Father John O'Connell's call—unprecedented in the late 1930s—for the establishment of

"Catholic Medical Bureaus" where reputable physicians would tutor couples in the successful practice of periodic continence.

Father O'Connell was frank when it came to his deep investment in rhythm's success. Without this new system, O'Connell intimated, a man could not function with integrity in the contemporary priesthood. "In the past our advice to married couples who for one reason or another are faced with the need of practicing birth limitation has been negligent, insincere, and worthy of criticism," as he boldly asserted. "Our Catholic people . . . are told in an offhand manner both by priests and Catholic social workers that they cannot practice birth control, and then they are given a 'pep talk' about the virtues of mortification." Far from being a solution, as O'Connell saw it, such an approach was "useless, futile, and worthless . . . for people who are not well grounded in their religion."[169] Should rhythm prove to be unreliable, what pastoral options were open to a man like O'Connell or to those probably many priests who shared his relatively advanced perspective? Their faith in rhythm had, indeed, done much to make the advanced perspective possible.

Despite the hopeful excitement that greeted rhythm, it was not without its clerical critics. A few were opposed to the method itself, despite an existing theological consensus that the practice of periodic continence was not gravely sinful. The evident certainty of the Ogino-Knaus safe period, such critics argued, cast the practice in a new moral light.[170] But most of the critics were only opposed to publicizing the method. Some feared, however implausibly, that widespread publicity would encourage adultery and especially fornication. An "experienced Capuchin missionary" objected to the *Pittsburgh Catholic*'s advertising of Latz's book on just such grounds: "He said," the paper's editor reported, "that he believed it to be far better that unmarried women heard nothing about the theory of 'The Rhythm;' that fear of the consequences of their sin kept many of our girls from committing that sin now, but with this barrier of fear removed there was no telling where it would all end." Others worried, perhaps equally implausibly, that general knowledge of the method would lead to an eventual decrease in the Catholic population.[171] Arguments like these were sometimes persuasive, as was the case at the *Pittsburgh Catholic*. "I removed all our advertising," the editor explained, "and any other reference to [Latz's] book and refused to accept any more orders for it unless we verified the fact that the woman ordering it was married."[172]

As these examples suggest, rhythm's critics were motivated by a deep animus against sexuality. Even those not given to alarmist views were typically convinced that the use of rhythm, when there was urgent cause to delay a pregnancy, was less virtuous than complete abstinence from intercourse. Where poverty or ill health required family limitation, it was "more Christian" to forego sex than to practice rhythm, as the priest protagonist of a Franciscan pamphlet explained in 1933, "although I do not condemn the man who uses periodic continence."[173] Indeed, if rhythm had any saving quality, it was the sexual discipline that the method invariably imposed. "Mere limitation of fertility is not the adequate end and purpose of periodic abstinence," the Jesuit Ignatius Cox told a radio audience in 1935, "it is limitation of fertility with limitation of sex indulgence."[174]

But the critics were also animated by moral and practical concerns that transcended the anti-sexual bias of their celibate formation. They worried about the inroads of materialism among Catholics and what they saw as a growing hostility to children in Western culture. They worried too that the widespread practice of rhythm would discourage Catholics from striving after sanctity or admiring those who did. Daniel Lord's Father Hall was among the latter, despite his conviction that the discovery of rhythm had been veritably providential. "'I'm getting,' he said, almost petulantly, 'awfully sick of telling people just how far they can go without actually going to hell.'" Catholics who could afford to do so, as Father Hall maintained, ought to rear large families in joyful fulfillment of the duties of their state in life.[175] And critics quite sensibly worried that the rhythm method might prove unreliable. Would those disappointed by rhythm not be more likely than other Catholics to embrace contraception? They had, after all, been led by rhythm's more enthusiastic promoters to regard the control of fertility as part of God's and nature's plan. At the very least, those disappointed by rhythm would harbor resentment against the priest whose counsel—or pamphlet—had originally led to its hopeful embrace.

Ultimately, the most compelling of the arguments against publicizing rhythm were political, both in terms of the Church itself and the secular debate over birth control. Nearly every critic was troubled by the moral authority such publicity vested in the laity. Confessors alone, in the view of a great many priests, should determine the circumstances in which a couple's practice of rhythm was truly legitimate. It was not that most moralists regarded the practice as illicit in and of itself; a majority regarded the practice of rhythm even for selfish reasons as no more than venially sinful. But it was all too easy, as many priests saw it, for couples to fall into what the Jesuit John Ford called "a 'birth-control-attitude' of mind," preferring material possessions and the pleasures of nonprocreative sex to the stern demands of Christian marriage.[176] Hence the need to consult a confessor. "It is the duty of the confessor to cause married people to conceive a higher idea of matrimony and to incite them to a manly exercise of the Christian virtues and a moderate use of the satisfactions of sense," as the moralist Valère Coucke explained. "Then only may he suggest something to them about the time of agenesis, when there exist serious reasons for believing that generation would be fraught with danger or for limiting the number of children."[177]

The critics also worried that the publicizing of rhythm would inevitably cloud, for all but the best-trained laity, the logic of contraception's intrinsic evil. "One hears, on both sides of the fence, the new phrase 'Catholic Birth control,'" as an unidentified priest wrote to a clerical journal in 1935.[178] Should the "Catholic" means of birth control prove ineffective or otherwise unsatisfactory, what would prevent many of those same laity from adopting a happier alternative? "To a mind untrained in the niceties of philosophical distinction, there is no great distance between using a calendar to take advantage of a recurrent safe period, and using a contraceptive instrument to make that period safe," as another priest correspondent explained. "To such a person it will be vain to explain that it is not so much the end of contraception that has drawn the fire of the church as it is the unnatural means advocated by the birth controllers."[179] Dark humorists among the laity would eventually parse the difference as having mainly to do with reliability and satisfaction. "Artificial" birth control, in other words, was different from the Catholic brand because it worked and did not notably frustrate a couple's sexual life. It might be wrong, but mostly because the Church declared it so.

The problem was obviously more than semantic. If periodic continence was licit, as no moralist denied that it sometimes was, then it was at least sometimes permissible for Catholics to deliberately separate the procreative function of marital sex from its allegedly secondary functions of enhancing affection and relieving sexual need. But if those functions deserved even sometimes to stand alone, should they really be defined as secondary? Were they not, at least for the duration of the safe period, the primary purpose of intercourse? The evident success of medical science in correctly identifying the probable boundaries of safety raised additional difficulties. If that same science could eventually pinpoint a woman's moment of ovulation, which would enable her to avoid pregnancy by abstaining for only two or three days, what genuine moral distinctiveness could the Catholic position claim? The last-mentioned was in the 1930s still a distant prospect. Perspicacious observers, however, could see even then that the logic of rhythm was fraught with consequence for traditional Catholic teaching on marital sex. "The Church permits the Rhythm Theory merely as something which may be tolerated—but tolerated almost fearfully," as Daniel Lord voiced the worry in 1936. "High authorities in the church are constantly warning priests and Catholic physicians to give out this theory only for good cause and to give it with a clear statement of the duties of parents and the obligations and social responsibilities of young men and women entering marriage."[180]

The most immediate problem, however, was the secular politics of birth control. Rhythm's more ardent proponents often testified eloquently to the moral and physical benefits of family limitation. As Father John Montgomery Cooper noted, with respect to Leo Latz's book, "I think he makes an excellent case for the birth controllers without intending to do so."[181] The "birth controllers" themselves evidently agreed, for Margaret Sanger was soon quoting Catholic rhythm literature, as were many of her colleagues. "At the recent birth control conference here in New York," an indignant Jesuit complained early in 1934, "the lady president read a passage which apparently gave all the reasons for birth control. She then stopped and said[,] that was written by the Catholic priest Dr. John O'Brien, and was taken from the *Sunday Visitor.*"[182] As the birth control lobby interpreted this literature, the Catholic Church had recently done an about-face with regard to family limitation. It no longer required its members to produce as many children as possible, probably because of radically altered economic circumstances. What remained was simply a "duel over methods," in the words of the *New Republic.*[183] "Face to face with the depression, the realistic leaders of the Church, one gathers, have been looking for a way of retreat that would not mean loss of face," as a pro-birth control article in *Harper*'s explained. "Some of them seem to think they have found it in the researches on the 'safe period' published during recent years."[184] Margaret Sanger made the case with her trademark pithiness, and in the dangerous context of a hearing before the House Judiciary Committee. "It comes down to a safe contraceptive or a safe period, and that is just about where both sides stand now."[185]

The situation was obviously alarming to Catholic leaders, and deeply frustrating, too. Most assumed that the birth control advocates were engaged in a willful distorting of Catholic teaching. This may have been true in some cases, although a good many birth control activists were probably close to invincibly ignorant when it came to Catholic sexual doctrine. "Up to now Catholic women have been forbidden to do anything to avoid child-bearing," as the normally well-informed Alice Hamilton told readers of the New York *Herald-Tribune,* "since thus they would be preventing the incarnation of waiting souls"[186] (Though Hamilton was wrong with regard to Catholic theology, her version came uncannily close to the logic enunciated by Cardinal Patrick Hayes in his 1921 rejoinder to Margaret Sanger.) Non-Catholic politicians too were easily confused, especially by talk about "Catholic" birth control. "After 'Rhythm,' the Catholic cause has no bright outlook," a discouraged Father John Burke reported with regard to Congressional debates over contraception in 1934.[187] Those debates turned mainly on amendment of the federal Comstock Act, which forbade the mailing of contraceptive information or devices. If books on rhythm could be sent through the mail, why not literature on contraceptives or indeed the devices themselves? Was this not rank favoritism on behalf of a putatively "Catholic" means of family limitation? The point was a telling one, though the birth control advocates went down to defeat in 1934. But the tide of public opinion had clearly turned in their favor. "We cannot, of course, refrain from continuing our opposition to birth control legislation," as Omaha's Bishop Joseph Rummel summed up the situation toward the end of 1934, "even though we must eventually lose the battle."[188]

The circumstances just described finally prompted the nation's bishops to attempt to curb the publicizing of the rhythm method. But this happened only at the end of 1934. Prior to that time, the advocates of rhythm could plausibly argue that they enjoyed episcopal support. The most prominent Catholic books on rhythm had, after all, been published with a bishop's approval and advertised in the Catholic press. But clerical opposition surfaced publicly even in the period of seeming official tolerance. Certain Jesuits were especially active. *America* magazine, the most visible of the American Jesuits' publications, ran a stinging editorial against rhythm publicity early in 1933. "With an enthusiasm hardly warranted by the facts some ill-advised persons have pushed into a nation-wide propaganda for the theory," editor Wilfrid Parsons declared, "and what is worse, have campaigned, for somewhat doubtful reasons, for the widespread and general distribution of books on the subject which by their very nature were intended . . . for physicians, nurses, social workers and clergymen." The promoters of rhythm, Parsons asserted, were running a "commercial racket"—pushing an obviously dubious theory for reasons of personal gain. In the process, they lent aid and comfort to the nation's pro-birth control forces.[189] Parsons had a kindred spirit in the Jesuit Ignatius Cox, an ethicist at Fordham College and national chaplain to the Guild of Catholic Physicians. Cox used the Guild's *Linacre Quarterly* to fire a second Jesuit shot across rhythm's bow, this time in the fall of 1933. "I did a job on the publicity given to the Safe Period, to appear in the September number of the Linacre, that will make your heart glow," he confided to Parsons.[190]

Leo Latz himself eventually felt the sting of Jesuit opposition. At the time of *The Rhythm*'s publication, Latz was a member of the medical faculty at Loyola University in Chicago, a Jesuit institution. He was abruptly fired from that position in August of 1934.[191] The firing was almost certainly a direct result of Latz's prominent association with the cause of rhythm, though the extant documents do not explicitly say so. Latz was initially told that his firing was occasioned by his having neglected to get proper departmental clearance for the publication of his book.[192] When he effectively countered that charge, he was told that his firing was part of an economically driven downsizing. A large number of faculty not engaged in regular teaching were being let go.[193] But correspondence between Latz supporter Joseph Reiner and two high-ranking Loyola officials suggests that rhythm was fundamentally at issue. Certain members of the medical faculty at Loyola had been hostile to rhythm from the outset, although Regent Terence Ahearn, S.J. seems not to have been among them. But Ahearn was implacably opposed to the theory by 1934, perhaps because of anxieties over its broad dissemination.[194] The dismissal was devastating to Latz, a devout Catholic who had earmarked proceeds from *The Rhythm* for various Catholic charities. Reiner alone, as Latz confessed in 1935, "knew the anguish and dishonor I . . . suffered, when people said: 'I heard you were thrown out of the University.'"[195]

Not every Jesuit was opposed to the publicizing of rhythm. No friend to the system was more whole-souled than Father Joseph Reiner. Nor were the Jesuits alone in their worries about rhythm publicity. "I canvassed the opinion of the Fathers of our Community, and found that they are unanimous in praising the main points of the article," as the Redemptorist Francis Connell, himself a moral theologian, told Wilfrid Parsons with regard to his *America* editorial.[196] Priests in religious orders may have gravitated in especially large numbers toward moral conservatism. But many in the diocesan clergy, for the multiple reasons discussed above, were concerned about rhythm, too. Various bishops also betrayed unease, despite the danger that such might be seen as criticism of those in their ranks who had given approval to a publication on rhythm. Fort Wayne's John Francis Noll had been one of the latter. But he was having second thoughts by the summer of 1934. He refused his imprimatur then to an expanded version of John O'Brien's *Legitimate Birth Control,* even contending—somewhat ingenuously—that substantial portions of that pamphlet had appeared in *Our Sunday Visitor* "by mistake."[197] (Noll was the paper's publisher and, perhaps incidentally, the fifth of nineteen children.[198]) His links to O'Brien on this delicate matter had become extremely embarrassing, as Noll readily acknowledged. "This embarrassment is keenly felt at this time when there is a reaction against the too much [*sic*] literature endorsing birth control by legitimate means."[199]

Matters reached a climax of sorts at the end of 1934. The Administrative Committee of the National Catholic Welfare Conference decided at its November meeting to adopt a statement of principle "governing the publication and dissemination of the Rhythm theory."[200] The Paulist John Burke, general secretary to the Conference, composed the statement's initial draft, which was then revised by various of the Administrative Committee's members. The final product was sent to every American bishop on December 22. "The Administrative Committee has found that misunderstanding, and in some cases a lowering of Christian ideals of the Sacrament of Matrimony, have resulted from the publication and indiscriminate circulation of books, pamphlets and occasional articles on rhythm," as the statement noted. "That the subject can be openly discussed and advocated," was, in the view of the Committee, "an unwarranted conclusion." The Sacred Penitentiary had warned even confessors "to deal cautiously with married persons on this subject matter." (The reference is to a ruling that dates from 1880.) "If the confessor in the sacred tribunal must be cautious in suggesting this means, certainly writers of popular books and pamphlets who give indiscriminate instruction on this delicate subject disregard the caution imposed by the Holy See."[201]

The Committee's statement was in no sense binding on any of the nation's bishops. It was sufficiently general, moreover, to permit even pliable recipients a good deal of latitude in terms of response. The Committee's members doubtless hoped for action from their brother bishops—"pressures upon our

Catholic booksellers and publishers," as Manchester's John Peterson put it bluntly, "and episcopal leashing of unrestrained clerics."[202] New York's Cardinal Hayes proved a model in both respects, if something of a slow starter. "Instead of [rhythm] being freely taught and commended, it is rather to be tolerated as an extreme remedy or means of preventing sin," he told his priests in 1936. Only confessors might broach the subject, and only in urgent cases or where penitents were habitual users of contraceptives. Hayes also forbade "the discussion of the question in any Catholic publication intended for the laity," as well as "any advertisement of the theory in a Catholic magazine."[203] Chicago's Cardinal Mundelein had even prior to the statement "expressed the opinion that the Bishops should insist upon a toning down of public utterances and Catholic newspaper publicity on birth control." It was already policy in his Archdiocese, he informed his fellow bishops in November 1934, that rhythm was "a matter for the confessional."[204] I have found no information on what other bishops did, but it seems overwhelmingly likely that they mostly hewed to the restrictive policies of Hayes and Mundelein. These were the nation's most prominent bishops, and both had been deeply involved in the evolving politics of rhythm.

That most bishops chose a conservative course is suggested by the nation's Catholic periodicals. Advertising for books and pamphlets on rhythm disappeared almost completely after the end of 1934, as did editorial reference to the topic. Clerical journals, which had earlier sponsored lively debates on the method, largely banned the subject from their pages. "It has been decided that further discussion of the problems of 'Natural Birth Control' shall not be carried on in these columns," as the *Acolyte* announced in November 1934.[205] Silence did not descend completely—pamphlet literature continued to be published, and books like those of Latz and O'Brien continued to be sold. The occasional priest, moreover, was apparently resistant to the newly restrictive regime. The bishop of Seattle, having refused an imprimatur to a pamphlet on rhythm written by one of his senior clergy, was startled to learn early in 1935 that the priest had nonetheless had the pamphlet published, along with a device—called "The Wheel of Life"—for calculating the putative safe period. Bishop Gerald Shaunessy required the assistance of the NCWC's John Burke and the Apostolic Delegate—the Vatican's representative to the American Church—to prevent national distribution of the pamphlet. (Shaunessy himself took care of the matter locally—"I saw to it that it was no longer for sale in Catholic book stores in Seattle, Portland, Vancouver and Spokane"—but does not seem to have disciplined the priest author, who was a former chancellor of the Seattle diocese.[206]) The Apostolic Delegate was called upon in at least one additional diocesan dustup over rhythm. He wrote to an unnamed prelate in 1936, apparently at the latter's behest, and essentially gave the force of law to the practice of Cardinal Hayes. "The theory in question," as the Delegate observed, is to be tolerated only "as an extreme remedy and a means to withhold the faithful from sin. . . . In addition, Your Excellency will kindly see that no Catholic periodical or newspaper, published in the diocese, advertises the theory in question, or discusses it otherwise than as directed above." The Delegate asked that the unnamed bishop "communicate the contents of this letter" to every priest in his diocese.[207]

By the mid-1930s, then, the subject of rhythm was shrouded in official silence. But rhythm did not thereby cease to be a factor in Catholic life. Confessors continued to commend it to penitents, and not necessarily only to those in extreme marital circumstances. "Married persons can by mutual consent restrict intercourse to the sterile period either temporarily or perpetually without offending against the moral law," the Jesuit moralist John Ford reminded seminarians in the late 1930s. "Nor does one need any excusing reason like poverty, ill health, etc. to justify this restriction." Ford was certainly opposed to publicizing rhythm, fearing—as mentioned above—that this would promote among Catholics a "birth control mentality." But in the privacy of the confessional, as Ford saw it, priests might speak of rhythm quite freely. "The penitentiary said that confessors giving information on this point should do it cautiously. But do not press this too far. It was over 55 years ago; times have changed."[208] Chicago's Reynold Hillenbrand seemed to share Ford's views, at least according to his fragmentary teaching notes. Tell penitents about the safe period, he urged his students. Never forget how many inducements presently exist for couples "to practice sinful birth control."[209] Not every moralist, of course, endorsed so relatively liberal a stance. But Ford and Hillenbrand were solidly mainstream in their thinking. Their counsels, moreover, permitted priests to respond humanely—as they saw it—to troubled penitents and, especially in the case of younger men, embrace a more positive view of marital sex than had characterized their Victorian forebears. The honest practice of their priesthood made both options necessary for growing numbers of clergy.

The laity too kept rhythm alive. They continued to buy literature on the subject, as well as the numerous devices available for calculating the safe period. (No bishop could prevent the sale of such, especially when it came to commercial publishers.) They talked about rhythm among themselves, sharing stories of success and failure. There were probably enough of the former to lend the theory a certain plausibility, particularly among those many Catholics for whom contraception was simply not an option. What the laity failed to do in the 1930s, or indeed for some years thereafter, was to speak publicly about the frustrations attendant on rhythm—the tensions it generated between spouses, the mechanical quality it sometimes afforded a couple's rationed sexual encounters, the relatively high rate of unintended pregnancies. A great many priests, in consequence, continued to regard the theory as a genuine solution to the admittedly hard problems attached to the Catholic stance on contraception.

So there was little in the way of validation, either in private encounters with priests or public discourse about rhythm, for those probably many Catholics whose recourse to rhythm ultimately failed. The public voice of rhythm at this juncture belonged mostly to commercial publishers with a vested interest in the theory. "Nature has come to the assistance of a bewildered people in this matter of controlling birth," in the typically optimistic view of Emmett J. Culligan's *Safeguarding Marital Happiness.* "As our new knowledge becomes known contraception and abortion will rapidly disappear. This great contribution of science should be heralded from house to house, as it is a message of joy and peace."[210] On those rare occasions when lay authors spoke critically of the practice, it was not rhythm's shortcomings that they had in mind but the theory's alleged abetting of lukewarm Catholicity. "It is the minimum for avoiding sin," in the words of a 1939 article in the *Catholic World.* "It substitutes a mean sort of prudence for a sublime trust in God."[211] In the circumstances, a frustrated veteran of the rhythm method might well impute its failings to her own want of care or her husband's want of self-restraint, and their joint distress to a want of faith.

If rhythm was at best a partial solution to the problem of fertility control among Catholics, its advent was nonetheless of immense importance. Their faith in rhythm almost certainly made it easier for priests to enforce Church teaching on contraception in more preemptive fashion. Absent rhythm, the Depression years would have been even harder for many would-be compassionate confessors. Rhythm enabled both its partisans and many of its critics to believe that Church teaching on contraception was not only right but humane—far more so, indeed, than the contraceptive ethic being promoted by their adversaries. Even men of highly restrictive views—those who would permit rhythm only in cases of extreme ill health or dire poverty—could console themselves in the conviction that God had provided for the needs of those whom the birth controllers wrongly saw as the tragic victims of Catholic teaching. "The Christian ideal is one of begetting children for time and for eternity," as a conservative Franciscan pointed out in 1940. "If a married couple honestly feel that for some reason they cannot meet that ideal, they know equally well that they may not commit a sin. They know that nature has so regulated their powers of reproduction that with a certain amount of periodic self-control they may arrange to have children as they may care for them—with no offense to God Who designed and regulated and gave them those powers."[212] Such easy confidence in rhythm deflected any number of hard problems from a good many clerical consciences.

The single most important development attached to rhythm, however, was the opening it created for a more positive clerical assessment of marital sex. At the outset of the 1930s, the extant clerical sources—professional journals, pamphlets, sermon texts—spoke of marriage almost solely in terms of its sexual dangers. Frequent sex in marriage was widely described as a barrier to the spouses' spiritual development, and an almost certain indication of at least one partner's gross physicality. "The marriage act must indeed be performed at times, for otherwise, as experience shows, estrangement or loveless coldness ensues, but this act must not be repeated too frequently, especially at the beginning of marriage, lest the sex instinct become increasingly impaired with accompanying evil consequences," in the view of Dominic Pruemmer, a German Dominican who also wrote for American clerical audiences.[213] Abstaining from sex, whether for purposes of family limitation or—much more rarely—for reasons of spiritual discipline, was regularly applauded in these same sources as a principal route to moral refinement and spiritual growth. Couples with legitimate reasons to limit their families, as the moralist Stanislaus Woywod argued, chose the better part when they opted for total abstinence rather than rhythm. "There is given by God a compensation for every sacrifice that is made in His honor, and in married life it will consist in a deeper and more spiritual love and affection for each other, a bond that is far superior to the ties of human love, a bond more enduring than that of flesh and blood."[214] Few priests doubted that procreation was the primary purpose of marriage, which might seem to run counter to the logic just enunciated. But fecundity was not infrequently praised precisely on the grounds of its anti-erotic consequences. "By the presence of children the mutual love of husband and wife is urged to still higher degrees of self-sacrifice and self-forgetfulness," as Ignatius Cox told a New York radio audience in the spring of 1930. "Children thus check and control sex."[215] Cox spoke with unusual bluntness, but his views were in the clerical mainstream.

By the 1930s, as we have seen, such views were already under challenge in the work of Dietrich von Hildebrand. Few American priests then were familiar with his arguments, although these would be quite widely known by the 1950s. But many priests knew from their own observations that regular sex was essential to the health of marriage. (Perhaps inevitably, given their formation, they thought primarily in terms of male sexual needs; a good woman's chief joy was assumed to derive from the pleasing of her mate.) The advent of a putatively reliable rhythm method freed men like these to speak in newly positive ways about marital sex—to begin to articulate a theology of marriage where sex both expressed and intensified love and thus supported a couple's journey toward holiness. Sex, in short, was increasingly seen as a force for spiritual good—a standard view by now among liberal and even some moderate Protestants.[216] So rhythm made it suddenly possible—always assuming faith in its efficacy—to elevate the so-called secondary ends of marriage to

Figure 3. Father John A. O'Brien (1893–1980), longtime champion of the rhythm method. Photo, probably late 1950s, courtesy of the University of Notre Dame Archives.

equal standing with the allegedly primary end of procreation. The more prescient critics of rhythm were well aware of this. "There are some who attempt to prove that the first end and purpose of marriage is the companionship of man and woman," as Monsignor Louis Nau began a vigorous assault on rhythm's promoters in 1934. "These pervert the order of nature. . . . Conjugal love is *per se* a means rather than an end and can only be considered a secondary purpose of marriage."[217]

The full implications of these developments were not apparent in the 1930s, save to the most farsighted. But they would ultimately have major impact on Catholic thinking about contraception. If marital sex had as much to do with the fostering of conjugal love as with procreation, should the latter good be permitted to nullify the former? That might easily happen when a couple had ample reason to fear a new pregnancy and equally ample reason to doubt that rhythm alone would prevent it. If fears like these came to undermine marriage as a community of love, did it really make sense to insist that each and every sexual act be open to procreation? It might in the circumstances be wiser to stipulate that the marriage itself must be open to children—though presumably no more than a couple believed that they could responsibly care for.

Such arguments came vigorously to the fore in the early-to-mid 1960s, at precisely the time—and precisely because—the laity gave public voice to their accumulated grievances with rhythm. Until that happened, even liberal priests were simply unable to engage the questions to which the logic of rhythm gave rise. John A. O'Brien, for one, eventually urged a change in Church teaching on contraception. But he did so only in the mid-1960s, at the end of a long career as rhythm's most famous clerical advocate. Lay testimony about rhythm was instrumental in this evolution, as O'Brien readily acknowledged. The laity doing the testifying, somewhat ironically, were products of the positive theology of marriage that men like O'Brien had done so much to popularize.

The Secular Politics of Birth Control

The political tide turned definitively in the 1930s against the Church and its dwindling number of anti-birth control allies. Change was evident first in the courts and various professional associations. The Second Circuit Court of Appeals rendered a decision in 1930 that made enforcement of the anti-contraceptive portions of the Comstock Act markedly more difficult. The commercial traffic in contraceptives immediately quickened and became more public. That same court significantly modified the Comstock Act in 1936, ruling that it should not be construed as preventing physicians from using the mails to send or receive contraceptive information or devices. Roosevelt's Solicitor General declined to appeal the case to the Supreme Court, effectively freeing physicians from even the outside chance of federal prosecution.[218] That the National Catholic Welfare Conference decided against a public protest of this decision suggests how rapidly the public climate was changing.[219]

The change was further accelerated by a 1937 resolution of the American Medical Association, which endorsed contraception under medical advisement as appropriate to nearly all marital circumstances. "Voluntary family limitation," in the words of the resolution, "is dependent largely on the judgment and wishes of individual parents." The Congress, it is true, did nothing in the 1930s to liberalize access to contraception, though it was widely known in Washington that federal relief programs sometimes underwrote the costs of contraception for their clients. (This was never authorized as policy and always done surreptitiously.) Nor did the various state legislatures modify their existing laws, much less pass new and more liberal ones. But legislators everywhere understood that the old restrictive laws were in most instances simply incapable of enforcement. Contraceptives were freely advertised in towns and cities across the country, while birth control clinics functioned openly in heavily Catholic cities like Chicago, Philadelphia, and New York.[220] By the late 1930s, indeed, birth control clinics in certain Southern jurisdictions were enjoying covert state support.[221]

Organized Catholic opposition was almost certainly the principal reason that legislators failed to act, though Catholics were not the only opponents of liberalized access to birth control. So Catholic leaders could pride themselves on their not inconsiderable political leverage.[222] But most were profoundly discouraged about the ultimate prospect. Though the pro-contraception forces often spoke of the Church as a rich and powerful adversary, things looked quite different to those in the Catholic trenches. "The Birth Control advocates have the money," as John J. Burke saw it. "They can afford to pay the expenses for attending a hearing to the specialists they bring here. We can do nothing of the kind."[223] Nor were Protestant allies nearly as numerous as in the 1920s, though certain denominations—most notably the Missouri Synod Lutherans—were still formally committed to an anti-birth control stance. This made it difficult for Catholic leaders to plausibly maintain that opposition to contraception was a Christian rather than a specifically Catholic position—something they regarded as essential to long-term political success. Protestant defections also meant that the anti-Catholic rhetoric of Margaret Sanger and her allies seemed ever more potent and threatening. "This fight, to my mind, is now more than a fight against birth control; it is a fight against the bitter enemies of the Catholic Church," as Ignatius Cox summarized the situation in 1935.[224] The drift of public opinion—politics in its broadest sense—was even more troubling. "It is my fear that the majority opinion of the country is in favor of Birth Control—the people, the legislatures, the Courts," a Catholic activist acknowledged in 1936.[225] Small wonder, then, that Catholic leaders were increasingly wont to attribute the success of the birth control movement to sinister forces—to corporate capitalism, to communism, even on occasion to the Prince of Darkness himself. In the words of the never phlegmatic Ignatius Cox, "I have always believed that the B.C. movement is characterised [*sic*] by signs of Satanic influence."[226]

Whatever their private discouragement, Catholic leaders did not doubt the necessity of continuing the fight. Those active in the struggle were honestly convinced that contraception was both gravely wrong and deleterious in its effects. Hence the moral obligation to soldier on, even in an ultimately losing battle. They were conscious too that at least some Catholics were capable of being swayed by the opposition's arguments. Hence the need to reply to those arguments as regularly as they were made. The opposition, indeed, was trying hard to appeal to Catholics, notwithstanding its frequent attacks on the Church. "They grab every appearance," as Chicago's Archbishop Samuel Stritch described the birth control forces locally, "and in their propaganda represent that only a small group of intransigents in the Catholic Church is opposed to birth control."[227] (That small group, needless to say, was alleged to be mostly composed of the celibate clergy.) The strategy of the movement, as Ignatius Cox quite plausibly saw it, was not only to "isolate Catholics" from other Americans "but also to isolate the *Catholic laity from their clerical leaders.*"[228] So Catholic engagement in the secular politics of birth control was only in part about law and policy, important though these were. It had also and more enduringly to do with the internal politics of the Church. The secular politics of birth control were simultaneously, from the Catholic perspective, a highly public means of catechizing the faithful.

The means employed to these dual ends were not particularly novel. Where Catholic leaders could not prevent the holding of legislative hearings on birth control, they appeared as more or less expert witnesses and tried to recruit non-Catholic allies to testify as well. (The staff of the NCWC in Washington was responsible for dealing with proposed federal legislation; the various bishops were responsible for developments in their own dioceses.) Lay witnesses were generally preferred to clerical ones, for obvious public relations reasons. Lay female witnesses were the most valued of all. "We should have trained, capable, experienced men and particularly women at our command," as John J. Burke noted in 1931.[229] Few of those witnesses, however, offered any but clerically vetted testimony. "We have no authority to speak on behalf of the Catholic Church," as a representative of the National Catholic Alumni Federation rather artlessly acknowledged before a Congressional committee. "That is strictly the province of the hierarchy of the church." The members of his organization spoke simply "as Catholic gentlemen and as American citizens." Their objections to proposed liberalization of the Comstock Act were accordingly couched in the language of negative social consequences rather than that of Catholic doctrine.[230]

Such pragmatic concerns—as opposed to the invoking of Scripture and papal statements or extended meditations on the natural law—dominated Catholic political discourse in the 1930s when it came to contraception. Birth control threatened the nation's security by dangerously lowering fertility. The threat was economic as well as military, with the current depression frequently attributed to long-term decline in the birthrate. "President Theodore Roosevelt called birth control by its true name, race suicide," as New York's Cardinal Patrick Hayes began an overtly political sermon in 1935. (It was preached in rejoinder to a birth control conference held in his see city and subsequently published in the New York's *Times.*) The American population "is no longer reproducing itself. If judged by this standard, the United States is already a dying nation."[231] Birth control violated the principles of social justice so warmly endorsed by the Roosevelt administration. The bishops' call for a "family wage" at their annual meeting in 1932 was explicitly linked to their opposition to birth control, as was their endorsement of the right to collective bargaining.[232] Liberalized access to birth control would erode public morals and undermine the health of marriage. "Panaceas" like birth control, in the words of lay activist Anna Dill Gamble, "appeal only to the weaknesses of human nature—to its inertia, to its hatred of self-restraint, to its reluctance to accept responsibility."[233] Contraceptives, moreover, were in at least some cases medically hazardous. Sterility and cancer had been reliably linked to the use of certain contraceptives, as New York's Father Edward Moore asserted in a heavily promoted book that appeared in 1931. Women were especially apt to suffer, and not just in the physical order. "Neurologists and psychiatrists talk in terms of neuroses and psychoses as a result of the refusal of parenthood."[234]

Catholic leaders were walking a delicate line in this regard. They were trying, on the one hand, to speak in nonsectarian terms to a broad American audience. They wanted, on the other hand, to remind Catholics of their religiously grounded obligation to adhere to Church teaching on contraception. Presumably they hoped to achieve both goals by marshaling lay opposition to the liberalization of birth control laws at the local, state, and national levels. Catholic leaders pursued this strategy far more broadly and successfully in the 1930s than they had earlier done, soliciting letters and statements from Catholic organizations and individual Catholics too at various critical junctures in the legislative war. A 1933 example from the Diocese of Brooklyn is instructive.

Patrick Scanlon, managing editor of the *Brooklyn Tablet,* directed this particular local effort to prevent amendment of the federal Comstock Act. He ran a front-page editorial in the diocesan weekly he edited to provide a model for letters of protest. "It states arguments against the bill from an American standpoint—the words Catholic, morality or religion are not mentioned," as he told the NCWC's John Burke. He then alerted "the heads of our diocesan organizations and . . . the heads of our colleges," as well as the parish-based conferences of the Society of St. Vincent de Paul, a lay charitable organization. ("Our poor [are] not asking for birth control but for a square deal.") Each of these organizations was requested to send a statement of opposition to members of the Congressional committee holding hearings on the offending bill. The *Tablet*'s readers were asked to send letters of their own to the Committee, while each of the diocese's roughly 300 seminarians was required to do so. The request was ultimately made from every pulpit in the diocese.[235]

Catholics involved in such campaigns nearly always spoke the secular language provided by men like Patrick Scanlon. But they acted as Catholics, in Catholic contexts, and under the guidance of an ultimately clerical leadership. Brooklyn's Scanlon was a layman, but he functioned in this campaign under direct episcopal control. Theirs was a kind of tribal warfare, in other words, but couched in the neutral discourse of patriotism and public welfare. While speaking as Americans to other Americans, mobilized Catholics were simultaneously reminded of their distinctiveness and especially of their Catholic obligations when it came to birth control. "Remind them frequently that they are 'the elect of God,'" as Bishop John Noll advised his priests in 1940, with regard to the Catholic laity, "and that they should readily recognize that they *must* live differently from others."[236] Insofar as the secular politics of birth control conveyed this message to the mass of Catholics, it was not from the Catholic perspective a wholly losing proposition.

Middle-class Catholic women were especially affected by the various political campaigns, given the assiduousness with which Catholic leaders encouraged their participation. Birth control, as we have seen, was widely regarded as an issue particularly affecting women. Male opponents of liberalized laws, not to mention celibate male opponents, were acutely aware of their disadvantage in this regard. Hence the need for Catholic women to testify at legislative hearings and for Catholic women's organizations to generate letters and statements of protest. Catholic women in the field of social work were especially well situated to monitor, and where necessary challenge, efforts by birth control advocacy groups to gain professional approbation and otherwise shape welfare policy at the state and local level. Only women, moreover, could plausibly speak for the Church when groups like the National Federation of Women's Clubs or the American Association of University Women veered in the mid-1930s toward public endorsement of birth control. St. Paul's Archbishop John Gregory Murray ordered Catholic women under his jurisdiction to resign their memberships when both organizations took this step in 1935. ("In an interview yesterday," according to the New York *Times,* the Archbishop likened birth-control groups to the 'Dillinger gang,' saying both were 'organized to commit murder.'"[237]) But his brother bishops at their annual meeting declined to endorse this approach. The Catholic members of both groups should instead be encouraged to work at rescinding the offending resolutions.[238]

Gently bred Catholic women were hardly accustomed to such roles, or indeed to regarding themselves as public actors. So more was involved for the newly minted activist than pious service to her Church, regardless of what the bishops intended. She was in fact being pushed toward a model of citizenship hitherto almost exclusively associated with educated Protestant and secular elites. Catholic women, after all, were expected to match their female opponents in any number of public venues—at hearings, in propaganda campaigns, at intra-organizational debates. Those who took the charge seriously were presumably changed by the experience, though little survives by way of evidence in this regard. Unlike Margaret Sanger, Catholic women activists were neither self-promoters—not in a public sense, at least—nor inclined to autobiography.

Perhaps this particular feature of the birth control wars is nothing but an ironic footnote. It was only a relative handful of women who were mobilized for extensive service, and in a cause that arguably denied the autonomy of their sex. But its import may well have been greater. Catholic leaders often argued that theirs was the truly pro-woman stand. Contraception, as they told it, reduced the female to a sexual object and undermined her security in marriage.

The chief victims of what Daniel Lord called the birth controllers' "vast experiment" would, according to the Catholic argument, come from that great majority of women who were simply unable to earn enough to support a family on their own.[239] Perhaps the new visibility of Catholic women as public opponents of birth control lent credibility to this position for a not insignificant number of their educated Catholic sisters. If Catholics could muster the likes of an Agnes Regan or Rita McGoldrick to take on Margaret Sanger herself, were they really as behind the times as the birth controllers claimed? (Regan was a longtime staff member at the National Catholic Welfare Conference, while McGoldrick was president of the National Council of Catholic Women. Both were skilled and prominent fixtures of the era's political battles over contraception.) Were Catholics not in fact the true feminists—those who protected the interests of all women rather than ministering to the misperceived needs of a privileged elite? Such was an increasingly popular argument among Catholic women writers, not only in the 1930s but for some years thereafter.[240] Logic like this may help to explain why the best-educated Catholic women in the late 1940s and the 1950s were particularly apt to support the Church's stand on contraception, and why their fertility in these years was so remarkably high.

The growing public acceptance of birth control gave rise on occasion to unusually creative political gestures on the part of certain Catholic leaders. Most of these were apparently intended to appeal especially to women. Chicago's Cardinal Mundelein, for example, endowed a subsidized maternity hospital in his see city in 1931. The cardinal was at once responding to the very real needs of his working-class flock and hoping to preach a sermon in stone on the social justice implications of the birth control debate. The wives of low-wage workers, according to the cardinal, had as much right to a hospital delivery as their more affluent sisters; they had a right to children, too, which the birth controllers would deny them. "In a word," as the cardinal told his priests with regard to the just-announced hospital, "it is our answer to the birth control propaganda." That the hospital was open only to Catholics "of the Caucasian races," apparently a condition of the chief donor's gift, underscores the extent to which Catholic thinking about social justice was as late as the 1930s still severely distorted by racism.[241] Nearly all Catholic hospitals then were either closed to African Americans or served them on a segregated basis.

A Redemptorist priest, one Father Joseph A. Schagemann, embarked in the early 1930s on a more modest version of Mundelein's scheme, founding what soon became known as the maternity guild movement. Maternity guilds were parish-based organizations, the management of which was in lay—especially lay female—hands. Their purpose was twofold. Each parish guild was charged with the raising of sufficient funds to assist needy families locally who expected the birth of a child. Ideally, this included the underwriting of hospitalization costs, though such might be hard for a less-than-affluent parish to sustain. Guild members were also expected to promote Church teaching on contraception among fellow Catholics.[242] "It is a necessary part of the fight upon birth-control," as a New York laywoman explained, especially in the context of widespread unemployment. "It was something of a shock to me to discover last summer that, despite the teachings of the Church on the sanctity of family life and the evil of birth-control, no Catholic hospital in New York City, with the exception of Misericordia, will accept free maternity cases . . . that, along with free public maternity care, in our city and others, goes birth control advice and even compulsory abortions and sterilization."[243] The movement sustained modest growth in the 1930s and '40s. By 1948, it claimed eighty-eight parish guilds in twenty-two different dioceses.[244]

Other Catholic leaders, equally creative, flirted with more coercive solutions. Fort Wayne's Bishop John Francis Noll proposed in 1937 that individual Catholics be asked to sign an anti-birth control pledge "after the manner of the Legion of Decency," in the words of the NCWC's John Burke, who thought the idea a bad one.[245] (The Legion of Decency pledge, publicly recited by Catholics on an annual basis, required adherence to Legion ratings when it came to movie-going.) Rochester's Bishop Edward Mooney, then chair of that body's Administrative Committee, was similarly unimpressed.[246] The matter apparently went no further, though most of the nation's bishops would eventually require those about to be married in their dioceses to sign statements acknowledging their familiarity with Church teaching on birth control and their obligation to observe it. Chicago's Mundelein, as we have seen, had adopted such a policy as early as 1932. A Benedictine priest proposed in 1938 that Catholic couples be directed to renew their marriage vows at a yearly public ceremony. "The husbands and wives, renewing the promises of fidelity to the great Sacrament, will be warned, at least this once a year, as if by a voice from Heaven against the insidious heresy of less children—and less heirs of Heaven."[247] No bishop, to my knowledge, endorsed the proposal or otherwise encouraged its implementation. The public nature of ventures like these risked alienating many laity, as nearly all bishops presumably knew, and would surely have provided grist for their opponents' propaganda mills.

Absent public coercion, what more could be done to stem the tide of contraceptive use among Catholics? The Administrative Committee of the NCWC debated the question early in 1941, mostly at the behest of Salt Lake City's Duane Hunt, who urged his fellow bishops to a national campaign against what he saw as widespread Catholic flouting of Church teaching.[248] But the Committee rejected his suggestion, albeit gently and with apologies. The most it thought possible was a closer monitoring of the activities of the national Birth Control Council and more frequent stories in the Catholic press explaining the Council's political methods.[249] The Committee's decision probably rested in part on want of funds and perhaps on chairman Mooney's doubts about the jurisdictional reach of the national bishop's conference.[250] Episcopal discouragement over birth control politics played a role as well. "It is not a new problem for us, as Your Excellency knows," a longtime staff member at the NCWC explained the Committee's decision, "and we have, through the years, endeavored to combat this wide-spread evil. It seemed an easier thing to do when the effort was confined chiefly to legislation in the National Congress." But recent court decisions had made propaganda for birth control "an entirely accepted thing."[251] Monsignor Michael Ready, author of this plaintive missive, said nothing directly about the problem of Catholic contraceptive use, which had been Bishop Hunt's original concern. Recent defeats in the secular realm had apparently made that problem less amenable of solution than had hitherto been acknowledged.

Catholic leaders thus entered the war years in a state of profound discouragement with regard to the nation's moral life. Many wartime developments worked to intensify their already gloomy collective mood. But contra the predictions of a good many doomsayers, the war was followed by an era of intense domesticity and a longer and larger baby boom than anyone had anticipated. Catholics, especially the best educated among them, led the way in this latter regard, many as a direct result of their Church's teaching on contraception. A healthy majority of Catholics in the immediate postwar years apparently did their earnest best to observe that teaching on a regular basis. Smaller but still significant numbers were ardent proponents of the teaching, which they saw as expressive of their most deeply held religious values.

Fertility control did continue in these years to be a principal cause of anxiety for married Catholics, and of pastoral problems for the clergy. This was perhaps especially true by the second half of the 1950s, when the baby boom crested and birthrates nationally began a slow creep downward. Lay resentments began to accumulate and eventually fueled an epoch-making challenge, not only to the teaching itself but the very authority on which it rested. This last-mentioned phenomenon, however, should not detract from the remarkable developments of the immediate postwar decade. It was then that the efforts of the 1930s bore their most luxuriant fruit.

4

"Life Is a Warfare"

Confession, Preaching, Politics,
1941–1962

Much changed for American Catholics between 1941 and 1962. When the United States entered the Second World War, its Catholic population was heavily urban and disproportionately concentrated in the industrial working class. Upward mobility had clearly been slowed by ten long years of depression. Though the near-cessation of immigration had helped to speed assimilation, ethnic consciousness was still strong among Catholics, particularly the more recent arrivals, who remained mostly clustered in so-called foreign language parishes. Even wholly assimilated Catholics, moreover, were unsure of their full acceptance as Americans. All adults but the youngest had lingering memories of the "tribal twenties," when foreign birth and Catholic faith—the two were often conflated—seemed in the view of many Americans to be equally incompatible with responsible citizenship. "You felt it was their country," as the novelist J. F. Powers evoked a Catholic boyhood amidst a sea of supremely confident Protestants, "handed down to them by the Pilgrims, George Washington, and others, and that they were taking a risk in letting you live in it."[1]

Things were quite otherwise by 1962, the year that saw the inaugural session of the Second Vatican Council. American Catholics then were far more numerous than just twenty years earlier—the Catholic population had doubled since 1940, thanks almost exclusively to a rising Catholic birthrate. This growing population was increasingly suburban, affluent, and educated. (By the mid-1970s, non-Hispanic Catholics would rank second only to American Jews in terms of family income.[2]) And Catholics by the early 1960s had largely outgrown their sense of being probationary Americans. The Second World War had proved more powerfully integrative for Catholics than any other American minority. The image of the Church in popular culture and indeed in public opinion polls was markedly positive in the postwar years, despite periodic episodes of interconfessional conflict, some of it having to do with the politics of contraception. The election of a Catholic president in 1960 was the greatest boon of all, though it mostly confirmed that enormous change had already taken place. Still, the event itself was for Catholics a new font of confident belongingness.

Despite the manifold changes, however, the years between 1941 and 1962 still form a coherent chapter in American Catholic history. These decades mark a culmination of sorts—the fullest flowering of a mostly clerical effort, several generations long, to effect among American Catholics remarkably high standards of religious loyalty and practice. Rates of Mass attendance and reception of the sacraments among American Catholics almost certainly reached their high-water mark in the 1950s, with the previous decade having recorded important progress in this regard. The waning of ethnic identities made room for an identity rooted mostly in religion. Simply being Catholic was increasingly a form of ethnicity in its own right, with predictable consequences in terms of loyalty to the Church and the values it championed. Partly for this reason, these same years saw the prohibition on birth control assume a more dominant role than ever before in American Catholic consciousness. It was almost inconceivable, in the view of a respected Jesuit moralist in the mid-1950s, that a practicing Catholic in the United States could "allege inculpable ignorance of the Church's position on contraception."[3] The teaching, after all, was quite literally everywhere—in the Catholic and secular media; local, state, and national politics, the Catholic pulpit; and especially the confessional—and Catholics were better primed than ever before to hear it.

Figure 4. "Ghetto Catholicism" at its zenith: First Communion breakfast at St. Peter's parish, Somerset, PA, with pastor J. P. Manion and four Sisters of Mercy. Photo courtesy of the American Catholic History Research Center and University Archives, Catholic University.

The postwar years also saw an abundant flowering of lay-led groups devoted to Catholic family life—groups that were increasingly supplemented by family life ministries in the various dioceses. These both reflected and strengthened a proud counterculturalism among the more devout laity. The teaching on birth control was in this context embraced by those same devout laity as an antidote to materialism and a statement of faith in the human future. It was an ironic means of lay empowerment, too. Who could preach more forcefully against the period's alleged secularism than couples who permitted God to determine the size of their families? Who better to persuade a cynical world that human purposes transcended its fears and false values? "The religion of Christ is revolutionary, radical, and of another world," as a lay magazine from Chicago articulated the ethos. "There is no place in it for mediocrity." Hence the obligation of Catholic couples to "prefer another baby to a new car."[4] The earnest editors spoke in this instance for a distinct minority of Catholics. But it was an articulate and highly visible minority, and one that did much in the postwar years to enhance the legitimacy among ordinary Catholics of the Church's teaching on marriage and sex. Lay activists and their clerical allies managed in the postwar years to infuse the teaching's presentation with an appealing idealism and even a certain romance. "As parents of a large family we've become teachers of life," a Chicago father of eleven explained in 1953, "and that's important."[5]

The teaching, of course, had another face, too—one that was far less attractive. A good many clerical writers kept to a fear-inducing and repressive mode, especially in the popular Catholic media. "You need to think about your real goals in life," the Redemptorist editor of the *Liguorian* lectured the allegedly many Catholics who had turned to contraception. "You need to think about heaven and hell. You need to think about death, and how God can call you in the very midst of your planning for a comfortable future on earth." True Christians kept their eyes on the last things; they trusted God, no matter how dark the circumstances, and were not overcome by fear or discouragement or hungers of the flesh. Prayer and the sacraments made them "equal to any sacrifice up to and including martyrdom."[6] A stern idealism was evident in perorations of this sort, which summoned ordinary Catholics to spiritual heroism. But the general flavor was punitive and rather sour. In this rhetorical universe, Catholics were not so much "teachers of life" as the stoic servants of an implacable God. "Life is a warfare," as our Redemptorist reminded his readers, citing Job for their edification. No one "can escape the battle and yet reach heaven."[7]

Catholic Birthrates and Contraceptive Practice

The general American birthrate rose significantly during the Second World War—more babies were born in 1943 than in any previous year of the century—and even more spectacularly thereafter. The average number of children per household had climbed from just under two to three by the late 1940s, though the "baby boom" was not to peak until 1957, when the total fertility rate for white American women exceeded 3.5. Birthrates did not resume their historic downward trend until the mid-1960s. The single state became much rarer in this same period, as did the postponing of childbearing. The marriage rate in the postwar years reached an all-time high, while the median age at first marriage for both sexes sank to historic lows. American women in the early 1950s were marrying at a median age of barely twenty years, with the average woman bearing her first child sooner after marriage than in the 1920s.

Every segment of the American population was affected by these developments. But Catholic fertility patterns were distinctive in two important ways. The Catholic birthrate in these years was higher than that of the nation as a whole—roughly 20 percent higher, according to some estimates, with the differential rising to perhaps as much as 40 percent in certain affluent locales.[8] Catholic families were typically larger than those of other Americans, sometimes spectacularly so. This was especially true of the families of college-educated Catholics, whose numbers were growing rapidly. College-educated Catholic women, particularly those from Catholic colleges, had among the nation's highest birthrates in the 1950s.[9] A Catholic college education was strongly predictive of preference for a numerous family, according to a study published in 1963. (This same study found a disproportionate number of Irish Americans attending Catholic colleges and universities, suggesting an ethnic dimension to the phenomenon.[10]) College education was also predictive of a woman's adhering to her church's teaching on contraception—something that did not change until the later 1960s. As late as 1965, college-trained Catholic women were significantly less likely to defy their church on this score than Catholic women who had not completed high school.[11]

The extent to which Catholics adhered to the teaching, hitherto mostly a mystery, can by the mid-1950s be plausibly documented. Beginning in 1955, the Office of Population Research at Princeton University conducted a series of national fertility studies that included religion among the variables. The studies were done at five-year intervals between 1955 and 1970.

In the sample surveyed in 1955, which consisted of currently married white women between the ages of 18 and 39, roughly 30 percent of the Catholic respondents admitted to having employed a means of family limitation other than abstinence or rhythm. This seems, at least in retrospect, a remarkably high degree of compliance with Church teaching, especially in light of the very young ages at which period couples married. Few clergy, however, saw it this way: that 30 percent translated into very large numbers of troubled penitents, even if the persons in question confessed infrequently. It translated as well into numerous bad examples, not only in terms of family planning but also in religious observance. The 1955 study, like subsequent ones, found that those who defied church teaching were typically less devout than those who did not—less likely to attend Mass on a weekly basis or to receive the sacraments regularly.

The Princeton fertility survey done in 1960 recorded a fairly significant increase in forbidden modes of contraceptive practice among married Catholics of childbearing age. About 38 percent of the sample admitted to such, with those aged 35 to 39 reporting the highest incidence of noncompliance. Forty-six percent of this age group had used or were using a prohibited means of family limitation. In other respects the survey's findings echoed those of its predecessor: high fertility among Catholics was positively correlated with levels of education and especially Catholic education, family income, regularity in religious practice, and to a lesser degree with Irish ethnicity. (Italian American respondents wanted the fewest children, with those of German and Slavic origin occupying the middle ground.) Catholics as a group, however, still expressed a preference for significantly larger families than Protestants or Jews. Notwithstanding these continuities, the survey had clearly detected an important change, and one that proved to be accelerating. More than half of the Catholic women polled by the Princeton survey in 1965 had used or were using a means of contraception forbidden by papal authority.[12]

The Princeton surveys thus suggest that the teaching on contraception was even in the 1950s in the early stages of what became a thoroughgoing delegitimization. This was partly the product of Catholics who rejected the teaching at the outset of their married lives. Their numbers were clearly growing: 30 percent of Catholic respondents aged 20 to 24 had defied Church teaching, according to the Princeton survey done in 1955. By 1960, that figure had risen to 43 percent. Less devout and less educated than their "conforming" age-mates, this group was presumably vulnerable to change in mainstream fertility values. American birthrates generally had begun to decline between 1955 and 1960, probably reflecting an increased premium on women's wage earning. Catholics like these had existed in previous generations, too, though we have no reliable figures with regard to their use of birth control. But by the 1950s, such Catholics were maturing in a society where marital contraception enjoyed widespread, public, and wholly unambiguous endorsement. This had not been the case for their parents. These younger Catholics, then, almost certainly embraced contraception with a greater ease and confidence than their parents had done, and presumably used it more effectively. They appear, in short, to have solved the problem of family limitation very much on their own terms—in good part, one suspects, because the problem had for them never loomed terribly large. Indifferent Catholics or no, they were still a force for change—functioning as such, indeed, before its advent was even remotely intuited.

It was a second group, however, whose experience had the greater impact on the intra-Catholic politics of birth control. I speak of those many Catholics who turned to forbidden modes of contraception only after a decade or more of marriage. Often devout and well educated, such Catholics had typically used rhythm to space or limit births, though surprising numbers claim to have taken no precautions at all. (Rhythm, according to several fertility studies, was very much the province of the highly educated.[13]) But most such couples usually achieved, well before the end of the wife's fertile years, what was for them a maximal family. Postwar Catholics, after all, were marrying at younger ages than their parents had done. Not every Catholic in such circumstances proceeded to flout Church teaching—prior to the mid-1960s, an apparent majority did not. But a growing minority felt it had no choice.[14] Hence the unusually large number of Catholic nonconformers in their later thirties who emerge in the 1960 Princeton survey. No other age group showed so dramatic an increase in disobedience to the teaching, from 28 percent in 1955 to 46 percent in 1960.

Catholics like these paid a price for disobedience. Many ceased to go regularly to the sacraments. Three local studies of Catholic religious practice, conducted variously between the early 1940s and the mid-1950s, show a marked decline among married Catholics in their thirties with regard to the frequency of confession and communion and even, though to a lesser extent, of attendance at Mass. We would normally expect Catholics in this age group, nearly all of them parents of school-age children, to be conscientious about modeling piety. But no other age group showed such low levels of observance. The principal reason for the decline, at least in the view of the studies' priest authors, was birth control: couples in their thirties, already the parents of at least two or three children, would naturally be vulnerable to the blandishments of contraceptives. None of the priest authors, interestingly, had much to say about the psychological suffering attendant on the situation, especially for Catholics who had once been reasonably devout.[15]

But psychological suffering—one might almost say anguish—was indeed a reality for many such Catholics, as we will later see. This had certainly been true as well for Catholics in previous generations. The postwar situation was nonetheless different and far more productive of deeply troubled consciences. Unlike Catholics in previous generations, the hard-pressed parents of the postwar years could make no claim to "good faith ignorance." Nearly all of them understood the absolute nature of the teaching. Significant numbers, moreover, had heard the teaching explained in attractively personalist language. Some had once embraced it—perhaps in some sense still embraced it—as emblematic of their deepest spiritual values. To challenge the teaching in such circumstances meant rejecting an image of the ideal self, as well as the religious authority that had hitherto structured one's life. Presumably because of this, open challenge to the teaching was slow to emerge, even on the part of those who quietly defied it. It was not until 1964 that the Catholic laity spoke publicly on the issue in any numbers at all. Many continued throughout the 1950s to give principled endorsement to the teaching, at least in public opinion polls. But it was a deeply conflicted laity that did so, as the angers of the 1960s might lead us to suspect.

The social climate of the postwar years was helpful in certain respects to Catholics who wished to comply with Church teaching. Americans of many backgrounds were positively inclined toward relatively large families.[16] Few seemed to doubt that marriage and motherhood were requisite life goals for the vast majority of women, with paid employment—should it occur at all—being tailored to fit the demands of one's family. Catholics, moreover, were widely admired for their certitude in matters both doctrinal and moral. They were admired too for their upward mobility—the evident reward of disciplined group norms. Large Catholic families had in a previous generation conjured up negative stereotypes of ignorance and immigrant poverty. In the postwar years they were far more apt to evoke abundance and rightly ordered values. Americans were deeply worried then about the well-being of youth and the family—about juvenile delinquency, premarital sex, adultery, and divorce. They worried too about the corrosive effects of materialism, even as they enjoyed an unprecedented prosperity. So the Catholic example, real or imagined, seemed to speak to public as well as purely private concerns.

But the postwar climate also challenged Catholic priorities in the realm of sex. A substantial majority of non-Catholic Americans by the 1940s endorsed contraceptive practice in marriage.[17] For many, indeed, it was integral to marital morality—only the selfish or irresponsible would risk a wife's health or a family's well-being by having too many children too rapidly. Margaret Sanger's once radical Birth Control Federation was rechristened Planned Parenthood in 1942, albeit over Sanger's objections, and successfully marketed as a sober exponent of responsible family values. Premier among these was sexual fulfillment in marriage, widely regarded in the postwar years as a sine qua non of marital health. Middlebrow culture by the 1950s was suffused with neo-Freudian logic—the hazards of sexual repression, the destructive effects of sexual shame—though usually in the context of a fulsome respect for marriage. Female frigidity generated especially intense anxiety: the sexually unresponsive wife was widely regarded as a principal cause of marital failure. Catholic writing on marital sex increasingly reflected such concerns, with more liberal moralists waxing lyrical on the salvific effects of sexual communion in marriage. But this view of sex was bound, in the not terribly long-term, to come into practical conflict with Catholic teaching on contraception.

Catholics were challenged as well by growing societal fears about overpopulation. Such fears were new—the opponents of birth control had hitherto trafficked in the specter of population decline, and with a certain plausibility. Many Catholic spokesmen, indeed, continued in this mode throughout the

1940s. But by the early 1950s, American elite opinion was increasingly focused on the dangers of unchecked population growth, especially but not exclusively in the world's poorest nations. By the later 1950s, their concerns were
the stuff of the popular media.[18] *Standing Room Only* was the typically alarmist title of a book published in 1955—one that managed to be both anti-
Catholic and anti-Communist. (Both the Kremlin and the Vatican, according
to the author, were enemies of population planning.[19]) A subsequent article,
widely cited, set 13 November 2026 as the putative date when "standing room
only" would be a literal reality.[20] But if period fears were exaggerated, they
were spurred nonetheless by very real problems. Third world poverty, exacerbated by rapid population growth, was indeed appalling. And widespread
poverty was clearly a cause of political instability and war. The issue, which
had become a national obsession by the early 1960s, was for Catholic leaders
extremely hard to negotiate. Accustomed to occupying the high ground in public debates on sex, they found themselves on the moral defensive.

The advent of an oral contraceptive—the justly famous "Pill"—also created
major problems for Catholic opponents of birth control. Tested in heavily
Catholic Puerto Rico in 1956, the Pill was first marketed in the United States
in 1960. Its advent raised potential difficulties for the standard Catholic argument against contraception, which turned on the "deordination" of a natural
act by means of artificial barriers or the act's lack of completeness. Neither factor was relevant, strictly speaking, to the Pill. Perhaps more important, the
anovular pill disassociated—at least for its consumer—the sexual act from the
fact of contraception. Women ignorant of their sexual anatomy or afflicted by
shame might especially appreciate this. So might women for whom contraceptive devices were redolent of guilt and cultural otherness. Those many
Catholic women who used contraceptives for the first time in the course of the
1960s turned in large numbers to the Pill, which by 1970 was among Catholics
the single most popular means of family limitation.[21] Psychologically speaking, then, the Pill profoundly altered the climate in which Catholics thought
about contraception. It also made for a new openness in terms of the theological debate. As John T. Noonan has noted, "the pill became the center and symbol of efforts to modify the Catholic position on birth control."[22] That process
was underway, in Europe if not the United States, even in the 1950s.

Catholic spokesmen and propagandists did their earnest best in the postwar
years to speak in terms consistent with the general social climate. They typically couched their appeals in a positive, pro-family idiom: non-contraceptive
marriages nurtured in both spouses the personal discipline and other-centeredness that made for a healthy family life. They placed heavier emphasis
than ever before on the psychic—as opposed to the physical—costs of contraception, especially for women. Birth control was a principal cause of neu-
rosis in American females, according to more than one Catholic pamphleteer.[23]

Especially popular were arguments that echoed the period's quasi-Freudian anxieties about gender: only generous fecundity would cure the peculiar "softness" alleged to afflict American men and the discontent that spurred their wives to neurotic envy of so-called male privilege. "When men and women deliberately keep children out of their lives," according to a pamphlet by the Jesuit Daniel Lord, "it is a sign that they are emotionally immature."[24] Catholic propaganda in the postwar years was less emphatic with regard to social justice than it had earlier been, presumably due to the period's greater prosperity and political conservatism. But it frequently condemned materialism. A "contraceptive mentality"—the phrase was increasingly popular among postwar Catholic apologists—meant the valuing of things over people. Most Americans would have agreed, at least in principle, that this was a very bad thing.

Postwar Catholic discourse about contraception was also, and quite strikingly, affected by the period's romanticization of marital sex. That marital sex was a form of prayer, productive of grace, a means of profoundly intimate communion with one's spouse and with God—these were new concepts for most American Catholics. They were undeniably attractive, however, especially in the context of period domesticity. This positive rhetoric of sex did not wholly displace an older tradition where sex was accorded at best a guarded blessing. There were Catholic propagandists still who touted the spiritual benefits of sexual abstinence in marriage. "A measure of voluntary continence on the part of both spouses contributes much to a satisfactory married life," as a 1942 publication—a product of the NCWC's Family Life Bureau—assured its readers.[25] The threat of hell continued to figure in mission sermons on birth control. One could even find the occasional publication where contraception was likened to murder.[26] But negative talk about marital sex became increasingly less common in the postwar years. The Family Life Bureau by the mid-1950s was fluent in the language of marital sex as quasi-sacrament, as was nearly every diocesan office for family life ministry.[27] The shift in rhetorical emphasis did not result in a totally transformed Catholicism: tactless confessors still plied their trade, as did tasteless mission sermonizers. But it did encourage many Catholics, especially the young and well educated, to claim as their spiritual portion a lyrically positive view of sex. Nothing was more consequential for the looming debate among Catholics over the morality of marital contraception.

So Catholics in the postwar years lived in the midst of great and growing contradictions. Most were still rooted in the Catholic subculture that had nurtured their parents and grandparents. Suburban Catholics were at least as committed as their immigrant forebears to parochial schooling and an organizationally vibrant parish life. But those same Catholics—increasingly affluent and well educated—moved successfully in the larger society to an extent unimaginable in any previous generation, and were the more vulnerable to its priorities and values. One might try to deny that vulnerability by adopting a critical stance with regard to those values. Hence the popularity among highly educated Catholics of extravagant talk about postwar decadence. "On every side, Catholics are subjected to a sea of secularism," in the typical words of a presumably mild-mannered civil servant. "We are assailed by a paganism which probably ranks in some respects with the most flagrant paganism of decadent Rome and Greece."[28] But for all the sincerity of their countercultural impulses, Catholics had so benign an experience of postwar America as to prompt among even the devout a generous appreciation of the society's foundational values. The result was a people increasingly caught between two moral systems—the one hierarchical and essentially communal, the other premised on the good of individual autonomy.

In the circumstances, which were real if not yet widely acknowledged, pastoral ministry became increasingly demanding. Younger Catholics, especially the more affluent, were typically resentful of clerical authoritarianism. They wanted at least a degree of psychological acuity in their priests, especially when it came to matters bearing on the family. Demanding of themselves, they were equally so of the clergy—expecting both holiness of life and professional competence. Happily for all concerned, the men ordained between 1941 and 1962 were a generally impressive lot—better educated than ever before and, overwhelmingly native born, accustomed to democratic norms. Few, in all likelihood, had chosen the priesthood for reasons of economic security; given the times, indeed, many bright young candidates were actually turning their backs on personal affluence. Did some choose the priesthood in a desperate effort to subdue internal demons, particularly in the realm of sex? Undoubtedly. But their lives as seminarians and even as priests were so closely governed that sexual acting out was probably far less common than in a subsequent generation. The internalized prohibitions against such acting out were almost certainly stronger, too. Priestly morale in these years was reliably reported to be high. High morale did much to sustain recruitment to the priesthood, which remained at levels close to those of the vocations-rich 1930s. It was also a source of strength for priests as they navigated the increasingly choppy sea of Catholic marital morality.

Confession

The 1930s, as we have seen, saw major changes in confession. Priests almost certainly questioned more frequently when it came to marital sex. The laity were more forthcoming, too—growing numbers of penitents were apparently apt to confess their contraceptive lapses, even in the absence of clerical prompting. Both trends continued, indeed became normative, in the 1940s and '50s. Men ordained then expected as a matter of course to speak frankly about contraception as confessors and counselors. Such frankness, in fact, was for growing numbers closely linked to a sense of professional competence. Faced with an increasingly educated laity, many clergy were made anxious about their own relative status as professionals. Hence such oddities as a Franciscan sermon on confession that praised priests not only for their "Christ-given power to take away sin" but for having "one of the best professional educations in the world."[29] An obvious analogy could be drawn between the work of the confessor and that of the psychiatrist, and Catholic writers were increasingly drawn to such—although with a certain understandable wariness.[30] (The immense prestige of psychoanalysis has few odder period acknowledgments.) The confessor's role, in the Catholic telling, was of infinitely greater value; he alone could communicate grace, just as he alone was sure to know the fullness of the moral law. But like the psychiatrist, a priest had to have encyclopedic knowledge of humanity's darker nature, for he too probed the mysteries of that nature with—ideally—calm omniscience and a kind of clinical detachment. Gentlemanly reticence with regard to sex was no more appropriate to the confessor than to his secular quasi-counterpart.

Notwithstanding their generally greater frankness, the men ordained in the 1940s and '50s were trained in most respects like those in previous generations. Seminary life was still minutely regulated. Radios and phonographs were typically forbidden, as were newspapers and magazines—though expurgated versions of such were sometimes allowed by the mid-1950s. Visits to and from one's family were strictly rationed. Prior to 1960, seminarians at Chicago's St. Mary of the Lake were not allowed to go home for Christmas, while summer vacations were spent at the archdiocesan "villa" in Wisconsin. Even the local seminary high school had its "free day" on Thursday rather than Saturday, "so we wouldn't mix with other people," in the words of Father Robert Ferrigan, ordained in 1961. "It just seem[ed] so anti-family and anti-relational. And I was going to be a diocesan priest."[31] Relations with one's fellow students were even more closely governed. Students were almost never allowed in one another's rooms; simply speaking to an occupant from the threshold was "a privilege not to be presumed," according to the rule at Boston's St. John's Seminary, "but must be sought from a member of the Faculty."[32] Rules like these were presumably not unconnected to fears of homosexuality. They had far more fundamentally to do, however, with a general subduing of the sensory self. Were his natural affections not rigorously disciplined, the seminarian would never belong wholly to God—or so his mentors had been taught and evidently believed. Hence the silence that was normally mandated outside the classroom and scheduled recreation periods. "Mortification should begin with the senses," in the words of a popular period treatise on mental prayer, "and when these are taught restraint, not much difficulty will be experienced in controlling the interior. . . . The imagination itself is starved of all that can excite in it pleasant, agreeable, and sensual images."[33]

Seminary life was not much changed either in terms of intellectual content, particularly when it came to moral theology. The single most widely used text for this subject, at least according to my priest informants, was that of Hieronymus Noldin, originally published in four volumes between 1906 and 1908. Students by the 1940s were using an allegedly updated edition, but little of substance had in fact been altered. The text was still in Latin, portions of which the student was expected to memorize verbatim. Lectures were sometimes in Latin, too, especially when the topic had to do with sex, though the typical instructor seems frequently to have lapsed into English. Joseph Connell, a widely respected moralist who taught for many years at the Catholic University, would normally conduct the first five minutes of his classes in Latin before getting down to business in the vernacular.[34] But there were certainly places—Chicago's St. Mary of the Lake was one—where spoken Latin was the classroom rule. That few seminarians were themselves fluent in the spoken language hardly mattered, given that students were not expected to engage in class discussion. "You didn't challenge anything that was said in class," in the words of Monsignor Vincent Howard, ordained in 1947 for the Archdiocese of Detroit. "There really was a wall between the faculty and the students."[35] Howard studied moral theology at Mt. St. Mary's near Cincinnati. But his recollections of the seminary classroom were echoed by nearly every man I interviewed. My moral theology professor "knew all the manuals and seemed to have no room for any kind of question," according to Chicago's Father Leo Mahan, ordained in 1951. "What he demanded of you was to repeat back what he had taught you."[36]

Critical engagement on the part of the student was also discouraged by the antihistorical nature of most seminary instruction. Moral theology was taught as a closed and timeless system, in the typical experience of Father Joseph Ryder, who studied at the Catholic University in the mid-1940s. "You didn't know the history of how [particular moral positions] evolved." The same was true of dogmatic theology and Scripture. "You knew there was something wrong . . . but you couldn't put your finger on it because, in those days, you never got a historical context to any of it."[37] Most students, however, do not seem to have known that something was wrong—not, at least, when it came to the teaching on contraception. Father Daniel Budzynski, ordained in Milwaukee in 1956, spoke for nearly all my informants when he summed up his thinking on birth control as a seminarian: "There was no controversy. . . . You have your children or else abstain." My informants were young when they entered the seminary—as young as fourteen in a good many cases. They were sexually inexperienced and, in some instances, sexually ignorant, too. Most came from fairly large families, as did many seminarians nationally in the postwar years; my informants still speak admiringly of their parents' generosity and evident devotion to duty.[38] Young men like these, enduring the rigors of a celibate's formation, simply lacked the resources—emotional as well as intellectual— to question a teaching on which the whole of Catholic sexual ethics turned. Reading about Planned Parenthood, evidently new to him, seminarian Budzynski was "horrified."[39]

Men so narrowly trained were hardly prepared to be empathetic confessors. The demands of their new role as priests only made things worse. "You're not confident when you start out," as Detroit's Father Edward Prus tells it. "There's an ill-at-ease kind of feeling, you know; you're hesitant about making any kind of decision."[40] Young priests often clung to the rules of their seminary textbooks and the preternaturally ordered moral world those rules evoked. "When I came out of the seminary, I knew everything," in the rueful words of Father Clifford Ruskowski, ordained in 1962 but wholly innocent then of the looming Catholic crisis with regard to contraception. "The issue of birth control, even when I was first ordained, was a non-problem—at least as far as our mentality went."[41] Many of my informants described their very youthful selves as rigid, particularly in the confessional; Father Anthony Kosnik, ordained in 1955, was not alone in lamenting "the sins of my early priesthood."[42] I doubt that any of my informants was ever cruel as a confessor, even at his most exacting. Nor was their putative rigidity necessarily experienced as such by many of their penitents—a confessor's general attitude can be far more important than his specific counsels. (According to Detroit's Father John Blaska, speaking of ministry in general, "All people want to know is, is the priest kind?"[43] This was nowhere more true than in the confessional.) I do, however, respect their memories of once very different selves. A newly ordained priest, Father Prus explained, hasn't yet realized the fullness of his vocation. "But the more you live with people and the more you try to pray and absorb God's word and try to see what's going on, then the more pastoral you become and the more confident you become in what you're doing."[44]

Not every priest, of course, responded with such generosity. Some priests never did learn to "live with people." The choleric confessors whom knowledgeable penitents tried to avoid, the men who "seem to regard it as their chief function to upbraid and humiliate the sinner," in the words of a clerical critic— priests like these found imperfect humanity a source of frustration and even rage.[45] "There are times when kindness is a weakness, a condoning of sin, or at its best, cheap sentimentality," as an irate priest responded to a laywoman's complaints about rude confessors. "In the summary of everything, hell will not be kind!"[46] Other priests retreated into themselves, unwilling and finally unable to respond to penitents in any but mechanical fashion. A confessor's "display of hurried indifference," in the view of an unhappy layman, could be quite as alienating to the penitent as an unbending rigorism. No penitent wanted to be "made to feel that the confessor is impatient."[47] The enormous numbers of confessions heard in the typical postwar parish made impatience a real occupational hazard, even for priests who might function acceptably in other areas of ministry. Younger priests often heard confessions for ten to fifteen hours a week, and more at the time of major feasts. (Pastors generally excused themselves from long hours in "the box," leaving most of the work to their assistants.) Baltimore's Joseph Gallagher, stationed in the late 1950s at the downtown Cathedral, once kept an annual tally: "I think that one year I did 5,327 confessions."[48] Gallagher's burden was lighter, however, than that of the priests at a large Bronx parish, who at about the same time were each hearing "almost 15,000" confessions a year, at least in the estimation of Jesuit sociologist Joseph Schuyler.[49]

But despite the press of numbers, the great majority of priests were conscientious confessors. They tried their manful best to be patient and compassionate, no matter how stuffy the confessional box or exasperating the penitent. "There are those who will do anything except to speak up," as a Cistercian priest explained. "Others are so reticent and incomplete in their answers that numerous questions are necessary before the confessor can drag out the information necessary to specify the sin. Others will insist on going into long details about venial sins, and glide over matters far more serious."[50] How do I know that most confessors tried to respond compassionately, even when faced with such provocations? I rely mostly on the literature of confession, which was vast and markedly pastoral in orientation. There was a large and eager audience for books like Gerald Kelly's *The Good Confessor,* first published in 1951. Kelly, a well-known Jesuit moralist, was hardly a liberal on sexual sin, though—as I was duly reminded by Father Joseph Ryder—it hardly makes sense in the American Church of the 1950s to speak with regard to sexual morality in terms of liberals and conservatives.[51] But Kelly's focus was very much on the penitent's experience of confession. The priest should put the penitent at ease, question as non-obtrusively as possible, offer words of encouragement, and always give the penitent the benefit of the doubt. Sermons preached on confession at priests' conferences and retreats nearly always had the same pastoral emphasis. "Priestly inconsiderateness in the confessional may produce eternally disastrous results," a Passionist typically cautioned priests on retreat in California and Idaho. "Remember it is your duty to draw, to attract the people to God. And in the confessional you do so by administering the Mercy of God and not His Justice."[52]

A similarly pastoral orientation was even communicated in the seminary, despite the rigidities of the curriculum. As several of my informants noted, one learns from more than the textbook in even the most structured classroom. The examples employed by an instructor, his evident conception of the confessor's role, the extent to which he revealed his personality—these things mattered, too. The redoutable Joseph Connell, imparting stern orthodoxy at the Catholic University, was remembered by even my liberal informants as a warm and engaging man. (He also had wide intellectual interests, including the morality of prizefighting and nuclear war. We called it "bombs and boxing," as Father Edward Scheuerman recounted Connell's course in moral theology.[53]) Seminarians, moreover, knew from their own weekly confessions how at least some of the faculty functioned as confessors. Few seminaries in the postwar years were so ill-managed that manifestly incompetent men were assigned to hear student confessions. We were taught a system, my informants said in effect, but also taught to work within it as humanely as possible. Even the textbooks helped, especially if one read the footnotes, to which practical applications and exceptions to the rule were sometimes relegated. "We look at [those textbooks] now and say that their vision was too narrow and so forth, it was too sin-centered, too juridical," as the late Jesuit Richard McCormick told me. "But when it came down to applying things to people, especially in the confessional setting, they were very pastoral."[54]

A pastoral orientation could obviously conflict with demands for confessors to be proactive when it came to a sin like marital contraception. Were priests in the postwar years in fact more likely than priests in the 1930s to question penitents in this regard? The answer is both yes and no. Relatively few priests seem to have followed the Chicago model, where confessors were expected to raise the question whenever a married penitent had been away from confession for several months. (Whether three or six months were the "trigger" is something on which my Chicago informants disagree.) The Chicago norms did have their non-Chicago defenders. The influential Joseph Connell was among them. "I believe that we can lay down the reasonable rule that every married person within child-bearing age who has been away from confession for three months or more should be prudently questioned whether or not he or she is guilty of this sin," as he told any number of priests' conferences, "for by the law of averages there is a good probability that every such person is included in that group of Catholics who are committing contraception and saying nothing about it in confession."[55] The Paulist Joseph McSorley, whose 1915 handbook on the hearing of Italian-language confessions made no mention at all of contraception, seemed to endorse Chicago rules in a 1942 guide for priests who were hearing confessions in Spanish. This latter publication, which provided a script of sorts for confessors with rudimentary Spanish, included the following sequence: "Are you married? Were you married by a priest? Have you taken precautions not to have children?"[56] Certain European theologians were arguing by the 1950s that marital contraception was in some locales so nearly universal that every married penitent had of necessity to be questioned about this sin.[57]

Most American moralists, however, simply disagreed. The views of Gerald Kelly were widely endorsed. Kelly could not "condemn" the practice of routinely asking married penitents about birth control. He understood the motivation of priests who did so: "it is said that some Catholics openly boast about the fact that what they do as regards birth control is no business of their confessor." But he still regarded the practice as unwise. One should never question, especially with regard to sexual sin, without a well-founded suspicion that the penitent was in fact guilty.[58] What constituted a well-founded suspicion on the confessor's part? Kelly, in company with many others, thought it largely a matter of intuition. "It is something they say, or the way they say it, or sometimes something akin to private inspiration," in the words of Monsignor John Linsenmeyer, speaking in 1945 at a clergy conference in Detroit.[59] A penitent's evident nervousness, her seeming to hold something back, her failure to confess a single grave sin after being long absent from confession—these were standard markers. But a locale's reputation for widespread contraceptive use was emphatically not sufficient grounds, at least according to respected American moralists. "Any given confession should be conducted on an exclusively individual basis," in the authoritative logic of the Jesuit John Lynch, "and presumption favors the sincerity of any penitent." One should not proceed in the confessional based on assumptions about married people generally.[60]

Despite the encouragement of weighty authorities, many priests were probably reluctant to question penitents based on intuitive suspicion alone. Only a handful of my interviewees remembered having done so, mainly as newly minted clergy. "I would say that as younger priests we were more inclined to question," in the words of Father Edward Scheuerman, ordained in 1950. "As we became more experienced in the pastoral field we questioned less and less."[61] Unsolicited probing with regard to sexual sin was always risky, in the view of most of my informants. One was apt to alienate penitents, particularly the excessively anxious or those who confessed infrequently. Gerald Kelly did not fundamentally disagree. A priest was indeed obliged to question if he had reason to suspect that a penitent was holding back. But the questioning was always to be indirect and tactful. "The confessor might say: 'You don't seem to feel at ease. . . . Is there something worrying you—something you find it hard to say—something in which I can help you?'" Should the penitent have nothing to offer at this juncture, the confessor should desist.[62] In the circumstances, an equally conscientious confessor might well opt to err on the side of caution—to seldom or never question about sins that a penitent had not mentioned. "A sensitive priest can always tell that there's something not being confessed," as Chicago's Leo Mahan summed up his own evolution as a confessor. "You can just feel it. And the more sensitive you are, the less you're inclined to ask. Because that's an abuse. If people can't get it into words and they haven't got the courage, it doesn't mean they're not sorry."[63]

Long lines of penitents were also a disincentive. The problem was especially acute on the eve of major feasts. The premium then was on speed, even for confessors who prided themselves on thoughtful attention to every penitent. "You couldn't really be pastoral at all" when the lines were unusually long, in the words of Father William Pettit, ordained in 1954. At Christmas and Easter, as he told it, there might be as many as two hundred penitents waiting on three or four confessors.[64] Penitents who confessed only once or twice a year were particularly likely to do so at the time of major feasts. And these were precisely the penitents most apt to be holding something back, or—in probably the greater number of cases—anxious to confess an embarrassing sin as expeditiously as possible. Even infrequent penitents knew that long lines nearly always precluded questioning, whether about sins not mentioned or, at least at any length, the particulars of those that were.

For all their reluctance to question, however, my informants were bedeviled as confessors by the problem of birth control. Though some penitents concealed this putative sin, many more confessed it—and in significantly larger numbers than ever before. They did so especially at major feasts and particularly during the Easter season, when Catholics were required to receive communion. The Saturday prior to Trinity Sunday—the final Sunday of the Easter Season—was perhaps the busiest time of all, at least according to Monsignor William Sherzer, ordained in 1945. "There would be lines around the block coming to confession. And it would all be birth control."[65] But feast or no, the problem was invariably there. Some birth control users suffered from guilt so extreme that confessing only once a year was psychologically impossible. Others longed to receive communion on something approaching a regular basis. And even lukewarm Catholics might find it socially necessary to receive communion more than once or twice a year—as the member of a wedding party, parent of a First Communicant, or mourner at a family funeral.

So nearly all priests had cause to agree with the postwar judgement of Francis Connell: "the most difficult and trying problem which confessors encounter in the United States at the present time is the sin of contraception."[66] Among my informants, it was only those who served primarily in African American or Hispanic parishes who did not remember birth control as a vexing constant in confession. Unlike their European-descended counterparts, black and Hispanic Catholics were even in the 1950s not generally given to frequent confession. They were also less apt to be regular users of contraception, and perhaps less likely to confess it when they were. "I can honestly say [that] I never remember the subject [birth control] ever coming up from blacks," as Chicago's Leo Mahan recounts his time in an African American parish on the city's south side, where the Church's prohibition on remarriage after divorce was the principal stumbling block to conversion. A subsequent stint among Spanish-speaking immigrants revealed a similar pattern. "The immigrant to Chicago, Puerto Ricans and Mexicans, *never* asked [about birth control]. Whatever their relationship to priests in their native lands or to the Church, that wasn't part of the experience."[67]

Once a penitent had confessed to contraception, the confessor was usually confronted by the need to question. Many penitents, evidently, confessed the sin in vague or colloquial language. They "lost the seed," "took precautions," "were careful."[68] Since the gravity of a penitent's sin might depend in part on the mode of contraception employed, it would presumably be necessary to ask for clarification.[69] Coitus interruptus, while seriously sinful, did not suggest the same malice aforethought as the use of a condom or diaphragm. There were implications too for the non-contracepting spouse, with gendered effects that we will soon explore. A wife might "never consent to condomistic inter-course," in the words of Francis J. Connell, while a husband's right to sex with a diaphragm-using wife was upheld by certain reputable moralists.[70] A peni-tent's imprecise language might even obscure the nature of the sin involved. As the Jesuit John Ford explained to class after class of seminarians, one should never assume the meaning of phrases like "I got rid of children" or "I tried to bring myself round." The "confessor should make sure he is dealing with abortion or attempted abortion and not with mere birth control before questioning further," Ford counseled. "'Do you mean you did something to prevent conception, committed the sin of birth control—or do you mean some-thing still worse?'"[71]

Confessors were invariably taught to ask how frequently a particular sin had been committed. When the sin in question was a typically habitual one, like contraception or masturbation, the priest was advised by good authority to go one step further. Penitents guilty of birth control sometimes moved from con-fessor to confessor, looking for leniency in part but also seeking to avoid priests who might know their histories. Others confessed only occasionally, giving up the practice of contraception for several weeks prior to receiving the sacrament.[72] Here too the goal was apparently to conceal the habitual nature of one's offense. So priests should not only ask the standard "how many times" when a sin like contraception was confessed, in the authoritative view of Ger-ald Kelly. They should also ask "in a kindly and rather casual manner whether the sin confessed concerns some habitual difficulty."[73] Since the question was relevant to a penitent's contrition and prospects for reform, even confessors who disliked probing might find it pastorally useful. Once a penitent had con-fessed to birth control, as Detroit's Father Lawrence Jackson explained, I was taught to ask about his difficulties—was he making an effort to change? What did that effort consist of?[74] The resulting narrative was almost bound to touch on the penitent's contraceptive past.

Absolution required a "firm purpose of amendment" on the penitent's part—an honest determination to mend her sinful ways. A confessor could hardly avoid asking questions in this regard. Was the penitent truly sorry for her sins? Did she intend to live rightly in the future? Most penitents, it seems, were plausibly contrite. According to my priest informants, penitents in the confessional almost never contested the substance of the teaching—not, at least, prior to the mid-1960s. Those inclined to argue simply stayed away from confession, at least as my informants saw it. A penitent's failure to object could easily be read as assent to the teaching, and many confessors seem to have done so. "Most of the people accepted the teaching of the Church on birth control," as Monsignor William Sherzer still maintains. "Now, they didn't all keep it, but they accepted it."[75]

It was not difficult for the vast majority of confessors to regard such submissive penitents as objectively sorry for their sins. But was their sorrow only fleeting? Were not many apparently submissive penitents so "addicted" to contraception—a favorite usage among period moralists—that they lacked anything approaching a firm purpose of amendment? Even the least intrusive confessors felt obliged to question in this regard. One had at the very least to elicit from the penitent a promise to try to avoid future lapses. Sterner or more scrupulous confessors might require the penitent to dispose of his store of contraceptive devices. "If he has been using a condom, or if a woman penitent has been using means such as vaginal jellies or lotions, or a diaphragm," in the words of a Vincentian moralist, "the only satisfactory reply to the confessor's interrogations will be a sincere and definite promise to get rid of these evil means, whatever they may be."[76] The point was less to make future lapses difficult—one could always buy more contraceptives—than to elicit what moralists called "extraordinary signs of contrition." Absent this, in the view of many moralists, confessors would normally be obliged to withhold absolution.[77]

Confessors, however, were part of a system that made generous room for pastoral judgment. Respected moralists could and did disagree when it came to the application of first principles. In the circumstances, a confessor was free to choose the less onerous interpretation and many apparently did. Few of my priest informants remember having ever denied absolution to a contracepting penitent; the rest recall doing so in only a handful of extreme and painful cases. "I thought at that time it would be a sacrilege on my part to absolve someone who said absolutely they were going to continue doing it," as a Boston priest remembered of the only such case in his career. "And I felt very, very bad about it."[78] A penitent's presence at confession was a powerful presumption in her favor—so I was repeatedly told. It signified sorrow for sin and a desire to amend one's life. "The very fact that the person's coming into confession shows a good disposition," as Monsignor Vincent Horkan explained. "And if they admit what they consider serious sins in confession, what more can you ask?" A confessor would naturally interrogate with regard to a penitent's purpose of amendment, especially when it came to a sin like contraception, whose "proximate occasions"—the spouse and the marriage bed—could hardly be avoided. But as Horkan pointed out, "You do the best you can under the circumstances. That's a firm purpose of amendment. There's no guarantee—no guarantee. I'm going to do my best with the help of God. That's as far as it can go."[79]

A self-styled conservative, ordained in 1941, Horkan found ample validation as a young priest for his markedly pastoral approach. Any number of reputable moralists endorsed it, although they—like Horkan himself—never questioned the rightness of the Church's stand on birth control. It was not necessary for even recidivist penitents—those who fell repeatedly into the same grave sins—to manifest more than "the ordinary signs of repentance," according to an Irish moralist, writing in 1950 for an American priests' magazine. Save in certain "exceptional" cases, the confessor should always presume in favor of the penitent. "The confessor can never be sure that there is no likelihood of future amendment. He may rather hope that the grace of absolution will enable the sinner at least to lessen the number of his falls and that the grace of repeated absolutions, if he comes to confession regularly, will gradually win him entirely from the error of his ways."[80]

I suspect that many confessors, though surely not all, were inclined to an equally pastoral approach. This presumably made life easier for both confessor and penitent. But birth control was still a source of great tension in the confessional, or so the evidence suggests. Most of my priest informants recall this subject as among the most painful they confronted as confessors. It was apt to embarrass the very young priest and challenge his fragile sense of competence. "We were so naïve when it came to sexuality," as Fr. Clifford Ruskowski recalled. "Even in the confessional I was scared to death of having sins of sex confessed because I didn't really know what I was talking about."[81] Many penitents faced circumstances so objectively difficult that a priest's pious counsels could seem at least momentarily hollow—to him as well as his penitent. "Don't be afraid to point to the celibacy of the clergy," in the standard advice of a clerical writer in 1956, "not to show that it can be done—but to show that you *understand* that self-control is difficult but possible."[82] Was a priest's protected life remotely like that of a man living intimately with his spouse? Many confessors came to doubt it. "What do you do with things that people can't change?" mused Milwaukee's Father John Michael Murphy, ordained in 1945. "And you're God; you're sitting in that confessional and they kind of think that this is what God thinks."[83] Perhaps most troubling was the crippling guilt experienced by all too many penitents, some of whom seemed to experience sex mainly as a font of anxiety and self-loathing. "You don't run into the bad kind of scrupulosity anymore," as Chicago's Father Tom Ventura noted. But he saw it when he was first ordained, in 1961.[84] Detroit's Gerald Martin agreed. "Sometimes you'd almost have to give sex instructions. . . . Whatever you do as husband and wife together is not sinful, as long as the semen ends up in the wife's body in the right place."[85]

The laity were doubtless grateful for humane confessors, especially when it came to sexual sin. The few lay-authored complaints about confession to appear in the postwar years nearly always centered on men who were cold or abrupt or actively rude. "Our skulls are often *very* thick," as a convert wrote of her fellow penitents, "but there's one universal language that we can grasp: kindness." Unkind confessors were a distinct minority, but even the discriminating penitent—one who "shopped" for an understanding man—could not invariably avoid them. "The name over the confessional may be 'Father McGillicuddy' but—and this is a dirty trick methinks—his assistant, Father Scorpion, may be occupying his box instead. Like Pandora, you don't know what you're going to find."[86]

A single encounter with a bad confessor, no matter how inadvertent his cruelty, might be devastating to a penitent. The Catholics who abandoned confession in such startling numbers in the mid-to-late 1960s were in some cases prompted by just such memories. But many of these same Catholics had no horror stories to retail. They had mostly been lucky with their confessors, some of whom had been admirably pastoral. What they resented—and many came to this awareness only in retrospect—was not simply the shame attendant on confessing to sexual sin, palpable though this was. They also resented, and perhaps more deeply, the seemingly mechanical way in which sexual sin was defined. This was particularly true of married Catholics who thought it necessary to practice birth control. Some were honestly persuaded that their conduct was not sinful. Others were less certain. But few of the latter, in all likelihood, thought of their conduct as a willful violation of God's law. It had instead to do with life's hard circumstances, with human finitude, and perhaps with human weakness. Even the gentlest confessor, however, had in the end to speak the language of the system. He might absolve you willingly, but always on the assumption that you had indeed committed a grave moral wrong.[87]

The rigidities of the system were a burden for confessors, too. Contraception was always a mortal sin, regardless of a penitent's circumstances or her motives. "You were forced to confront people with an absolute," in the words of Monsignor William Sherzer, and this could be "terribly painful."[88] The logic behind that absolute was never easy to explain, as priests in an earlier generation had already discovered. Nor was it easy to justify the system's seemingly disparate impact on the female sex. Only women, after all, were candidates for literal martyrdom in the teaching's cause. The moral culpability of the non-contracepting spouse—an issue that surfaced frequently in confession—raised questions of gender equity, too, and particularly in the postwar years, when coitus interruptus was widely abandoned in favor of contraceptive devices. A woman whose husband planned to use a condom was obliged to resist his sexual advances "as a virgin would an assailant." If she feared grave harm—death or perhaps desertion—she might "submit passively," but only on the condition that she experience no sexual pleasure. "If there is grave danger that she will yield to this pleasure, not even the certain knowledge that she will be killed . . . will justify non-resistance on her part," in the stern but orthodox words of Francis Connell.[89] But a man whose wife used a diaphragm might, in the view of certain reputable moralists, engage in guiltless sexual inter-course—assuming that he voiced displeasure at her contraceptive doings. "The requirements of a lawful marital act seem to be adequately fulfilled on the part of the husband if he emits semen into his wife's vagina, even though this organ has been artificially shut off from the uterus," as a proponent of the position explained.[90] The debate was not simply academic: its logic was ap-plied to real cases in real confessionals and was almost certainly the stuff of rumor among the laity. "For the layman a mechanical device is apt to be a me-chanical device," as Gerald Kelly correctly noted, and the laity "might well wonder" why women were governed by such evidently different rules than men.[91]

Certain European theologians, troubled by what they regarded as the system's undue legalism, argued in the postwar years for something akin to a reforma-tion in Catholic moral theology. In place of an act-centered morality—"ab-stract, negative, individualistic, asocial, and juridical," in the characterization of one critic[92]—the reformers called for an ethic of charity. What mattered was an actor's fundamental moral orientation. Was he responsive to the love of God? Generously concerned for the well-being of others? As these would-be reformers were quick to point out, theirs was not a purely subjective approach to morality. An objective moral order did indeed exist, and all actions had ul-timately to be judged by it. But particular acts could be adequately evaluated only in the context of an actor's motivation and her journey toward Christian maturity. "The author envisions truly Christian morality in the framework of a dialogue between God and man," as the Jesuit John Lynch explained the the-sis of Bernard Häring's *The Law of Christ,* published in German to wide ac-claim in 1955. "God calls, man responds; acceptance is our *metanoia* or conversion, refusal is sin."[93]

Many of these same reformers also urged a greater psychological sophisti-cation when it came to judging culpability for sin. It was a flawed and dimin-ished humanity that strove to respond to God's infinite love. Precisely because of their inherent limitations, most humans were not wholly free agents when it came to moral choice. This was particularly true in the realm of sexual sin. "Almost all mankind is so sexually immature, and so dominated consciously or unconsciously by passion," as a disapproving John Ford explained the thinking of Abbé Marc Oraison, "that in practice and as a general rule we must presume sexual sins to be only materially grave."[94] The logic was most fre-quently applied to masturbation and "conjugal onanism," sins committed by very large numbers of otherwise faithful Catholics. Such putative sinners of-ten failed to grasp the intrinsic evil of their acts; the need for intimacy and sexual release often compromised their ability to obey the moral law, which particularly in the case of birth control sometimes demanded the humanly impossible. It was therefore most unlikely that such putative sinners were guilty of any but minor offenses, especially if they regretted their inability to conform to what they accepted on faith as the law of God.[95] "The tendency to broaden the area of irresponsibility even among those who would be considered mentally and emotionally normal and to take a benign attitude toward human weakness is quite prevalent in current thinking," worried the Jesuit John Connery. "Someone asks in *L'Ami du clergé* [a prominent French clerical journal] whether it is only for sins of malice that one will be condemned to hell. The question clearly reflects this tendency to remove all serious guilt from sins of weakness."[96]

Few American priests in the postwar years were directly affected by such arguments, which circulated widely in the United States only after the early 1960s. The dissenting theologians wrote mostly in French or German; their books and articles appeared belatedly in English, if at all; a few of the bolder offerings were eventually placed on the Index of Forbidden Books or withdrawn from general circulation at the Vatican's behest. But once these ideas began their American circulation, they fell on fertile ground—particularly though not exclusively among the younger clergy. That ground had been substantially prepared by priests' experience as confessors, and especially the anguish of their many penitents who wrestled with the problem of family limitation. Though he did not personally question the teaching on contraception until 1964, the late Monsignor John Egan, ordained for Chicago in 1943, spoke for many of his confreres when he described that teaching as a "terrible burden."[97] Monsignor Vincent Howard agreed. "These people come in, and it's such a strain on their marriage, you know. How can we force that tension into their lives, you know, what right do we have to do that? I used to feel so sorry for some of those people who'd come in."[98]

The conflicted emotions of men like these were strikingly embodied in a remarkable confessors' manual published in an American edition in 1960—a sign of what soon emerged as transitional times. Dom Desmond Schlegel did not directly challenge Church teaching with regard to birth control: "birth prevention," as he told it, was "of course" objectively immoral. But he doubted that many who confessed to this sin were actually guilty of a grave offense. The penitent's situation mattered—"we must listen patiently to the penitent's account of the circumstances in which he is placed." So did a penitent's grasp of the teaching's logic. "Are we always quite sure ourselves why the practice is wrong, and are we capable of giving a reasonable account of its immorality to others?" as Schlegel asked with startling candor. "And then is the penitent quite sure why the practice is wrong, and can he give a reasonable account to himself of its immorality?" Confessors should especially remember how readily the biblical Jesus forgave sins of impurity, which offended Him far less deeply than "hypocrisy, pride, avarice, hardness." So the truly Christ-like confessor would presumably grant absolution to most if not all of his contracepting penitents—although Schlegel, interestingly enough, did not dare to say so directly.[99]

Many American priests as of 1960 were in fact behaving as Schlegel implicitly advised. "We never questioned . . . the teaching," as the Jesuit Richard McCormick summed things up with regard to the 1950s and early 1960s. "We accepted it. The question was, how would you go about—in the confessional—dealing with people who had the problem? How would you go about [it] in a very sympathetic way, without turning them off? And I think we succeeded eminently in doing that."[100] I do not quarrel with McCormick's assessment—not in terms of priests' intentions. But it glides too easily over the experience of a great many penitents. The gentlest confessor had to ask for a firm purpose of amendment. Most conscientious Catholics took the resulting obligation seriously. The outcome was often an intense internal conflict—guilt at one's inability or unwillingness to live as the Church mandated; growing resentment, and simultaneous anxieties about that resentment, at guilt endured in the cause of a teaching that growing numbers of Catholics were coming to doubt. Once these painful emotions went public, as was happening by the latter part of 1963, the confidence of many confessors was badly undermined. Confession itself was soon under assault by a portion of the laity, and quietly abandoned by many more. The gentlest confessors were perhaps the most surprised. "Back in the '40s and '50s, if anybody'd told us what was going to happen to the sacrament of penance," in the bemused words of Monsignor Vincent Howard, "we would *not* have believed it. We would absolutely not have believed it."[101]

Preaching

Preaching continued in the 1940s and '50s to play a relatively minor role in Catholic religious life and, by extension, the consciousness of the clergy. Few of my priest informants remember having ever preached a Sunday sermon on birth control. But in fact many of them did. The archdioceses of Milwaukee and Chicago had mandatory sermon outlines by the 1940s, which every priest was expected to use; Detroit followed suit in 1954. In each of these dioceses, the prescribed sermon sequences included occasional instruction on the evils of contraception. ("I'm sure I gave what was in the book," as Detroit's Father William Carolin quite typically described a priest's relationship to these Chancery-provided scripts. "I can remember taking those outlines into the pulpit."[102]) The "birth control" sermons in question were usually brief and always rhetorically restrained. They point nonetheless to a much greater boldness in

Sunday preaching when it came to marital sex. Particularly in the 1950s, prescribed sermons of this sort were couched in terms that even adolescents might grasp. "Artificial birth control is the prevention of conception by the use of mechanical, chemical, and other similar means," as the Detroit outlines sketched the opening of a 1956 instruction. "It is evil because it perverts a natural faculty. It makes sex enjoyment an end in itself, not a means to an end."[103] Such sermons, moreover, were routinely assigned to even the youngest clergy. Gone were the days when pastors alone were thought to possess sufficient gravitas to broach so delicate a topic.

Not every American diocese in the postwar years had mandatory sermon outlines. They seem to have been most common in the Midwest. None of my informants in Philadelphia, Baltimore, or Boston remembers such, nor have I found references to their existence—much less surviving copies—for any of the major East Coast dioceses. Did priests in dioceses like these preach even occasional sermons against birth control? While I cannot say for certain, I suspect that many did. Contraception was so public a topic by the 1940s and its proponents so aggressive that the climate surrounding Sunday preaching was almost bound to be affected, no matter how cautious the local Chancery. A study done during World War II, which involved the detailed questioning of thirty-five pastors on family life issues in ministry, had most informants saying that marital sex was now a topic of at least occasional preaching in their parishes or dioceses. Even in the absence of diocesan sermon outlines, according to this study, some bishops required an annual sermon or sermons on marriage. "The subjects include such points as the dignity, privileges, obligations of the married state," as one informant explained—which meant that contraception would inevitably be addressed.[104]

How frankly was this done? A sermon text from Boston is perhaps indicative. All priests in that archdiocese were ordered by then-Archbishop Richard Cushing to preach on birth control on the second Sunday of October 1948. (The occasion was a statewide referendum to amend a law, anomalous for the 1940s, that forbade the sale or distribution of contraceptive information and devices.) The model sermon provided by the Boston Chancery was fairly straightforward in its diction, despite the mixed congregations to whom it would be preached. "The law of God unequivocally and absolutely condemns every artificial intervention designed to defeat the sacred purpose of marriage, which is the procreation of children," explained the text, which featured repeated use of the term "birth control"—once strictly off-limits for Sunday sermonizing.[105] Every priest in the archdiocese, even the youngest, was expected to preach along these lines.

Almost no Sunday preacher addressed this hard subject on more than an occasional basis. The Feast of the Holy Family might provide a suitable venue; Lent was also a favored time for sermons of this sort. Nor did they typically break new apologetical ground. Few texts dwelled at length on the natural law basis of the teaching, though it usually merited a respectful nod. "There is not much use in talking to people about frustrated faculties in the pulpit," as John Ford bluntly reminded a class of young Jesuits. "They do not understand it and it does not convince."[106] Sermons focused instead on the Church's authority and, to a lesser extent, the deleterious social consequences of widespread contraceptive use. The encyclical *Casti Connubii* was regularly invoked, along with more occasional references to various Church Fathers. Scripture was frequently cited, too. The story of Onan was a staple of sermons as late as the early 1960s, although mainstream Scripture scholars by then had long since abandoned the view that Onan was slain for the practice of coitus interruptus.[107] Preachers sometimes also invoked God's original blessing on Adam and Eve, but seldom as bluntly as a Polish American mission preacher in the mid-1940s. "God did not bring Adam and Eve together and command them, 'Enjoy yourselves and have fun' but creating Adam a man and Eve a woman He did order them to 'increase and multiply.'"[108]

Whatever the specific warrant, sermons repeatedly stressed that the Church's teaching on contraception was and would remain unchanging. The law in question, after all, was not a matter of ecclesial discipline but a fundamental law of God. "If we believe in the Church, if we believe that Christ and the Holy Spirit are with the Church, could we admit that the Church has made a mistake in so grave a matter?" asked Bishop Albert Meyer in a Lenten sermon, probably in the late 1940s. "We might as well deny the Church itself!" (Meyer was bishop at the time of Superior, Wisconsin; he later served as archbishop of Milwaukee and cardinal-archbishop of Chicago.) So even those Catholics who did not understand why contraception was intrinsically evil were obliged to accept the teaching. To reject or question it was tantamount to rejecting Christ.[109] "Holy Mother Church looks sadly at those who defy her, even as Christ looked upon the disciples who refused to believe (cf. John 6, 67)," as the Milwaukee sermon guide sketched a 1949 offering, this one for the Feast of Christ the King, "but the Church cannot annul one word of the divine law. The beautiful feast of the Kingship of Christ offers us the opportunity to reaffirm our stand on His side."[110] The proposed diction of the Milwaukee sermon was markedly temperate, whatever its guilt-inducing purposes. But given period anxieties, temperance did not invariably rule. A Catholic woman who merely set foot in a birth control clinic, according to a 1941 Lenten pastoral letter by Rochester's Bishop James E. Kearney, "denies her faith, repudiates the teaching authority of Christ's Church, and sets at naught the divine law." In the eyes of the Church, she is "a renegade."[111] Bishop Kearney's impassioned words were presumably read from every pulpit in his diocese.

Period preachers were fairly predictable too when it came to the negative social effects of contraception. The specter of underpopulation was quietly retired from rhetorical duty in the late 1940s. And younger priests in particular increasingly steered clear of extravagant claims with regard to the physical harm that allegedly flowed from contraceptive use. But postwar priests were as one with their Depression-era predecessors when it came to the impact of contraception on public morals. "The breakdown of chastity in the marriage relation leads to breakdown all along the line," as John Ford summed things up for soon-to-be Jesuit preachers.[112] It meant an increase in divorce and a growing acceptance of divorce. It spurred adultery and fornication. It meant the devaluation of children, expressed in its most horrific form by permissive attitudes toward abortion, and ultimately of women, too. "When the modern woman, in the name of freedom, urges easy divorce and artificial sterility, she is in effect urging womanhood to enslave itself," as Father Hugh Calkins warned darkly in a 1946 radio sermon. "When will today's women see that the Church's fight to preserve intact decent marriage morals is really a fight to keep decency in man's treatment of women?"[113] A contraceptive society was the domain of grasping individualists—unjust economically and coarse in its popular culture. A world like this had little room for the radically dependent—the old, the chronically sick—and little tolerance for large families, save perhaps among the affluent. Catholic preaching at its most attractive defended the teaching on contraception by invoking an ethic of solidarity and especially the claims of the young. "Someone has sneeringly remarked that Catholic[s] teach that marriage is nothing but a 'child-factory,'" according to the previously quoted Bishop Albert Meyer. "What great baseness underlies such a statement I feel sure must be evident to all here present. Is not a child God's handiwork, likeness, darling? A new lamb, a new voice, a future dweller in God's heaven, a fellow citizen of the angels, a flower that blooms in the desert[?]"[114]

What was new to Catholic preaching in the postwar years was a positive rhetoric of marital sex. "Married people should be taught . . . that God wishes them to become holy and saints through marriage," as Milwaukee's priests were told in 1949, with regard to the sermon for the Feast of All Saints. "Explain also that it is an heretical notion that there is anything sinful or shameful about the physical expression of marriage love."[115] The sermon outlines for Detroit and Chicago incorporated a similar emphasis. Such positive talk was not wholly unknown prior to the 1940s, though it was rare, with the good of sex nearly always linked primarily to procreation. Nor had it fully carried the day, even in the 1950s. Sermons extolling the benefits of marital abstinence were certainly less common then but they were still preached, especially in the context of parish missions. And even those preachers who extolled the good—indeed the holiness—of sexual communion had of necessity to praise continence, too, given the hard realities of the teaching on contraception. "If you *sincerely want* to control the sex appetite, you *can*," in the words of a Chicago model sermon addressed to the married as well as the single. "At first you may not succeed. But if you pick yourself up after each failure, make a humble and sincere confession, and start again, you *will* get it. The trouble is in really *wanting* it." God did not command the impossible, as period sermonizers repeatedly stressed. The strength to live rightly could be readily derived from the grace of the sacraments—confession, communion, and marriage itself. "Married life is one continuous sacrament in which each moment of each day finds the partners using the graces of this huge reservoir to help them live up to the duties of their state," explained a Redemptorist priest from the Sunday pulpit. "Realizing then the true dignity of this sacrament, do not join with those who see nothing in marriage but an outlet for lust and pleasure."[116]

Many postwar sermons were also distinguished by a gentler treatment of the female sex, at least by the standards of a previous generation. Not that women were off the hook altogether—there were still preachers, especially at missions, who held them primarily responsible for marital contraception. "And now the women themselves are stabbing the Church right in the back," as a Passionist elaborated on this venerable theme during the Second World War. "This is one of the great reasons for the destruction of the home."[117] Such blatantly accusatory rhetoric, however, was increasingly less common, especially in the 1950s. The decade's high birthrate was presumably a factor; so too was a growing awareness among priests, particularly those in family life ministries, of longstanding female resentment at talk like this. The sermon guidelines for Milwaukee, Detroit, and Chicago are tellingly free of anti-female language, although not of what a later generation would call sexism. "If the young woman is working, she should give up her job as soon as she becomes a wife or at least in ample time before the birth of her first child," according to a Chicago model sermon for 1951. "And this first child should in the normal course of nature, come in the first year of marriage." Motherhood, in the logic of this and innumerable other sermons, was the high and inevitable destiny of every married woman—the veritable essence of her being. "No matter what the reason, you cannot violate the basic rules of nature without endangering both your eternal salvation and the very success of your marriage." Even rhythm was off-limits in the early years of marriage, though no Sunday preacher in the 1950s would have dared to speak rhythm's name. But the meaning was evident: "By nature the husband desires the union of 'two in one flesh.' So any plan to limit this union or to prevent it will lead to severe, overpowering temptations, and to unfaithfulness that endangers the permanence of your marriage."[118]

We obviously cannot know for certain what the laity actually heard in the course of Sunday preaching. The sermon was hardly central to the pre-Vatican II liturgy. Nor were most priests yet adequately trained in homiletics. "I think in my four years in the seminary, I recall only once having to give a sermon in class," in the words of Monsignor Vincent Howard.[119] Boston's Monsignor Edward Sviokla, ordained in 1951, learned early in his career that pulpit eloquence was not essential to a priest's sense of competence. He should preach for "no more than ten minutes," the more senior priests at his first parish told him. "You know, if they want to listen to Fulton Sheen, they get him on television."[120] The results of such counsel were predictable, especially in those many dioceses where sermon guides or outlines were not mandated. "From the point of view of the listener and recorder it was frequently difficult to discern the 'leading idea' in the sermons," according to a priest sociologist, who studied a Southern urban parish for a year in the late 1940s. "Most of the sermons showed a lack of unity and cohesion, touching on three or four main concepts and mixing together both doctrine and admonition."[121] The typical Sunday congregation, moreover, was large and crowded; many of its adult members were preoccupied with the needs of their young children or distracted by those who were sitting nearby. This last-mentioned problem was especially acute by the 1950s, and not only because of the Catholic birthrate. Family masses were widely popular then, particularly in suburban parishes.

So there were genuine obstacles to hearing a preacher's message, quite apart from its possibly troublesome content. Perhaps these explain the complaint of one suburban Chicago layman, who claimed in 1954 to have "heard very little . . . from the pulpit about birth control. . . . I think the clergy are going soft on telling the people *from the pulpit* what the story is on this point."[122] The sermons he called for were being preached, though less frequently than our zealous reporter would evidently have prescribed. A priest writing nine years earlier had a very different view. Even a passing reference to birth control in the pulpit made most Catholics uneasy, in the assessment of Pittsburgh's Thomas Murphy. "There seemed to be quite a tension in the air," as he recalled of a recent brush with this delicate subject, which suggests at least a momentarily attentive congregation.[123] This perhaps had to do with Murphy himself, who seems to have prepared his sermons conscientiously. He was given to arresting rhetoric, too. "Even some of our own, traitors to our Catholic heritage of suffering for our Christlike ideals, are going over to the side of the enemy and scoffing at the idea of marital chastity, are proclaiming that the Catholic code of marriage ethics is not practicable in these days," he declared in a sermon devoted mainly to an alleged decline in family prayer. "Would to God those people would not stay with us so we would know just how many real Catholics we truly have!"[124]

In the view of one of my priest informants, even polished sermons like the one just quoted were not terribly significant in themselves. Father Anthony Kosnik, ordained for Detroit in 1955, had dim recollections of preaching occasional sermons on "marital morality." But nothing I said, he insisted, was news to any adult. Churchgoing Catholics by the 1950s were well aware of the Church's stand on birth control. Nor was my preaching particularly persuasive; other exponents of the teaching made the Church's case far more effectively.

Father Kosnik had the Catholic media principally in mind, and it was indeed more slickly professional by the 1950s than ever before. The "Catholic Mother of the Year"—a brilliant media creation—was in Kosnik's view a far more potent sermonizer than the most eloquent priest.[125] She invariably had an enormous brood, typically at least ten, though the African American woman so honored in 1952—a touching Catholic "first"—was mother to only nine exemplary sons and daughters. Like every Mother of the Year, Mrs. Maceo Thomas exuded a deeply spiritual serenity: "On each occasion that I met her," in the words of an admiring priest, "she impressed me with her motherliness, unselfishness, devotion to her husband and children, her graciousness, poise, [and] charm."[126] Nearly every parish had her equivalent. "The first four or five children are most difficult for a mother when they are little," explained a Chicago mother of sixteen. "As the family grows, the simpler it becomes to manage."[127] Svelte and lovely as well as serene, Alma Fitzpatrick was doubtless a standing reproach to those many women in her southside parish whose lives and persons were less well ordered. She and other women like her preached sermons, too, of a sort not easy to ignore.

Mission preaching, as we have seen, differed from the Sunday variety in both its floridness and frankness. It was also attended more or less voluntarily. So we can probably assume that mission sermons were heard with greater attentiveness than Sunday preaching, though perhaps with growing distaste as well. Missions continued in the postwar years to draw substantial crowds. But the numbers were widely reported to be gradually diminishing, and relatively smaller at their best than had been the case in the 1930s. There was greater competition now when it came to the Catholic evening. Television was a major factor; so too was the growth in specialized ministries, particularly those aimed at families. "Many pastors today seem to think that the old-style mission is out-of-date—incapable of drawing crowds or of really interesting those who do attend," as a Passionist assessed the situation in 1961. "They prefer novenas, even week-end retreats, Cana and Pre-Cana Conferences, groups like C[hristian] F[amily] M[ovement] or the Legion of Mary."[128] Activities like these, in the view of numerous Catholic leaders, could speak more authentically than missions to an increasingly mobile and educated laity. Unlike missions, they addressed the needs and experiences of particular subgroups in the Catholic population—college students, for example, or the parents of young children. And they typically made room for at least a modicum of lay leadership.

The alleged outdatedness of missions had much to do with their perceived negativity. Missions, their critics argued, focused far too much on sin, fear, and punishment. Nor did they pay sufficient attention to the social justice dimensions of morality, at least in the view of the more advanced critics. Such opinions had occasionally been voiced in earlier decades, too, but mostly sotto voce. By the 1950s, however, the dissenters were sufficiently numerous to command respect in the Catholic media and shape the behavior of certain pastors.[129] The dissenting ranks included laity, especially the highly educated, who were increasingly apt to voice their discontents. Parish missions, in the acerbic but typical view of one such dissenter, were intellectually stultifying and even spiritually damaging. There was too much emphasis on hell, too little on positive helps to a deeper spiritual life. And there was too much talk about sex, especially contraception. "I'm willing to accept the experts when they say that the evil of birth control does damn more souls of the men and women I know than I, in my naivete, dream," April Oursler Armstrong wrote in 1959, in the telling venue of a mainstream clerical journal. "Still, I can't help seeing the families in this parish who have more children than I—7, 10, even 12, to my 6—and wondering if Father's in the right hall tonight." Those who flouted Church teaching on contraception "just are not in the audience."[130]

Birth control was indeed a staple of postwar mission preaching. "Of all sins mentioned in the average Mission, birth control gets the biggest play," in Armstrong's only mildly exaggerated formulation, "about 10 to 1 against other mortal sins, with adultery and heavy petting running close seconds."[131] Missioners typically defended their ministry by reminding the growing ranks of critics that birth control was widely practiced even by churchgoing Catholics. "It is normally quite difficult for a pastor to explain the sin of birth control in his Sunday sermons," as one proponent of missions explained in 1949. "When will the people have a chance to hear what is right and wrong in this matter outside of the special sermons of a mission?"[132] Those rights and wrongs, as we have seen, had emerged by the 1940s as the stuff of occasional Sunday sermons. But such sermons could not be as blunt or emotional as the usual mission offering. Sunday sermons could not linger on contraceptive specifics—could not elaborate, as a Passionist was wont to do, on "prophylactics, diaphragms, douches . . . the non-completion of the marriage act and wasting of the male sperm outside the body of the wife. . . . jellies, pills, foams, abortions."[133] Nor could the Sunday preacher speak vividly of eternal punishment. Most missioners, by contrast, were proud of their inventive preaching on this hard and, it seems, increasingly repellant topic. Witness the following, from a Passionist ordained in 1939: "Did you ever try to picture the soul of a habitual sinner, who is in mortal sin day after day? He goes through life chained to a corpse. He drags that corpse with him to work, to his recreation, and at night he lies down and clasps to his bosom, that horrid, putrid thing, a soul in mortal sin."[134]

As these excerpts suggest, mission preachers continued in the postwar years to appropriate the language of their blunt-spoken predecessors. The God of the mission was still an all-seeing Judge. One's secret sins, including those of the marriage bed, were still scheduled for exposure on the Last Day, when—

in the telling of at least the occasional preacher—aborted children would appear to accuse their guilty parents and "all who have actively shared in this slaughter."[135] Unrepentant contraceptionists still went to hell for all eternity. "Father O'Hallohan then gave the main sermon on the Last Judgment," as a Jesuit sociologist recounted a mission in a Southern parish. "He described the kinds of women who would be on Christ's right side: the woman who preferred parochial activity to social climbing; the mother who was the queen of the home and not a birth-controller; the young lady who knew how to behave at a party and which men to date; the high-school girl who followed her conscience rather than the crowd. 'Get used to saying, "Lord, I want to prepare now for the day when the books are open for all to see.'"[136] Father Flannon Gannon made the point more piquantly by looking at those on Christ's left—"birth controllers, adulterers, fornicators, prostitutes, drunkards, Mass Skippers . . . ," all of whom had purchased hell through "the madness of the senses."[137] Sermons like these were suffused by a palpable hostility to sex and perhaps especially sex in marriage, given the missioner's near-obsession with contraceptive sins. "The gratification of concupiscence is but incidental to child bearing and can never be satisfied for itself alone," in the not wholly orthodox words of an earlier-quoted priest, whose order preached missions to Polish Americans.[138]

Despite the persistence of such tropes, mission preaching was changing—and presumably in direct response to evolving lay sensibilities. Postwar texts were less likely than those from earlier decades to belittle women or hold them especially responsible for "sins against marriage." They trafficked less frequently in lurid descriptions of the physical torments of hell, though the reality of hell—an apparently well-populated place—was regularly affirmed.[139] And many more missioners than ever before did their sometimes clumsy best to speak a positive language of marriage. A "storm of invectives," as an experienced preacher advised his confreres, was increasingly apt to alienate one's hearers; marital morality was better promoted by evoking the "beauty and peace of a truly Catholic family."[140] Various preachers developed the theme with varying degrees of skill. "The more children God gives a man and wife the happier family will they have," in the artless phrasing of a Passionist, who was obviously trying to avoid a punitive rhetoric of prohibitions. "The more desirable will be their home. The more successful their marriage."[141] An elderly Capuchin commanded greater eloquence. "The greatest mystery in this visible creation is the beginning of human life. God and man working together! It is all love! . . . Fathers! Mothers! Keep this high ideal of your holy vocation always before your eyes. Never oppose the will of the Creator when using your God-given privileges! Never say 'No!' when God says 'Yes!'"[142]

The more positive content of many missions was not in the end sufficient to save this venerable form of preaching. Large numbers of parishes were abandoning missions by the mid-1960s, when the mission-preaching orders themselves were losing the first of what would soon be a flood of younger members. When those leaner orders reinvented the mission, as they eventually did, its substance was markedly different. The new mission was far more Biblical in orientation than its predecessor, where Scripture rarely featured, save for purposes of doctrinal proof-texting. It evoked a tenderly loving God, rather than a punitive or judgmental One, and seldom or never mentioned hell. The whole spirit was "up, up, up with people," as a not entirely approving Father Donald Dacey evoked a Redemptorist mission he had recently attended in suburban Detroit. "You're all wonderful, and that's all there is to it."[143] The new mission spoke of morality primarily in terms of the individual's openness to God and her willingness to serve God by caring for His creation and especially the poor. And it virtually never addressed the subject of birth control. Typically preached to congregations mixed in terms of sex and age, the reinvented mission—like the contemporary Sunday pulpit—steered away from problems of sexual morality in general.

The demise of the old-style parish mission was clearly linked to its near-obsession with birth control. But more was at issue than a single hard teaching. By rejecting the Church's stand on contraception, growing numbers of Catholics were rejecting a legalist's approach to morality and an ahistorical understanding of their Church's teaching authority. Mission preaching trafficked in both. For all practical purposes, moreover, they were also rejecting the intense eschatological consciousness that permeated mission preaching. That this life should be regarded as a time of probation, that earthly suffering should be embraced as a means of spiritual purification—such notions were increasingly apt to offend the educated Catholic. Had God not endowed His people with creative intelligence? Did He not wish them to make this world a better place—to minimize suffering rather than simply endure it? Catholics were hardly the first to raise such questions, nor were those questions invariably linked to struggles over contraception. (The European Holocaust worked more powerfully than most Catholic leaders realized to delegitimize the cult of suffering.) But many postwar Catholics, relative children of privilege, faced hard moral choices for the very first time in the context of marriage and parenthood. Minor though their suffering was by the century's terrible standards, it was often sufficient to prompt reflection on the purposes of sex and life and the relative claims of authority and conscience.

Politics

Even during the Second World War, American Catholic leaders were conscious of fighting a rearguard action when it came to the secular politics of contraception. The bishops knew that birth control activists worked closely in many localities with state and federal public health agencies. "I do not know of any

Federal or state appropriation made specifically for this purpose," a staffer at the National Catholic Welfare Conference noted in mid-1941, "but there probably are numerous occasions on which Public Health officers give birth control advice and distribute birth control devices for prophylactic purposes in the course of their regular practice."[144] A peacetime draft, instituted in 1940, and subsequent American declarations of war on Japan and Germany brought further unnerving developments. Even prior to Pearl Harbor, the U.S. Surgeon General had ordered the various armed forces to make condoms available to all military personnel, which was done in some camps via vending machines— necessarily highly public.[145] Films shown in every training center routinely provided instruction in the use of prophylactics. Concerted efforts on the part of the NCWC finally resulted in minor modifications of the policy, but nothing more. By 1942, indeed, agents of the Public Health service were distributing fairly graphic instructions on condom use to civilian defense plant workers, though apparently without official authorization.[146]

The postwar years brought new instances of failure, mostly at the local level, and a handful of Pyrrhic victories. The latter chiefly involved the frustration of efforts to provide contraceptive services at various public hospitals. Where Catholics were numerous this was easily done, but at a heavy cost in terms of public relations. The proponents of such services played skillfully on their humane intent and the obvious benefits to taxpayers. (It was mainly the poor and dependent who were public hospital clients.) Catholics encountered a similar problem at the end of the 1950s, when Planned Parenthood and other groups inaugurated a campaign to include family planning assistance in various programs sponsored by the United Nations and, ultimately, by means of American foreign aid. It was not initially hard for Catholic leaders to prevent such action. But it was increasingly difficult for them to justify what seemed to many Americans—including growing numbers of Catholics—like heartless indifference to the suffering of the Third World poor. Throughout the period, needless to say, Catholics were accused of imposing their distinctly minority views on a nation clearly in favor of marital contraception. The anti-contraception laws that remained on the books in Connecticut and Massachusetts were for many Americans particularly emblematic of the tension. Catholics managed to protect those laws until 1965, in what were perhaps the most Pyrrhic victories of all.

These various political skirmishes seemed at first to function for Catholics as earlier bouts in the contraceptive wars had done. They reinforced tribal boundaries and provided occasions for mobilizing the larger Catholic organizations. In these as in previous battles, the more active laity wrote letters of protest, signed petitions, and sent delegates to public hearings. But as the postwar years wore on, growing numbers of Catholics came to doubt the wisdom of the battle, if not necessarily the principles it sought to protect. It was painfully evident that Catholics had few allies when it came to contraception, and none who shared their particular moral logic. Was it right for Catholics in a democracy to override majority opinion, especially on a matter that most Americans now regarded as unambiguously private? Was their ability to do so not inevitably temporary, even where Catholics currently enjoyed the necessary political clout? Were short-term victories worth the cost in public resentment of the Church? It was evident, too, at least among more thoughtful Catholics, that the opposition had principles of its own. Planned Parenthood by the 1950s could deploy its own religious spokesmen to bless an agenda of family stability and social amelioration. Its supporters might be mostly wrong when it came to the purposes of sex, but it was almost impossible now to regard them as wild-eyed radicals or fanatical self-promoters.

So even as the nation prepared to elect its first Catholic president, Catholic leaders were absorbing some difficult lessons on the limits of politics. Some were ready by the late 1950s to concede defeat in precisely those places where Catholic power was greatest. Catholics might currently be able to prevent the establishment of birth control clinics in big-city public hospitals, as such critics readily conceded, but the victory would inevitably be temporary and the cost to the Church prohibitive. "I believe that little permanent good will be accomplished and much harm done by continued intransigent efforts to maintain this admirable regulation," as Monsignor J. D. Conway remarked of a highly publicized contest in New York, in the interesting venue of a column that featured in many diocesan papers.[147] Similar views were increasingly voiced with regard to state laws in Connecticut and Massachusetts. Protecting outmoded laws against contraception, as *Commonweal* editorialized in 1960, "strengthen[ed] in the non-Catholic mind the ever-present fear of Catholic power and [did] much to nullify the persuasive force of Catholic teaching."[148] *Commonweal*'s editors were still publicly committed to the Church's stand on contraception. But they did not ask the obvious. What would the generality of Catholics conclude should their leaders abandon such highly symbolic redoubts? It seemed inevitable, at least to the likes of Monsignor John S. Kennedy, that repealing such laws would result in "a probably popular impression that the Church had changed its teaching on the morality of contraception."[149] If political action risked harm to the Church, accommodation was risky, too—or so it was frequently argued.

This era of hard choices opened on an appropriately difficult note. The American bishops, as previously mentioned, were embroiled throughout the Second World War in a heated debate with the federal government over its various efforts to combat venereal disease. The government's work in this regard, which was not confined to the military services, deeply shocked most bishops. Fargo's Aloysius Muensch was presumably referring to officers of the public health when he spoke in a 1943 pastoral letter of "evil men" who "shamelessly" promoted "sin and disease" among members of the armed forces. "They are saboteurs of the country's defense, and ought to be dealt with as such."[150] Chicago's Samuel Stritch, a leading figure in the NCWC, asked a moralist at his diocesan seminary whether condom distribution in the armed forces did not render the war unjust, at least for Catholic combatants. "Our Government's sin in issuing contraceptives to our soldiers does not change the character of that war from a just to an unjust war," the Jesuit John J. Clifford reassured him in September 1943. "For we were attacked and are still under attack."[151] That Catholic conscripts might feel obliged to refuse military service had already been suggested in an NCWC letter to Navy Secretary Frank Knox, sent shortly before Pearl Harbor.[152] The implied threat was partly tactical. It also measured the dismay with which many bishops reacted to early news of their government's "sin."

The bishops protested the government's policies on several occasions, both before and after Pearl Harbor. They sent strongly worded letters to Knox and Secretary of War Henry Stimson in the fall of 1941. Detroit's Cardinal Edward Mooney, chairman of the NCWC's Administrative Committee, wrote personally to President Roosevelt in 1943 and in terms that were unusually direct for this most diplomatic of prelates. "When the representatives of the Government force our Catholic young men to listen to lectures and to witness demonstrations whose clear implications directly contravene the teaching of their Church, it seems to us that the Government is violating freedom of conscience in an important matter."[153] Editorials to this effect appeared in the Catholic press as well, some of them probably at the behest of individual bishops. The NCWC was also a repeated critic of the anti-venereal disease campaign that the U.S. Public Health Service inaugurated for civilian audiences in 1942. The campaign, which included both pamphlets and film shorts, frankly promoted the use of condoms—an opening sometimes exploited by local birth control groups. "The Bishops are reliably informed that in certain localities this booklet is mailed to married couples whose names appear in the announcements of births," as the NCWC noted in response to a 1942 pamphlet, whose "how to" pages were apparently quite explicit.[154]

The bishops' efforts, not surprisingly, bore very limited fruit. Their protests had little effect on practice in the military, save to deter certain base commanders from requiring men who left the base to have condoms in their possession. (Secretary Stimson had at the bishops' request reversed such an order in Puerto Rico.[155]) The bishops had somewhat greater impact on policy aimed at civilians. NCWC protests resulted in early 1943 in the formation of a committee to vet the various productions of the U.S. Public Health service with regard to venereal disease. The Jesuit Alphonse Schwitalla, himself a medical doctor, served as the Catholic representative on this five-member group, where his patient and eminently intelligent counsel changed the tone of numerous publications.[156] But while he might win from his committee colleagues "a strong condemnation of promiscuity," something that Schwitalla had initially doubted "would ever be possible," he could not prevent the endorsement of condoms in the pamphlets, posters, and even the films approved by the committee.[157] For this reason, certain bishops were deeply troubled by his presence there. "It seems to me that Father Schwitalla, by implication, is tolerating the use of contraceptives in illicit sex relations," as a New Jersey prelate complained.[158] This view had been given forceful expression at an almost-disastrous exploratory meeting that preceded formation of the committee on which Schwitalla so controversially sat. Francis Connell had accompanied Schwitalla to this gathering, but in no mood to negotiate. "You gentlemen believe then in providing a bullet-proof vest to a thief?" he demanded at one point. "In our minds it is far better to have all sorts of physical evils take place than one immoral act. The Catholic Church will not compromise."[159]

Wartime policy with regard to condoms had just the effects that even the most judicious bishops had predicted. Commercial advertising of contraceptives even during the war achieved a new boldness and sophistication. The condom itself, long regarded as the most shameful of the various contraceptives, gained in both familiarity and respectability—despite its wartime associations with nonmarital sex. Public discussion of contraception lost much of its remaining aura of impropriety. Perhaps most important, the wartime campaigns simply assumed the common sense of contraceptive practice. The situation redounded to the benefit of the recently renamed Planned Parenthood, which emerged from the war with a sober new visage and faintly clerical air. "This vicious movement is being definitely cloaked with the garb of religion," an NCWC memo lamented in 1946, when the theme of Planned Parenthood's annual convention was "Religion's Responsibility in Marriage and Parenthood."[160] Robed in its new respectability, the organization in many locales sought membership in the Community Chest and local social service councils, initiatives always resisted by Catholics but increasingly—if grudgingly—accepted as inevitable. Planned Parenthood, according to the NCWC, had joined the Community Chest in at least twenty-one cities by late 1947. "In five cities, the Catholic charities withdrew when Planned Parenthood was admitted to the Chest; in sixteen others they did not."[161]

Local battles like these were the stuff of politics until the late 1950s. Occasional conflicts drew national attention, like the dustup in New York City over public hospital policy. Public hospitals there had for many years refused to provide their patients with contraceptive information or devices. When the policy was publicly challenged in 1958, the Catholic leadership locally went to great lengths to defend it, though the test case at issue—that of a diabetic African American woman who was a Protestant—made their task especially hard. Elite opinion nationally was sharply critical of the Church. "It is, in fact, astonishing that there should be any doubt on the matter," the New York *Times* concluded with regard to a change in the policy, whose survival to date was largely due to local Catholic power.[162] "The general non-Catholic attitude in this City opposed what they regarded as the imposition of Catholic morality on non-Catholics," as the chancellor of the New York Archdiocese later conceded. The policy was finally reversed, not by an elected official—the mayor himself had refused to do so on explicitly religious grounds—but by the non-elected Board of Hospitals.[163] The rewritten policy, however, was still quite restrictive, at least on paper. Physicians might prescribe contraceptives only for women—married, of course—whose "life or health . . . may be jeopardized by pregnancy."[164]

The New York victory, for all its seeming inevitability, was an early one for the pro-contraception forces. Publicly supported birth control clinics were not numerous in the United States prior to the mid-1960s, mainly—though not exclusively—because of Catholic opposition. That opposition, however, was seldom as public or intransigent as had been the case in New York, where Catholic leaders learned important lessons. Publicity was generally damaging to the Catholic cause and productive of widespread resentment toward the Church. As the National Council of Churches pointedly noted in 1961, laws or public policies that restricted access to contraception for the married "violate the civil and religious liberties of all citizens, including Protestants."[165] Better, in the circumstances, for Catholic leaders to voice their objections quietly, hoping to delay the advent of public clinics locally. Once such clinics were judged to be inevitable, Church leaders typically sought guarantees that public hospital patients would not be coerced into contraception and that Catholic hospital personnel would not be forced to participate in providing birth control services.

Catholic opposition to family planning programs for underdeveloped countries, an issue that surfaced in the late 1950s, was initially easier to market. The leaders of many poor countries were themselves opposed to such programs, which the more militant linked to a racist agenda. But growing domestic worry about overpopulation, at near-epidemic levels by the early 1960s, soon put Catholic leaders on the defensive. It was simply inadequate, in such a climate, to speak the language of long-term solutions—increased food production, liberalized trade and immigration laws, rising levels of education and a concomitant rise in the age at marriage. Nor was it persuasive, even for growing numbers of Catholics, to speak hopefully of rhythm's potential as a global means of family limitation. Rhythm's perceived inadequacies were only heightened by period excitement about the Pill and the seeming promise of the intrauterine device, the latter especially favored by international family planners. Simple and apparently foolproof, such devices suggested to many Americans that medical science held the key to a safer, more stable and orderly world.

Though they mostly lost in the court of public opinion, the American bishops had short-term success when it came to affecting policy. The international politics of fertility control were sufficiently complex that the United Nations did not endorse or support any family planning initiatives in the early 1960s. Nor did American foreign aid programs include such services prior to 1966, despite recommendation to the contrary by the so-called Draper Committee report of 1959.[166] President Eisenhower declined to endorse this controversial recommendation, though only in part due to Catholic opposition. (The American bishops had issued a vigorous critique of the Draper Committee's conclusions.) Foreign aid in any form was bitterly opposed by many on the Republican right, while the Catholic bishops—and a majority of Catholic voters—had been its long-term supporters. It hardly made sense to risk the future of foreign assistance in the service of a still-divisive cause. The Catholic bishops and their constituents had also been staunch American friends of the United Nations, as Catholic spokesmen did not fail to stress in their many interventions with the American delegation. "I reminded Mr. Gardner that in preponderant part U.S. Catholics have been stalwart and constant supporters of the United Nations since its advent, and that alienation of such support at a time when that organization needs all the help it can get would be almost calamitous," an NCWC staffer reported of a recent encounter with a high-ranking official in the State Department. "I sense this point hit the mark and with timely persuasiveness."[167]

Catholic leaders had short-term success as well with the most quixotic of their political objectives, though here too the cost in public opinion was distressingly high. The objective at issue was the protecting of anti-contraception laws in Massachusetts and Connecticut, by far the strictest in the United States. The laws were unamended relics of the nineteenth century and predictably extreme; the Connecticut law forbade not only the sale and distribution of contraceptives but their use, even by married couples. Neither law was seriously enforced in the postwar years, at least when it came to physicians in private practice. Even condoms could be sold, though only for purposes of disease prevention—as their labels obligingly stated. But the laws effectively prevented the establishment of public birth control clinics and inhibited contraceptive advertising. They had symbolic value, too, particularly for Catholic residents of the two states in question, which had unusually bitter histories of interconfessional rivalry. Every American Catholic, however, was ultimately implicated, given that these repressive laws—ironically the products of Protestant-dominated legislatures—were widely seen by the 1940s as monuments to Catholic power.

The Connecticut law was never amended, nor was its amendment ever the subject of a popular referendum. It was finally overturned in 1965, by action of the U.S. Supreme Court in the landmark *Griswold* decision, the language of which helped to pave the way for *Roe v. Wade* in 1973. (The majority in *Roe,* which legalized abortion in every American jurisdiction, elaborated on a "right to privacy" first articulated in *Griswold.*) The Massachusetts law, by contrast, was twice the subject of statewide referenda—first in 1942 and again in 1948. Proposed amendment of the law was defeated on both occasions. Catholics did not achieve these results unaided, not being a majority in the state, and Catholic leaders tried in both campaigns to speak ecumenically. But the contest was widely regarded as confessional in nature, whatever the role additionally played by ethnicity, class, and historical accident. Particularly in 1948, the campaign against liberalization was prominently led by the state's Catholic bishops, with Boston's Richard Cushing assuming the role of commander-in-chief. The pro-amendment cause was in that same year endorsed by a number of mainstream Protestant bodies, including the Massachusetts Council of Churches.

Having failed in their efforts to prevent the question from being placed on the ballot, Catholic leaders in 1942 waged a determined campaign but one that was in important respects less aggressive than 1948. The Boston *Pilot,* the archdiocesan weekly, editorialized against the proposed amendment, which— according to the paper—Catholics were "solemnly bound" to oppose.[168] Every pastor was ordered by the Boston Chancery to preach against the proposed amendment on a Sunday prior to the election, although no model text was provided.[169] The Chancery also seems to have funded a fairly extensive advertising campaign, which apparently included radio spots and "dramalogues," as well as a predictable assortment of pamphlets and flyers.[170] There were anti-amendment billboards, too, according to the recollections of a then-adolescent John T. Noonan.[171] But based on the extant record, there was no systematic effort to increase registration among Catholics or otherwise swell the Catholic vote. Nor does the propaganda seem to have been aggressively Catholic in content. An evidently popular radio "dramalogue"—it was subsequently used in the 1948 campaign—featured the improbably ecumenical trio of Mesdames Perkins, O'Malley, and Levine, who shake their heads over birth control foolishness as they hang the Monday wash.[172] Even the campaign's principal slogan—"Birth control is against God's law!"—was probably seen at the Boston Chancery as religiously neutral, couched in "moral" as opposed to sectarian language. As for Cardinal William O'Connell, no stranger in the past to politics, he mostly stayed behind the scenes. O'Connell was old and ailing and probably confident as to results. The forces of liberalization went down to defeat in 1942 by a margin of roughly 200,000 votes.[173]

The 1948 campaign was quite different. The Boston Chancery of Archbishop Richard Cushing was the highly visible command center of the anti-amendment forces, with Catholic voters aggressively mobilized by their priests. "It is of prime importance for us to secure a maximum registration of voters for the Fall elections and referenda," as Cushing told his clergy in July. It was "the responsibility of parish priests to secure a maximum registration of our people." Every pastor was to ensure that the duty of registration was regularly preached from the pulpit; he was also to establish a committee of reliable lay activists to carry the registration effort door-to-door.[174] As an evident guard against slacking off, Cushing required each pastor to report "the precise result of these efforts" on three separate occasions during the fall.[175] Leaflets, flyers, and window cards were distributed to Catholics throughout the state—a Boston-based "central committee" coordinated these and other efforts—while radio spots and longer features flooded the airwaves.[176] As election day drew near, every priest in the Boston Archdiocese was instructed to preach three successive sermons—model texts were provided—on the moral obligation to vote and the evils of contraception.[177] On election day itself, pastors were told to arrange for anti-amendment literature to be distributed at the local polls. Never in the history of the birth control wars had Catholics been so extensively mobilized, and the effort quite naturally came to national attention. The short-term effect was a Catholic victory: the proposed amendment was defeated by some 278,000 votes.[178] But the cost to the Church was high, and not only in Massachusetts, where interreligious tensions were greatly exacerbated. Non-Catholics nationally were also troubled by this seemingly unchecked deployment of the Church's political muscle.

The 1948 campaign was noteworthy for an additional reason. As in 1942, most Catholic propaganda was couched in what passed for ecumenical terms. "Religious and medical leaders of all faiths unite in opposing the proposed change in our state laws," as a radio spot maintained. Protestants, Catholics and Jews alike believe "in the preservation of the home . . . the sanctity of the family . . . the maintenance of public and personal morality."[179] But in 1948, this same propaganda favored language that seemed to conflate contraception and abortion.[180] The proposed amendment was "anti-baby," intent on denying life to those who would otherwise come into being.[181] "Unnatural Birth Control is against God's Law," according to a radio spot that ran statewide. "It's like abortion of the unwanted and certain other perversions which some people may rationalize and defend, but which God's law forbids."[182] The *Catholic Mirror,* the official organ of the Diocese of Springfield, ran a chilling illustration of a sleeping infant about to be murdered by a knife-wielding arm, prominently labeled "Planned Parenthood." The baby stood for "tomorrow's children"; the knife itself for "birth control."[183] An image like this lent ominous and distinctly unecumenical import to the campaign's principal slogan: "Birth control is *still* against God's law!" But it was effective, at least in the not unbiased view of local Planned Parenthood activists. The 1948 referendum "asked that physicians be allowed 'to provide medical contraceptive care to married women for the protection of life or health,'" as one such explained in 1950. "It was defeated largely because of misunderstanding on the part of the voters, many of whom confused 'contraceptive care' with abortion, sterilization, or state control of family numbers."[184]

The rhetorical excesses of the 1948 campaign had in part to do with the age

Figure 5. Anti-amendment propaganda in the Springfield *Catholic Mirror* during the 1948 "birth control referendum" in Massachusetts. Image courtesy of the Archives of the Archdiocese of Boston.

of its clerical leadership. All had been raised in a world where the line between contraception and abortion was not uncommonly blurred. But it probably had to do as well with that leadership's growing anxiety about its opponents—their confidence, their staying power, the evident force of their arguments. "They'll never say die," a discouraged Cushing remarked to a political confidant in the early 1950s. "I hate to think of going through another battle in 1954."[185] (The state constitution required that two biennial elections take place before a previously rejected referendum could again be placed on the ballot.) Planned Parenthood might have been badly beaten in 1948, when voter turnout in Massachusetts was unusually high. They had, however, drawn many more votes than in 1942.[186] Given trends in public opinion, was it not likely—even inevitable—that the group would enjoy continued gains in future referenda? The "anti-baby" rhetoric of 1948 seemed at the time to stem from Catholic arrogance, at least in the view of the Church's adversaries. But it may have spoken more fundamentally to Catholic fears. Men sure of their cause would hardly have stooped to such theologically dubious appeals—for such they were by the late 1940s—or risked their divisive consequences.

The Massachusetts law in question survived unamended into the mid-1960s. It was terribly vulnerable by then to challenge from the courts. But before this could happen, Boston's Catholic leaders brokered its strategic amendment, which legalized the provision of contraception to married couples for any reason.[187] After surprisingly extended wrangling, the measure passed the legislature in 1966. It fell to Richard Cushing—Cardinal Cushing as of 1958—to publicly bless the compromise, which he did with the ghostwriterly aid of the *Pilot*'s Monsignor Francis Lally and the Jesuit John Courtney Murray. "In the present case, especially in the light of the position taken by other religious groups in our plural society, it does not seem reasonable to me to forbid in civil law a practice that can be considered a matter of private morality," as Cushing told a public hearing in 1965. "Again let me say, that Catholics do not share the views of many of their neighbors in this regard, but they respect them as conscientious religious commitments on the part of responsible citizens."[188] The logic could hardly have been more remote from the world of 1948, when contraception—in the Catholic telling—seemed at times to be tantamount to murder. The contrast was not lost on Cushing's Catholic constituents, many of whom heard more in his statement than a graceful acknowledgment of religious pluralism. They heard as well a tacit admission of Catholic error with regard to contraception, which—unlike murder or indeed other forms of seriously antisocial conduct—was now conceded to be a purely private matter. "It all depends on how much of an evil you think birth control is," as John Ford put it bluntly with regard to the wisdom of amending the Massachusetts law.[189]

The Catholic capitulation in Massachusetts marked the end of a political era—one increasingly characterized by Catholic losses and instances of strategic retreat. By the mid-1960s, growing numbers of Catholic leaders had essentially abandoned efforts to thwart the contraceptive cause, at least by means of the state. Those who remained in the battle were soon overwhelmed by the period's increasingly radical individualism. The amended Massachusetts law—proud monument to interreligious cooperation—survived only until 1972, when it was overturned by the U.S. Supreme Court. That law, in the Court's judgment, discriminated in unconstitutional fashion against unmarried adults. The amended law, after all, had legalized contraception only for the state's married couples.[190]

5

"It Isn't Easy to Be a Catholic"

Rhythm, Education for Marriage,
Lay Voices, 1941–1962

The postwar years saw an explosion of creative energy in American Catholicism, especially with regard to marriage and the family. Genuine innovation occurred in terms of family life ministry, spurred in a good many cases by local lay activism. Catholic colleges and even high schools embarked in large numbers on courses in marriage and family life—not a new development, to be sure, but far more widespread now than ever before. A devout elite among the laity, many of them highly educated, were active in organizations of their own, where they promoted a near-heroic vision of Christian family living. Above all there was talk—about the nature of man and woman, the meaning of sex, the place of rhythm in a truly Christian marriage. Theologians held forth on these and related subjects in unprecedented volume, mostly in publications aimed at fellow priests but sometimes those meant for the laity. Priests in family life ministry had their own venues—local newsletters, couples' retreats, conferences for the betrothed. Priests trained as marriage counselors—a postwar innovation—deployed their counsel privately. But it was enhanced by a new aura of professionalism.

The laity talked, too, and more publicly than ever before. Their voices were initially heard in support of uncompromising idealism. "Let those who marry have children as God sends them," as a typical article in the lay-edited *Integrity* articulated the ethos in 1947. "It will comfort them to remember that God is not bound by the laws of a bad economic system, and that He will provide, somehow, extra (extra rooms and extra food) for the children He sends."[1] In the world of *Integrity* and like-minded lay publications, holy foolishness was the order of the day. "It isn't easy to be a Catholic," was the proud boast of a student sodality publication from Chicago, citing as one of its principal examples "the mother who welcomes her seventh child." (The magazine's pantheon of exemplary Catholics also included those who refused to condone racism or political corruption.) "People will smile, or sigh, or smirk, or sneer, and it will be hard to take."[2]

By the mid-1950s, however, dissenting voices were beginning to be heard, sometimes in accents of great bitterness. Church teaching on birth control is fundamentally destructive, these voices said. It undermines married love, creates family discord, drives too many people from the practice of their religion. "It doesn't seem that having a baby every year is right for mother or children," a twenty-nine-year-old mother of four young children told the priest editors of the *Liguorian* in 1955. "I believe that Christ never meant marriage to be this hard. . . . I feel that the Church does not really understand about birth-control and that by keeping silent about it I am doing wrong." Obviously devout, this troubled woman had not yet reached the point of open rebellion, though her convert husband was emphatically in favor of using contraceptives. "My husband says it will be Christ Himself before whom we will have to stand in judgment when we die and not the priests of the Church."[3] Like growing numbers of her equally devout contemporaries, however, she had come to doubt the morality of the teaching on contraception—a potentially fatal development for her faith in ecclesial authority.

This rising chorus of talk—about marriage, sex, contraception, authority—is the primary focus of the present chapter. We look first at the debate over rhythm, which emerged in the postwar years with renewed visibility and vigor. We then examine developments in premarital instruction and marriage education. We listen finally to lay voices—to the advocates of domestic sanctity, the doubtful, the angry, and the distressed. Amid the sometimes Babel sounds, one thing is clear: this was a church that took its sexual teaching seriously. Some of the brightest and most pastorally minded of its clergy worked hard to present that teaching in contemporaneously persuasive terms. Many of its most devout laity were equally ardent in the teaching's defense, sometimes seeming to outdo their priests. Even the disaffected laity often remained obedient, no longer convinced of the teaching's truth but bound for complex reasons to the Church's structures of authority. The troubled mother invoked above was one of them: "I suggest that the Church grant the use of a medically approved contraceptive for at least six months after a baby is born," she proposed by way of solution to her own and others' problems. "I also suggest that in each diocese a special board of priests who are especially informed on these matters be granted the power to permit married couples in special circumstances to practice contraception."[4] At least at this juncture, in the mid-1950s, she was emotionally unprepared to act on the socially mainstream values—individual autonomy, rational planning, sexual fulfillment in marriage—in which she so obviously believed.

Rhythm and Its Discontents

Nearly all Catholic adults in the postwar years knew at least in broad outline about the rhythm method, despite the reluctance of many priests to address the matter publicly. The pioneering literature of the early 1930s was still in print and apparently selling steadily. Leo Latz's *The Rhythm,* which first publicized the method for American audiences, had sold over 400,000 copies by 1950. Commercial publishers were active, too, promoting not only "calendar wheels" but wildly inflated expectations. "From available statistics the method is reliable in 97 per cent of all cases," in the heartening words of *The Modern Method of Birth Control,* in its third edition by 1943 and obviously marketed especially to Catholics. As for the laity, especially women, they talked about rhythm among themselves, apparently on the general assumption that the method had been approved by the Church—an illusion furthered by Planned Parenthood and by many of rhythm's commercial promoters. "APPROVED BY THE CLERGY, BLESSED BY THE CHURCH" in the words of a fairly typical ad, this one for *Natural Control of Conception.*[5] "The zeal of some of its Catholic advocates would do justice to a crusader," as the editors of *Integrity* rather sourly noted in 1948. "The attitude among many of the young Catholic couples is that Rhythm is a recommended practice, verging on a precept. On more than one occasion Catholic friends have told us that it is *more* Catholic to plan families by the use of Rhythm than to take the children as they come!"[6]

The clergy were far more divided and of necessity more reticent, especially in the 1940s. Rhythm was still a forbidden subject when it came to Sunday preaching. "There can be no public promulgation of the theory from the pulpit, or from any other place," in the stern but typical words of Monsignor John Linsenmeyer, addressing a Detroit clergy conference in 1945.[7] Even mission preachers, famed for their frankness, were cautioned against explicit talk on this seemingly innocuous topic. "Make no more than a reference to the 'safe period,'" as Redemptorist preachers were told in the 1940s. "But do not use the words 'safe period.' Rather say 'self-control' or 'continence.'"[8] The problem was not so much the moral status of rhythm—a solid majority of theologians upheld periodic continence as a licit means of family limitation. The difficulties lay in the practical order, as they had earlier done. Many priests still worried that endorsing rhythm meant the unwitting promotion of a contraceptive mentality. Were the clergy to bless rhythm publicly, Catholics would inevitably come to believe that they had a right to plan their families. What would happen in such circumstances when the rhythm method failed, as, in the view of many experts, it was ultimately bound to do? And how did one counter the argument, still deployed by the advocates of birth control, that rhythm was simply the "Catholic" means to an end endorsed by all right-thinking Americans? "People in general are not theologians," as a conservative moralist quite sensibly noted. They would not necessarily grasp distinctions that were evident to the clergy. Besides, rhythm publicity undermined the "Catholic ideal of fecund marriage."[9]

Despite these concerns, however, growing numbers of priests were willing to speak approvingly of rhythm, and not only as confessors and counselors. By the late 1940s, priests were regularly addressing the subject at Cana conferences for married couples, at pre-Cana gatherings for the engaged, and even in college classes on marriage—although not invariably of their own volition.[10] In settings like these, the laity asked about rhythm; priding themselves on a new closeness to the people, their priests could hardly refuse to respond. Rhythm was also increasingly mentioned in premarital instruction, especially when younger priests were involved, with couples sometimes steered toward knowledgeable Catholic physicians. (Father Hugh Calkins, a near-apoplectic critic of rhythm, wrote angrily in 1948 about "parish priests giving a copy of a book on Rhythm to each engaged couple with a word of approval."[11]) Students in Catholic medical schools were taught the method and apparently confidence in it, since Catholic doctors were far more certain of its efficacy than their Protestant and Jewish counterparts.[12] Rhythm even made its oblique way into preaching, as a mission instruction on confession neatly demonstrates. We should look to confession for help with our seemingly insoluble problems, Father Valentine Leitsch told innumerable congregations in the 1940s and 50s. "Let me give you an example. I am taking it for granted that I am speaking most[ly] to married people." You know that birth control is forbidden, he continued. And yet you have more children already than you can easily provide for. Or perhaps several reputable doctors have said that your wife must not become pregnant again. "Why not take this to the Confessional and talk it over with the priest. I am not saying he will tell you to practice birth-control—by no means. But he will tell you what is the right thing to do. Many times when you find the answer (right) you will be very much relieved."[13] Father Leitsch in this sermon never breathed the word rhythm, or even such euphemisms as periodic continence. But he was nonetheless its promoter, given the laity's state of awareness and the hopefulness with which he alluded to this obviously moral—if mysteriously unmentionable—means of family limitation.

Rhythm's increased visibility in the postwar years seems to have led to its growing practice, especially among the highly educated. National data suggest a substantial increase in the practice of rhythm in the 1940s and especially the first half of the 1950s, mostly but not exclusively among Catholics.[14] The extent of Catholic usage, and its strong correlation with levels of education, was documented by consecutive national fertility surveys in 1955 and 1960. About 65 percent of the Catholic wives sampled in 1955 had used or were currently using rhythm, with the figure rising to 80 percent for those with college training. The equivalent figures for 1960 were 70 percent and 89 percent.[15] Just under half of the Catholics sampled had never used any method but rhythm to space or limit births—47 percent in 1955, 45 percent in 1960. The rest of those who reported its practice had also used forbidden methods, either in lieu of rhythm or in tandem with it.[16]

This last-mentioned behavior is especially intriguing. There were obviously those who tried rhythm and found it wanting. Some then turned, presumably in desperation, to an alternative mode of contraception—an "appliance" method was the most likely—either on a permanent basis or temporarily, for purposes of child-spacing. But what of those—probably a smaller number—who practiced rhythm in tandem with additional contraceptive strategies, either habitually or on those occasions when a couple had sex at unsafe times? The latter behavior makes logical sense, though it did confirm the darker suspicions of rhythm's clerical critics. But the former is rather puzzling. Why bother with rhythm's restrictive schedule if one were already taking contraceptive precautions? Some couples—not all of them Catholics—apparently did so to increase their margin of contraceptive safety.[17] Others—nearly all of them Catholics—were engaged in a kind of symbolic obedience to a teaching whose burdens had become at least temporarily intolerable. John Ford was consulted in the mid-1950s on a case where the husband insisted on using a condom, though his wife had thus far contrived to keep him on a rhythm schedule for intercourse. "She honestly believed that on her side the actions were guiltless since she was practicing rhythm, and that only her husband was sinning." Thus persuaded, she saw no need to mention the odd arrangement in confession. It was only chance probing by a confessor—spurred, one rather suspects, by his penitent's nervous demeanor—that brought the matter to clerical notice. She "trembles and shakes in the presence of a priest," as Ford's correspondent described the woman in question, whose improbable fiction of innocence—essential, perhaps, to her psychic well-being—had by now been thoroughly undermined.[18]

Rhythm's postwar popularity was enhanced in part by its putatively greater reliability. With the advent of the basal temperature method, first publicized in the late 1940s, women could more surely determine their approximate moment of ovulation.[19] The method was cumbersome, to be sure: every morning, prior to rising, a woman took her rectal temperature, carefully charting its minute changes. Ovulation occurred at the temperature's low point and was followed by a telltale if modest temperature rise. After two or three days of an elevated temperature, the woman was reliably sterile for the rest of her menstrual cycle—always assuming that the woman in question ovulated only once a month. The preovulatory phase was more problematic, save for women—rare indeed—whose time of ovulation never varied. Intercourse shortly before ovulation, the fact of which could not be detected before it actually took place, could easily result in pregnancy. The basal temperature method, then, did not necessarily mean more sex for Catholic couples using rhythm, though long-term users could come to know the probable parameters of a woman's fertile days.[20] But correctly observed—no mean feat for a busy mother—it was certainly more reliable than rhythm based on the calendar alone.

Other innovations followed. A product called "Tes-Tape" appeared on the market in 1957, followed in 1959 by the "Fertility Testor." Both purported to signal the moment of ovulation by detecting change in the chemistry of cervical secretions. Tes-Tape was a particular disappointment, being prone to false positives; the Fertility Testor, an alleged improvement, simply ceased to be relevant as the practice of rhythm declined in the mid-1960s and after.[21] But even the Fertility Testor had its share of disappointed users. "Catholic magazines make it sound so wonderful," a jaundiced laywoman commented, with specific reference to the device, "and then it all comes to nothing."[22] The significance of devices like these lay principally in the optimism they generated among the promoters of rhythm. As "the most scientific method of birth control," to borrow from one of this numerous tribe, rhythm was bound before long to be rendered very nearly foolproof and even easier to use than "the Pill."[23] The logic was parodied many years later by British novelist David Lodge: "Father Brierly's Parish Priest, in the course of a heated argument, assured him that 'the Yanks were working on a little gadget like a wristwatch that would make it as simple as telling the time.'"[24]

Optimism of this sort was especially consoling for priests, who were regularly faced with hard questions in the realm of marital sex. "I would not say the case is hopeless," John Ford assured a clerical correspondent, who had consulted him on an objectively grim situation, this one involving a mother with apparently severe mental illness. "There is now a new refinement in the techniques for determining the exact time of ovulation. . . . Certain women whose periods are too irregular to be calculated by other methods can determine their sterile days with the help of this method." Ford, who referred to the Fertility Testor, was appropriately cautious in his counsel. "Do not raise their hopes unduly about this method."[25] But he was clearly pleased to be able to offer assistance that went beyond the usual exhortations to prayer and the sacraments. Faith in rhythm's perfectibility helped as well when restive penitents objected that the method had repeatedly failed them. Complaints of this sort, in the typical view of the Redemptorist Hugh J. O'Connell, were nearly always rooted in ignorance. The basal temperature method, coupled with use of the Fertility Testor, promised results that in his view were "equal or almost equal" to "artificial contraceptives," always assuming that said techniques were employed with the requisite care.[26]

Talk like this, omnipresent in Catholic circles by the early 1960s, was seen at the time as a way of defending Church teaching. But its main effect, at least for the laity, was probably to blur the distinction between rhythm and forbidden modes of family limitation. Rhythm's defenders, after all, were essentially touting its growing contraceptive efficacy. Relatively few laity were yet persuaded on this score, as the Jesuit John L. Thomas conceded in his admirably pastoral book on rhythm. "Because of a current, widespread misunderstanding on this question, we must point out at once that rhythm is not merely tolerated on the grounds that it is a highly unreliable method of avoiding pregnancy."[27] Still, rhythm's defenders by the late 1950s were clearly endorsing the laity's desire for certainty when it came to family planning—a long step away from the world of "let[ing] the babies come, confident somehow that God will provide for them," to borrow from a period mission sermon.[28] And if rhythm were really one day to become as reliable as the Pill, what difference would remain—apart from questions of cost, health, or convenience—between what were, for all practical purposes, two highly effective modes of birth control?

Rhythm's critics had been aware of such dangers long before the advent of fertility tape and basal temperature charts. "Even many of the intellectual class are slow to see the difference between material contraception and the 'safe period' practice," as Father N. Orville Griese observed in 1944, when he emerged as rhythm's single most influential critic. His attack was not simply on rhythm publicity, though Griese like other of rhythm's detractors was certainly opposed to this. It centered instead on the morality of rhythm itself, as Griese explained in his widely cited *The 'Rhythm' in Marriage and Christian Morality.* Griese acknowledged that his was a distinctly minority view: "the majority of contemporary theologians seem to hold that the application of the 'safe period' method is objectively indifferent from a moral viewpoint." But this was because they thought in terms of isolated acts, likening rhythm to intercourse between naturally infertile spouses. Rightly understood, rhythm was actually "a system of marital relations"—one "designed to prevent the realization of the primary end of marital union." As a system, Griese argued, rhythm was objectively "illicit," though circumstances might render it at least temporarily sinless in individual cases. Rhythm could be morally justified, in other words, only in those cases where a couple had truly grave reasons for avoiding childbirth—a serious threat to the mother's health, crushing poverty, well-founded fear of stillbirth or severe congenital abnormalities. "The practice must be presented as something appropriate only for a limited number of circumstances," as Griese advised his priest readers, "and even then, as less worthy than complete abstinence."[29]

Even after its publication, Griese's remained a minority position, though a central thrust of his argument was seemingly endorsed by Pope Pius XII, when he made his first public statement on rhythm in 1951. Until that time, however, a majority of moralists held that rhythm per se was perfectly licit. Couples who practiced rhythm for objectively selfish reasons might sin by so doing, but seldom more than venially. No one, after all, was obliged to have children. "The law of fecundity obliges only the race in general," as Father Hugh O'Connell articulated the mainstream view. "It prohibits the frustration of marriage by contraception; but does not place a positive obligation on any individuals."[30] A couple might, at least in theory, practice rhythm for the whole of their marital life and not fall into mortal sin, particularly if both spouses freely agreed to the program. Their conduct might be deplorably selfish—much depended on their motives. But their failure to reproduce—for purposes of argument, moral theologians blithely assumed the total efficacy of rhythm—was not itself sinful, no matter that Catholic teaching on marriage defined procreation as its primary end.

Griese, however, did give heart to a varied assortment of critics, who mounted a furious assault on rhythm during the later 1940s. Much of it was angry in tone, sometimes overtly hostile to sex and invariably so toward the laity. Father Hugh Calkins epitomized the reigning mood of intemperance, charging in 1948 that "Catholic couples have gone hog-wild in the abusive employment of rhythm. . . . A method meant to be a temporary solution of a critical problem has become a way of life, a very selfish, luxury-loving, materialistic way of life." Too many of the Catholic laity, in Calkins' view, had become "promoters of sterility," more concerned with ease and comfort than children and obedience to God. Well-educated Catholics in particular had absorbed a "pagan" approach to life, assuming that a family's size should depend on the parents' ability to provide extended schooling and material security. "But heaven, not security, is the goal set for the babies God sends. . . . Every couple should have the children God wants them to have." Determined to outwit God, the practitioners of rhythm were eventually punished by the very same ills that so often afflicted the devotees of artificial contraception. The women endured neuroses and ultimate sterility; the men lost respect for their wives and were regularly unfaithful, impelled in a good many cases by the sexual frustrations attendant on rhythm, which Calkins appeared to regard as a mostly female plot.[31] Father Joseph Donovan, the Vincentian rector of Kenrick Seminary in St. Louis, even spoke of rhythm's "viciousness." Couples who practiced rhythm without a "sufficiently justifying cause" were as prone to divorce and adultery as those who used contraceptives, "since such couples equivalently shut out all thought of God from their hearts and their minds and are wholly intent on their lust."[32]

Other critics of rhythm, many of them lay, spoke in tones of passionate idealism—more appealing than their carping counterparts but no less absolute in their logic. Ours, they argued, is an age gone mad for material possessions and sensate pleasure. Catholics can be its saving remnant, but only if they live according to standards of heroic virtue. For the great majority of Catholics, this would necessarily mean a form of domestic sanctity—a commitment most often epitomized by extravagantly generous parenthood. Have numerous children, these idealists counseled, if that is what God wills to send. "Six Isn't Enough!" according to the hortatory title of an article in a 1948 issue of *Integrity*.[33] "It will take heroic faith to act upon this principle, and a willingness to sacrifice a materialistic way of life," as another *Integrity* author noted. "It is characteristic of our day that nothing less than an heroic faith will suffice." A wife's ill health might occasionally justify the temporary practice of rhythm. But worries about the material morrow were never an adequate excuse. Hard-pressed couples should trust in God, Who would provide, and offer their lives as witness against false values. "Let us preach the *un*importance of being well-dressed," in the words of the above-quoted author. "Let us forget all about the American Way of Life, and start the Godly Way of Life, which will bring down graces upon us to rectify all the messes we have made of things."[34]

The debate over rhythm was changed abruptly in 1951, when Pope Pius XII addressed the subject in a talk to the Italian Catholic Society of Midwives. The pope spoke of rhythm with surprising warmth, implying that the method was permissible in a potentially very large number of cases. Couples who used rhythm were required to have a "serious motive" for so doing. But such motives might be "not rarely present" in the form of medical, economic, eugenic, and social "indications," with the last-mentioned quite easily being construed to include concern about overpopulation. Given the exceedingly grudging content of previous Roman statements on rhythm, Pius's tone and logic signaled a new and far more generous spirit—a genuine break with the past. He obviously knew that some moral theologians were still quoting as gospel the Sacred Penitentiary's instructions from 1880, which permitted confessors to "cautiously insinuate" information about rhythm—incorrect information, as we now know—but only to penitents already ensnared in the clutches of "onanism." The pope addressed the subject again just one month later, this time using the phrase "regulation of offspring" to describe what use of the sterile period might lawfully accomplish. As John T. Noonan has aptly noted, "This was the first time that a Pope had spoken with approval of the regulation of birth." The pope, moreover, expressed the hope that medical science "will develop for this method a sufficiently secure base" to render it truly effective.[35]

Rhythm's defenders, overjoyed, regarded the pope's twin statements as a full-fledged blessing of the method. No longer could the critics claim that the Church "merely tolerates" rhythm, to borrow from Father Hugh Calkins, for whom toleration in this instance meant no more than "reluctant permission"—and that in a limited number of cases.[36] But the pope also spoke, if only in passing, of a "duty to procreate," something missing from *Casti Connubii* and other Roman statements on marriage.[37] The duty was apparently binding on individual couples as well as the race—logic that seemed to vindicate a central thesis of Father Orville Griese, at least in the view of rhythm's critics.[38] So, rhythm's defenders, albeit victorious, had a new problem with which to wrestle. Was there indeed an "affirmative obligation on individual couples to procreate," in the phrasing of the Jesuits John Ford and Gerald Kelly? (The pope's seemingly casual reference to this alleged duty, invoked for purposes of explaining why couples were required to have a reason for the long-term practice of rhythm, raised doubts for some theologians as to its binding nature.[39]) And if such an obligation existed, how many children must a couple produce in order to satisfy it?

In the wake of the pope's pronouncements, the advocates of rhythm became much bolder. Speaking openly about the method was obviously easier now that the pope himself had done so, and indeed before lay audiences. John Ford, like nearly every moralist, had routinely warned seminarians against "too much publicity" when it came to rhythm. He ceased to do so in the 1950s, at least according to his teaching notes.[40] Periodicals aimed at the laity, which even in the 1940s had seldom or never referred to rhythm, now carried features on the subject that were typically frank and sometimes markedly sympathetic. Most couples had good reason to limit the size of their families—or so much of this literature assumed, despite its mostly clerical authorship. Those who chose to do so by means of rhythm were admirably Christian. "Couples who are unwilling to follow the example of so many of their contemporaries in the use of contraceptives and who conscientiously resort to the more difficult practice of rhythm reveal a respect for God's law worthy of commendation," in the words of the Jesuit John L. Thomas, whose *Marriage and Rhythm* was published in 1957.[41] Such couples, moreover, need not seek clerical permission to make use of rhythm, even for an extended period—such, at least, was the view of prominent moralists.[42] "The decision is up to them," in the typical phrasing of the Jesuit Paul Hilsdale, "and not—as many seem to think—up to their confessor." It was obviously necessary that the laity know "the Church's teaching about what reasons give sufficient justification."[43] But the laity, as they emerged in the most pastoral of the new rhythm literature, were informed and eminently responsible—a far cry from the selfish and willfully ignorant tribe who peopled the writings of a Father Hugh Calkins.

Certain priests in the 1950s resisted the trend toward liberalization. There were still those, not all of them elderly, who associated rhythm with selfishness and gross sensuality. Many believed that its practice required not only a genuinely grave reason but also a confessor's permission. (Busy priests often failed to keep up with the writings of prominent moralists.) "Even when an excusing cause is present," in the not-so-unusual words of Boston's Msgr. Lawrence Riley, "often it will be more advisable and more praiseworthy for a couple to continue to build a family, placing their trust in Divine Providence."[44] Some even denied absolution to penitents who were practicing rhythm for allegedly insufficient reasons, though the question of rhythm's potential sinfulness was so clearly disputed as to warrant the penitent's being given the benefit of the doubt.[45] "Do not refuse absolution in [the] present state of the discussion," John Ford flatly told his advanced theological students.[46] There was also the occasional confessor who commended abstinence in marriage, presumably as a higher good than the practice of periodic continence.

Men like these, however, went against the advice of most of their mainstream confreres. "The practice of total abstinence would normally arouse a strain and tension that might be harmful, psychologically and spiritually, to the peace and joy of domestic life," in the 1959 words of a clerical journal not noted for its liberalism.[47] The Jesuit John Thomas spoke almost despairingly of those who "fail to appreciate the complexities of sex in marriage when they so lightly recommend total abstinence."[48]

Despite the critics' persistence, rhythm's advocates in the 1950s mostly carried the day. The method was freely, almost casually, discussed by the laity and the younger clergy, and in terms that assumed not only its virtue but that of frank talk on this hitherto delicate subject. How else, as rhythm's supporters asked, could Catholics mount a plausible defense of their Church's hard teaching on marital sex? As for the typical confessor, he was far more apt to suggest rhythm to his married penitents than to challenge them about its use. (Those hearing confessions in uncertain Spanish could recommend rhythm by 1960, thanks to a new bilingual handbook.[49]) Priests in family life ministry had of necessity to keep up with the latest in rhythm news, though this now involved such decidedly unclerical topics as rectal thermometers and cervical mucous. "Really, Father, is there nothing sacred to women?" in the amused words of a Wisconsin laywoman. "Yet the times demand it. We pin you against the wall and insist that you answer 'why, when, where, how and why.'"[50] Presentations on rhythm were standard to most marriage and premarriage programs by the mid-1950s, when their tone and content were typically positive. A physician would generally handle the "how-to" portion of the program. But "Father" was expected to know the particulars of the system, his expertise being widely seen as a kind of blessing on its practice.

If rhythm's proponents mostly carried the day, they did not thereby silence their more tenacious critics. The debate went on, in muted fashion, into the 1960s. The laity for the most part were not disturbed by this, since all but the most scrupulous simply assumed that they had a right to practice rhythm. The users of rhythm, indeed, were popularly regarded as a kind of spiritual elite. The "general feeling" in her parish, according to a New Jersey laywomen, "seems to be that anyone who uses rhythm is very religious."[51] But scrupulous Catholics were often troubled by conflicting clerical counsels on rhythm, and increasingly annoyed by such. One Mrs. D. M. was "baffled" by Redemptorist Father Henry Sattler, who claimed in a 1960 edition of *Marriage* magazine that the spacing of children was in itself an insufficient reason to practice rhythm. "I have been told explicitly by a priest that it is permissible to practice rhythm one year after the birth of a child to space children for reasons of a mother's health."[52] Absent clerical unanimity, what was a good Catholic to do? She had evidently to abide by the judgment of her own informed conscience. The seemingly uniform edifice of Catholic moral theology, resplendent in its glistening coat of black and white, was perhaps not so uniform after all, or without its shades of gray. The lesson was clearly relevant to the looming debate among Catholics over the morality of contraception.

The debate on rhythm in the 1950s was noteworthy, at least in retrospect, for two additional developments. The first has to do with the putative "duty to procreate"—something seemingly enunciated by Pius XII in 1951. As early as 1952, Gerald Kelly proposed that "four or five children" would normally constitute fulfillment of this duty, at least in the United States. That number might rise or fall in the future, depending on population trends, which were obviously relevant to what was required for "conservation of the race."[53] (Kelly was writing, it should be noted, prior to popular panic about too-rapid population growth; by 1963, he was speaking in terms of three or four children per family.[54]) It would be "ideal," in Kelly's view, for a couple to have more than five

Figure 6. Five children, according to Gerald Kelly, S.J., would normally fulfill a couple's obligation to procreate. These exemplary parents also took seriously their duty to oversee the religious education of their children. Photo courtesy of the American Catholic History Research Center and University Archives, Catholic University.

children—though not, he hastened to add, where additional pregnancies would be medically hazardous or financially ruinous to the family. But even a healthy and affluent couple who had already borne five children was not required to have more. Having done their procreative duty, they might in good conscience practice rhythm for the rest of their fertile lives. A sufficient number of moralists agreed with Kelly's logic as to render it eminently "probable," in the view of John Ford and many others.[55] This meant that the faithful might safely proceed according to his counsel.

The second noteworthy development concerns the dangers that rhythm allegedly posed to marital happiness. Priests had long worried that its practice would unduly frustrate husbands, disposing them to masturbation or even infidelity. But most had not been worried in principle about sexual abstinence in marriage, the practice of which was widely believed to be a commendable spiritual discipline. By the 1950s, however, many younger clergy were subscribing to a positive theology of marriage—one that stressed the importance of frequent sexual intercourse. "The marital act is the most important way by which a husband and wife express their mutual love," as Father George Kelly explained in his 1958 *Catholic Marriage Manual.* The sexual droughts prescribed by rhythm clearly compromised a couple's ability to express that love with requisite generosity. "It is not natural that they should consult the calendar before deciding whether to carry their spontaneous relations to the natural conclusion." When they did have sex, this most intimate species of spousal communion might be experienced by rhythm's practitioners primarily in terms of physical release, at the palpable expense of affection and tenderness. One or both partners might eventually come to feel "open or unconscious resentment" toward the other, even permanent bitterness at what was seen as coldness or sexual rationing. "Practicing rhythm is particularly inadvisable for young couples," as Kelly advised, echoing many others. "During the early years of marriage, the emotional and physical needs for intercourse are at their greatest."[56]

It was easy for Kelly to raise such objections, given his obvious ambivalence about rhythm generally. Deeply conservative when it came to gender, he believed that large families should be the Catholic norm. Wholehearted clerical proponents of rhythm had more trouble on this score, since they too championed a positive view of marital sex. Some simply denied that its practice resulted in significant frustration, typically claiming for the method a greater certainty than experience warranted. Others conceded the problem but emphasized its fleeting nature. In the not-too-distant future, the method would be so substantially refined that couples would not normally have to abstain for more than a few days. But even these reluctant critics reinforced a growing anxiety about rhythm and the health of marriage. The fear was inseparable from the positive rhetoric that Catholic leaders increasingly deployed to talk about marital sex, the "spiritual and emotional aspects" of which, to borrow from Father George Kelly, were key to the meaning of marriage.[57]

Such lyrical talk about marital sex was bound in the nature of things to undermine its anti-contraceptive purposes. If regular, loving, and spontaneous sex was essential to the health of marriage, would reliable contraception not seem to be indicated—especially when a couple had already been blessed with several children? Given the prevailing age at marriage and the robust health of the typical young American, would not such a sexual program result—absent reliable contraception—in a good many very large families? "For the couple married in their early twenties, who meet with no great obstacles in having and rearing children, it is quite normal for the number of children born to their union to range between eight and twelve," in the blunt but honest words of Father Lawrence Lovasik, still dubious about rhythm's employment in 1962.[58] Few laity, needless to say, were eager to raise so large a brood; nor did most see the prospect as economically feasible, given the period's increased expectations with regard to extended schooling. If rhythm indeed posed a threat to marital happiness, as a swelling chorus of putative experts claimed that it did, what recourse was left to the conscientious Catholic? Was serious injury to one's marriage—the principal venue, after all, where most laity worked out their salvation—any less a violation of God's law than the prayerful, responsible use of, say, the anovular Pill?

Talk about fulfilling one's duty to procreate also had inadvertent affinities to contraceptive logic, though these are much less obvious. To speak the language of projected family size, as men like Gerald Kelly were doing, was to talk—however unwittingly—in a mode long familiar to Planned Parenthood. To attempt the spacing of one's offspring is, psychologically speaking, quite different from planning the births of a specified number of children—a goal that might well be achieved long before the end of a woman's fertile years. A good many Catholics in the postwar years were already behaving according to the norms of late modernity, producing a desired number of children and then simply stopping, usually by forbidden contraceptive means. But many more, at least in the 1950s, operated quite differently, using rhythm or bouts of abstinence to space a family whose ultimate size was unknown. Behavior like this, which most Catholics eventually abandoned, had little support beyond an increasingly permeable Catholic subculture. So it made a difference, if at first a largely subliminal one, when eminent moralists endorsed what was in effect a "stopping" approach to family limitation—so many children and then no more. That rhythm was seldom sufficiently reliable to guarantee such results was a separate problem, though hardly one that the Catholic laity could ignore.

Official Church support for rhythm peaked in the first half of the 1960s. The Diocese of Buffalo opened a rhythm clinic in 1961, followed a year later by the first of numerous rhythm conferences held in Chicago under the auspices of the Catholic Family Information Service—a lay-run organization with the wholehearted backing of Cardinal Albert Meyer.[59] Similar clinic-type programs were operating by 1965 in some thirty American dioceses.[60] Clerical voices were heard, as early as 1960, calling for private and government funds to underwrite a massive program of rhythm research. "With half the money and energy spent on trying to perfect 'The Pill,'" the Paulist Louis McKernan told readers of the *Catholic World* in that year, "the rhythm system could, according to informed medical opinion, be perfected rather quickly."[61] Father John A. O'Brien, a proponent of rhythm since the early 1930s, spoke glowingly of the method on a national telecast in 1962—the ostensible subject was "Birth Control and the Law"—and likewise urged federal support for research into its refinement.[62] The Family Life Bureau of the NCWC convened an International Symposium on Rhythm in 1964, precisely to spur such research and to publicize hopeful new findings. Among the latter, according to the Bureau's priest director, was clinical proof "that the form of Rhythm which uses the basal body temperature method has the same degree of effectiveness as the contraceptive pill."[63] No wonder John Ford was convinced, even in 1962, that rhythm's critics had been routed. "I'm working on rhythm," as he wrote to Gerald Kelly, his coauthor on the then-in-progress *Contemporary Moral Theology,* "and we certainly don't have to be afraid to say that we don't think it's mortal[ly sinful] to practice it without reasons. In fact we would be safe in playing down the affirmative obligation [to procreate], I think."[64]

This surge in high-profile support for rhythm was largely explained by three developments: obsessive popular anxiety about overpopulation, commercial advent of the anovular pill, and a newly public lay restiveness with regard to the teaching on contraception. The resulting climate was hardly one where a quietly permissive rhythm policy would suffice. Church leaders, in effect, were forced to enter the contraceptive lists—to offer a Catholic alternative to the Pill that promised in the near term to perform as effectively. Almost no one outside the Catholic camp believed that this was possible; growing numbers of Catholics doubted it, too, and were willing to say so publicly. Rhythm's seemingly definitive triumph, then, was really the moment of Catholic capitulation, when even moderate Catholic leaders embraced the opposition's agenda, at least when it came to marital sex. The Church is not "opposed to the regulation of offspring," as Father John A. O'Brien assured a national television audience early in 1964. "On the contrary, the church stresses the need for responsible parenthood, which is but another name for family planning." The means to such planning, as O'Brien duly insisted, had to conform to the natural law. But nature herself provided a means that was surer and inestimably safer than the vaunted Pill. "A scientific breakthrough that will either pinpoint the time of ovulation several days in advance or will bring about ovulation on a definite day in the middle of each twenty-eight to thirty day cycle is expected at any time." In the meantime, women with severely irregular cycles might in good conscience use the Pill "to regularize the menstrual cycle and thus render periodic abstinence not only more effective but virtually 100 per cent perfect and foolproof."[65]

O'Brien's last-mentioned assertion refers to one of the more ironic twists in rhythm's strange career. Even in the late 1950s, certain Catholic moralists were proposing that the not-yet-marketed Pill might licitly be used to correct menstrual irregularity. It was not wholly certain, they conceded, that the Pill would have this effect long term. But if it did—if taking the Pill for a limited time would result in a permanently regular cycle—then, in the view of some theologians, it might properly be used by women who wanted to practice rhythm but had been unable to do so. The purpose of taking the drug, after all, would not in this instance be directly contraceptive; ovulation might be temporarily suppressed but as the indirect effect of correcting a defective cycle.[66] How long could the Pill be used for this reason? Most moralists set an outside limit of six months, though a certain flexibility was obviously mandated, given physiological unknowns. Father O'Brien, in the above-mentioned broadcast, spoke of taking the pill for "as long as necessary."[67] Certain moralists also proposed, again as early as the late 1950s, that the Pill might also be used to guarantee sterility during lactation—a time when the effective practice of rhythm was virtually impossible. Nature intended this interlude to be sterile, according to Canon Louis Janssens, a prominent Belgian theologian. "If the natural mechanism was in default," then the Pill might legitimately be used to correct the defect.[68]

A sufficient number of moralists had endorsed the first-mentioned position by the early 1960s as to render it solidly "probable." (The use of the Pill during lactation was more problematic, since its direct purpose was the suppression of ovulation.[69]) So priests were free to suggest, in those inevitably many cases where rhythm had not worked, that short-term use of the Pill might rectify matters, or to bless this solution should it be proposed by a well-read member of the laity.[70] How many priests actually did so? That is obviously impossible to know. But some clearly did, especially among the younger clergy, many of whom were beginning to question—if only privately—the absolute nature of the prohibition on contraception. Thus an unknown number of Catholic women had their first experience of the Pill with priestly approval and even at priestly behest. A great many more were presumably aware that such a thing was possible, since the secular media were devoting unprecedented attention to the intra-Catholic politics of birth control.

The logic behind such use of the Pill was easily misunderstood—it was virtually incomprehensible to non-Catholics—and the plausible stuff of derisory humor. But it was ultimately no more paradoxical than rhythm itself, as the method's more prescient critics had long understood. The defense of rhythm, after all, was defense of deliberately non-procreative sex. The more public and generous that defense, the harder it was to explain why, short of abortion, other means to the same non-procreative end were not acceptable, too. "Very few Catholics understand this reasoning," a Baltimore priest acknowledged, "and most have to make an act of faith if they want to follow the Church in her stand."[71]

Premarital Instruction and Marriage Education

Catholic leaders in the 1940s and '50s paid greatly enhanced attention to premarital instruction, spurred in good part by a sense of crisis with regard to the health of the family. "The spirit of materialism has so far infected our Catholic young women that the ideal of Christian Marriage had in some instances been completely lost and in a great many more had been alarmingly weakened," as the Brooklyn Diocesan Council of Catholic Women explained its cosponsorship of a marriage education program for "girls" aged sixteen and over that began in 1945. "The increase in divorce among Catholics, the increase in birth control, were stark evidences of this fact."[72] Bishops in every part of the country, even the most remote, clearly felt new pressure to ensure that every soon-to-be married couple received adequate instruction from a priest, including an explanation of the Church's teaching on contraception. In a growing number of dioceses, couples were asked to swear obedience to Church teaching on birth control and divorce. Many of the more populous dioceses developed new programs for the engaged, where priests and sometimes lay couples presented the Catholic perspective on marriage more thoroughly and attractively than ever before. Birth control figured prominently in these venues, too. "Here is the straight goods on the marriage act, on conception and contraception, on rhythm pro and con," a priest approvingly noted of a pilot premarital program in Brooklyn in 1949. "The straight goods, more inspiring and of more lasting value simply because it is so plain-spoken and practical."[73]

The reader will recall that Chicago's Cardinal George Mundelein, by way of endorsing *Casti Connubii,* required as of 1932 that Catholics marrying in his archdiocese solemnly promise to refrain from "birth control practices."[74] Other bishops at the time were apparently reluctant to follow suit, at least in precipitous fashion. But by the early 1940s, Mundelein's policy was apparently being widely adopted, though initially in some locales only with regard to religiously mixed marriages.[75] By 1947, the *American Ecclesiastical Review* was casually referring to the item on birth control "usually found in the pre-marital questionnaire."[76] The wording of such questions may have varied from diocese to diocese, though the purpose was invariably that articulated by Peoria's Bishop Joseph Schlarman: "Both parties must promise they will lead a married life in conformity with the teaching of the Catholic Church regarding birth control; fully realizing the attitude of the Catholic church in this regard."[77] Both spouses-to-be were questioned separately on this and other issues, and ultimately obliged to swear to the truth of their statements. "They separately and solemnly swear with their hand on the Bible that they are free to marry and, not being coerced in any way, that they will not practice birth control, etc.," as Joseph Fichter explained the practice in what was probably the Archdiocese of New Orleans.[78]

The bishops who moved in this direction were motivated largely by worries about Catholic contraceptive use. (A 1941 Vatican instruction on the necessity of premarital questionnaires left the issue of contraception to the discretion of individual ordinaries, who might include or omit its mention as local conditions seemed to warrant.[79]) At the very least, such a policy required priests— not all of them eager for the job—to address the issue of birth control in the course of premarital instruction. That couples had to swear obedience to the teaching lent its presentation an aura of seriousness, even of urgency. Certainly it discouraged dissent, at least in the rectory parlor: when even one of the parties refused to so swear, in the view of certain authoritative moralists, the couple could not be married in the Church without a bishop's permission.[80] Perhaps the wording of the question itself sometimes eased lay consciences, though most young laity did not think like casuists. A form in use as of 1960 in the Diocese of Saginaw, Michigan, seems to afford a certain wiggle room: "Do you know that the primary purpose of marriage, as ordained by God, is the procreation and education of children? Do you intend to enter this marriage with such a purpose?" Was the Saginaw wording typical of other dioceses— Saginaw not then being distinguished by a liberal bishop or other relevant marks of singularity? Was it found in Saginaw much earlier than 1960? Since documents of this sort are rarely available in diocesan archives, I simply cannot say. The Saginaw document, perhaps tellingly, permits no wiggle room at all when it comes to remarriage after divorce: "Do you realize that you cannot marry again, once you have contracted this marriage, unless death dissolve the bond?"[81]

Faced with a probably blushing couple, how frankly did priests address the embarrassing subject of birth control? Most found it hard to speak in anything approaching clinical terms, preferring the more familiar language of theological precept. "These are not sex instructions," as Joseph Fichter explained of the premarital talks given at the southern parish where he spent a year in sociological observation, "except in so far as they deal with the morality of sex relations."[82] Priests had necessarily to explain the Church's stand on contraception, though many apparently did so in the arcane terms of the natural law or simply by reference to the Church's authority. They had also to instruct the couple in their mutual obligation to render the so-called marital debt—to consent to a spouse's reasonable requests for sexual intercourse. In this limited sense the subject of sex could not be avoided. That subject, however, was usually confined to the last of the two or three meetings that typically constituted individual premarital instruction. Some priests even preferred to deliver this delicate sermonette in the relative anonymity of the confessional on the very eve of the wedding. So while birth control now figured in premarital instruction more widely and prominently than ever before, that instruction still possessed—at least in a good many cases—an oddly evasive quality. The couple was reminded of a prohibition about which they already knew, at least in broad outline, and reminded quite forcefully of their Catholic obligation to observe it. But they were not necessarily enlightened with regard to the logic on which that prohibition rested.

There were certainly those who wished to go further, especially among the younger clergy. Premarital instruction, in the view of such men, was an excellent venue for imparting a genuinely Christian approach to sex—for enlarging on its spiritual meaning in the context of generous procreation. But inexperience all around—assumed of the couple as well as the priest—made plain speaking very hard, sometimes impossibly so. He and his seminary classmates were told that they ought to give premarital instruction, as Monsignor Vincent Howard recalled with a certain incredulity, "but we were never [pause]—it wasn't even hinted to us what we ought to be saying to them."[83] Better, in the circumstances, to find a helpful booklet that could do the job instead. One apparently popular candidate was *Happiness in Marriage: An Ethico-Medical Interpretation,* a succinct but eminently useful guide to the basics of intercourse that also explained—in plausibly pragmatic terms—why birth control was wrong. The booklet's central message, however, was the good of marital sex. "A moment's reflection will convince the reader that the exercise of marital rights by proper intercourse is altogether pure and honorable." Catholic couples had a right to know what would make for joyous and mutually satisfying sex—information that *Happiness in Marriage* was unabashedly aimed at providing. Couples should take their lovemaking seriously, striving for the ultimate goal of simultaneous orgasm. Patience was called for in this regard, and candor, too. "At a later time let them discuss those things that each notices might be done to improve their performance. . . . It is necessary that both husband and wife take a genuine interest in their love-union: a matter of far greater moment than their meals or purses."[84]

Happiness in Marriage was issued anonymously and without a publication date, though it was almost certainly a product of the later 1940s. Two of my interviewees from the Archdiocese of Detroit, ordained respectively in 1945 and 1947, remembered using the booklet prior to its Vatican condemnation in the spring of 1952 and finding it extremely helpful.[85] (Their memories came without my prompting, in response to a general question about premarital instruction.) The Vatican condemnation was issued by the Holy Office, evidently because of the booklet's sexual frankness. The pope himself, in the ironic context of his famous talk to the Italian Catholic Society of Midwives, had already expressed grave reservations about literature of this sort, especially when it was distributed under Catholic auspices. "Do your best to stop the diffusion of literature that thinks it is a duty to describe in full detail the intimacy of conjugal life under the pretext of instructing, directing and reassuring," as he told his immediate audience and a broader one, too—the latter made up of bishops and priests.[86] The clergy were thus abruptly deprived of an evidently useful tool for making premarriage instruction more relevant to the lived experience of the laity. Perhaps in the end it hardly mattered, though it would probably be fairer to say that it mattered more to priests than the laity. *Happiness in Marriage,* while admirably humane, was simply unable to address the problem eventually confronted by most devout Catholics. Sexual satisfaction in marriage was nearly always compromised, sometimes sooner rather than later, by worries about excess fertility.

What filled the gap for many priests were diocesan programs for the engaged, the earliest of which date from the Second World War. Detroit inaugurated such a program in 1943, its priest director later claiming that it was the first in the country.[87] By 1947, the Archdiocese of Chicago had a burgeoning program of this sort, which included a "day of recollection," followed by three evening sessions.[88] The Chicago program had evolved out of Cana Conference, a swiftly growing and mostly lay-led movement that aimed at the Christianization of family life. As Cana Conferences proliferated, so-called Pre-Cana programs nearly always developed in their wake. Thirty-six dioceses by 1950 reported the existence of such, when the closely linked movements were still expanding rapidly.[89] The large urban dioceses were particularly well represented among the early Pre-Cana enthusiasts, including Brooklyn, Baltimore, Cincinnati, New York, Milwaukee, and St. Louis, as well as the aforementioned Detroit and Chicago. By the second half of the 1950s, nearly every American diocese had a program for the engaged, some of them very large. Many pastors by then required attendance at courses of this sort for every soon-to-be married couple in their respective parishes.

The content of such programs was invariably based on a lyrically positive theology of marriage. "Young engaged couples have many fears—about housing, about high costs, about war, about too many children, about material security," a priest pioneer in the movement explained. "They must be told again and again that God is just as interested in them and their vocation as He is in priests and nuns."[90] Rather than trafficking in prohibitions, Pre-Cana spoke the language of high aspirations. "Marriage will make you better men and women and give you new ways to love one another and to be good to one another," as priests in Chicago told innumerable gatherings of generally very young couples. "Because marriage will make you better, it will also bring you closer to

God." Truly Christian couples grew in holiness as their marriages progressed; their love deepened with the passage of time and especially the birth of children. And no matter what trials they encountered in their supremely noble vocation as spouses, the lives of truly Christian couples were suffused with serenity and joy—the happy fruits of their having transcended the culturally sanctioned temptations of selfishness and greed. Genuinely Christian households were "domestic churches"—islands of holiness in a sea of materialism, beacons of hope to a jaded world. "You will discover how your love can comfort and inspire each other," Chicago's Pre-Cana attendees were confidently assured. "You will taste the anxious joys of new parenthood with all its new responsibilities; and you will see with new clearness that sanctity makes sense because it is the basis of your home life."[91]

Pre-Cana priests were hardly the first to speak of marriage as a route to sanctity. But this venerable Christian theme had not loomed large, especially prior to the Second World War, in American Catholic preaching on marriage or in the hurried encounters that often passed for premarital instruction. Pre-Cana exposed unprecedented numbers of young Catholics to an attractive logic, novel to many, and did so with warmth and congenial informality. Pre-Cana was also remarkably frank when it came to sex, which played a central role in the drama of conjugal sanctity. The standard Pre-Cana program nearly always included at least one talk by a medical doctor, who addressed the men and women separately on reproductive physiology and the mechanics of intercourse. A married couple also spoke at nearly every conference, though this was not standard in certain dioceses until the mid-1950s. They too addressed the question of sex, and in terms that purported to be deeply personal. What had they learned as a couple about the meaning of sex in marriage? The answer was always rendered in accents of tender idealism: intercourse "is an expression of married love at every level of the human personality, the unity of body, mind, soul," as Chicago's Pre-Cana proposed in its model outline for the couple's talk.[92] Priest presenters embraced a similarly positive rhetoric. "Do not be afraid of your passion, do not be ashamed of it," in the words of a typical priest's talk from Chicago, where Pre-Cana clergy often worried that some of their hearers were unhealthily repressed. "Your bodies will respond to each other, and this is as it should be; give yourselves to each other." The authentically Christian attitude toward sex was one of "frank reverence. Our bodies are good and beautiful; using them as God intends us to is wholesome and indeed sacred."[93]

The marital sex so earnestly celebrated—this use of our bodies as God intended—was emphatically non-contraceptive, as every Pre-Cana Conference made clear. The Church's teaching was always invoked, typically in terms that echoed the romantic idealism surrounding Pre-Cana's discussions of sex. "In general: do not present just a negative approach—no birth control, no divorce, no promiscuity—but a very positive approach, making the ideal very attractive and desirable, showing that children are not penalties but *included* in the object of mature conjugal love," as Chicago Pre-Cana, whose literature was used in many dioceses, advised its priest presenters.[94] Procreative sex meant trust in God and joyous embrace of His purposes—a triumph over selfishness, materialism, and fear. It meant speaking the language of perfect communion with one's body—holding nothing back from the beloved in the realm of flesh or spirit. "Accept marriage as God made it—a life-long, faithful, creative love affair," as Chicago's priests urged, "and He will make you happier than you can imagine."[95] Pre-Cana participants accepted such counsels with apparent docility, though they did ask regularly about rhythm, the use of which was discouraged in the early years of marriage.[96] Their own fertility as yet happily untested, engaged couples had no immediate reason to challenge Pre-Cana's logic when it came to birth control, save perhaps for those who expected the wife to continue her paid employment. This was something else that Pre-Cana's leaders actively discouraged.[97]

The situation was quite different in Catholic programs for the married, which also proliferated widely in the postwar years. The largest and most influential were the previously mentioned Cana Conference and the Christian Family Movement, both of which date—for all practical purposes—from the mid-1940s. Cana was the more conventionally educational of the two, primarily oriented to the support of a distinctively Catholic family life by means of retreat-like group programs and the sponsoring of local clubs, where five to six couples, meeting regularly, discussed their particular problems and needs with regard to Christian living. The Christian Family Movement, as it was called as of 1950, thought in somewhat broader terms: the problems of individual families could not be fully addressed without simultaneously addressing societal patterns of injustice. Members of the CFM, as it was generally known, met regularly in small groups, too, just like the more active members of Cana. But they were as apt to discuss the wrongs of racial segregation as topics like "the Mass and the family"—a perennial Cana favorite. CFM couples, however, were still deeply committed to modeling Christian virtue in their individual family lives, a project that necessarily included wholehearted adherence to the Church's stand on contraception. Like their Cana counterparts, most CFM couples eventually struggled with problems of excess fertility. How to live the gospel of sacralized sex, as central to the CFM as it was to Cana, when fears of yet another pregnancy haunted every marital embrace?

The members of both groups were highly educated and reasonably affluent, which does much to explain their insistence on strong and at least nominally independent lay leadership.[98] In both organizations, small-group meetings were led by "presider-couples," with the chaplain—should he be present— permitted to speak only at the meeting's conclusion. Many members were also

Figure 7. The family rosary, a favored devotion in the postwar years for couples active in Cana Conference and the Christian Family Movement. Photo courtesy of the American Catholic History Research Center and University Archives, Catholic University.

intensely idealistic—bent, in a startling number of cases, on lives of heroic sanctity. The mostly young priests who served these movements were attractive idealists, too, and often endorsed their constituents' high spiritual ambitions. "We had as a Spiritual Director a young, newly-ordained, idealistic priest," a Michigan woman recalled of her first encounter with CFM in the late 1950s, when she and her husband had six children. "He recommended our *not* using Rhythm. This quite suited our plans to live an 'extra-special' life for Christ."[99] Several Cana groups in Milwaukee by the late 1940s had organized around the idea "that they want to have as many children as possible," as an admiring priest explained, "that God is going to plan their family, and that they need to get together to give each other social approval, trade ideas about

[C]hristian attitudes in the home, and material help." These zealous couples somehow found time to print a proselytizing newsletter and sustain a cooperative-buying scheme for infant food and supplies.[100] Both Cana and CFM, in consequence, were suffused by a kind of competitive natalism. "In our first group in L.A.," a CFM veteran remembered, "we were all newly married and each of us seemed to have a baby in turn. There was a really fierce competitive spirit"—something that she felt especially acutely when medical problems forced her to "drop out of the race" after only three births.[101]

Both groups approached the subject of marital sex with the same intense idealism, and perhaps a subliminal competitiveness, too. Lovemaking is "intended to be prayer," in the typical words of a couple from Washington, D.C. It is "intended by God to be a step toward union with Him—a giant step toward heaven."[102] Husbands and wives, according to the oft-repeated language of the Chicago Cana manual, "should realize [that] the marriage act is a source of grace."[103] Lack of sexual satisfaction was a principal cause of unhappiness in marriage, according to a longtime Cana priest presenter, who regularly lamented in his talks the "statistics" that "tell us that 50 percent of women do not experience full satisfaction in the marriage act." Only "1 out of 5 experience satisfaction consistently"—a particular sadness, given that "the marriage act" was meant to be "a means of grace and merit."[104] Surrounded by talk like this, the frustrations attendant on rhythm or sustained periods of abstinence were especially hard to endure and, increasingly, hard to justify, though anxieties on this latter score were seldom aired publicly prior to the 1960s. A relatively young widow spoke for many of her contemporaries when, in 1964, she finally reflected for public consumption on fifteen years of carefully rationed sex: "Now that he is gone from me for the rest of my days I look back and wonder if all this self-denial of the expression of the deep passion we held for each other was so right. It seems that I spent those years wishing for the later years when there would be no question of consequences."[105]

But whatever their private tribulations, most Cana and CFM couples stayed loyal to their shared procreative ideology. Those who could no longer abide by its tenets simply left the group. "It is no solution for a Catholic of vital persuasion to try to save himself or his wife or his marriage by using proscribed methods of birth control," as a Catholic college professor explained in 1963. "You make up in guilt and fear what you save in babies."[106] The fear of hell was indeed at work, despite—or perhaps because of—the high educational status of the Catholics in question. But devotion to principle was a factor, too. These were couples, as one of their number described them, who "would like, without planning, to welcome every child as a unique expression of their love"—for whom "not planning" was a core ideal.[107] "It is as if parents of large broods have a tangible proof of their own inner strength, worth, trust in God, what have you that those of lesser numbers lack," in the rueful words of a CFM activist, who was finally after "many years" dispelling what she now described as "the silly romantic notions of adolescence."[108] This obviously intelligent woman was not held in thrall to the ideal simply because of her own immaturity, though the explanation was a popular one in the 1960s. She had been drawn to its almost breathtaking generosity and to the models of Christian virtue that it so obviously inspired. Milwaukee's Father John Michael Murphy, ordained in 1945, still remembers with something approaching awe the determination of a former seminary classmate—one who left prior to ordination—to let God plan his nascent family. The decision eventually resulted in twelve children. "Just imagine it. It's almost what's at the bottom of the mystics: whatever You say, I say thank you for. It's a complete release of all control, except the will of God. . . . I'm not there yet."[109]

Couples like the ones just mentioned were not typical Catholics, even in the domesticated 1950s. But the values they embodied had far-reaching effect, not only on other lay Catholics but many priests as well—especially the more consciously pastoral. That the prohibition on contraception could transcend the merely negative, that it could be intimately associated with other than ascetic virtues and demonstrable happiness in the here-and-now—this was a great boon to priests who were not for the most part eager to impose excessively heavy burdens on their people. The impact on the laity was generally more ambiguous. It was good to see the married state honored by priests and even bishops to an extent that was genuinely new. Truly Christian marriage was now extolled, at least by clergy in family life ministry, as fully equal to the celibate's vocation and just as apostolic. The resulting lay feistiness was readily apparent at any Cana or CFM gathering. "It was quite a revelation to me, used as I am to talking to people of meagre [*sic*] education who prefer just to listen," in the words of rather shaken Redemptorist, who had just preached his first Cana conference in 1948. "It seemed to me that your group gathers rather to assert itself."[110] But spiritual heroism among the laity had its downside, too, at least for those many Catholics who were not prepared to live accordingly. It was one thing to flout Church teaching on the grounds that a celibate clergy knew nothing about the realities of marriage, quite another to fail a test of virtue that certain of one's fellow parishioners had passed with evident aplomb.

By thus encouraging the clergy and stimulating guilt among many of their less-committed contemporaries, this spiritual elite among the laity—articulate and highly visible—gave extended life in the postwar years to the Catholic teaching on contraception. Their eventual defection from the teaching, something that dates from the mid-1960s, was equally consequential. The accelerating defections were caused by societal change as well as the amply compelling reality of too many children. Highly educated Catholics like these were particularly prey to period worries about overpopulation. The women among them were often attracted to the period's nascent feminism, which proceeded according to quite different assumptions from the world of domestic sanctity. "Woman's essential mission in the world is to be to mankind a living example of the spirit of total dedication to God," in the typical words of a Cana discussion outline, this one from Washington, D.C. "This complete surrender of self to God is the pattern of her place in the home."[111] Such couples were also wholly committed to sexual fulfillment in marriage, which they embraced—as we have seen—for religious as well as secular reasons. Not for them the solution of Catholic lore where, in the words of Boston's Monsignor George Casey, "dad was resolutely thrust out of the bedroom and that was that."[112] "To live a continent marriage is, to us, no marriage at all," as a mother of seven explained in 1965, when she had just gone on the Pill.[113] She was indeed a product of her society, but also of change in the postwar Church, at least some of whose priests now agreed with her—about continent marriage if not the Pill—and were willing to say so.

Few Catholics were ready, prior to the mid-1960s, to make such statements publicly. By the time most felt able to do so, a great deal of bitterness had accumulated, perhaps especially among the devout, many of whom had built their lives around a teaching that no longer made sense to them. It was hardly surprising that some should feel an acute sense of betrayal—of having been sold, in effect, a romanticized and inherently contradictory bill of goods. "His dilemma is that many moral demands, of seemingly equal weight, are made on him at once," as Michael Novak explained in 1964 of the "married layman," who wished to be true to his simultaneous callings as spousal lover and responsible parent. "It is not aberrant good will but frustrated good will which sometimes fatigues him and introduces him to bitterness." Though the Second Vatican Council was even then in session, the subject of family planning had been removed from its agenda and faced an uncertain future. The frustrated "layman"—and presumably his wife—was thereby immersed in a situation of "enforced dishonesty." The solution, in Novak's view, was for the laity to begin to speak "as frankly and as clearly as they can of what Catholic marriage is as they have come to know it."[114]

Novak was right. It was indeed the laity's willingness to speak publicly that ultimately caused change to happen—change in Catholic thought and behavior if not a formal change in Church teaching. The flood of frank lay talk that began to rise in 1964 created a new world for Catholics—for the hitherto timorous laity, their priests, and even their bishops, almost none of whom had been aware that a crisis over birth control was in the offing. "I see very little evidence that our Bishops and priests realize that for the vast majority of Catholic married couples the most serious moral problems revolve around the questions of rhythm and birth control," a *Commonweal* contributor rightly asserted in 1962, in an article prompted by hopes for the upcoming ecumenical council.[115]

(The writer was tellingly unwilling to call for a change in the teaching. He spoke instead of more money for rhythm research.) Given the volume and significance of lay talk in the mid-1960s, it is easy to ignore the talk that came before, which mostly took the form of occasional letters to Catholic publications concerned with marriage and family life—magazines like *The Sign, The Grail* (later *Marriage*), and especially *The Liguorian*. But the limited talk of the 1950s was in fact a force for change, and intimately connected to the flood of debate that followed. So it behooves us to listen to these mostly forgotten voices, if only to remind ourselves that the Church of the later 1960s did not spring de novo from the Council. Like nearly every revolution, it was the product of incremental change.

The Laity Begin to Speak

Catholic periodicals prior to the mid-1950s carried very few letters or lay-authored features on the subject of family limitation. What little appeared came mostly from the holy foolishness camp. "The world would be a happier and more blessed place if there were more 'Thy Will Be Done' attitudes and less selfish 'planning,'" a California mother of six quite typically told the *Sign* in 1950, responding approvingly to an article called "The Baby-Spacing Legend." It was simply untrue that a woman's health suffered when babies were born less than two years apart; her own six, after all, had been born in as many years.[116] The same issue of the *Sign* carried a mildly dissenting letter, this one from an Oregon mother of three, who noted that articles of the aforementioned sort were invariably "written by men, never the overworked mothers of these large families they advocate." But for all the palpable irritation, hers was hardly a call for deep reform, save perhaps by extreme indirection. "The Church has not condemned the Rhythm system and I believe the person who practices abstinence should be commended. . . . the *Sign* and all Catholic publications should not play up the large family idea so much." Since this Oregon woman defined a large family as one with "more than four children," she was clearly moving toward a personal confrontation with her Church's teaching on contraception.[117] But she was not there yet, or at least not ready to say so publicly.

That even mildly dissenting letters were rare until 1955 does not mean that dissent did not exist. We must not forget the married thirty-somethings who stayed away from the sacraments in significantly larger numbers than other Catholics, as several sociological studies attested. Couples like these were widely assumed to be practicing forbidden modes of contraception—dissenters in terms of behavior if not in the realm of opinion. There is also poll data to suggest that very large numbers of Catholics disagreed with Church teaching, even when they continued to obey it. A 1952 survey done for the

Catholic Digest found that 51 percent of the Catholics questioned did not regard "mechanical birth control" as inherently sinful. The finding was so disturbing to the *Digest*'s priest editor that he declined to publish it, along with an equally distressing response to a question on divorce and remarriage. (Roughly the same percentage disagreed with Church teaching on this matter, too.) "We do think that this information is important enough to be given to Your Excellency," he wrote to Philadelphia's Archbishop John F. O'Hara, who agreed "that the table should not go beyond the Hierarchy." The offending data was apparently later sent to every American bishop, with what effect we simply do not know.[118]

By the mid-1950s, lay views on family planning were making their way into print in notably larger numbers, mainly through readers' letters. These letters were increasingly blunt and increasingly apt to challenge the teaching, though support was plentifully evident, too. Was the increased volume mainly due to a suddenly more outspoken laity? Or were the editors in question, nearly all of them priests, now willing—for the very first time—to countenance such debate? Journalist Daniel Callahan was inclined toward the former explanation, at least from the vantage point of 1964. "Up until about the middle of the fifties there was a remarkable harmony among the ideals of the magisterium, the theologians and the married laity," he asserted, though with reference to "zealous" Catholics only. "A large family was accepted as the norm of a Catholic marriage." By the second half of the decade, as Callahan saw it, even zealous Catholics were beginning to question these assumptions, if only because of too many babies that had come too fast.[119] How to cope, as more and more couples were asking, when three or four of these now-grown babies were simultaneously in college? Perhaps priest editors were also aware of a greater lay restiveness. Silence might not be pastorally prudent if the problem of family planning was generating increased resentment of the Church. "It is good that such letters are written," the priest editors of the *Liguorian* noted of the angry missives they received with regard to birth control, "because they point up a job of instruction that is yet to be done."[120]

Published by the Redemptorist Fathers, the *Liguorian* gave unusually generous space to readers' views on family planning, presumably as an extension of the order's work in mission preaching. Every dissenting letter was accompanied by a corrective rejoinder. Almost no correspondence on this topic appeared before 1955, though the readers' letters feature dated from 1947. After the mid-1950s, however, the magazine regularly carried such, with the volume increasing perceptibly in the early 1960s. Many of the published letters expressed support for the teaching, as did a majority of those that failed to make their way into print—at least according to the editors. A few of the letters in support were mechanically pious. "Our main concern is for our eternal salvation and the necessities of life just come automatically."[121] One or two were distinctly odd, at least in terms of today's expectations. "It was during a novena to Our Mother of Perpetual Help that I was made to realize my need of psychotherapy, which, approved by my confessors, finally resulted in my growing up emotionally."[122] (This in response to a woman who had earlier written about her fears of another pregnancy.) But most such letters were sincere affirmations of a teaching that the writers were obviously living, often enough in daunting circumstances. A truculent self-righteousness did sometimes diminish their impact as lay-authored "sermons." The most candid, however, were genuinely moving—a source of reproach, one imagines, to a reader on the brink of disobedience, but of inspiration, too.

It was the dissenting letters, however, that took the palm for passion and seemingly for honesty, though the anger of some correspondents made for hyperbolic moments. Most *Liguorian* readers, a solidly middle-class lot, were devout Catholics or had at least been raised that way. They tended, in consequence, to be guilt-wracked dissenters—a condition that occasionally gave rise to fierce jeremiads against the clergy. "How can you know anything about our problems?" demanded a particularly choleric correspondent from Maine in 1958, a man who had left the Church over birth control. "Living fat, smug and complacent in a nice, large, warm rectory, with no more worries than whether the car will start when you want to go for a ride! What do you know of the bills that confront a man and wife when they are trying to take care of several children?"[123] A California mother pregnant with her third made the point more gently but with far greater effectiveness. "You take a vow of poverty," as she pointed out to the *Liguorian*'s Redemptorist editors in 1959, "but have everything provided for you." Your admittedly busy existence, moreover, is ordered and fundamentally tranquil: "You have everything nicely scheduled—meals, prayers, chapel exercises, recreation on time." Life was very different for young parents. "My husband returns home from work to find a disorderly home, a sick wife, and crying babies." He "hasn't sat down to relax for a long time."[124]

Most dissenting letters to the *Liguorian* spoke the language of experience—very much in the spirit of the one just quoted. This is precisely what gave them their power. We simply can't afford more children, even ignoring the eventual costs of college, many writers asserted—proceeding at their most effective to offer persuasive, if mundane, details. "He is a ready worker," a twenty-nine-year-old mother of six young children noted of her husband, "and over the years he has given up fishing, hunting, his occasional beer, barber shop haircuts, and now cigarettes, to save money for the children."[125] Nor can we adequately nurture our children when the babies come too fast. "Does it bring a pleasant picture to your mind to think of a mother of four or more feeding an infant in arms while a year-old baby sits at her feet begging to be held?" demanded a Michigan woman in 1955.[126] There were ample complaints about rhythm, too, both with regard to its efficacy and the strains it often placed on the couple's relationship. "I have had seven children within eight years, despite frantic and distressing efforts to follow rhythm on many occasions," a mother wrote in 1960. "It seems unjust that we who have accepted the responsibilities of marriage should have to practice continence."[127] As for priests who prescribed prayer and the sacraments for the strength to endure such trials, they were wildly impractical—at least in the view of an overburdened Colorado woman writing in 1958. "We cannot possibly take time out for Mass, rosary, other prayers, to alleviate the suffering of giving up our expressions of love. If we took time out for one half hour of extra devotions a day, we would not have time to feed the children."[128]

Experience was a language that was hard for priests to counter. Their rejoinders were typically couched in abstractions—the demands of the natural law, the teaching authority of the Church—and increasingly contested abstractions, at that. "I can't believe what the Church says about birth-control, when the proof of what not being able to space children a little means is before me every day," as a despairing mother put it bluntly in 1955.[129] Her four children had been conceived in fewer than five years. Clerical logic, moreover, allowed no room for exceptions, which could easily make priests seem heartless. Even gentle confessors, as we shall see, came in for their share of resentment in the early-to-mid 1960s, mainly from devout penitents who wanted explicit permission to use the Pill—something that most liberal clergy still felt unable to give. The large population of many Catholic parishes often compounded the problem, with troubled laity feeling that their problems were simply unreal to a clergy who did not necessarily know them by name. "Our two priests know us only slightly," in the typical words of a guilty young mother who had turned to contraception after six births in close succession. The year was 1957. "This is a huge parish and they are overworked. I would tell them our problem but I know their answer already."[130]

In circumstances such as these, the growing boldness of the laity was of vast potential consequence. Dissident laity like the ones just quoted were making the case for experience—for its legitimacy as a resource in moral decision making and even the building of moral systems. By speaking publicly, they helped to validate the private trials of hitherto silent laity: such putatively private troubles, the dissidents argued, had to be taken into account when it came to moral deliberation. Abstractions alone would not suffice. Would it not be "a lesser evil" to practice birth control, as a correspondent asked the *Liguorian*'s editors in 1961, "and preserve a happy home, peace of mind and mental equilibrium," rather than "to struggle through raising a family when you are depressed, scared of becoming pregnant, and in tears much of the time[?]"[131] The editors answered in predictable fashion: mortal sin could never be justified, no matter what the circumstances; God never sends trials without sending the graces needed to overcome them. "He may ask for a form of modified martyrdom, as He Himself was martyred for us all; He never makes sin inescapable."[132] But the very posing of the question suggested a different moral equation. Perhaps God is found, at least for the married laity, precisely in "a happy home"; perhaps only the married laity know what is needed for its creation in their individual circumstances. "Parents have to gauge what they can bear with the grace the Lord gives them," as a lay writer had earlier noted, in the unlikely precincts of the Jesuit's *America*. "For happy, healthy parents give glory to God, too."[133]

The process of change in the Church was greatly accelerated by the Second Vatican Council, the first session of which convened late in 1962. Among its many effects was a further emboldening of the laity, whose willingness to speak publicly on marriage and marital sex grew exponentially in the mid-1960s. Their talk, as already noted, was a major cause of change, not only in Catholic thinking but Catholic practice, too. By the mid-1960s, even devout couples were turning to forbidden modes of contraception, though not necessarily without residual guilt, despite what was in many cases the tacit permission of a priest. The clergy, for their part, were increasingly troubled, particularly the liberals among them. With the Church still formally opposed to contraception, how far could one go as a confessor or counselor? What did one do with the scrupulous penitent who insisted on more than tacit permission? The bishops were conflicted, too, simultaneously aware of a pastoral crisis but loyal, if not to the teaching itself, then to the authority of Rome. (Many were loyal to the teaching, too, though their numbers had clearly diminished by 1968.) All parties looked eagerly to the pope, many hoping for a change in the teaching, others for revivified leadership with regard to its enforcement. But Paul VI failed to speak, save for occasional ambiguous utterances, during fully five years of accelerating change. By the time he finally did so, in the justly famous *Humanae Vitae,* the gospel of experience had already triumphed, at least in the affluent industrialized countries. The effect of his long-awaited encyclical was mostly the further polarization of an already divided Church.

6

The Church's First Duty Is Charity

The "People Of God" in a Time
of Upheaval, 1962–July 1968

The "Catholic 1960s" began on 11 October 1962, with the formal opening of the Second Vatican Council in Rome. First announced in 1959, the upcoming Council had elicited only mild curiosity from most American Catholics, including the clergy. Few anticipated that the gathering would result in major reform of a Church that prided itself on an alleged imperviousness to change. But the Council, which soon developed into a major media event, proved partly for this reason to be a powerful spur to change in Catholic thought and practice. It was not long before the generality of Catholics were following news about the Council, which many saw—thanks to the tenor of mass media coverage—as a contest between "progressivism" and the unyielding claims of tradition. These perceptions were bolstered by an altered national mood—one increasingly open to reform and increasingly optimistic when it came to the prospects of the activist liberal state. Grateful heirs of the New Deal and the state's largesse in the realm of higher education, American Catholics were for the most part instinctive "progressives"—ready admirers of the new Catholic president and a pope whose populist touch seemed made for a world redefined by television. Increasingly at home in mainstream American culture, they were also less protected from its cult of expressive individualism.

The new climate in Church and nation transformed the nascent debate over marital contraception. Initiated by an educated laity, that debate grew suddenly louder, more public, and more insistent. Priests and especially bishops were initially surprised by this, and increasingly divided in terms of their response. Long-suppressed doubts on the clerical side were finally aired in public, though typically in more guarded terms than those employed by the laity. Was the Church's teaching on contraception adequate to the needs of present-day believers? Did it faithfully reflect the tradition's core wisdom with regard to marriage? "Where lies the answer I wish I knew," as a Baltimore priest told his archbishop in the spring of 1966, when Lawrence Shehan asked his clergy for their assessment of the teaching's impact on pastoral ministry—itself a sign of changing times. "Many Catholics frequently confess that they have used 'illegitimate' means of preventing conception," the priest acknowledged, although "the majority of Catholics who use these illegitimate means feel that they are wrong simply because the Church says that they are." Were such penitents, many of them devout, guilty of serious sin? The priest in question admitted to confusion. "But this I know: the Church's first task and duty is charity, love for her children, especially for the children who dearly love her, who never intend to leave her, yet are trapped in an impossible situation."[1]

Invoking charity was a commonplace of the 1960's debate over contraception. Reformers of every stripe invoked the claims of love over law and the need to be in solidarity with a suffering humanity. "What our times demand is a pastoral approach, demonstrating the love and kindness that flow from our religion," as Cardinal Augustin Bea told the first session of the Council.[2] But the debate over contraception tended by its very nature toward polarization. Proponents of change and their opponents thought in equally absolute terms. Change in the teaching, according to one side, was essential to the happiness, perhaps even the salvation, of countless married Catholics. Change, according to the other, would eviscerate the magisterium—the teaching authority of the Church. Because authority was crucially at issue, with one camp invoking the logic of lay experience and the other the statements of recent popes, the debate transcended the knotty question of sex and its purposes. It was also a debate about the Church—its structures, its claim to infallibility in matters of doctrine and morals, its right to rule dissent out of bounds. Small wonder that the debate grew increasingly shrill, and—like other period contests—was less and less marked by charity. "Schism is a breakdown in patience before it is a conflict of creed," as theologian James Burtchaell wrote in the turbulent wake of *Humanae Vitae*. "And if the Church has at times been dismembered over the date of Easter, over the *filioque*, and even over the preference of grape juice to wine, then the present squabble over contraception is not too trivial to generate the mood and to provide the pretext for schism."[3]

The "Catholic 1960s": The Council and Cultural Change

The Second Vatican Council met in four sessions between October 1962 and December 1965. Prior to its climactic fourth session, the Council's achievements had been relatively modest, apart from reform of the liturgy. With the fourth session came major Council statements on religious liberty, ecumenism, non-Christian religions, and the earthly mission of the Church. Most observers saw in these statements a new mode of Catholic self-understanding—historically informed, Biblically rooted, preeminently pastoral. Council documents spoke of the Church as "the people of God"—an egalitarian image, whatever the intentions of the Council Fathers. The documents also spoke ecumenically: ours is a pilgrim Church, they asserted, in solidarity not only with non-Catholic

Christians, who are kin to us by means of baptism, but also adherents of other faiths. The new language defined an ecclesiology far removed from the juridical model favored by Council traditionalists. Cardinal Alfredo Ottaviani, head of the Vatican's Holy Office and chief among the traditionalists, was not alone in his post-Council fears of "overboldness on the part of the laity," although laity had played no part at all in the Council's formal proceedings.[4] The move from a monarchical language of church to an essentially communal one did indeed enhance the role and status of the laity, as Ottaviani rather gracelessly recognized, and suggested a diminished scope for clerical authority.

More important than the Council's documents were the drama it embodied and the spirit it appeared to bless. Though the Council's sessions were closed to the press and its participants initially sworn to secrecy, the Council was still widely covered by the media. The regnant story line, only sometimes exaggerated, was that of a progressive majority repeatedly and sometimes unscrupulously frustrated by a small clique of reactionaries, most of them members of the Vatican bureaucracy. It was shocking enough for American Catholics to witness their allegedly changeless Church changing, even confessing to past errors. How much more astonishing to learn that this change had emerged from a politics reminiscent of City Hall. As unlikely a source as the *Ladies' Home Journal* rang changes on the theme, in this case with regard to the papal commission created in the course of the Council to consider the related problems of family limitation and global population growth. "Liberal commission members, who favor some changes in the teachings of the Church, assert that the commission's work is being sabotaged by a denial of funds to hold meetings and provide such essential working tools as adequate translation services. They say that some documents fail to reach the higher authorities for whom they are intended and that the texts of others have been tampered with in transmission. They freely impugn the motives of the opposition."[5] Here was a narrative almost bound to tarnish the mystique of ecclesiastical authority.

At the same time, the secular media projected a church with an engagingly human face—one stumbling toward a fuller grasp of its own complex past and a world whose contradictions spoke simultaneously of hope and unimaginable disaster. (The Council's first session had coincided with the Cuban missile crisis.) At the Council, or so it seemed, even the mightiest bishop had something to learn, and the Council's growing progressive majority suggested that many were embracing the task. The Council also abounded with symbolic gestures, nearly all of them affirming the Church's new status as a pilgrim people. The Protestant and Orthodox observers, present from the first session; the welcoming rhetoric with regard to other faith traditions; the eventual presence of lay observers—such deceptively modest developments bespoke a new openness to a pluralist world and a nod to egalitarianism. Hence the "spirit of the

Council," regularly invoked after 1965 by Catholic reformers of every variety. The very fact of the Council, these reformers argued, mandated continued change in the Church. As pilgrim people, Catholics were obliged to read the "signs of the times" and to strive unremittingly for a deeper understanding of Scripture and the Christian past.

Given its near-revolutionary consequences, the Council had obvious import for the nascent debate on contraception. Because of complicated Vatican politics, however, the issue of birth control was not on the Council's agenda. Pope John XXIII did establish a commission—mentioned above—to discuss the question, mostly in the context of period worries about overpopulation. Hence its formal name: the Pontifical Commission for the Study of Population, Family and Births, and the expertise of its six initial members in demography, medicine, and sociology. This commission was enlarged by John's successor, Pope Paul VI, late in 1963 and on several subsequent occasions; its membership stood at seventy-two in the summer of 1966, when it met for the final time. By then, the Commission included both bishops and priest theologians, notably absent from the original group, as well as additional lay experts in relevant academic subjects and even three married couples. As the group was enlarged, its initially secret existence went public and its doings were more and more the stuff of media speculation. They were the stuff of speculation among lay Catholics, too, for whom the Commission's very existence kept hope alive for a change in Church teaching. The Commission, a purely advisory body, did endorse such a change in the summer of 1966, though this fact was kept secret for nearly a year. Despite the Commission's recommendation, Pope Paul reaffirmed the Church's ban on artificial contraception in his encyclical *Humanae Vitae,* issued on 29 July 1968.[6]

Dissenting talk about birth control, seemingly ubiquitous by the mid-1960s, was spurred by more than the Council and meetings of the Commission. Stimulus to change was everywhere: in a newly critical Catholic press and particularly such lay-edited publications as *Commonweal* and the brand-new *National Catholic Reporter;* in highly publicized lecture tours by progressive theologians like Hans Küng, Charles Curran, and Bernard Häring; and perhaps especially in the rapidly mutating texture of Catholic practice. Remarkable changes took place in the Mass, which prior to the Council had been said entirely in Latin and almost entirely by the priest celebrant. Beginning in 1964, the ritual was increasingly conducted in the vernacular, with the congregation encouraged to take a more active liturgical role. The priest, who had hitherto faced the altar for nearly the whole of the service, now faced the people instead, while the ritual was progressively simplified and endowed with a more communal ethos. The process of reform culminated in 1969, with the promulgation of a completely revised order of the Mass, now wholly said in the vernacular. Devotions to the saints and even the Blessed Virgin faded in many parishes, sometimes for want of clients but at least as often by the unceremonious fiat of a reform-minded pastor. Friday abstinence from meat, a similarly evocative marker of Catholic distinctiveness, was ended by the American bishops in 1966. Attendance at Protestant rituals, once strictly forbidden, was now approved in enlightened quarters as generously ecumenical.

Changes like these removed for many Catholics the final bricks from what had once been a ghetto wall—the last protections against full psychic absorption into an increasingly secularized culture and the sometimes disconcerting demands of religious pluralism. Not surprisingly, their own behavior began to change: attendance at Mass declined after the mid-1960s and even regularly observant Catholics went less and less frequently to confession. As for priests and women religious, once regarded by nearly every Catholic as bound by their vows for eternity, they began to resign in the wake of the Council in unprecedented numbers—often to marry. Fewer and fewer young Catholics were willing to take their places, with predictable consequences for a wide range of Catholic institutions, particularly schools and colleges.

Compounding the Catholic ethos of change were changes in secular culture. If "the sixties" was something of a global phenomenon, no Western nation was more altered by this time of upheaval than the United States. The immediate postwar years—the famously domestic interlude between 1945 and the very early 1960s—had lulled a majority of Americans into a deceptive sense of national purpose and cohesion. The situation was ultimately conducive both to restlessness, especially on the part of the young, and to confidence in the nation's ability to wrestle with long-ignored social problems. The decade was born amid calls to end poverty, racism, and the nuclear arms race. Social movements to these ends developed rapidly thereafter, eventually posing genuine challenges to the established political leadership. At its best, the new mood was attentive to individual rights in a deeper and more generous way than had hitherto been characteristic of the nation's public life. But the period had a dark side, too, which became increasingly evident. Distrust of authority grew apace and was frequently melded with a self-absorbed focus on rights—often defined with unprecedented expansiveness—that paid little or no attention to communal needs. The dominant mood turned sour in the latter half of the decade, with the country embroiled in an unpopular war and race-based angers leading to urban rioting. Some Americans moved left in response, both culturally and politically; many more moved to the right. Like the Church, the nation was increasingly polarized and less and less able to apprehend what had previously held it together.

It was largely a historical accident—whether happy or otherwise, I leave to the reader—that the Council ended just as the "sixties" was moving into its most extreme and polarized phase. Implementing reform was enormously difficult in such a climate, particularly when it came to limiting the inevitable unintended consequences. This was particularly true with regard to sexual morality. Various movements for sexual liberation—from the strictures of marriage and the nuclear family, from allegedly outmoded expectations of premarital chastity, from what poet Adrienne Rich dubbed "compulsory heterosexuality"[7]—took root at mid-decade, infecting popular culture. A resurgent feminism challenged conventional gender roles in marriage. The cult of sexual fulfillment—freed, now, from the exclusive context of marriage—invaded even the soberer reaches of the middle class, presumably aided by the now-ubiquitous anovular pill and the apparent medical conquest of venereal disease. Despite the altered climate, Americans continued to marry in record numbers. But the divorce rate rose sharply after mid-decade, as the birthrate resumed its historic downward trend. The large family, once admired—at least in the abstract—as a sign of hope and the parents' psychic maturity, abruptly lost its appeal. By 1974, a distinct minority of Americans was endorsing a family of four or more children as "ideal." Decline in this regard had been sharpest among Catholics, followed closely by that among women generally.[8]

In cultural circumstances like these, Catholic efforts to talk about sex were seriously handicapped. Could the Church endorse contraception in marriage and not find itself on a slippery slope where every sexual prohibition was suddenly up for renegotiation? Nearly all conservatives doubted it. That the altered cultural climate had led to a grassroots campaign to legalize abortion only made matters more grave. Maintaining the prohibition on contraception in marriage was self-evidently necessary, in the view of many worried observers, as a kind of hedge against tolerant attitudes toward abortion, not to mention sexual permissiveness. Whatever the alleged suffering of married Catholics, it was a small price to pay. Couples who favored a change in the teaching were understandably angered by such arguments, which seemed to reduce their own needs and experiences to the merest footnote in a not terribly persuasive brief. "Honestly, most couples are bored to nausea by the constant negative theology of marriage they've been fed," as an angry correspondent told Father Walter Imbiorski, the eminently gentle advisor to Chicago's Christian Family Movement, who was edging toward moderate reformism by 1965. "'It's only the second best state of life, and that only if it imitates as nearly as possible the celibate state or engages in fantastic bursts of procreativity.' What will make better marriages is the junking of this entire mentality."[9] Lay anger like this was hardly a new thing, nor indeed were anxieties over the social consequences of endorsing contraception for the married. But in the context of a new sexual radicalism, both anger and fear were intensified. Thoughtful debate was increasingly hard, and the situation of would-be moderates made increasingly untenable.

Thus American Catholics embarked on their great debate over contraception in something approaching tumultuous circumstances. Old certainties were everywhere in retreat. The experience was probably most easily negotiated by younger, well-educated members of the laity, for whom the erosion of certainty often felt like emancipation. Having forced the debate over contraception and having in many cases claimed the right to decide for themselves in the matter, such men and women took pride in their new Christian maturity. "Against the current, if necessary, accepting the risks inherent in responsible choice, morally serious, the theonomous Catholic tastes the joy of the free man," as Michael Novak articulated the ethos in 1967, with explicit reference to individual decision making about birth control.[10] Matters were more problematic for the clergy, especially those who worked in parishes. Caught between the needs of their people and continued stasis in Rome, many priests were unsure of how to respond to their troubled married penitents. "Encounters with extreme cases of this sort have led this confessor to what almost amounts to a crisis of conscience," in the words of a young parish assistant from Baltimore, who in his two years of priesthood had met with apparently numerous penitents who were either abstaining from intercourse, to the great detriment of their marriages, or using contraceptives and remaining away from communion.[11] Loss of confidence in the confessional simply fed what was widely reported, by 1965, to be a crisis in priestly identity. What did it mean to be a priest in the post-conciliar church? What was his status as moral teacher in a world of rapidly shifting standards and a newly empowered laity?

Even bishops were caught in the rising dispute over contraception's legitimacy, although they had as a group been mostly protected from lay grievances on this score. Limiting public dissent on the question, if this were in fact to be done, was a task that logically fell to a bishop in his capacity as local ordinary. So did the monitoring of seminary teaching, particularly since dissenting views were rumored by the mid-1960s to be common on seminary faculties. As the teaching was rendered increasingly uncertain, due in part to the pope's long silence, the various bishops had to guide their priests in their work as preachers, counselors, and especially confessors. They might feel obliged to offer instruction to the married laity, too. None of these were easy assignments, given the tide of public opinion. Certain bishops, moreover, suffered genuine crises of conscience, both as defenders of the teaching and as opponents. One of the latter, indeed—James Shannon, a young auxiliary bishop of St. Paul-Minneapolis—actually resigned his episcopal office in the wake of *Humanae Vitae*.[12] But for all their difficulties, the bishops as a group were not as demoralized as the parish clergy by the public debate over birth control. The damage done to the episcopacy was less immediately visible.

The Laity: Finding a Public Voice

Two 1963 publications were instrumental in bringing lay discontent with Church teaching definitively into the public sphere. The first, in order of time, was John Rock's *The Time Has Come: A Catholic Doctor's Proposals to End the Battle over Birth Control.* Rock, a Boston gynecologist on the faculty of the Harvard Medical School, was hardly a conventional Catholic, for all his evident devoutness and numerous children. He had been publicly associated since 1931 with various efforts to modify Massachusetts' strict anti-contraception law. He was also one of the principal developers of the anovular pill—the main occasion of his famous book. Use of the Pill, Rock argued, was simply a refinement of the rhythm method and thus, from a Catholic perspective, morally acceptable. Women were naturally sterile for a portion of each menstrual cycle; the Pill achieved an extension of that natural sterility by means of externally administered hormones. Rock proposed an analogy: just as ovulation was inhibited by natural hormonal secretions during pregnancy to protect the developing fetus, so couples who judged it necessary to delay a new pregnancy for the good of their existing children might employ the Pill to this end. "One might even tend to think it immoral for husband and wife . . . to reject their God-given intellect and trust only to the automatic action of female sex glands or to their ability to suppress the powerful love urge which their Creator fused with their sex instinct." Most Catholic moralists at this juncture condemned the Pill as an agent of temporary sterility and, as such, gravely sinful when used for directly contraceptive purposes. Rock disagreed. The Pill did not mutilate any of the reproductive organs but instead induced a state of ovarian repose. The woman's reproductive function was not suppressed but suspended.[13]

Something of a latter-day Leo Latz, Rock was even more adept when it came to publicizing his message. He wrote for popular publications, including mass-circulation women's magazines and was an attractive interviewee, appearing in such venues as *LIFE,* the *Saturday Evening Post,* and a cover story in *Newsweek.* He was also an authoritative television presence. Rock's appeal lay less in his aristocratic good looks and professional competence than in his willingness to speak plainly—a rare quality in Catholic public life when it came to contraception. "Unless he simply repeats verbatim the formulas in theological manuals," as *Commonweal* described the Catholic scholar who wished to write about birth control or problems of overpopulation, "he is likely to arouse hostility, suspicion or condemnation." The result was a dreary scholarly conformity and what *Commonweal* aptly called a "stilted, circumlocutionary" mode of expressing even the mildest dissent.[14] Especially in the American context, Rock's was a new mode of speaking—direct, pragmatic, alert to contemporary social problems. (Alarm about surging global population was a principal theme in Rock's book.) Clerical reviewers might plausibly deplore his want of theological precision. But of what value was precision if theologians could not address the actual moral dilemmas of the laity? Hence Rock's emancipatory effect on Catholic public discourse, which was welcomed not only by laity but even some priests. "I must say that I like to see Dr. Rock stir-

ring up the theologians," Father Michael O'Leary informed the probably startled readers of the *Michigan Catholic,* "and I hope with him that through a
more exhaustive study of the problem [of family limitation] they may some-
day come up with more welcome answers."[15]

Rock's book, coupled with the excitement generated by the Second Vatican
Council, helped to persuade the American media that Catholic dissent over
contraception was a safe, even profitable, topic to explore. Many of the earliest explorations centered wholly or mainly on Rock himself. But soon the focus was broadened to include the allegedly many Catholics who, like Rock,
wanted a reformulation of Church teaching, if not its outright repudiation.
"Discussions among both the clergy and the laity turn often to birth control
now," the New York *Times* told its readers in August 1963, "as increasing numbers of Catholics discover that the issue, which they have looked upon as a
matter of faith and morals beyond their right to question, actually falls within
their province to examine."[16] The *Times*'s four-article series was subsequently
abridged in the *Readers' Digest,* where the inevitably less nuanced contents
were absorbed by a probably large Catholic readership. "Throughout the entire article, there runs the same smug, scarcely concealed attitude that the
Church is wrong," according to Hugh O'Connell, a Redemptorist priest and
theologian, "and that it is only a matter of time when she must change her view
on the sinfulness of contraceptive methods." Father O'Connell was especially
annoyed by the *Digest*'s promotion of the piece, with newspaper ads an-
nouncing that "there's a sharp division on this subject *within the Church.*"
Since O'Connell defined "the Church" in terms of its formal teaching office,
he could in good conscience assert that the *Digest*'s claim was wholly untrue.[17]
"Those who try to cast doubt on the Church's position merely quote the statements of some individual Catholics, such as Doctor Rock."[18] But like growing numbers of his confreres, he was deeply worried by the secular media's de
facto legitimization of Catholic dissent.

What the laity still lacked, however, were plausible public embodiments of
their own difficulties with Church teaching. The redoubtable Dr. Rock was
too old and rich to fill the bill. His own private experience of the teaching,
moreover, was absent from his widely referenced book. Even the *Times*'s four
articles failed to quote dissenting lay sources by name or identify their situations in any specific way. Hence the importance of a second 1963 publication—second in order of time to Rock's volume: the December issue of *Jubilee*
magazine, which carried two lay-authored essays bluntly critical of Church
teaching. The first was by Rosemary Radford Reuther, then a graduate student
in church history and the mother of three young children; the other was written by Bruce Cooper, an English father of five, whose remarks had previously
appeared in the London *Spectator.* Cooper's essay was the more acerbic, perhaps because English Catholics of a certain class have historically been less

than deferential to their mostly Irish clergy. Particularly critical of rhythm, whose paraphernalia he dismissed as "reminiscent of the stud farm," Cooper inveighed against the teaching as a source not just of personal distress but serious social problems, too, including high rates of delinquency among Catholic youth in Great Britain.[19] Rosemary Reuther was no less critical but politer and more academic in tone, as probably befitted a very young woman presuming to voice public dissent on so intimate a topic. She dissected the weaknesses in the natural law argument and noted that rhythm was not only frustrating and anxiety laden, but least apt to work for the poor and ill educated. "Is it too much to ask that Catholics be willing to recognize that their traditional arguments on this subject are at best unsatisfactory and that we might be less dogmatic in proclaiming them? Perhaps the matter should be regarded as morally 'optional'—as some European theologians seem to be hinting."[20]

Jubilee's lay editors solicited comments on the two essays, the first features of their kind to have appeared in an American Catholic venue, and printed a representative selection of readers' letters in subsequent issues. What they thereby produced was a new kind of forum—very different from those provided by such clerically edited publications as the *Liguorian* and *Marriage*. The latter journals were printing an unprecedented number of dissenting lay letters on birth control by the early 1960s, but invariably in the context of corrective commentary by their priest editors. *Jubilee,* by contrast, offered something akin to a free exchange among adults, where frankness about one's experience provided the substance of collective theological reflection rather than triggering a potted reproof. For this reason alone, the *Jubilee* letters had an effect well beyond the magazine's small circulation. They were evidently discussed at neighborhood parties and parish study groups, exhilarating not only for their content but as an image of a church where an educated laity had at last come into its own.

Jubilee's editors apparently received several hundred letters from the magazine's readership, which was in the main both devout and well educated. Most favored a change in Church teaching or at least voiced doubts about the teaching's rationale. Only a handful defended it, mostly as a bulwark against selfishness. It was clerical correspondents, and they alone, who worried that a change in the teaching would call into question what one called "the Church's inerrancy in interpreting moral issues where there is no clear revealed dogma."[21] Nearly every letter writer, regardless of views, betrayed a sense of belonging to a beleaguered minority—an early sign of polarization among devout Catholics. Those struggling with the teaching's effects and doubting its rightness often spoke of the clergy as indifferent to the laity's suffering. "We are not rebellious Catholics," as a mother of nine contended, "but we have met nothing but closed faces when we sought to discuss our family situation."[22] Few appeared to anticipate an imminent change in the teaching, whatever ten-

tative hopes they harbored. Those who defended the teaching or worried about
the consequences of its abandonment, felt equally misunderstood, usually by
other lay Catholics. "Of course, we are of that fast-fading older school," in the
words of another mother of nine, this one from Indiana. "We stupidly believe
a child's eternal salvation is our first concern so we have not hesitated to give
him life—and thereby an opportunity for heaven—thinking that more important than any college degree."[23]

What was most remarkable about the *Jubilee* letters was their literacy and
theological sophistication. Numerous correspondents, mostly males, challenged the natural law reasoning that had long undergirded the teaching, and
did so with seeming authority. "After much reading of the writings of moralists on this point," according to a father of four, whose letter included a cita-
tion to *Theological Studies,* "it becomes more and more clear to me that the
validity of the Church's position cannot be proved by reason alone, as it must
be able to be if it is based upon the natural law. This position becomes convincing only if one makes a large unwarranted assumption: that the generative
aspect of sex is the only worthy aspect of it."[24] The sprinkling of letters from
priests and seminarians suffered by contrast: either the writer confessed to his
private doubts about the teaching, which he nonetheless felt obliged to uphold
as a confessor and counselor, or he engaged in what probably looked to most
readers like specious reasoning. The lay correspondents emerged as the more
theologically confident, honest, and humane. "Who am I to buck this mono-
lith of teaching of the Church's theologians?" asked a missionary priest stationed in Africa, whose own brother was currently struggling with the burden
of a too-numerous family. He had great sympathy for his brother "and his prolific wife." But despite private misgivings about the teaching's rationale, this
priest still felt that "I had no right to tell them directly that they could use artificial means and do so with a clear conscience."[25] How telling the contrast
posed by the crisp judgments of a college-trained mother of six: "Once it is decided that the number of conceptions can morally be limited it follows that the
most effective and practical methods of limitation should be used. Rhythm and
abstinence are not the most effective methods. To refuse the use of others is
fanatical and somewhat akin to the Jehovah's Witnesses' refusal of blood trans-
fusions."[26]

For all their seeming confidence as moral arbiters, the lay correspondents to
Jubilee were not for the most part using contraceptives. This was true of the
woman just quoted, though the oldest of her six youngsters was only seven.
"Completely out of obedience to the Church, I follow her teachings," as she
explained, "but there are times when I feel like a victim of religious tyranny
and times when I have many doubts about my faith." In this respect, the laity
were behaving like those clerical letter writers who doubted the teaching but
still continued to enforce it. The laity, however, suffered for their obedience

far more than the clergy did, at least as the laity saw it. A priest might be briefly troubled by having to insist on a firm purpose of amendment from a married penitent whose too-large family had prompted her to contraception. But he could readily console himself by invoking the claims of institutional authority. "I have reached the conclusion that in committing myself to the priesthood," as a New Jersey priest told *Jubilee*'s readers, "I also committed myself implicitly to the obligation of presenting to others the approved moral doctrine of the Church, even in areas where I happen to disagree with that doctrine."[27]

The penitent, by contrast, had either to abide by a teaching that was causing her grief, and about which she herself might have doubts, or deprive herself of the sacraments. "I do not go to confession (and therefore Communion)," as the mother of five young children explained, having recently opted for contraception, "for how can I be sorry for something I believe is right? How can I promise not to sin again when I intend to do the same thing again[?]" She felt estranged from the Church and worried spasmodically about going to hell. But the alternative, as she saw it, was to employ a method—to wit, rhythm—that she did not hesitate to call "immoral" and still have more children than she was emotionally equipped to nurture. "I feel that I have a moral obligation to raise my children to the best of my ability and by having a child every year, my best would be mighty poor indeed."[28]

The most gripping portions of the *Jubilee* letters center on just such dilemmas. How to handle one's equally grave obligations to spouse, children, and Church? Many of the writers were bitter veterans of the rhythm method, which they typically excoriated as destructive of marital happiness and of dubious value as a means of family limitation. Nearly all were limiting intercourse to the post-ovulatory phase of the wife's menstrual cycle, which in certain extreme cases meant a safe period of less than a week. "This almost total abstinence has taken a terrible toll on our marriage and on the entire emotional atmosphere in our home," according to a suburban mother of six, who held a Master's Degree in psychiatric social work. "Everyone is extremely nervous and quarrelsome and the children particularly have been damaged emotionally."[29] Even under less taxing circumstances, rhythm was said to result in "constant friction, unending pregnancies, confused children who cannot understand the tension in their home," in the words of another mother of six, this one from Canada.[30] It was the "unending pregnancies" that especially distressed a rancher from California, who had fathered five children in less than eight years of marriage. "Prudent use of rhythm has so far given us an average of eight months' time between the birth of one child and the conception of the next. . . . Do you see why our non-Catholic friends believe we are all at the Mad Hatter's Tea Party?"[31]

Both women and men cited sexual frustration as a principal drawback to rhythm, although women were the more likely to discuss the problem in terms of its emotional costs. "What warmth and tenderness has gone out of our marriage," in the wistful phrasing of a New York mother of three.[32] The male perspective was often more bitter. Should the Church eventually consent to marital contraception, one man asked, how would the clergy justify their having imposed so frustrating a regime as rhythm on countless married men? Not entirely tongue-in-check, he predicted "a March on Rome by millions of men, who[,] having been rejected by their wives, live lives of continence in close proximity to the opposite sex."[33] Women were also the more apt to worry about the impact of too-frequent births on their children's emotional well-being. Socially mobile and well educated, Catholics like these were particularly vulnerable to the period's heightened standards of child nurture, for which women were held primarily responsible. "Only a mother can know the manifold needs of a small child," according to one correspondent, "and only a mother knows when a child is not being given the best of care. Not even a father, to say nothing of a priest, is aware of all these needs." She went on to cite allegedly exemplary Catholic families—exemplary, at least, in the eyes of the parish clergy—where overburdened mothers had of necessity to neglect the care of their too-numerous offspring. "The priest does not see a baby's buttocks bleeding from diaper rash; he does not see the baby who has its bottle 'propped.'"[34]

Beyond physical neglect with its attendant emotional consequences were larger issues of character development. It was not just that educated parents wanted college for their children, and the disciplined achievement orientation that this goal implied. They also wished, some more consciously than others, to nurture an intellectual independence appropriate to life in a world of affluent professionals. "I cannot pass on to my children the naïve and over-simplified view of human nature and marriage that my husband and I accepted so quiescently," a suburban mother of four explained. "As with the old position toward heretics, in the present controversy on contraceptives the Catholic position has overlooked the rights and integrity of the human personality as well as the integrity of family life."[35]

Women letter writers were also the more eloquent when it came to the psychological costs of being a serious sinner in the eyes of the church. Some of the *Jubilee* correspondents had used forbidden modes of contraception in the past, presumably in the wake of childbirth or at other times when rhythm's uncertainties were simply unendurable. Others, albeit an evident handful, were currently engaged in forbidden contraceptive practice, with varying degrees of guilt. Even those intellectually convinced that contraception was not wrong, especially when accomplished by means of the Pill, had still to wrestle with the fact of their disobedience to church teaching and the many examples around them of couples who continued to obey despite great personal cost. "I had a very real sense of something within me that was dark and dead, as though a great light had been switched off and I was a walking shell of a body," a military wife and mother of seven explained with regard to an earlier period of contraceptive use. "I do not think my husband had any such feeling."[36] The most conscientious stayed away from confession during such interludes, unable to promise honestly to try to amend their lives. Deprived of the sacraments, they invariably felt estranged from the Church and sometimes even from God. "When one uses artificial birth control," in the words of a New York mother of three, "one becomes part of the 'gray Church.' You can sometimes guess at who is in this sad plight by seeing who receives communion. There are many teenagers and many older people, but too often those between 25 and 40 remain seated, or if they do go, they are expecting." One's children asked difficult questions about the cause of their parents' behavior, and the stay-at-home mother was sometimes denied the consolations of parish social life. Most parish organizations, after all, had regular communion Sundays. "I would love to be a Cub Scout or Brownie leader," as the New York mother confessed. "But I am held back by the realization that I could not receive holy communion with them."[37]

Conscientious Catholics like these were usually aware that others in their circumstances continued to frequent the sacraments, either neglecting to confess their sins of contraception or squelching their scruples with regard to a firm purpose of amendment. "There are those . . . who do receive [communion]," in the words of the above-mentioned New York mother, "and, as one woman I know said, tell their *other* sins to the Blessed Virgin's statue after confession."[38] Expectations generated by the Second Vatican Council probably increased the numbers. "With the hope that some of the 'fresh air' that is to be breathed into the Church will be applied to birth control," as a Nevada woman saw it, "some undoubtedly hope that what they are doing may turn out not to be wrong after all and try to forget that it is considered wrong now."[39] The situation was obviously difficult for those who remained obedient and especially for those who obeyed despite their doubts. "It is difficult to practice 'heroic virtue' when you are not even sure that you believe in what you are doing," as a Virginia mother of four acknowledged ruefully.[40] Like the well-conducted siblings in a family whose stern parents neglected to discipline their large brood equitably, Catholics of the *Jubilee* stripe not infrequently felt toward clerical authority an odd mix of dependence and rage. They were quick to note encounters with unsympathetic priests and to give their opinions disproportionate weight, no matter how extreme these opinions might be. "If there is one thing our religious educations have taught us, it is the conviction of sin," a Catholic college professor reminded *Jubilee*'s readers.[41] The unprecedented ecumenical rhetoric emanating from the Council simply made matters worse, despite its being welcomed by most highly educated laity. If devout Protestants who employed contraception were candidates for heaven, asked an Illinois father of four, why was it that "Catholics who do the same, and who die without confessing this mortal sin, will be damned forever[?]"[42]

Jubilee's new openness was soon echoed in other Catholic publications, especially those that were lay controlled. *Commonweal,* for example, devoted a full issue in June 1964 to what it called responsible parenthood, where the editor demanded a prominent role for "the layman" in working out an updated Catholic morality of marriage. "His voice is needed, even if (and especially when) his approach is different from those attempting to establish norms of his conduct."[43] The secular media were even more hospitable to stories about what *Look* described as "an anguished Catholic debate now coming out into the open . . . in almost every Catholic publication."[44] Rosemary Reuther's *Jubilee* essay appeared in an expanded form in the *Saturday Evening Post* and then in the *Reader's Digest.* Dr. John Rock was generously featured at about the same time in a David Brinkley television special, where he briefly debated Father John A. O'Brien, the pioneer proponent of rhythm. O'Brien was genuinely surprised by "the very considerable number of professing Catholics" who wrote in the wake of the program to express their agreement with Rock, and who "branded the Church's position as 'medieval' and 'hopelessly outdated.'"[45]

By mid-1964 few Catholics were unaware that their Church's teaching on contraception was under public attack, and by precisely the sorts of devout college graduates who just a few years earlier had been among its most articulate champions. Two anthologies appearing toward the end of the year, edited respectively by Michael Novak and William Birmingham, showcased those voices in their most attractive mode—thoughtful, articulate, theologically informed.[46] Reading the lay-authored essays in Novak's *The Experience of Marriage,* according to theology professor Charles Curran, "made me reconsider my own role as a priest, a confessor, and a theologian. . . . What values are preserved in the present teaching of the Church? Are there other ways to preserve the same values?"[47]

The rising tide of lay testimony was similar in content to the *Jubilee* essays and letters. Many lay writers were sufficiently knowledgeable to quarrel with the regnant understanding of natural law, at least as it applied to the Catholic doctrine on contraception. But most spoke the language of personal experience, in frank and often affecting fashion, particularly when it came to sex. "Marital union was accomplished in fear, apprehension and, on occasion, tears," according to a young teacher, who had fathered three children in five years of marriage, despite what he described as conscientious use of the rhythm method. "Instead of being the fount of mutual comfort, our marriage was, in some ways, becoming the very source of our unhappiness." Like many of his contemporaries, he also worried about the rising cost of college: "as a teacher, I was becoming afraid that I would find myself unable to give my own children the very education which had been so important in my own life."[48] Catholics like this young man, who had been educated solely in Catholic schools, had previously been inclined to regard the teaching as a noble embodiment of anti-materialism and even a source of spiritual discipline. That impulse was largely absent from lay writing by the mid-1960s, replaced in a growing number of cases by suspicion that the teaching might actually be a cause of moral mischief. "Cannot one sin by *having* a child?" asked the father of five young children, whose wife had recently been afflicted by stress-induced psychological problems. Quite apart from the damage that rhythm did to most couples' sexual lives, were not the burdens on mothers of large families often so great that the children's psychological—and hence spiritual—development suffered? "When this is the case, when children already born are not put firmly on the path of salvation because of the general chaotic conditions and inadequate attention occasioned by still more births, I would question the responsibility of the parents."[49]

The Novak and Birmingham anthologies did introduce one important new element to the debate—something almost entirely absent from the *Jubilee* letters. This was an explicitly feminist language and logic. "Many women find a radical discrepancy between their sense of themselves as individuals and the Church's virtual identification of their nature with the maternal role," as Sally Sullivan noted in her Birmingham essay, pointedly titled "Woman: Mother or Person?" "The problem of finding a Christian solution to family planning cannot be solved until we answer these questions about woman's nature and hence her rights." The product of a secular women's college, Sullivan fluently invoked such authorities as Simone de Beauvoir and Betty Friedan.[50] If psychological wholeness was essential to spiritual health, as highly educated young Catholics did not doubt, what of the woman whose wholeness depended on work as well as love? "I have always known that I had a 'double vocation,' to be a wife and mother and a sculptor," Anne Martin explained. A wife of two years and expecting her first child, Martin had not yet directly experienced the conflict inherent—at least for a Catholic—in these dual goals. But she knew that it loomed: "at a certain point circumstances will be overwhelming; eventually a choice must be made." That seemingly inevitable choice was for her the epitome of unfairness. "I don't think a woman should be required to see her existence only in terms of motherhood. I do not feel that I should make a career out of producing children." Her creative work, enhanced thus far by the joy of marriage and anticipated childbirth, was as much "a part of my salvation" as her family role.[51] Sentiments like these were not readily appreciated by most American Catholics, even in 1964. "We are surprised by how many priests, especially, expect that a woman will naturally drop her interest in personal development for the sake of her family," as a woman wrote in the Novak anthology, speaking for her husband as well as herself. "Perhaps they base their attitudes on sentimental portraits of their mothers."[52] It would not be long, however, before feminist claims like these seemed to many younger Catholics—and particularly the women among them—to embody an elemental justice.

The swelling chorus of dissent almost certainly helped to generate change in the family planning behavior of the devout and well educated. College-trained Catholic wives who received communion at least once a month were still, in 1965, the most likely to conform to their Church's teaching on contraception. But their conduct had changed quite significantly in this regard since 1960—more, in fact, than that of any other subgroup in the Catholic population. "Between 1955 and 1960 the increase in nonconformity was inversely associated with amount of education," as sociologist Raymond Potvin noted, "but between 1960 and 1965 the differential was completely reversed, with education being directly related to increase in nonconformity." Devout college graduates were belatedly joining what by 1965 had become a rush to "nonconformity" on the birth control front: 53 percent of Catholic wives aged eighteen to thirty-nine were either presently using a forbidden means of contraception or had done so in the past, according to a national study. Nearly all respondents in this category, it should be noted, were regular users of contraception at the time the study was done. A similar study in 1955 had found only 30 percent of Catholic wives admitting to such behavior. Even in 1965, Catholic family planning choices were still notably different from those of other Americans. But something had clearly shifted by then: conformity to Church teaching was no longer the statistical norm, and the loyalty of so-called core Catholics was being significantly eroded.[53]

Despite their steadily diminishing numbers, a good many Catholics in 1965 were still obedient to Church teaching. (The rate of diminution was impressive: by 1970, fully 68 percent of Catholic wives in their childbearing years were limiting their families by a means other than abstinence or rhythm.[54]) To remain obedient in such circumstances was apt to be difficult. The circle of friends who shared your problems was almost certainly growing smaller, while rumors abounded of priests who encouraged married penitents to decide for themselves when it came to contraceptive use. "Anyone wanting to practice birth control today can do so if he looks for the right priest," in the words of a couple from Syracuse, writing in 1965.[55] Then there was the expectation, increasingly widespread, of an eventual change in Church teaching. More than 60 percent of the laity expected such a change, according to a Gallup poll in mid-1965, with 55 percent of those expecting that change within the next five years.[56]

Perhaps hardest to bear for the reluctantly obedient was the rhetoric of "maturity" and "responsibility" that accompanied many endorsements of change. The exemplary Catholic now seemed to be one who limited her family out of concern for the health of her marriage, the well-being of her children, and the future of a dangerously overcrowded planet. Obedience, it was often suggested, was a less genuinely Christian virtue than the courage required by independent moral choice. With Chicago's Cana Conference, once the champion of generous procreation, now cosponsoring a series of conferences on global population problems at the University of Notre Dame, it was sometimes hard for the still-obedient layman to see that his burden of personal sacrifice made moral sense any longer. Perhaps it never had. "What do we tell the kids? That we were stupid sheep?" demanded a newspaper editor from Minneapolis. "Artificial birth control was a mortal sin because it violated the divine and natural law. Now in a magazine I urge my children to read, there is promotion for 'contraception and holiness'"—the last-mentioned words in reference to a 1964 book of essays by the same title, in which prominent theologians made a case for responsible use of birth control in marriage.[57]

The dilemma of the still-obedient laity is painfully apparent in a remarkable set of letters, collected in 1965 by Pat and Patty Crowley, longtime leaders in the Christian Family Movement. The Crowleys were among the three lay couples appointed by Pope Paul VI to his expanded birth control commission late in 1964.[58] They arrived at their first commission meeting, in March 1965, armed with the results of a small survey done among CFM members, where respondents were asked if they favored liberalization of the Church's teaching on contraception. Most respondents "definitely" favored reform, often explaining their stance—through letters accompanying the survey form—in terms of their own experience of marriage. "Many of them gave their history," as the Crowleys explained at the time, "which was really an eye-opener to many of the priests and theologians at the Commission meeting."[59] The Crowleys and the other lay couples—one from Canada, the other from France—were asked by several commission members to undertake additional survey work. The Crowleys' assignment was to use their vast network of CFM contacts to solicit personal accounts of how the rhythm method was actually experienced as a means of family planning.

In this second survey, the Crowleys asked only two questions: In what ways, if any, had rhythm been helpful to the couple's marriage? In what ways, if any, had it been harmful? They eventually received some three thousand responses, mostly from North America—many in the form of highly personal letters.[60] Although none were subsequently published, those letters apparently had a major impact on the papal commission's deliberations and particularly the thinking of its clerical members. Britain's Cardinal John Heenan was a case in point. He had been a vocal proponent of the Church's stand on contraception prior to his 1966 commission appointment, perhaps partly because his days of routinely hearing confessions were long in the past. He evolved, albeit reluctantly, into an advocate of reform during his commission tenure. "On this I take my stand," as the cardinal told the commission's other archbishops during its final session. "I am *quite* sure that relief must be brought to Catholic couples and I cannot bring myself to accept that the thermometer and the calendar are a good way of keeping men and women from mortal sin."[61] Heenan's rhetoric

CFM'ers *throughout the World*

CANADA	12.00	TANGANYIKA	60
MALTA	150	URUGUAY	400
PHILLIPINES	100	HAWAII	150
UGANDA	40	PUERTO RICO	20
	40	PAKISTAN	20
	60	DENMARK	60
	500	JAPAN	100
	1,000	IRELAND	30
	200	ENGLAND	80
	00	COLOMBIA	150
		CHILI	500

Figure 8. Pat and Patty Crowley, probably in the mid-1950s, with Fr. Louis Putz, C.S.C. and Monsignor—later Bishop—William McManus. The setting is a CFM convention. Photo courtesy of the University of Notre Dame Archives.

in this regard was very much that of the Crowley letters and indeed of the other lay testimony to which commission members had been exposed.

The Crowley letters were written by unusually devout Catholics—an important reason for their authority with a man like Heenan. Nearly all of the authors were active in CFM; many were parents of large families. Most of the letter writers still adhered to the rhythm method, though few had confidence in its efficacy and many were no longer convinced by the Church's arguments against contraception. Some had recently opted for the Pill, mostly in desperation, and were typically staying away from the sacraments in consequence. Even those who believed that their putative disobedience in this matter was the morally better option were often haunted by guilt—an emotion accompanied by resentment and sometimes a kind of shame. Was it fully adult to invest the Church, imagined almost exclusively in terms of the hierarchy, with an authority equal to that of God? For historically conscious Catholics, it was hard to defend such behavior as admirable or indeed as invariably moral. "Through it all I felt that I was disobeying the Church rather than God," as one woman explained of her anguished decision to take the Pill. She admitted with a certain discomfiture that "God and the church are synonymous to me," which meant that the Church could rightly demand obedience and exclude her from the Eucharist when she withheld it. "But I never truly believed that God would condemn me forever for my decision." A medically mandated hysterectomy would soon "end the dilemma for us," as she related with obvious relief, and enable the couple to return to the sacraments.[62]

Parish priests were often the targets of guilt-related anger, something else that may have affected the thinking of a man like Cardinal Heenan. Even gentle confessors were increasingly excoriated for failing to understand the needs of the married. "I have tried to communicate with intelligent young priests concerning my personal physical-emotional-financial conflict brought about by the fear of having additional children," as an obviously bitter young father wrote. "The reply usually suggests that I should pray harder and ask God for greater understanding. . . . I frequently got the feeling that if I wanted to be baptized or buried they probably would do a good job, it was the interim that caused all their problems."[63] Clerical endorsements of rhythm, only recently a mark of pastoral liberalism, now provoked undisguised scorn. "It is our opinion that if the clergy took rectal temperatures that Catholic marrieds would not still be waiting for an answer on contraception," in the jaundiced view of a father of six, asserting that "the use of rhythm nearly destroyed our marriage."[64] Arguments like these were hardly new, though they had in the past been largely voiced in purely private contexts. But such arguments had not characterized the most devout laity and certainly not those who were active in family life movements. The latter were far more likely than other Catholics to know at least one priest well, and he most probably an attractively pastoral soul. That the clergy seemed increasingly wanting to such Catholics—increasingly disqualified by the fact of their celibacy to speak authoritatively on marriage—was an ominous sign of changing times.

Many writers were almost as troubled by conflicting counsel in the confessional, despite its liberating implications. "We have moved around from one parish to another and find that priests differ greatly in their views on the subject," one Crowley writer quite typically reported. "This alone has made us wonder, 'Who is right and who is wrong?'"[65] One could in fact "shop around" for a priest who would give at least temporary permission to use the Pill, often on the flimsiest of medical excuses. But some devout Catholics were too scrupulous—or too neurotic, as a critic might have it—to accept such permission as definitive, though the very disagreement evident among confessors suggested a teaching in the throes of de facto reform. A Navy wife who had recently helped to establish a rhythm clinic in her parish told the Crowleys that among her numerous contacts were women who were taking the Pill, nearly always with a priest's permission, but who still thought it necessary to stay away from communion. "While many told the priest they were taking them for regulation [of the menstrual cycle], they realized that primarily the effect they desired was safety from pregnancy."[66] A Canadian mother of six, who had endured seven miscarriages, dealt with her guilt at using the Pill by accusing the clerical Church of something akin to felonious negligence with regard to this "terribly important question." No priest, she contended, "would advise her in any way"—which probably meant that no priest would tell her that she could use the Pill for overtly contraceptive purposes. "We feel strongly that the Church has done our marriage irreparable harm because of her refusal to speak."[67] Note that she singled out priests for blame and not the pope or bishops, who were presumably too distant and sacrosanct to be public objects of her anger.

The Crowley letters had little new to offer with regard to the practice of rhythm. The various writers attested to the method's fallibility as a means of family limitation and its damaging impact on a couple's sexual and emotional lives. Even Cardinal Heenan would have been familiar with such arguments, given their prominence in lay writing on marriage since 1963. What gave the Crowley letters their power was a wealth of homely particulars and a sometimes rather startling frankness. "I tried the temperature-taking method but found it quite repulsive and degrading," as a middle-aged mother of eight explained, who had recently gone on the Pill. "The rhythm cycle limited us to about four or five days a month. We could not always limit our need for each other to those particular days. We went to confession constantly to ask forgiveness for the incomplete acts of love. . . . I can remember crying in despair, praying to God to let me die rather than continue living as a source of sin for my husband."[68] Busy mothers outlined the difficulties of taking one's rectal temperature prior to morning rising in a household filled with small children. "I usually awaken to a scream for a bottle," as the mother of four young children pointed out.[69] Other women noted that practicing rhythm meant abbreviating or even foregoing breastfeeding, since women do not normally menstruate during lactation—a fact unknown to at least one confessor, whom a letter writer described as "quite surprised to hear that while nursing no periods were gotten."[70] It seemed distinctly odd, in the view of one correspondent, that the natural feeding of one's infant should be incompatible with an allegedly natural mode of birth control.[71] Both husbands and wives explained that a spouse who traveled might stretch the required period of sexual abstinence to more than a month, should the spouse's time away from home coincide with the putative safe period. "Life was full of unnecessary frustrations because of rhythm," in the words of a mother of eight. "With a husband in the Military Service and away from home 60 percent of the time—it all seemed very unnatural. Life seemed a constant sacrifice as the 'time' was never 'right'. . . . Since having a hysterectomy we now feel that there is beauty in sex instead of frustration, fear and tension."[72]

A greatly expanded papal commission assembled for its last spate of meet-ings—a three-month marathon—in April 1966. The new members were bish-ops and cardinals, sixteen of whom now formed the body that would formally offer advice to the pope. The commission's lay members, along with its priest theologians, were relegated at the final meeting to the status of *periti,* or advi-sory experts, although they continued to exercise enormous influence at com-mission meetings. (For this reason I will still refer to them as commission members.) Britain's Cardinal Heenan was among the augmented episcopal ranks; so were Archbishops, soon-to-be Cardinals, John Dearden of Detroit and Lawrence Shehan of Baltimore. The new episcopal appointments were ap-parently occasioned by Pope Paul's fear that the commission was drifting in a dangerously liberal direction, which would also explain his elevating Cardinal Alfredo Ottaviani to the commission's cochairmanship.[73] But not all of those appointments were hard-line opponents of change: Dearden was known to be a liberal, as were Cardinals Julius Doepfner of Munich and Leo Suenens of Malines, Belgium. So perhaps the pope's mind was still open, as the contin-ued existence of the commission and its free-ranging deliberations might be taken to indicate. "It is not logical to insist in the strongest language that the solemn doctrine of C[asti] C[onnubii] must be upheld and at the same time al-low discussions to be conducted in his own commission which make sense only in the supposition that the doctrine can be rejected," as the Jesuit theolo-gian John Ford noted, after one of several private interventions with the pope to warn him about the commission's growing liberal majority. "I wonder if he realizes the inconsistency of this position?"[74]

Notwithstanding its expanded episcopal membership, the final session of the commission gave pride of place to lay testimony. Several lay members re-ported at length on the Crowley and other related surveys, while the lay women on the commission were invited to address the group during what was dubbed the "pastoral week." Patty Crowley spoke with particular effect, only to be out-done by Madame Colette Potvin, a Francophone Canadian who with her physi-cian husband was a longtime advocate of rhythm clinics. Crowley briefly summarized the results of the CFM surveys: nearly all the respondents, she emphasized, thought that rhythm had negative effects on the spousal relation-ship and an often deleterious impact on family life generally. She noted that women were especially burdened by the system, and not only because of their greater fear of an untimely pregnancy. "Over and over, respondents pointed out that nature prepares a woman at the time of ovulation to have the greatest urge to mate with her husband. . . . She craves his love."[75] To be forced to deny her husband at such times was damaging both to the marriage and the woman's psyche, since "woman by her very nature is a loving creature and needs ten-derness and love in return. If denied this love she may even become emotion-ally disturbed."[76] Crowley's sentiments on this score, hardly those of a militant feminist, reflected the ethos of sex-as-sacrament so central to Catholic family life ministries in the neo-Freudian 1950s. Her testimony, however, was not without its feminist impulses, tentative though these seem today. "The time may have come to put less emphasis on a woman's duty to be submissive and to stress more the equal dignity and worth of husband and wife."[77] Crowley pleaded in conclusion for the Church to "demonstrate her trust in her children" by leaving decisions about family limitation wholly up to their informed consciences. "Couples want children and will have them generously and love and cherish them," she assured the group. "They do not need the impetus of legislation to procreate[;] it is the very instinct of life, love and sexuality."[78]

Madame Potvin's statement derived its power from its remarkable candor. She spoke as a wife of seventeen years and the mother of five, as she told the assembled commission members. "I am not a doctor or a psychologist, and I have no university diploma." She also spoke as a woman who had suffered three miscarriages and undergone a hysterectomy. Personally "disengaged from the problem of fecundity," as she phrased it, she was well-positioned to reflect on the multiple meanings of marital sex. Hers was a distinctively feminine perspective, she reminded the audience—"lost in a crowd of theologians and scientists," she wanted to bring them "face to face with a real woman, to reveal her soul to them, to show them how she thinks, how she reacts, how she suffers, how she lives." But the various members would miss the point if they insisted on regarding woman "as a diminished man, an occasion of sin for man, an incarnation of the demon of sensuality." Woman ought to be seen as man's companion, to employ the language of Genesis. Because she was so, a woman experienced the "conjugal act" as a free and joyous self-offering—"a gift of pleasure to her husband, of physical and psychic well-being, which makes the man wonderfully happy." Woman, at least in Western culture, married primarily to live with a beloved man; children were "the normal consequence of authentic love but not its goal." Potvin spoke especially lyrically about what she called the "conjugal orgasm"—an intense experience of sexual communion possible only to those whose souls were as strongly attracted as their bodies. "The day after such a communion with her husband, the wife is more serene, all her duties seem light, she is more patient with the children, more loving with them, she radiates joy even beyond the family circle."[79]

The various commission members were so moved by Madame Potvin's testimony that she was asked to repeat it before the body's bishops and cardinals, absent from the "pastoral week" but due to arrive in June for the commission's final sessions.[80] She gamely agreed to do so. What this exercise cost her can only be imagined; both she and Patty Crowley, traditionally bred women for all their personal strengths, had spoken during the pastoral week in a state approaching fear and trembling. (Potvin admitted publicly to experiencing "a great helplessness."[81]) How infinitely more difficult to speak of intimate matters before men whom Potvin had been taught to regard as "princes of the church." Perhaps her courage gave heart to certain commission prelates, who sensed that a change in the teaching was pastorally necessary but still feared its possible consequences. The substance of her message was important, too, bringing home with particular force the point made again and again in the surveys and letters that had had such impact on the commission's priest theologians. It was time, Potvin stated simply, to think about sexuality in terms of its several positive functions in Christian married life—"to see how sex is encompassed by God's great commandment to love one another as we love ourselves."[82]

The bishops and cardinals who assembled for the commission's final meeting seem to have agreed. They approved a report, drawn up by a subset of the commission's theologian advisors and slightly amended by the prelates, that called for a change in the Church's teaching on contraception. Such a change would not repudiate the essential wisdom of past teaching, according to the report, but only adapt that wisdom to altered circumstances. "Social changes in matrimony and the family, especially in the role of the woman; lowering of the infant mortality rates; new bodies of knowledge in biology, psychology, sexuality and demography; a changed estimation of the value and meaning of human sexuality and of conjugal relations"—all these things mandated a less rigid and absolute approach to the problem of family limitation.[83] What the Church had to protect at all costs was the good of fecundity—the essential orientation of marriage to the generation of new life. But this good could be protected, indeed would be best protected, by defining Christian marriage itself as open to the transmission of life, rather than requiring this openness of every conjugal act. The report was evasive when it came to which modes of contraception were morally acceptable, saying only that those most consonant with the dignity of the spouses should be employed. But in a clear victory for the many lay voices to which the commission had been privy, the final report dismissed rhythm as a frequently ineffective and frustrating method of family planning.[84]

What soon came to be known as the majority report of the papal commission was forwarded to Pope Paul in late June. It was followed shortly thereafter by the so-called minority report, largely written by Germain Grisez, then a Georgetown University theologian, and the Jesuit John Ford, who was probably the most articulate of the commission's conservative minority. That minority was very small by the end of the commission's deliberations—probably no more than five, including the redoubtable Cardinal Ottaviani. Their report enshrined the points repeatedly made by Father Ford in his interventions at the commission's various meetings. The teaching on contraception "was not *substantially* reformable," Ford maintained. The Church was not free to say that contraception is not intrinsically evil.[85] That teaching embodied the Church's commitment to the inviolability of human life and to God's dominion with regard to life's inception and end. "Just as already existing human life is removed from the dominion of man," in the words of the report, "so also in some similar way is human life as it comes to be; that is, the act and the generative process, inasmuch as they are generative, are removed from his dominion."[86] Then there was the vexing problem of ecclesial authority. "This particular doctrine of the Church is one which has affected the intimate lives of millions upon millions of Christians throughout the centuries," as Ford told his fellow members of the commission. "It is my position that the Church could not have made such a very grave mistake through all the centuries or even through one century, imposing very heavy burdens in the name of Jesus Christ, unless Jesus Christ imposed them. . . . If the Church can have erred so egregiously, then the faithful can no longer believe in her teaching authority."[87]

The end of the commission's work was followed by a long papal silence, save for Paul's brief instruction, in the fall of 1966, for the faithful to abide by the traditional teaching while he studied the commission's findings and deliberated over what he called an enormously complex problem. The practical effect, for a great many priests, was to cast grave doubt on the binding nature of that teaching. With numerous theologians saying that contraception might sometimes be licit and the pope refusing to pronounce on what even he seemed to regard as a matter of great uncertainty, what was the conscientious confessor to do? "There is great confusion with regard to birth control," as a Detroit priest reported early in 1967. "Regardless of statements from the Holy See to the contrary, a real state of doubt exists if not theologically then certainly psychologically. . . . My personal experience has been that a number of priests leave the matter to individual conscience or, in some instances, actually teach that it is morally acceptable."[88] The situation, while hard on all parties, worked fundamentally in the interests of reform, as conservatives were uncomfortably aware. "They feel that if the delay continues it will be a legitimate step to interpret it as consent on the part of the magisterium to the so-called 'progressive' position," explained Bishop Alexander Zaleski, with specific reference to the Jesuits John Ford and John Lynch.[89] Another Detroit priest, sympathetic to the liberal side, concurred with the analysis. "The Pope is quickly being confronted with a de facto solution to birth control," William Sherzer wrote in January 1967. "I am quite sure, from conversations with many theologians and parish priests both, that a new consensus is rapidly forming which is contrary to the established teaching of the magisterium."[90]

Matters were further complicated in April 1967, when the *National Catholic Reporter*—lay owned and edited—reprinted the still-secret majority and minority reports of the papal commission. (The commission actually issued only one report; the so-called minority offering was independently produced after the commission had adjourned for the last time.) The story made for front-page news in the secular as well as the Catholic media and greatly intensified expectations, at least among the laity, that the teaching would soon be amended.[91] It also endowed the reformist ranks with a welcome aura of legitimacy: especially in the context of papal silence, the commission majority seemed to speak with something approaching true ecclesial authority, despite the body's advisory status. Not surprisingly, even hitherto obedient laity turned in ever-increasing numbers to modes of contraception still formally forbidden by the Church. Change in this regard occurred more rapidly between 1965 and 1970 than in any five-year interval since 1955.[92]

Growing numbers of Catholics, some devout and some less so, also changed their behavior with regard to confession. "I note a considerable decline in the frequency and taste for confession, as it is now administered, on the part of our more intelligent laity," an Ohio priest quite typically reported very early in 1967.[93] Birth control was usually a factor, at least for adults. Growing numbers of priests might now be willing to grant routine absolution to their contracepting penitents. But permissiveness in this regard sometimes had the effect of stimulating lay resentment over earlier painful confessions that had centered on birth control. What purpose had that agony served if contraception was not in fact intrinsically immoral? Many laity were surprisingly willing to forgive, if not forget, encounters of this sort. But some were sufficiently angry to be deterred from continued frequent confession.

More fundamental was a new way of thinking about sin—something stimulated in a great many cases by individual deliberations over birth control. Was it sometimes right to employ a prohibited mode of contraception? Growing numbers of Catholics thought so. No matter what the Church taught, Catholics like these did not believe that contraception was wrong in and of itself. Its morality depended instead on the user's disposition, motivation, and circumstances—a logic that was readily applied to a wide range of moral dilemmas. Of what relevance, then, was a penitential ritual that almost invariably required a rapid-fire itemization of sins defined according to a rule book? Confession "as it is now administered," to echo the Ohio priest just quoted, had little room for exploring individual motives and circumstances. It also presumed that the priest, rather than the penitent, was the appropriate judge of the penitent's conduct. Their wrestling with the birth control question had caused many laity to doubt this, especially in light of the clergy's celibacy. "Confession has become a stylized ritual—stand—advance a few paces—enter the box—use only [the] socially determined amount of time for accusing one's self," in the words of a highly educated Catholic woman, responding to a 1966 survey. "Exploring the conscience, or rather forming it, is a solitary experience—not for the confessional."[94]

So matters stood for the laity on the eve of *Humanae Vitae,* the pope's belated affirmation of the traditional teaching. He spoke to an American laity firmly in favor of change: 73 percent of adult Catholics polled by a *Newsweek* survey in 1967 favored a change in the Church's stance on contraception, with the young and college educated even more apt to endorse reform.[95] More important, he spoke to a laity moving rapidly toward an unprecedented consciousness of moral autonomy. "The encyclical *Humanae Vitae* was for all practical purposes an appeal to pure authority," as Andrew Greeley saw matters in 1972, " a pure authority which the Pope mistakenly assumed that he still had."[96] Most American Catholics still regarded the pope as a powerful symbol of their faith tradition and a principal spokesman for Christianity. But his pronouncements now had to be judged, for essentially moral reasons, by the individual's own understanding of what was right and wrong. "It seems to me that Christ met each person as an individual with individual problems," a Baltimore laywoman wrote to her cardinal-archbishop in the immediate wake of *Humanae Vitae.* "He was more concerned about the welfare of each person than the Letter of the Law. . . . In the last analysis, I feel, we cannot let Pope Paul make our decisions for us. Certainly, we must listen to him carefully; we must let the Church guide our decisions—but we must also realize that God speaks to each one of us personally."[97]

What was new by 1968 was not lay disobedience to Church teaching, or even lay doubts that the teaching was right, at least with regard to its rigidity. Many Catholic couples in the 1930s effectively rejected *Casti Connubii,* if we judge by their behavior. But they did not publicly dissent from the encyclical, and even in private were apt to couch their objections in narrowly pragmatic terms. The teaching was simply too hard to observe, especially in the context of a global depression. That individual laity were morally obliged to weigh the merits of Church teaching "through our own insights and experiences," in the words of the just-quoted Baltimore woman, would have seemed to most Depression-era Catholics like a working definition of Protestantism. However independent their behavior might be, they did not speak a principled language of individual choice—not when it came to religion.

Many laity thought differently by the later 1960s, particularly the young and well educated. Their own individualism did not seem to them inconsistent with Catholicism, and certainly not with an understanding of the Church as the people of God. "In the belief that Christ is truly present in His Church, and that the Holy Spirit guides her not only through the hierarchy, but through the laity as well, I should like to offer you my witness as a Catholic married woman," as another Baltimorean began her letter of protest to Cardinal Shehan with regard to *Humanae Vitae.*[98] Might the Spirit, indeed, not speak through other churches than the Roman Catholic? A graduate student at Notre Dame, writing to challenge the pope on his reigning assumptions in the encyclical, was prepared to assert that the Anglicans had probably been right at Lambeth about the morality of contraception. In that likely event, Catholics were obliged to submit to the Spirit's dictates "in humility." "Was Vatican II to deny us a vernacular liturgy because it would seem that the Spirit guided Luther and the other reformers hundreds of years before the Catholic Church?"[99]

Not every American Catholic in the later 1960s moved in this direction. But since young Catholics were so powerfully affected by this mode of thinking and since diminishing numbers of priests were willing to challenge it, the correspondents just quoted represent what soon became the lay Catholic mainstream. The situation was fraught with certain grave difficulties. In the context of a vitiated teaching authority, how were Catholics to determine what constituted the essentials of doctrine? How were they to agree on a distinctively Christian code of morality and pass it on to the next generation? Some once-ardent proponents of change would eventually conclude that its costs outweighed the benefits. Hence Michael Novak's eventual rebirth as a religious and political conservative. Many laity, however, experienced change as a source of personal liberation, or so period rhetoric would suggest. As popular parlance had it, they became adults in the Church and in relation to their faith. Moral responsibility might be a heavy burden, but it represented a valued form of independence—one appropriate to a laity now more than ever defined by middle-class status and college training. The truly adult Catholic, as a still-radical Michael Novak articulated the ideal in 1967, "enters the community of those whose faith has ceased to be a reflected light, and has become a flame in the center of the self. His own informed conscience is his primary source of responsibility; he chooses his own identity and destiny."[100]

Trained as they were to obedience, most Catholics came gradually to a full sense of moral autonomy—a process nearly always connected to agonizing over contraception. Deciding that the teaching was wrong, at least with regard to one's own circumstances, was only the first step. One had subsequently to wrestle with the wrongness or not of disobeying even a flawed Church teaching. Could one use contraceptives and still receive the Eucharist? Especially among the more devout, this step was hard to negotiate. According to a study done early in 1967, only a small minority of hitherto devout Catholics who had opted for a forbidden means of birth control was still receiving communion. A majority of Catholics polled for this study, regardless of their birth control practice, "held that a loss of faith could result if a person makes decisions about which Church teachings he will (or will not) follow"—thus revealing their fear of moral autonomy even as they edged toward it. Fewer than 30 percent of the Protestants polled as a kind of control group agreed with the statement.[101] Once the pope finally spoke in *Humanae Vitae,* the issue was joined with particular intensity. Only the authority of one's own conscience could justify continued disobedience. Thus untold numbers of Catholics had moral autonomy thrust upon them by a pope who had hoped to achieve just the opposite. Some left the Church in consequence; many more resumed the full practice of their religion, notwithstanding their use of contraception. It was a Reformation of

sorts, accomplished in the minds and hearts of the people if not in terms of ecclesiastical structures. The contradictions thereby generated still haunt the
American Church.

The Clergy: Negotiating Identity

As the laity moved toward moral autonomy, and sin was increasingly seen in
largely subjective terms, a crisis loomed for the clergy. "What is confusing and
disturbing for the priest are the implications for his traditional role as moral
guide, judge and confidential advisor," a Midwestern priest noted in 1968, in
the midst of what he rightly regarded as a cultural revolution. "Not only is the
efficient and clever 'outside world' rather skeptical of his traditional moral
role, it seems that his own church community is in two minds about it."[102] As
early as 1964, priests were talking in terms of an identity crisis. What did it
mean to be a priest, given "the rapid rate of change in the Church and temporal society[?]," as a clerical gathering in Chicago phrased an increasingly urgent question.[103] The grievances initially centered on a perceived lack of
respect. Assistant priests—those who served under the potentially absolute
sway of a pastor—often felt like "'errand boys, valets, hired help' for whom
the cardinal virtue of obedience is a nearly unendurable burden," according to
the aforementioned priests' meeting in Chicago, which took place at the end
of 1963. The advanced age of many assistants only made matters worse: in a
great many dioceses, including Chicago, men waited twenty years and more
prior to becoming pastors.

Long waits like these had been a fact of clerical life since the 1930s, so this
particular problem was not exactly new. But by the early 1960s, the climate
was right for the airing of suppressed grievances. Younger men especially were
conscious that an increasingly well-schooled laity expected more from their
priests in terms of professional competence, and posed an implicit challenge
to clerical authority by virtue of their own occupational achievements and ease
in the larger society. One's priestly status was no longer sufficient to command
automatic respect, or so it seemed to growing numbers of clergy. At just this
time, moreover, the laity were emerging as articulate public critics of the
Church—mostly in the context of the debate over contraception. Their example almost certainly encouraged priests to present their own discontents for
public consideration. Thus the public debate over mandatory celibacy for
priests followed close on the heels of the public debate over contraception. But
lay criticism was also a cause of further demoralization among the clergy.
Priests were the frequent targets of such criticism, given their role as the frontline enforcers of the Church's sexual teaching. And even more troubling was
the claim—ubiquitous by the mid-1960s—that a celibate clergy was seriously
compromised when it came to an understanding of sex. Experience was all.

Prey to the romanticization of marriage that lay at the heart of the various family life movements, growing numbers of priests began to doubt that their celibacy conveyed any meaningful moral witness. Was marriage not the preeminent model of self-giving—of truly other-centered love? "I believe many priests would be less selfish and egotistical if they had a family to share their immediate attention and distract them from self," as a clerical critic of mandatory celibacy articulated the argument in 1964.[104]

The reforms of the Second Vatican Council had the inadvertent effect of exacerbating the nascent crisis in priestly identity. This was particularly true of liturgical reform. Many priests welcomed the vernacular Mass and endorsed the Council's efforts to involve the laity more fully in this great prayer of the Church. But it meant relearning the whole of a complex ritual that had lain at the heart of one's long schooling. "We were perfectly trained to serve in a world that disintegrated as soon as we stepped into it," as Baltimore's Father Joseph Gallagher put it, with regard to liturgical reform and a great deal more.[105] The reformed liturgy also put a new premium on a priest's personality, even as it undermined his exalted status as ritual mediator. Now that he faced the congregation and spoke their language, the priest could no longer take refuge in the arcane recesses of the Latin Mass—in its elaborate ritual gestures and archaic cadences. His performance depended more than ever before on his perceived warmth and sincerity, and his gifts—or otherwise—as a preacher, since the reformed liturgy gave new prominence to the sermon. Not even the youngest priests had been adequately trained as homilists, and nearly all had been socialized to a formal and rather remote public persona—of dubious value in their reformed liturgical role. The transition was hard for most clergy to negotiate, though young men generally found it easier to move from the old ritual world to the new.

The pre-conciliar Latin Mass had been very much the priest's preserve. The congregation was mostly silent, with many absorbed in their own private prayers. Few laity were permitted on the altar, which was separated from the body of the church by an elaborate railing. People knelt to receive communion, which was taken on the tongue. Only the priest was permitted to touch the consecrated Host with his hands and drink the consecrated wine. The reformed liturgy, by contrast, was marked by a kind of communal ethos, with new roles permitted to the laity and a diminution of the symbolic barriers separating celebrant from congregation. By means of its structure, gestures, and language, the ritual emphasized the collective nature of the Eucharistic offering. The priest's role as mediator—as the ritual conduit between God and humanity—was thereby eroded, despite his central place in the liturgy itself. Hence the growing tendency among Catholics to speak of the Eucharist as a meal or banquet—a communal phenomenon par excellence—rather than a sacrifice, which suggested the solitary action of a man set apart for this ritual purpose.

The effect for some priests was to call into question the importance of their sacramental role—traditionally the essence of priesthood. That role, in the view of a young Dominican, "doesn't require much time, nor is it typically very difficult. So if priesthood is understood primarily as a sacramental ministry, many young priests begin to question the value of their calling."[106] Theological speculation with regard to the Eucharist simply compounded the confusion. Catholics have historically been taught that the consecrated bread and wine are the literal body and blood of Christ—made so by the ritual action of a validly ordained priest. The reformed liturgy, by its very horizontalism, seemed to lend tacit support to those theologians—very much a product of the radical 1960s—who understood the sacrament more subjectively. Such theologians, in the words of Baltimore's Cardinal Shehan, appeared "to say that Christ's presence in the Eucharist is real *when* and *because* I *believe* He is present, in reaction to the 'bread and wine' sign."[107] The faith of the people, in other words, was the efficacious cause of Christ's sacramental presence, however this presence might be individually understood.

Weakened support for the priest's sacramental role, which included the rapidly diminishing traffic in the confessional, made the issue of mandatory celibacy all the more problematic. Nearly everyone intuited that a priest's celibacy was bound up with antique concepts of ritual purity, although contemporary defenders of the practice seldom employed such language. The priest's role as mediator, it was usually argued, required a single-hearted devotion to God; his celibacy was a powerful symbol of that devotion.[108] But with the priest's status as mediator being called into question, the principal justification for mandatory celibacy was seriously undermined. A communal ritual—one increasingly understood in other than sacrificial terms—was consonant with a presider who resembled the community he represented. A markedly positive theology of marriage, dominant by the 1960s, reinforced the new liturgical logic. It had once been a Catholic commonplace, though mostly articulated by the clergy, that consecrated virginity was superior to marriage. By the mid-1960s, even clerical conservatives were reluctant to press the claim, at least in public. "The current emphasis on the sanctity of sex makes it impossible to defend celibacy as a negation of something tainted or not quite pure," as a priest from Washington State observed in 1968.[109] In the new ideological climate, marriage sometimes seemed the better part. "I think that celibacy has been narrowed over the years to such an extent that it is typically thought of and taught as a closing off of a person rather than an opening up of a person to human experience," in the words of a Chicago priest psychologist, who eventually left the active priesthood to marry.[110]

The debate over mandatory celibacy reached its zenith in the second half of the 1960s. A solid majority of American priests apparently favored the clergy's being free to marry: 62 percent of respondents in a 1966 survey endorsed voluntary celibacy, as did 56 percent of those in a 1970 study. The younger the priest, the more apt he was to favor a policy of voluntary celibacy: 84 percent of the 1970 respondents who were under the age of thirty-six wanted to see such a change in church law.[111] Any change in the discipline, however, rested with Rome—as was also the case with the teaching on contraception. Pope Paul was evidently the more certain with regard to the discipline of celibacy, issuing an encyclical "on priestly celibacy" in June 1967, when he was still agonizing over what to do about birth control. *Sacerdotalis Caelibatus* reaffirmed the obligation to clerical celibacy in the Latin rite, endorsing this ancient discipline as peculiarly "fitting" to the sacramental priesthood.[112] Paul's arguments were greeted derisively by many of celibacy's critics, in what proved to be a precursor of the protests that met *Humanae Vitae*. *Commonweal* exemplified the dissenters' mood with an editorial headed "Bachelor Psychosis."[113] The apparently numerous priests who had hoped for a change in the discipline were especially embittered, much as their lay counterparts would soon be with regard to contraception and for much the same reasons. "It has been my experience, in lectures and seminars, that a good deal of hostility has been generated on this topic among priests and seminarians," as a Midwestern priest explained. "This hostility centers around the experience of having their central life commitment discussed at higher levels without their being involved in any consultation."[114]

The unprecedented number of priests who left the active ministry after 1965 is most often explained by invoking frustrations over celibacy. Most of those who left, after all, married shortly thereafter. Others claimed that the wave of resignations—at least 10 percent of the active clergy in the United States departed between 1966 and 1971—had more fundamentally to do with a crisis of belief, either in an ultimate sense or with regard to the priesthood.[115] Either explanation suggests a priestly caste in disarray. The unprecedented resignations were both evidence of this distressing reality and a cause of its progressive intensification, especially given the simultaneous erosion of once-healthy seminary enrollments. "The priest is not alone as he questions the meaning of his life," in the words of a working paper generated by a Chicago priests' organization. "Young people too are wondering why his work is said to be such an important contribution."[116] It did not escape the notice of an increasingly alienated clergy that the Second Vatican Council, for all its revolutionary effects, had had little to say about the priesthood. The Council Fathers had acknowledged that an increasingly educated laity had of necessity to play a more prominent role in the Church and indeed an evangelizing role in the world. As for the world's bishops, their Council experience was a powerful source of new morale and a spur to the organization of national episcopal conferences. "But no fresh rationales for being a priest or a religious emerged," as Martin Marty has cogently noted, "while the old ones were effectively undercut by the advances in understanding of bishop and lay person."[117]

The gathering crisis of the priesthood—"quite clearly seen" by some, "rather uneasily sensed" by most, in the words of a clerical observer[118]—was connected in multiple ways to the gathering crisis over contraception. Many priests were probably disposed, by the very fact of their own alienation, to a greater sympathy for reform of the teaching on birth control. The laity were not alone in regarding the hierarchy as deaf to those whom they governed—as inclined, in the view of one Michigan priest, to consult "the 'palace guard' . . . to the detriment of the real people who have to execute these decisions."[119] The prospect of a married clergy—devoutly if wishfully to be hoped for—led nearly all advocates of voluntary celibacy to endorse reform. "It is difficult to believe that if priests, bishops, cardinals and the pope himself were married that they [would] not learn from their wives the suffering and agony which result from too frequent pregnancies," in the words of Father John A. O'Brien, now a convert both to contraception and clerical marriage.[120] Those priests who became sexually active—a not inconsiderable number in the later 1960s, albeit a distinct minority—presumably used contraceptives themselves. They were seldom involved in relationships that had immediate room for a child.[121]

At the same time, the birth control crisis further weakened the already shaken self-confidence of a great many clergy. "Lay people who had been taught all their lives to turn to the priest for the teaching of the Church on moral questions were now asking in vain for any sure guidance," as a thoughtful priest observer summed up the mid-1960s. "This more than anything else has highlighted the confusion and role uncertainty of the clergy."[122] Those who privately doubted the teaching were for the most part unable to say so to their penitents, believing themselves obliged to hew to the traditional doctrine—at least in principle. One could grant absolution without dwelling at length on the penitent's purpose of amendment. One could even encourage troubled penitents to follow their own consciences. Neither option left the priest with much sense of authority. Nor were such approaches particularly helpful to penitents who wanted assistance in forming their consciences, or the comfort of a priest's "permission" to use birth control. "As a confessor I . . . feel the need of some solid absolutes as tools to work with in the confessional," a military chaplain explained in 1966. "Each Saturday I feel that I have been excavated of everything I have to offer in the way of acceptable advice."[123] Even those willing to enforce the teaching were increasingly troubled by having to "refuse absolution to some of [their] best parishioners"—a reflection, no doubt, of the growing use of contraception among the devout—and on grounds that were regularly challenged in the Catholic press.[124] Hearing confessions in the mid-1960s often left priests feeling helpless. They felt even more so as their erstwhile penitents began to abandon the sacrament. "The custom of hearing confessions and forgiving sin is not only central to the priest's self-understanding," in the words of a sensitive period observer, "it is one of his striking claims which makes him different from other clergymen."[125]

Few priests at the outset of the 1960s were aware that contraception was about to explode as a highly divisive issue among Catholics. The teaching seemed unshakable. According to Bishop Kenneth Untener, ordained for Detroit in 1963, his training in moral theology was "totally unchanged" by the Second Vatican Council. At the time of his ordination, he regarded the teaching on contraception as "a given, and not a big issue."[126] Even young priests knew that the teaching was hard for most laity to observe—something they quickly learned from their penitents, who were increasingly apt to be frank with regard to sex. "It affected me very deeply, the struggles of people saying, 'I can't make love by a thermometer, by a test, and it's really destroying my relationship with my wife,'" as Chicago's Father Robert Ferrigan remembered his early years of priesthood, having been ordained in 1961. "I'm a twenty-five year old celibate listening to this, thinking—'yeah, we're not machines,' what they were saying is that they were not machines, and they felt that our moral code was about treating the body as a machine."[127] But few priests, at least in the early 1960s, believed that the teaching's burden was unbearable. They were sure that empathetic confessors could substantially lighten the load. Father Ferrigan, for example, quickly chose to omit close questioning with regard to "sins against marriage" and was always generous with encouragement and absolution. Like nearly all my priest informants, he regarded himself as a good confessor—or, to be more exact, believed that he soon matured into one. Despite the rigidities of his training, as Baltimore's Joseph Gallagher quite typically put it, "I certainly had the notion that the confessor was to be kind and patient."[128]

Lay-authored publications were for many priests the first intimation that gentle confessors were not the solution to the laity's birth control problems. "The current problem here is birth control," a Wisconsin seminarian informed a friend in the spring of 1964. "The article [i.e., Rosemary Reuther's] that appeared in the recent issue of [the *Saturday Evening*] *Post* and the letters that have appeared in *Jubilee* have raised the storm."[129] Presumably emboldened by the rise of public dissent, many hitherto quiescent Catholics began to speak frankly to their clergy—both in the confessional and outside of it. "A sizeable number of good Catholics have told me that they are practicing birth control," as a young Baltimore priest reported. "After some discussion I am convinced that they are in good conscience. . . . For these people it's the intention that makes the difference between morality and immorality."[130] Some priests even learned from lay sources about theologians in Europe who were querying the traditional teaching's logic. Rosemary Ruether, it will be recalled, invoked their authority in her *Jubilee* essay, while Dr. John Rock claimed on national television that an unnamed Dutch bishop had recently given a public quasi-endorsement to the Pill. (Rock presumably made reference to Bishop William Bekkers, who asserted in a televised address in Holland in 1963 that the Pill was not contraceptive in the usual sense; he also noted that most married couples had compelling cause to limit their families and were not equally endowed with the qualities necessary to achieve this by means of periodic continence.[131]) Once the secular media lit on the story of lay dissent over contraception, venturesome theologians became the stuff of everyday news. "About a year and a half ago, I began to hear reports from 'progressive' Catholics that the European moralists were about to shift the Church's whole doctrine on this subject," an American Jesuit told a confrere in the spring of 1964. "These reports will gain much greater currency now, as a result of Bob Kaiser's article in the current number of *Time,* which I presume you have seen."[132]

Most priests adjusted easily to the new situation in terms of their preaching role. Liturgical reformers—in the ascendancy now, given their triumph at the Council—called for preaching to be more explicitly rooted in Scripture. What Biblical warrants against contraception were there, save for the venerable story of Onan? And even Onan had been dethroned, thanks to a greater freedom for Catholic scripture scholars. "The passage about Onan must be discounted, since the reason why God punished him is unclear," a New Jersey priest explained.[133] Even John Ford and Gerald Kelly conceded the story's diminished utility in their magisterial treatment of *Marriage Questions,* published in 1963. They looked instead to St. Paul's alleged condemnation of homosexuality for an implicit prohibition of contraception, but without success—at least according to the respected Jesuit scripture scholar Joseph Fitzmyer: "I frankly know of no passage in the N[ew] T[estament] which forbids it [contraception."][134] A more scriptural orientation also meant that explicitly dogmatic sermons were increasingly rare, which further decreased the likelihood that birth control would be addressed. There are no references to contraception in the sermon outlines for the Archdioceses of Detroit and Milwaukee after 1962, and only one in those for the Archdiocese of Chicago.[135] Nor did the principal homiletics journal any longer feature texts denouncing this putative sin.

Even greater changes took place with regard to mission preaching—historically the venue where sins against marriage were deplored in the most extreme and explicit language. Afflicted by declining attendance throughout the 1950s, missions had very nearly collapsed by the mid-1960s, at least in urban and suburban settings.[136] Hence the Passionist preacher, a veteran of the mission circuit, who in 1964 lamented "the painful, embarrassing fact of preaching many missions to churches half empty. . . . Or sometimes, it seems, just empty."[137] Growing numbers of pastors, seeing the trend, simply dispensed with the parish mission and "no longer feel bound by the regulation of Canon Law that a mission should be given to their people at regular intervals," in the words of a disappointed Redemptorist.[138] Certain religious orders responded by quietly dismantling their "mission bands," as the Jesuits seem to have done in the mid-1960s.[139] Others tried to update the mission, repudiating what a Paulist described as "the old moralizing, fire-and-brimstone, picture-painting, pulpit-pounding, anecdotic story-telling, sobbing, ham-acting, berating, and oratorical soaring that have characterized the 'old-time religion' mission."[140] The updated mission "must proclaim Salvation history to the People of God," in the words of the Passionist quoted above, and orient its hearers to the Gospel virtues of "mildness, goodness, charity."[141] It ought to be preached to mixed congregations of men and women—separation of the sexes "is an artificial distinction that no longer has any value." Nor should it deal with the problem of contraception, at least in the view of the just-quoted Paulist, who thought that the subject was best left to the Pre-Cana programs now existing in almost every diocese.[142]

Like preaching, premarital instruction was relatively easy for most '60s priests to negotiate, despite a more restive laity. With Pre-Cana programs now so ubiquitous, many priests depended on Pre-Cana staff to address the issue of birth control. In Milwaukee, for example, a well-developed Pre-Cana program served roughly 72 percent of the city's eligible couples in 1964.[143] Pre-Cana programs were invariably orthodox with regard to contraception. But over the course of the 1960s they came to place increasingly heavy emphasis on the practice of rhythm—a subject once off-limits to Pre-Cana presenters, save when asked directly about it, mostly because the program's priest sponsors feared that rhythm talk led to a "contraceptive mentality." By the 1960s, moreover, talk about rhythm meant talk about the Pill, if only as an adjunct to the system—a means of allegedly correcting an irregular menstrual cycle.[144] By mid-decade, many Pre-Cana programs were also talking the language of "responsible parenthood"—the moral obligation of parents to bear only the number of children for whom they could adequately care. This provided an obvious opening to contraception and might well have been read, given the climate, as an oblique endorsement of such, at least in the form of the Pill. Pre-Cana audiences appear to have been quite docile, despite the period's growing turbulence. Various programs, however, were reporting diminished attendance by the later 1960s. A hard-line lecture on contraception was capable by then of eliciting overt audience resistance. "Needless to say, the students objected vehemently to this view," as a priest psychologist recounted a 1969 premarital conference in Ames, Iowa, where he decried the widespread practice of delaying the birth of the first child for several years after marriage. "And, with embarrassing honesty (or stupidity?) they complained that they did not like the *words* I was using—such as 'intravaginal masturbation.'"[145]

As has been previously indicated, most priests in the 1960s faced their greatest difficulties with regard to birth control in their role as confessors. Penitents in objectively hard circumstances had always made for heartrending encounters. But until the mid-1960s, encounters like these took place in what was for priests a psychologically secure environment. Prior to this time, nearly all American priests were sure that the teaching on contraception was of divine origin—infallibly taught by the Church from its very beginning. Even those who doubted the teaching's logic—and such did exist—were certain of its authority. "Who am I to argue with centuries of Church teaching—the Church that's inspired by the Holy Spirit?" as Father Anthony Kosnik described his youthful self, having been ordained in 1955.[146] (Kosnik eventually evolved into a quite radical critic of Church teaching with regard to sexual questions generally.) Once doubts about the teaching's infallible status were raised, as happened with almost breathtaking rapidity after 1963, hard cases in confession posed a genuine moral dilemma for growing numbers of clergy. "The theologians had better come up with a better answer or else I and many other priests will not be able to justify our own consciences in the confessional," as a priest from Boston told the editors of *Jubilee* in 1964.[147]

The anovular pill occasioned particular difficulties in confession, since it alone among contraceptives was sometimes licit for Catholics to employ. Women religious in the Congo had received a Vatican congregation's permission to take the Pill as a means of proactive protection in the event of rape, since the struggle for national independence there had turned increasingly violent. (Not surprisingly, given its piquant blend of sex, race, and religion, the story was widely featured in the secular media.) Why could this logic not also apply to a woman whose health would be severely threatened by another pregnancy, but who could not—perhaps because of an uncooperative spouse— make effective use of rhythm?[148] Might such a woman not properly regard her husband as an "unjust aggressor"—like the "natives who were bent on rape"— and thus take the Pill? A priest asked a clerical journal just this question late in 1963. It was easily answered, at least in the abstract: a husband, "unlike the rapist, has a right to marital relations in virtue of the marriage bond."[149] But by giving its blessing to this indisputably contraceptive use of the Pill, the Vatican congregation in question had opened a can of theological worms. Husbands, after all, did not have an unlimited right to intercourse: an adulterous or inebriated spouse forfeited the right, at least temporarily. Why could the wife of a chronic alcoholic, to pick an obvious example, not protect her own rights by means of the Pill, if nuns in the missions were permitted to do so?

A far more frequent cause of difficulty was the opinion, broadly subscribed to by 1963, that a woman might take the Pill to regulate her menstrual cycle, the better to practice rhythm. But what degree of irregularity justified such use? And for how long could it legitimately continue? It was no easy matter for parish priests—busy men, all—to keep up with such debates, particularly as matters were evolving rapidly. The use of the Pill during lactation, once regarded by nearly all moralists as overtly contraceptive, had come by 1965 to be quite widely regarded as licit.[150] One could deal with scrupulous penitents—those incapable of making an independent decision in favor of contraception—by recommending the Pill for a yearlong period of lactation, followed by a year's use to regulate the cycle, according to a Jesuit moralist in the spring of 1965.[151] Chicago's newly ordained priests were told, in 1966, that pill use during lactation was permissible for nine months only—but permissible whether or not a woman intended to breastfeed her infant.[152] Father Bernard Häring, a well-known German moralist, was advising American priests by 1964 that the Pill might also be used to establish a regular cycle during perimenopause. "Many physicians and gynecologists have tried it for a period of 4–5–6 months. . . . After that they should then try the use of rhythm."[153]

The problem for confessors was not simply judging when the Pill might be licitly employed, difficult though that might be. Many penitents could not understand why a contraceptive that was sometimes acceptable was gravely sinful on other occasions. Hitherto docile penitents began to answer back—a new experience for both parties. "They commonly engage in long arguments in the Confessional stating that different priests give contradictory answers and do not agree with each other," as a Baltimore priest recounted his recent experiences as a confessor in 1966.[154] If a penitent honestly disagreed with Church teaching and invoked her own conscience as justification for practicing birth control, what was the confessor to do? Much depended on whose advice he sought. Joseph Connell, an invincibly conservative moralist, asserted flatly in late 1964 that no penitent of this description could receive absolution. The priest "must simply tell the penitent that he is not allowed to administer sacramental absolution to him if he knowingly refuses to accept the authoritative teaching of the Church."[155] But the Jesuit moralist quoted above—one Father Edwin Faltaisek—was telling his students at about the same time that even a poorly formed conscience had to be respected. "Perhaps his [the penitent's] conscience has been formed erroneously, but then it falls under the heading of good faith ignorance."[156]

The debate over conscience accelerated as the debate over contraception became more general. Liberals had the upper hand, since the teaching was under a broad and sustained public challenge. A doubtful law does not bind, as every seminarian knew. But could the teaching really be doubtful, given that Pope Paul had on at least two occasions told the faithful to observe the traditional norms, regardless of the debate that was effectively institutionalized in his birth control commission? Conservative theologians like John Ford and most American bishops did not think so. A number of the bishops issued instructions to this effect: "It is therefore most important," Baltimore's Lawrence Shehan quite typically told his priests, "that when the occasion requires, the confessor state clearly and unmistakably what the teaching authority of the Church holds on this subject." Only rhythm and abstinence were acceptable means of family limitation, even in difficult circumstances.[157] By 1966, however, probably most American moralists regarded the teaching as doubtful. Even Richard McCormick, the highly respected Jesuit who had ably defended the teaching as recently as 1965, had opted for doubt by 1967—a change that carried great weight with clerical middle-of-the-roaders.[158] As conservative a theologian as the Jesuit John Lynch was apparently teetering on the brink by the summer of 1968, just prior to *Humanae Vitae.* A New York bishop had heard from a reliable informant that Lynch "feels he will have to admit doubt and teach that one can follow the opinion that it [contraception] is permissible," if the pope did not speak by September.[159]

Some priests—albeit a minority—were so firmly committed to the traditional teaching that their work as confessors was not much disturbed, save for a probable diminution in the number of penitents who sought them out. Hardline confessors had always had reputations that preceded them, but especially so in the 1960s. Some men in this camp were quite gentle confessors in practice, and would just a few years earlier have been so regarded by the great majority of penitents. Though he believed contraception to be "unnatural and objectively sinful," a Jesuit based in Baltimore told Cardinal Shehan in 1966, he prided himself on treating his penitents with compassion. "Practically, I think absolution should be given as readily [for sins of contraception] as it is for other serious sins."[160] Other conservatives, however, were so hostile to sex and so agitated by the cultural climate that their demeanor in the confessional probably became even more punitive. "All that has to be done is to make the husband sleep on the floor from time to time," in the view of an elderly priest in Baltimore, whose regular assignment—happily for that city's laity—was as chaplain to a women's religious order. "Married couples certainly have sufficient opportunities to satisfy themselves in accordance with God's law as we know it."[161]

In Baltimore, it was older priests who were most likely to oppose a change in the teaching, though most of the Baltimore clergy by 1966—including a number of older men—were proponents of reform.[162] Surveys done of priests nationally in the wake of *Humanae Vitae* show the same age-related bias, which is hardly surprising. Not every older conservative, however, was pathologically hostile to sex. Many feared that a change in the teaching would fatally undermine the Church's authority and accelerate the society's rush toward a purely instrumental sexual ethic. "One of our leading neo-pagan periodicals, devoured by millions of our college-age youth, has followed what seems to me the logical and inevitable path from eliminating the physical structure of the act in marriage, to defending extra-marital relations, to denying the existence of any type of sexual perversion whatsoever," in the view of a small-town priest in Maryland. "The latest element of sexual activity to be thrown out is *affection.*"[163]

Probably a majority of priests by the mid-1960s were less than wholly committed to the Church's traditional teaching, with some in a frankly questioning state. They found themselves in a kind of confessor's limbo. What to do when a penitent contested the sinfulness of contraception, at least in her particular circumstances? What to say when a penitent simply refused to amend his contraceptive ways? The problem was especially acute for the sensitive confessor—the man who could hear what his penitent was actually saying. Growing numbers were no longer simply seeking absolution, which could sometimes be had in exchange for even an oblique acknowledgement of contraception's sinfulness. "And I can remember—'are you sorry for this?'" as Detroit's Father Louis Grandpre recounted his evolution as a confessor during these turbulent years. "'No, I'm not sorry.' 'Are you sorry that you're not sorry?' 'Well, yeah, I can say that.' 'Well, that's good enough. Say an act of contrition and let's get on with it.'"[164] But absolution was not sufficient. What many penitents wanted was priestly approval of the moral judgment to which the penitent had at least tentatively come, though not necessarily without fear and trembling. "I think they were coming to confession to kind of get a support for their position," as Monsignor Dennis Harrity remembered of such penitents in the mid-1960s.[165]

Many priests, particularly younger ones, eventually responded by telling their married penitents to follow their informed consciences with regard to contraception. This was usually a difficult step to take, given the implicit acknowledgement that the teaching these same priests had once enforced was less than absolute. What did such counsel suggest about the teaching authority of the Church? "I would say that it took some years of conscientious reading, reflection, study and discussion to come to a deeper view," as Detroit's Father William John Murphy recounted his own evolution in this regard. "Probably somewhere in the mid-'60s I began to feel much freer."[166] It helped that growing numbers of priests were members by then of clerical discussion groups—Father Murphy joined one in 1965—where pastoral problems were deliberated in the light of new theological writing. Others found comfort in solitary reading and reflection. Father Ralph Kowalski, an eminently scholarly man, still remembers the liberating impact of John T. Noonan's magisterial *Contraception,* a history of Catholic doctrine that was published in 1965. Noonan did not dispute the antiquity of the teaching but documented the variety of sometimes contradictory arguments that had historically been deployed on its behalf, and also the many periods in Church history when the teaching had received little attention. Reading Noonan's book was for Kowalski a source of "great relief. . . . The veil was lifted, as far as I was concerned."[167]

By the mid-1960s, then, the penitent who confessed to contraception faced an unprecedented variety of possible responses. Some priests insisted on its status as a mortal sin and demanded that the penitent reform her life. She might be denied absolution, if her purpose of amendment was judged insufficient. Other confessors made no comment at all in response to a penitent's acknowledging birth control but granted absolution without further ado. John Ford, not surprisingly, regarded this approach as "a guilty connivance with the sin of contraception" and practically irrefutable evidence that the confessor in question did not really believe "that contraception is always immoral."[168] Still other confessors, as we have seen, might tell at least the argumentative penitent that she should follow the dictates of conscience. A few priests were even prepared to give the explicit blessing to contraception—at least in the form of the anovular pill—that so many of their penitents obviously craved. Since the Church no longer spoke with a single voice, it was harder and harder to maintain—for priests and laity alike—that the teaching was not in fact doubtful. Potentially liberating for the laity, the situation was difficult for most clergy. A doubtful law might not bind. But neither did it make for a dynamic show of priestly authority. If the laity, moreover, could make judgments in conscience with regard to birth control, what was to stop them from doing so in other matters? And if they did, what substance would remain to the priest's historic role as moral authority, guide, and judge?

In the end, most penitents simply stopped mentioning birth control when they itemized their sins. This was probably a relief to a great many priests, as few of them relished the moral choice they were suddenly called on to exercise as confessors. Consider the case of a young California woman, a semi-invalid because of rapidly progressing multiple sclerosis, who could find no confessor in 1965 who would give her an unambiguous permission to use the Pill—despite pregnancy's posing a clear danger to her life. One priest allegedly "said that he wished I would have had my tubes tied and then come to him for counsel." Penitents like these, unable for complex reasons to make up their own minds with regard to birth control, simultaneously affirmed a priest's authority and robbed him of the confidence he had until recently been assured of when it came to dealing with sexual sin. In this particular case, a physician broke the logjam. The doctor insisted that his desperately ill patient take the Pill, allegedly to alleviate menstrual cramps. "When the priest gives me absolution he tells me to try and stifle, in my mind, the contraceptive effect and keep in mind that I need them for cramps. So I am permitted to receive the Eucharist with a 'clear' (but a disturbed) conscience."[169]

As we have previously seen, many laity also eventually ceased to go regularly to confession. Priests were commenting on declining numbers as early as 1966, with the sacrament being widely described as in a state of collapse by 1969. "The once familiar steady flow of penitents has in most places slowed

Figure 9. Cartoonist Marty Murphy makes gentle but pointed fun of the long delay in the pope's issuance of an encyclical on contraception. The cartoon appeared on the cover of the April/May 1968 edition of the *Critic* magazine. Photo used by permission of the Thomas More Association.

down to a very unsteady trickle," a Detroit priest quite typically noted in the latter year. "Even the big feasts no longer draw crowds to the confessional."[170] Despite the rigors of hearing many confessions and the moral difficulties of recent years, most priests were anything but relieved at this particular development. "Is confession, as some supposedly knowledgeable theologians predict, on the way out?" asked a young priest from Syracuse in 1968. "If so, where do I fit in as a priest? How am I valuable to people? What is my role, my identity in the world?"[171] Given the large size of most Catholic parishes, it was probably true—as a Jesuit claimed in 1965—that for most Catholics "confession is the only personal contact with a priest."[172] There was not much chance of replicating this contact in other forums, and certainly not its peculiar intimacy. "I thought it was a tremendous compliment to a priest to have a person come in and talk to them like that, even though the screen was there," in the words of Father Kevin O'Brien, ordained in 1954.[173] Nor did the priest enjoy a more authoritative role than as a confessor, particularly now that the reformed liturgy had demystified his role in the Mass. But with confession in decline, what good was the priest's prodigious learning in moral theology—his preparation to be both judge and doctor of souls? Where did he fit in a world of seemingly omnicompetent secular professionals—the psychiatrists, social workers, and marriage counselors whom more and more Catholics now consulted rather than their clergy? Priests used to hear confessions for hours on end, as Father Jerome Krieg remembered of his long career, which began in 1938. He was in the confessional one Holy Saturday for more than eight hours—hearing "one after another, one after another. . . . Where did all those people come from? Where did they all go?"[174]

It does not take much imagination to hear in Father Krieg's plaintive query a more fundamental set of questions about priesthood and its seeming evisceration. Why, he was effectively asking, did the priestly vocation once elicit reverence from so many of our people? Why did they once accept our authority in the moral realm—confessing their sins on a regular basis, even if they often fell again into the very same ones? Why was our example once so compelling that the seminaries were filled to bursting? "In some ways, I envy older priests," as a young Dominican in 1966 articulated his sense of ominously changing times. "I think that they are surer of themselves than those of us ordained in the last ten or twelve years. There is more peace in them, more solidity to them. They are less mixed up, personally and theologically."[175] While the young Dominican was clearly romanticizing the situation of his elders, many of whom felt battered by the pace and direction of period change, he was right to see the younger clergy as particularly prey to demoralization, if only because their careers coincided with an unprecedented lay awakening—complicated in the 1960s by a new theological radicalism. "The role of laity and clergy is becoming vaguer day by day," in the words of two CFM activists from Milwaukee, writing in 1966 and obviously delighted by the trend. "Priests do not know what their role is. They all say that."[176]

The debate over contraception was also a major cause of priestly demoralization. The awakened laity of the 1950s had typically endorsed their tradition's highly restrictive understanding of sexuality, attractively packaged by then in a tender rhetoric of sex-as-sacrament, and its equally restrictive understanding of gender. Priests active in the various family life movements were able to promote the leadership of an educated laity and still feel possessed of an authoritative role. Once this same lay constituency began to challenge the tradition's assumptions and—very much in conjunction with this challenge—to insist on experience as a principal criterion for moral decision making, priests felt increasingly like marginal men. "As regards birth control, we were trained like lawyers," in the words of Boston's Father Francis Delaney.[177] But what was achieved in the 1960s was precisely the delegalization of the Church.[178] "The Catholic priest, the social guardian of the traditional morality, becomes increasingly uncertain," as a priest professor summed things up in 1968. "His own professional training in this area of sexuality seems increasingly inadequate and irrelevant."[179] Being consigned in the mid-1960s to an equivocal role in the confessional simply exacerbated the problem, especially in a cultural context that placed a premium on personal witness and authenticity. With the issuance of *Humanae Vitae,* as we shall shortly see, the clergy's crisis of identity—fused, now, in a great many cases with individual crises of conscience—reached its climax. It was priests who were that encyclical's principal victims.

The American Bishops: Renegotiating Leadership

Probably no American bishop on the eve of the Second Vatican Council anticipated any change in the Church's teaching on contraception, or thought that such was necessary. None seem to have raised the issue in the documents most bishops sent to Rome in preparation for the Council.[180] Few, in all likelihood, were aware that the teaching was under quiet siege by certain European moralists. The American bishops were regarded in Europe as "hard-working, ingenuous but theologically deficient," to quote the pseudonymous Xavier Rynne, whose riveting, first-person accounts of the Council appeared in the *New Yorker.*[181] Unfair as the assessment was, it contained a germ of truth.

Beyond their unfamiliarity with the theological avant-garde, nearly every bishop had ample cause to assume the teaching's immutability. Working primarily as administrators and in carefully orchestrated ceremonial roles, they had little contact with the sufferings of the married laity and little sense of their growing restiveness. All had been trained to regard the teaching as infallible. Perhaps most important, they presided over a church that looked to be in a state of robust health. "It is not our people who miss Mass on Sunday, refuse the sacraments and vote the Communist ticket," as San Antonio's Steven Leven reminded his European confreres at the Council, in one of the feistier moments for the American delegation. "We have not lost the working class. They are the foundation and support of the Church."[182] The bishops were far less optimistic about the health of the larger American society, which seemed to them caught in the throes of an excessive individualism and drifting toward a shocking degree of sexualization. Patriots to a man, they undoubtedly saw Catholic sexual teaching as a source of salvation not only for Catholics but, in an oddly secular sense, for the country they loved.

It was European bishops and their theological advisors who raised the problem of contraception at the Council. A vigorous tradition of theological enquiry in countries like Germany, Belgium, and Holland helps to explain this; so does the increasingly parlous state of the Church in continental Europe, where Mass attendance and reception of the sacraments had long been in decline. The prohibition on marital contraception kept countless baptized Catholics away from the sacraments, it was frequently argued. It also offended the educated, who saw marriage in highly personalist terms and worried—notwithstanding Europe's low birthrates—about the exploding global population. Given the existence of the papal commission, contraception was not on the Council's formal agenda, save—as we shall see—in the form of the Council's brief statement on marriage and the family. But it surfaced repeatedly in the informal discussions that surrounded the Council's various sessions, where probably most of the Council's educational impact occurred. "My whole attitude toward birth control was changed one night at the Vatican Council," as the late Monsignor John Egan remembered of a 1964 discussion at "the Villanova common room," where theological debates regularly took place. On this particular evening, four prominent theologians were present—John Courtney Murray, Gregory Baum, Charles Davis and, to the best of Egan's recollection, Bernard Cooke. All four, according to Egan, agreed that a married couple who had good reasons might licitly practice contraception. Conscience was determinative in the matter. "That solved it for me," as Egan explained. "I had at least a strong probable opinion," given the quality of the theologians involved.[183]

The conciliar buzz about birth control was sufficiently intense that, at Pope Paul's request, the Vatican Secretariat of State polled the various national hierarchies early in 1964 with regard to the status—broadly defined—of contraception in their countries. To what extent did Catholics practice birth control? What about non-Catholics? How was contraception treated in law and public policy? What doctrinal and pastoral tendencies were evident on the part of theologians and the parish clergy? True to its reputation for efficiency, the National Catholic Welfare Conference commissioned papers in response to each of these queries, then asked its members for their comments, since the Vatican also wished to know the view of the nation's bishops "on this whole question."[184] The pope was evidently impressed. "I might mention that His Holiness took personal note of these documents," Egidio Vagnozzi, the Apostolic Delegate to the United States, told Archbishop Patrick O'Boyle, "and highly commended the organizational effort that went into their preparation."[185]

John C. Ford wrote the paper on doctrinal and pastoral tendencies—the most important of the documents sent to the bishops and subsequently to the Holy See. Given the positive response it elicited from most of the American hierarchy and Ford's probable contributions to *Humanae Vitae,* the contents are worth exploring. Ford began by acknowledging widespread confusion among American Catholics, "both priests and people," about Church teaching on contraception and their own obligations in this regard. The confusion stemmed not from the country's professional theologians, who in Ford's view were thoroughly orthodox on the question, but instead from "a good deal of bootleg moral theology." Chief among the miscreants was Dr. John Rock, whom Ford privately thought should be barred from the sacraments. Certain European theologians were also muddying the waters, aided by publications like *Commonweal* and even the diocesan press. Ford seemed particularly worried about Bernard Häring, who traveled frequently to the United States to lecture on moral theology: Häring had allegedly left an unknown number of priests and seminarians "under the impression that in some cases those who intend to continue practicing contraception may be absolved." Although it was impossible to be precise as to numbers, it was clear that at least some confessors were giving obliquely permissive counsel about the Pill and that at least some laity were taking it to heart.[186]

The situation was such, in Ford's view, that "the Church"—defined as the pope, possibly in concert with the bishops—had to speak. Otherwise growing numbers of Catholics would be led to "believe that a substantial change is coming." But what, exactly, should "the Church" say? Certainly it had to endorse the doctrine enunciated in *Casti Connubii* and subsequently affirmed in various statements by Pope Pius XII, "including his rejection of the pill for contraceptive reasons." Failure to do so would result in "devastating" effects, both pastorally and doctrinally. "Nobody could say any longer what moral doctrines of the Church were binding on the conscience of the faithful. . . . The whole field of sexual morality could be called into question." In these relativist and sexualized times, moreover, the Church was obliged to remind the world that the human generative function has "in some special sense a sacred and inviolable character from nature and from God." As with other functions of the body, humans could sometimes intervene to enhance the generative function— to enable it to work more perfectly. But because that function had to do with the origins of life, human powers of intervention had special limits when it came to generativity. "We know this much with certainty, at least from ecclesiastical authority, that contraception and contraceptive sterilization go beyond these limits." If contraception was not murder—and Ford was far too sophisticated to make such an argument—it nonetheless bore directly on the inviolability of human life.[187]

Affirming the traditional teaching, however, entailed at least two major problems. The first had to do with the teaching's still shaky intellectual foundations. The natural law argument, as Ford had long argued, simply did not convince. The second problem had to do with the development of doctrine, which Ford—for all his conservatism—both endorsed and regarded as necessary, at least in the realm of morality. Catholic teaching on marriage had changed enormously in the course of Ford's own lifetime, with sex now accorded a far higher value and one independent of procreation, thanks largely to rhythm—"now firmly established as a legitimate means of controlling conception and limiting family size." Any reaffirmation of the teaching on contraception had to make room for continued development of this sort, which Ford assumed would occur primarily by "perfecting the security of periodic continence for those couples who are entitled to practice it." Ford, in other words, was convinced—and trying to convince the bishops—that medical science would soon make it possible to predict the moment of ovulation more or less exactly, even to cause ovulation to occur on a particular day. Developments like these would render the practice of rhythm almost foolproof and not terribly burdensome, since couples would have to abstain for a few days only. The pope should encourage not just medical research into these promising possibilities but theological explorations to meet such eventualities as a drug that enabled a woman to set a date for her monthly fertile period.[188]

Although Ford was deeply loyal to the pope, he wanted the Council to issue the much-needed statement on contraception. A Council pronouncement would frustrate those too-numerous dissenters who "ignore or minimize previous Papal pronouncements and still more the decrees of Roman congregations." The statement should invoke Church authority only—"there is no real theological consensus" on the reasons for the teaching—and leave "open for discussion the regulation and correction of abnormal sterility-fertility." (Ford referred in the latter phrase to various strategies for perfecting the practice of rhythm.) He proposed, albeit tentatively, that the statement might be accompanied by "an instruction which among other things would make it clear that Catholics who refuse to accept the teaching of the Church on birth control are ineligible to receive the Sacraments." Perhaps he sensed that the bishops would regard such a step as pastorally imprudent. How many otherwise upstanding Catholics would abandon the sacraments if such an instruction were promulgated? How many would drift away from the Church? Ford himself, however, seemed to think that firmness was in order: "Without some such sanction there will be many another Dr. Rock."[189]

The 105 bishops who voiced their opinion on birth control in response to the NCWC's solicitation were generally in sympathy with Ford's views. Only eight were opposed to the issuing of a statement on contraception, which would of necessity have been one that affirmed the traditional teaching. None of the eight, to all appearances, voiced doubts about the teaching itself, although St. Louis's Cardinal Joseph Ritter was clearly worried about the pastoral problems it was creating. A statement of the sort proposed by Ford, in Ritter's opinion, "would serve to put many in bad faith and result in greater alienation from the Church." The overwhelming majority of the bishop respondents—97, to be exact—favored such a statement, to be issued expeditiously. "If action is not soon, clear, authoritative and united we shall be generations repairing the damage," as one unidentified prelate articulated the consensus view. Fifty-two bishops wanted the Council to speak; twenty-three thought the job best done by the pope. Most apparently wanted the statement, no matter who its author, to be couched in pastoral language; it "should avoid, inasmuch as possible, a negative and condemnatory approach and emphasis should be placed upon the positive aspects in order to inform and to inspire our people," as one bishop put it. But the statement should also be clear as to principles, and in that sense firm. "This is needed by priests," as another respondent opined, "even more than by [the] faithful."[190]

Shortly after the bishops were polled, John Ford traveled to Rome, at least partly to prod the pope or the Council to issue a statement on contraception. The journey confirmed anew that such was urgently needed. The students at Louvain's American College—historically an incubator for the next generation of U.S. theologians—responded to a Ford lecture on marital morality with undisguised skepticism. "They question that procreation is primary end [of intercourse]," as Ford's diary records. "Question whole tradition on birth control. Don't accept auth[ority] of Pius XII on pill. Question authority of papal statements more generally." Much of the blame, in Ford's opinion, rested with Canon Louis Janssens, famous far beyond Belgium for his permissive views on the Pill, who taught moral theology at Louvain. ("Vatican II was Louvain I," as Michigan's Father Tom McDevitt likes to say, being a 1958 graduate of the institution. He remembers Janssens as "a wonderful man."[191]) But Bernard Häring was culpable, too. He had recently lectured at Louvain, telling the students—according to Ford—that "they were not only permitted to advise people to use [the] pill a la J[anssens] but were *obliged* to inform penitents of their liberty to follow this opinion because it is a truly probable opinion."[192]

Once in Rome, Ford quickly secured an interview with Cardinal Alfredo Ottaviani and then, presumably through Ottaviani's good offices, a private audience with the pope. Ottaviani poured scorn on the notion of the Council's issuing a statement on contraception—something that would inevitably require the assembled bishops to discuss the subject. "Impossible. Never finish," Ford's notes on the meeting have Ottaviani saying. "Besides, so many of the Bishops knew nothing about the subject."[193] Ford found a readier response from Pope Paul, to whom he presented a copy of the report he had done for the American bishops. "He was affable, cordial, alert, a little tired, a little sad perhaps, seemed to understand everything, gave me his attention." Ford talked "fast and furious"—sometimes in English, sometimes in Italian, sometimes even in Latin for purposes of clarity. (The pope "seemed to understand my Latin very well.") He stressed what he saw as the reigning confusion, using his recent experience at Louvain as an example, although without mentioning either the college or Häring by name—perhaps partly because Häring was personally close to the pope. Only a definitive affirmation of the teaching could end the confusion, Ford argued; "I also made much of the authority of [the] ordinary magisterium, how failure to sustain Pius XII would undermine it etc." Never one to hold back, Ford proceeded to instruct the pope on just what such an affirmation should include.[194]

Pope Paul did indeed issue a statement on contraception but hardly of the sort that Ford had wanted. The pope announced on 23 June 1964 that "the matter was under study, a study as wide and deep as possible." For the time being, however, the faithful were to observe the traditional teaching: "so far we do not have sufficient reason to regard the norms given by Pope Pius XII in this matter as surpassed and therefore not binding; they must therefore be considered as valid, at least until we feel in conscience bound to modify them."[195] A more equivocal formulation could hardly be imagined. Paul not only suggested that the teaching might change, presumably as a result of his commission's deliberations, but that he himself had an open mind. How else to explain his intimation that the strictures of Pius XII—which involved not only the Pill but the teaching on contraception per se—were mutable, in the event of new evidence? A fuller understanding of how the Pill worked, new developments in moral theology—either a quite likely eventuality, the pope could be read as saying—might clear the way for a new approach to the morality of contraception.

Ford's distress at the pope's uncertain leadership involved him in a two-front war. One front was in Rome, where Ford tried simultaneously to encourage the pope to issue a sterner pronouncement[196] and to ensure that the Council's language on marriage was consonant with the logic of *Casti Connubii*. The latter effort is discussed below. The other front was at home, where Ford was involved in efforts to have the American bishops issue a statement of their own. Ford himself wrote a document for the bishops' consideration, which elaborated on the arguments of his earlier report to the NCWC. The document possessed Ford's characteristic clarity, logic, and theological acuity; it stressed the antiquity of the teaching, its intimate connection to the sacredness of life, its openness to development. It was also blunt. Many Catholics had come to believe that "the Catholic Church is about to repudiate her teaching on the immorality of contraception. This is not the case."[197]

The bishops were initially eager to issue a statement, at least according to Washington's Archbishop Patrick O'Boyle, chairman of the NCWC's Administrative Committee.[198] But the Committee tabled an initial draft, one presumably written by Ford, in April 1965.[199] A document definitely written by Ford was given to the Administrative Committee in August of the same year, and evidently also sent to all the American cardinals. It failed to secure the Committee's approval. Most thought that Ford's statement was too long and diffuse. It "should be more succinct, more quotable," in the words of Pittsburgh's John Wright.[200] More worrying was the expectation, seemingly general among the bishops, that the pope would soon issue a birth control encyclical. Should this occur, as the rector of St. Mary's Seminary in Baltimore asked, "how will your statement harmonize with the encyclical? You may be on the side of the angels—fine, but you may not be—and then there will be even more confusion."[201] Manchester's Ernest Primeau reminded his confreres that Pope Paul himself had early in 1965 called for an end to public discussion of contraception by Catholics. Primarily for this reason, Primeau was "unequivocally opposed" to issuing a statement.[202]

Ford was undoubtedly disappointed by the bishops' refusal to speak but not one to surrender his colors. His rejected statement was soon in the hands of the pope—or at least those of Cardinal Amleto Cicognani, whom Ford asked to serve as his emissary. Ford's purposes at this point were twofold. He wanted the pope to reject a proposed "pastoral instruction" recently drafted by a working group from the papal commission and markedly latitudinarian in its provisions, especially with regard to confession. Publication of the instruction, as Ford saw it, "will open wide the doors to the practice of all kinds of contraception as being in accordance with probable opinions tolerated by the Church." (The instruction was never published.) Ford also wanted to alert the pope to troubling developments with regard to the so-called schema on marriage, currently being discussed at the Second Vatican Council. In this venue, too, Ford worried that the liberal forces were about to outwit the guardians of tradition, too many of whom—perhaps even the pope—appeared to be asleep at their posts.[203]

The Council spoke to marriage in the context of its declaration on "The Church in the Modern World," promulgated during the Council's fourth session late in 1965. The chapter on marriage and family life was principally drafted by Bernard Häring, whose generously personalist views informed its logic. The text as initially drafted not only proposed that the nurturing of spousal love was as primary a purpose of marital sex as the begetting of children. It also suggested that the teaching on contraception was open to revision. Neither *Casti Connubii* nor the various allocutions of Pius XII were mentioned in the document, which in fact devoted little space to contraceptive matters. It had been the intention of reformers, as a fellow Jesuit warned Ford in the summer of 1964, to "build up their moral arguments on the basis of silence." If the teaching were really set in stone, how could the Council have promulgated a document that failed to make this clear, especially given the public controversy currently surrounding the subject? This "liberal argument from silence," according to Ford's informant, "fits precisely with what Canon Janssens said to us at his home in May: neither Pope nor Council would speak against the pill and it would thus become accepted merely with the passage of time."[204]

Ford, in reaction, alerted sympathetic officials at the NCWC, who in turn warned at least some American bishops about "the purported strategy of the 'pro pill' [faction] in the Council."[205] Ford himself alerted Detroit's Archbishop John Dearden, head of the Council's subcommission on marriage and the family, who Ford assumed—wrongly, as it happened—was an ally. He subsequently submitted to the pope his critique of the Council's text on marriage, which was due to be voted on in late November 1965. Ford was in Rome during the fourth session of the Council, when he tried to get an audience with Pope Paul to discuss his misgivings about the liberal drift of the papal birth control commission—confident, perhaps, that others were working to undermine the Council's alleged "pro-pill" forces.[206] The pope initially refused to see him, but—suggesting that others had indeed been at work—called Ford abruptly to a private audience on Nov. 22, mainly to discuss the Council's chapter on marriage.[207]

Ford deftly exploited the opening. At the hour-long audience, he urged the necessity of the Council's "safeguard[ing] the doctrine of *Casti Connubii*," which the current text on marriage conspicuously failed to do.[208] It also failed to acknowledge what Ford called the Church's "historic constant" of prohibiting sterilizing drugs, which Ford believed the Pill to be. Was this true even of drugs that rendered a woman sterile only temporarily? the pope asked—at least according to Ford. Yes, said Ford, it was. What about "onanism?" asked the pope, by which he meant coitus interruptus—historically treated more tolerantly by confessors than barrier contraceptives. That too was forbidden, said Ford. But a solution was in the offing—a "drug determining the time of ovulation." The pope "was very interested." "It would be ironic," Ford told him, "if the Church gave in just when a good solution is coming."[209] The audience ended—again, according to Ford—with the pope's asking Ford "to write down the points which I considered absolutely indispensable to make the document acceptable" and to return the next day for further discussion, "which I did."[210]

On the day after Ford's second conversation with the pope—Nov. 23—the Dearden subcommission was thrown into temporary pandemonium by an announcement from the chair, occupied on that day by Cardinal Ottaviani. A letter had just arrived from the Vatican Secretariat of State, in the name of a "higher authority"—which could only mean the pope. The letter concerned the chapter on marriage, currently in the final stages of revision by the subcommission. Those revisions, the letter stated, should include explicit mention of *Casti Connubii* and Pius XII's allocution to midwives, a 1951 statement premised on the intrinsic evil of contraception but generous in its endorsement of rhythm. They should also incorporate four statements or *modi,* which were attached to the letter. The *modi* were clearly intended to make the chapter more orthodox—as Ford would have phrased it—with regard to contraception and the purposes of marriage. "When the *modi* were read, to the consternation of the subcommission members, there was a look of triumph on the faces of the American Jesuit John Ford and the Franciscan Father Ermenegildo Lio, advocates of an intransigent position on the subject of birth control," in the not entirely neutral words of Xavier Rynne.[211]

The proffered *modi* were at least partly Ford's work.[212] Certainly he gets credit for the pope's insistence that the chapter on marriage explicitly condemn *artes anticonceptionales*—loosely translated as "contraceptive practices."[213] For this reason, he was both distressed and angered by the subsequent disposition of those amendments, which were not so much ignored—as indeed, they could not have been—as watered down. *Artes anticonceptionales,* for example, was rendered—after a period of subcommission wrangling—as *usibus illicitis contra generationem,* or "illicit practices against human generation."[214] The latter phrase, as Ford readily recognized, was supremely ambiguous, as such "illicit practices" might not include every form of contraception or even contraception at all. The references to *Casti Connubii* and the allocution to midwives were relegated to a footnote and accompanied by mention of the still-sitting papal commission.[215] "It was very clear that the Lo[u]vanians came well prepared," a bitter Ford noted in his diary, "and that practically every intention of the sub-com[mission] . . . tended *to weaken* the mind and intent of the Pope."[216] Archbishop Dearden, the subcommission head and a man who generally kept his counsel, apparently worked hand-in-glove with the reformers. Bernard Häring, writing years later in his autobiography, was still grateful for Dearden's chairing of the session where the chapter was finally revised: "All I can say is that he was simply tremendous."[217] John Ford was of a different mind: "Dearden was no help at all."[218]

The chapter on marriage in *The Church in the Modern World* did not endorse contraception. What "the Louvanians" managed to do was to keep it from being an unambiguous condemnation of the Pill. The amended chapter was "much better than we feared, much poorer than we hoped," in the words of Germain Grisez, then a Ford confederate. Gains had been made, but these would melt "like a snow in May, if the Bishops and also the Pope himself" did not now speak publicly in defense of the traditional teaching. "If the Bishops do not teach," he warned, "the Church will not lack teachers."[219] The media— religious as well as secular—were among the most noxious of these false teachers, at least according to John Ford. "It has been reported very widely that the chapter on marriage leaves the 'door open' and even 'more than open' to a change in the Church's condemnation of contraception," he told the NCWC's Paul Tanner, once again urging the American bishops to make a definitive statement on the immorality of contraceptive birth control. "The implication is that a fundamental change can now take place so that contraception will become permissible."[220] Without firm leadership from the bishops and pope, the laity and even many clergy would inevitably assume that a Catholic could lic-

Figure 10. John C. Ford, S.J. in front of St. Peter's Basilica in Rome, June 1964. Photo courtesy of the Archives of the New England Province of the Society of Jesus.

itly practice contraception, if only because this opinion was now probable. "It would be almost impossible, or at least extremely difficult and fraught with practical danger, to allow a probable opinion in favor of contraception to flourish for two or three years . . . and then try to make a decision against contraception."[221]

By early 1966, Ford seems to have abandoned efforts to get the American bishops to speak. "Only the Holy Father can now remedy this situation," he told St. Paul's Archbishop Leo Binz, whose help he sought in conveying a model statement—a jump starter of sorts—to the pope, "something drafted by

Professor Germain G. Grisez of Georgetown University and myself."[222] The continued silence of the American bishops was caused in part by their expectation that the pope would soon speak, Binz probably not being the only one who knew about Ford's proposed statement. By 1966, moreover, at least some of those bishops had themselves come to something like doubt about the teaching—its practical applicability if not its core wisdom. This seems to have happened to Detroit's John Dearden, if his behavior is any evidence. (He never spoke publicly on contraception, or—to my admittedly incomplete knowledge—committed his thoughts on the question to paper.) A shy and by most accounts rather rigid churchman, Dearden was said by those who knew him to have been transformed by the Council—by exposure to a global church in all its variety, and new ideas, too. Dearden "changed more than any man I've ever seen in my life," the late Monsignor George Higgins told me.[223] Nearly all of my Detroit priest informants agreed, one going so far as to call Dearden's change a true conversion or *"metanoia*—just like St. Paul."[224]

Dearden's new sympathies for reform did not harm his standing with his fellow bishops. He was elected first chairman of the National Conference of Catholic Bishops—successor as of 1967 to the NCWC—in which position he served as the bishops' national spokesman. But notwithstanding the respect accorded a man like Dearden, the episcopal ranks were clearly divided over the issue of contraception—a principal reason for the bishops' collective silence on the issue, which was not broken until after the promulgation of *Humanae Vitae* and then in clearly compromise fashion. The bishops' long silence made them look like most uncertain shepherds—an unhappy development for those who were worried about the general erosion of episcopal authority. A frustrated Monsignor George Kelly, longtime director of the Family Life Bureau for the Archdiocese of New York, reflected on the situation with a certain bitterness in 1965. "While the opponents of Catholic doctrine have not been the least timorous about disputing the Holy See itself, and in fact have flagrantly violated the Papal directive not to speak against the present Catholic norms, the teaching voice of the bishops has hardly been heard at all."[225] The effect was to endow dissent with its own brand of magisterial authority, if only because the opposition was—at least in a public sense—so weak. "It is a long time now since I have heard anyone argue for the truth of the traditional teaching," Detroit's Monsignor William Sherzer commented early in 1967.[226]

The bishops' long silence also had an effect on the secular politics of birth control, which evolved after 1964 with astonishing speed. In a number of states by the mid-1960s, welfare programs had come to include the provision of contraceptive services, initially to married women only but soon to the unmarried, too. Reinforcing the link between family planning and period efforts to alleviate poverty, the federal Department of Health, Education, and Welfare and the Office of Economic Opportunity (OEO) lifted their restrictions in 1966 on the use of agency funds for birth control programs. Legislation passed the Congress in 1967 mandating a family planning program in each of the fifty states, to be funded at least in part by federal dollars. Foreign-aid programs by 1967, better funded now than ever before, included provisions for family planning assistance.[227] Most ominous were moves in a number of states to liberalize laws that governed access to abortion; California in 1967 effectively legalized abortion during the first three months of pregnancy, albeit with a physician's permission. Catholic leaders were convinced that these various developments were intimately linked. "It is a matter of record in other states that Bills in the abortion area have been introduced only after the successful passing of Bills supporting contraceptives for the unmarried," as Milwaukee's Archbishop William Cousins told his clergy in 1968.[228]

Matters moved so rapidly on this particular policy front for a number of reasons. The seeming passivity of the bishops was certainly one of them. "To date there has been no general policy adopted by the American bishops" with regard to the provision of contraceptive services by the various antipoverty agencies, the NCWC's Paul Tanner told a chancery official from Trenton, New Jersey, in 1965. An NCWC committee was currently at work "on a possible set of guidelines for dealing with questions of birth control as they affect the poverty program. If suitable guidelines that can be generally accepted are devised, they will be circulated among the Bishops."[229] Tanner's tentative phrasing was telling, as was a failed attempt by the NCWC's Administrative Committee to agree on a statement in the spring of 1965.[230] Save for sending the occasional witness to the occasional Congressional hearing, the NCWC kept silent until late 1966, despite being twice encouraged by Rome "to take a vital interest in this delicate and grave matter."[231] Staff from the NCWC did keep in touch with various members of the Johnson administration, and expressed their "mounting concern . . . over the continual expansion of governmentally sponsored birth control programs."[232] But that was not the same, either in terms of secular or intra-Catholic politics, as going public with their collective opposition. "The silence of the bishops is leading to unwarranted conclusions that the Church agrees with the government's policy," as a note taker summed up "the consensus" at the fall 1966 meeting of the NCWC Administrative Committee.[233]

Individual bishops were free, at least in the confines of their own dioceses, to take a more aggressive stance. Some did indeed issue statements opposing various family planning initiatives, although these were nearly always local or statewide in scope. The Illinois bishops, for example, publicly opposed a 1965 effort to make contraceptives available to the state's unmarried mothers who were receiving welfare, when their public arguments mostly turned on the deleterious social consequences of nonmarital sex. No grassroots campaign followed. The bishops decided against an effort to mobilize Catholic voters, simply because, in the words of Joliet's Martin McNamara, "the campaign would fail. . . . We would be scandalized at the number of Catholics who would not join in." An abortive campaign of this nature "would weaken whatever political influence we have in the minds of politicians."[234] Bishops in other places were similarly cautious as to strategy, apparently for the same reason.

The recalcitrant laity were a factor in national politics, too, where they presumably help to account for the bishops' collective reluctance to speak. A series of population conferences, held between 1963 and 1967 at the University of Notre Dame, allowed Catholic liberals to make alliances with activists from such groups as the Population Council and Planned Parenthood, who were veterans of national birth control politics. One outcome was a spate of dissenting books and articles, in which Catholic scholars joined their case for reform of Church teaching to bleak assessments of the future in the event of unchecked population growth.[235] Another was the Catholic Committee on Population and Government Policy, which by early 1966 was publicly backing "government assistance for family planning programs at home and abroad." Sociologist William D'Antonio, not long before a warm proponent of generous fecundity, was now—as the group's chairman—eager to make a case before Congress for just such programs.[236] The Notre Dame conferences seem to have fueled a growing radicalism among their participants, at least according to an admittedly conservative observer in 1965. "At the last meeting on population at Notre Dame University, which was stacked with the left bank, Dick McCormick said to one confrere: 'Suppose the Holy See recondemns contraception?' The response: 'We will not accept it.'"[237] Nor could Catholic officials within the Johnson administration be relied on as allies. Sargent Shriver, the head of the OEO, was both a practicing Catholic and a proponent of government-funded family planning programs.

When the bishops finally spoke to the issue, late in 1966, they did so in terms of human freedom. Government-sponsored birth control programs, at least when aimed at those on welfare, were inevitably coercive. "Birth control is not a universal obligation, as is often implied; moreover, true freedom of choice must provide even for those who wish to raise a larger family without being subject to criticism and without forfeiting for themselves the benefits or for their children the educational opportunities which have become part of the value system of a truly free society." Foreign assistance programs that included provisions for family planning were equally coercive, since aid might easily be seen by recipients as contingent on initiatives "for birth limitation." The statement made only passing and less than emphatic reference to the intrinsic wrongness of contraception. "A responsible decision," with regard to family planning, "will always be one which is open to life rather than intent upon the prevention of life"—an apparent reference to rhythm.[238] The casual reader, even the casual Catholic reader, might be forgiven for thinking that the bishops were speaking in their typically progressive social idiom—that the statement was more about care for the poor than about contraception per se. Absent coercion, the bishops might be read as saying, family planning programs posed no particular moral difficulties.

The bishops did succeed, by means of their public statement, in alarming Lyndon Johnson, whose long career had made him exquisitely sensitive to the dangers attendant on birth control politics. Delegates from the Johnson White House met on several occasions with NCWC staffers to try to mend fences. In the course of one such meeting, Father Francis Hurley—the NCWC's assistant general secretary—allegedly told White House aide Joseph Califano that the statement represented "the last trumpet of the older American bishops."[239] Hurley was probably not wholly right; even a liberal like John Dearden was concerned that government birth control programs might eventually lead to widespread sterilization and the legalization of abortion.[240] But he seems to have reassured the Johnson White House, which moved with a new decisiveness in 1967 when it came to issues of family planning. A bipartisan coalition in Congress was even more enthusiastic, and continued to be so once Johnson left office—despite the issuance of *Humanae Vitae.* "During the Nixon years," as historian Donald Critchlow has noted, "federal family planning not only was expanded but it also became institutionalized as domestic social policy."[241]

The difficult years of the mid-1960s—difficult, at least, from the bishops' perspective—were marked by occasional dustups over contraception where individual bishops behaved as if the old Church were still intact. What is remarkable, at least in retrospect, is how few such instances there were. New York's Cardinal Francis Spellman and Archbishop Leo Binz of St. Paul-Minneapolis were apparently largely responsible for the last-minute cancellation of a four-part television series, produced by the National Council of Catholic Men, on Catholics and contraception. The program was canceled just days before its scheduled airing in January 1965, ostensibly because the pope had requested an end to public discussion among Catholics of the birth control problem. The real reason, however, was probably its script, which was written by John Leo, then an associate editor of *Commonweal.* The interpretive framework for the four programs was relentlessly evolutionary: as the centuries pass, the Christian tradition—at least in terms of sexual teaching—becomes increasingly humane. The current debate over contraception is simply the latest chapter in this long history. "Those who are now asking the Church to reconsider its stand on birth control argue that our grasp of the natural law is never complete, that the Church should always remain open to new insights as they reveal themselves in time," the narrator explained in the second program, which dealt with the views of present-day theologians. "What scholars once considered natural, such as slavery, the use of torture, the subservience of women, are not considered natural today."[242] Conservative views were well represented in the script, which in this sense was admirably balanced. But the four programs were still an effective brief for an imminent change in the teaching. Given a potential audience of 1.5 million—the series was part of the *Catholic Hour,* which was broadcast on NBC—it is not surprising that a powerful conservative like Spellman should think it worth a moment's bad press to keep the series off the air.[243]

Washington's Archbishop Patrick O'Boyle, who certainly approved of the *Catholic Hour* cancellation, courted a bad press of his own by preaching in August 1966 on "Birth Control and Public Policy"—a rare subject indeed for Catholic sermons by the mid-1960s. His seat in the nation's capital gave the sermon high visibility. "The sermon . . . received wide circulation throughout the country," as an obviously pleased O'Boyle told the Apostolic Delegate. "I have received letters from many parts of the country, some commendatory and some not approving. This was to be expected."[244] O'Boyle spoke in part about public policy, where his argument emphasized the dangers attendant on state intervention in family life. "Violations of human privacy become inevitable in the relationship between government and the indigent people who comprise the target group for government-sponsored birth control," he told the congregation at St. Matthew's Cathedral. In this respect, his sermon anticipated the statement of the NCWC's Administrative Committee that was issued just three months later. But unlike the Committee, O'Boyle dwelt unambiguously on the intrinsic evil of contraception, "whether mechanical or chemical." Many non-Catholics, O'Boyle conceded, rejected this logic in evident good conscience, which had to be respected. It would be wrong for Catholics, assuming for the moment that it was possible, "to impose their own moral code upon the rest of the country by civil legislation." But by virtue of their membership "in the Mystical Body of Christ," Catholics themselves were obliged to accept "the official teaching of the Church in matters of faith and morals. And, my dear good people, the Church's teaching with regard to contraception has been both clear and consistent."[245]

Archbishop, soon to be Cardinal, O'Boyle was also central to the single most publicized instance of episcopal high-handedness with regard to the debate over birth control. The setting was the Catholic University of America, whose chancellorship belonged to O'Boyle by virtue of his being archbishop of Washington. The University's theology faculty in 1965 had hired Charles Curran, a priest of the Diocese of Rochester and on the faculty of its seminary, as Francis Connell's replacement in moral theology. Given Connell's intransigent views on sexual matters, almost any younger man would have meant a changing of the ideological guard. But Curran was—intellectually, if not temperamentally—something of a young Turk. To make matters worse, he wrote frequently for popular periodicals, particularly—given the times—on the subject of contraception. Curran was frank about his hopes for a change in Church teaching, which would—in his view—represent a legitimate development of doctrine, necessary in order to preserve the wisdom at the teaching's heart. He was certainly not a sexual radical. "As contrasted with what is written by some Europeans (Adolfs, for example) and some other North Americans (Father Baum, notably), the contents of this book are relatively temperate," as Pittsburgh's John Wright, a moral conservative, observed with regard to Curran's *Christian Morality Today*.[246] The more liberal Richard McCormick agreed. "His theological orientations are what I would call 'middle of the road'. . . . I have always felt that his recent troubles with the Catholic University Board of Trustees was a case of 'getting the wrong heretic.'"[247]

It was Curran's bad luck to have been so visible a dissenter at a university whose board was dominated by bishops and chaired by a man—Archbishop O'Boyle—who firmly, even passionately, believed that contraception was immoral. Despite the theology faculty's having voted unanimously to grant Father Curran a promotion, the board of trustees voted late in 1966 to terminate his appointment. When its action became known, the theology faculty went on strike—followed rapidly by other faculties across the university. Due process and academic freedom were the understandable rallying cries. With the campus in turmoil, the board of trustees hurriedly reversed itself.[248] Now-Cardinal O'Boyle, perhaps as a hoped-for prelude to subsequent action against Father Curran, then asked the Committee on Doctrine of the bishops' conference to review Curran's various writings. But not even John Ford, one of three theologians recruited for the task, could muster a wholehearted condemnation. "If private theologians teach all kinds of novelties while the Bishops remain silent, not only are the faithful confused, but the private theologians conclude, with some justification, that silence gives consent."[249]

In the end, it all came down to silence—a silence that bespoke uncertainty as well as creating it. The American bishops in the past had sometimes been accused of being "weak and dilatory" with regard to social doctrine, as New York's Monsignor George Kelly noted in 1965. "Historically this has never until recent years been said of Episcopal statements on marriage and family life."[250] Many laity were probably not distressed by their ecclesial shepherds' reticence, since it constituted a kind of permission to solve the birth control problem on one's own. But there were certainly those for whom the bishops' silence compounded a growing sense of normlessness. Older clergy too were sometimes troubled by the want of guidance from the Chancery. Others—young men, especially—grew to welcome the flexibility that episcopal silence afforded them, particularly in confession.

The most serious damage was probably done to the bishops themselves. Their standing as moral teachers was clearly undermined, given that so few of them offered guidance to their people at a time of agonizing moral reappraisal.

They seemed to fail the period test for authenticity, too. If honest speaking was a prerequisite for leadership, what to make of an episcopate that moved from silence into what looked to a great many Catholics like equivocation? Having issued a compromise statement on *Humanae Vitae,* the bishops retreated from the problem. "A peculiar, implicit gentleman's agreement has developed between clergy and hierarchy in which the hierarchy commits itself not to try seriously to enforce compliance with *Humanae Vitae* so long as the clergy is not too open and public in its opposition to the encyclical," Andrew Greeley asserted in 1972.[251] The solution, such as it was, was very bad for authority, at least of the hierarchical sort. Many Catholics and their priests simply lost confidence in the Church's leaders, who could no longer count on their office to command respect, much less obedience. The bishops now had to earn their authority. But that was not easy to do, not for men whose roles kept them aloof from most laity and whose circumstances made for a certain dishonesty, or at least the appearance of such, when it came to disputed questions of sexual morality. "Like it or not, justified or unjustified, the fact is many people think that church leaders say one thing publicly and another privately," Saginaw's Kenneth Untener remarked with regard to his fellow bishops. "When we profess our public support for *Humanae Vitae,* or when we engage in 'a conspiracy of silence,' they feel we lack integrity."[252]

Epilogue

Humanae Vitae *and Its Aftermath*

Pope Paul broke his long silence on birth control on 29 July 1968, when he issued the encyclical *Humanae Vitae—Of Human Life*. The title provided an immediate clue to the contents. Sexual intercourse, a gift "proper and exclusive" to marriage, was—in the "objective moral order established by God"—inseparably bound up with the begetting of new life. Its very structure attested to this, as did the "constant" teaching of the Church. Spouses, therefore, were "not free . . . to proceed at will" with regard to family limitation, but "must conform their actions to the creative intention of God." This meant, according to the encyclical's most frequently quoted sentence, "that each and every marriage act must remain open to the transmission of life." It was wrong to argue, as some had done, that "the procreative finality pertains to conjugal life as a whole, rather than to its single acts." The "unitive significance" of the conjugal act should never be deliberately severed from its "procreative significance." Couples who had good reason to delay the birth of a child might "make use of marriage during the infertile times only"—an obvious reference to rhythm, the practice of which was said to result in more fully developed personalities and enhanced "spiritual values."[1]

Despite its traditional conclusions, the encyclical broke new ground. It spoke of marital love in almost ardent terms—far more lyrically than *Casti Connubii* had done. It acknowledged the changing status of women and the problems attendant on too-rapid growth in the global population. It was frank in its hope that medical science would soon discover "a sufficiently secure basis" for family limitation by means of rhythm. Perhaps most important, it spoke in terms of high aspirations rather than serious sin. Couples were summoned to embrace the teaching joyfully, despite the difficulties it entailed. They should draw strength from the Eucharist and have regular recourse to confession. Even those still caught in the snares of contraception should not separate themselves from the sacraments—assuming, of course, that they aspired to live according to Church teaching. Priests, who were instructed to "expound without ambiguity the Church's teaching on marriage," were also told to be merciful to their struggling penitents and lavish with encouragement. "In their difficulties may married couples always find in the words and in the heart of the priest, the echo of the voice and love of the Redeemer."[2] Nowhere did the pope speak in terms of mortal sin, despite his insistence that contraception was "intrinsically disordered" and contrary to nature. Subjectively speaking, the pope might be read to say, many contracepting couples were guilty of no more than a minor offense against morality.

The nuances of the pope's argument were undoubtedly lost on most American Catholics. Relatively few of them, in all likelihood, read the encyclical itself, which in its initial English translation was rather turgid. Instead, they read and heard about it in the media, where the dominant story was simply that the pope had said no to contraception. "The headlines—'Pope Against Birth Control'—made the Pope, I think, look antiquarian, like he simply was not facing up to the realities of the times," in the words of Father Bernard Marthaler, who was himself a critic of the encyclical. "There were many positive things in that encyclical, but they were being ignored because of the negative points which the people were interested in."[3] Media coverage was not only oversimplified but typically hostile. "Reactions around the world—in the Italian and American press, for example—are just as sharp as they were at the time of the *Syllabus of Errors* of Pius IX," as Bernard Häring observed. "There is the difference, of course, that this time anti-Catholic feelings have been rarely expressed. The storm has broken over the heads of the curial advisors of the Pope and often of the Pope himself."[4] The negative coverage intensified an already palpable division among Catholics with regard not just to contraception but the larger question of authority. The Jesuit Avery Dulles, himself a proponent of the ban on contraception, remembers being "greatly troubled" by news of the encyclical. "I sensed that public opinion among Catholics had already swung so far in the direction of change that the pope's decision would be vehemently opposed. I was worried about the internal rifts that would arise in the church. My apprehensions were borne out by the events."[5]

The events to which Dulles refers have mostly to do with the unprecedented storm of protest that greeted *Humanae Vitae*. Encyclicals—an increasingly common form of papal communication in the past century and a half[6]—typically elicit comment from theologians only, which is usually confined to Catholic or scholarly outlets. In this instance, however, the laity were heard—most of them in accents of incredulity and anger. Theologians, for their part, went public—speaking for attribution in the media, sometimes in overtly confrontational fashion. Criticism of earlier encyclicals, always rare, had been articulated both respectfully and obliquely. "I am . . . ill at ease with the style and to some degree with the content of the dissent which has taken place," as one moderate bishop phrased his reaction.[7] It seemed, and not only in the United States, that the encyclical was being actively rejected by many Catholics—a very different proposition from failing to accord it wholehearted attention. But were Catholics free to reject a definitive statement by the pope in the realm of morality? Could individual conscience be legitimately invoked in such circumstances? On what grounds might a Catholic plausibly chide the pope, as many did, for failing to be sufficiently collegial in his decision making—for rejecting the recommendations of the papal commission's majority and failing to consult the world's bishops? Such questions came quickly to dominate the debate. "Contraception, as a moral issue, was virtually smothered in the ecclesiological tumult," as the Jesuit Richard McCormick summarized the situation.[8]

Some laity reacted publicly to the encyclical by writing letters to the media—secular as well as Catholic; others wrote to their bishops and, on occasion, the pope. The American lay members of the papal birth control commission even held a Washington press conference, where spokesman John T. Noonan likened *Humanae Vitae* to earlier papal statements, now discredited, condemning freedom of conscience and religious liberty.[9] Not every lay voice was a dissenting one. "I was taught that the Pope, when speaking on matters of faith and morals, is God's representative on earth; therefore, he is infallible," a Baltimore woman wrote to Cardinal Shehan in the encyclical's wake. How could this logic not apply to *Humanae Vitae*?[10] Laity who supported the pope founded Catholics United for the Faith, an organization devoted to the defense of papal authority generally and the encyclical's doctrine in particular.[11] But if national polls were remotely accurate, Catholics like these constituted a distinct minority. Of those Catholics who had heard of the encyclical—astonishingly, there were those who had not—only 28 percent agreed with the pope's position, according to a Gallup survey done less than a month after *Humanae Vitae* was promulgated. Fifty-four percent disagreed with the pope, while the remainder—presumably for various reasons—claimed to have no opinion.[12] Subsequent polling indicated that age was a major predictor of dissent from the teaching: the older the respondent, the more likely she was to agree with the pope—particularly when the respondent in question was beyond her childbearing years. So was religious fervor, as measured by frequency of attendance at Mass. The more devout the respondent, not surprisingly, the less likely she was to dissent from the teaching—although even among the devout fewer than half of those polled supported *Humanae Vitae*.[13]

Contraceptive practice among the laity was apparently unaffected by the encyclical: the trend toward nonconformity with Church teaching continued unabated. This was especially true among the young. Fully 78 percent of Catholic married women aged twenty to twenty-four, according to a study done in 1970, were limiting their families by a means other than abstinence or rhythm. Since earlier fertility surveys had shown that Catholic women's nonconformity tended to increase with age, it seemed to demographers that the youngest cohort of

Catholic wives would eventually behave, with regard to contraception, like other American women of their generation.[14] One could hardly offer more definitive evidence of *Humanae Vitae*'s nonreception on the part of most laity. "For millions of lay people, the birth control question has been confronted, prayed over and settled—and not in the direction of the Pope's encyclical," as *Commonweal* asserted.[15] This was true in the Diocese of Erie, Pennsylvania, according to a CFM couple there who had polled their very large circle of CFM contacts. Most Catholics locally, the couple believed, were practicing forbidden forms of contraception. Some in this group were lukewarm Catholics, who seldom paid attention to Church teaching. But many more took it seriously. Prior to the encyclical, committed Catholics like these "had agonizingly come to the decision that birth control was moral." Now, having assessed the document, they "could not change their minds."[16]

There were certainly lay Catholics for whom the encyclical generated personal crises. "A year ago I received permission from my confessor to use contraceptive pills," a Bronx woman, obviously troubled, wrote to the *Sign*—a magazine run by the Passionist Fathers. "It was a very relaxing and wonderful year." But "the Pope's encyclical has outlawed the use of the pills. . . . What can I do now? I don't know if I will be able to live up to what we are asked." Passionist Father Cronon Regan was wonderfully sympathetic in his reply, praising the questioner's faith and desire to obey the pope. He encouraged her to frequent the sacraments, even if a momentary weakness should cause her to revert to contraception. He also suggested—and this was daring—that "individual conscience and personal pastoral guidance still have an irreplaceable role to play."[17] But he could not give his questioner the explicit permission to contracept that she so obviously wanted; "the state of doubt that many theologians appealed to in 1967 no longer exists," as Father Regan explained. Was his questioner capable, psychologically speaking, of making an independent decision in these difficult circumstances? There were certainly some who were not. Consider the Baltimore couple, parents of six and in objectively grim circumstances, who wrote to Cardinal Shehan in 1971 to ask for "special permission to practice birth control. . . . We have heard of special permissions being granted in individual cases."[18]

Most Catholic couples, however, seem to have made their peace not only with contraception but independent decision making—if not before the encyclical then shortly thereafter. A survey of U.S. priests, done ten months after the issuance of *Humanae Vitae,* found only 14 percent being "frequently" consulted by the laity on the morality of birth control. (The study defined "frequently" as "several people each week."[19]) The precipitous decline in confession was clearly a factor. More and more Catholics, even regular churchgoers, were making confession an annual affair—rather in the fashion of their immigrant forebears. When they did confess, they were less and less apt to mention contraception. Shortly after the encyclical, "I didn't hear much birth control at all," as Detroit's Father Louis Grandpre remembers, along with other of my priest informants.[20] Perhaps some laity were afraid that the post-encyclical confessor would take a harder line, though a man like Grandpre was surely known as tolerant and sympathetic. But probably most Catholics had come by this time to a radically altered understanding of Church authority, which amounted in practice to a new individualism. With regard to contraception, and especially in the wake of the encyclical, conscience had of necessity to guide the faithful, or so the majority of Catholics seemed to believe. "The Pope's word is but one of the words to be heard," the seemingly ubiquitous Michael Novak commented with regard to *Humanae Vitae.* "It is not, on its own merits, a very perceptive or illuminating word. We have heard that word before, in fact, and have measured its inadequacy."[21] Novak's mood was reflective of the hour, especially among educated Catholics. And his logic could obviously be applied to a wide range of moral decision making.

Matters were more difficult for priests, roughly half of whom—according to surveys—disagreed with the encyclical's conclusions.[22] They were bound to the hierarchy, and thus the pope, by deeper and more immediate ties than all but a handful of laity. Priests received their sacramental powers by virtue of the apostolic succession—by an episcopal laying on of hands that allegedly went back to St. Peter. Even off duty, they stood for the Church—or so nearly all had been taught. As ordained celibates, they belonged—emotionally and culturally—to the world of the hierarchy, no matter what resentments might infect their view of the local bishop. To oppose a definitive papal teaching, particularly in public, had a whiff of patricide about it—even for avowed liberals. The dissenter might also find himself progressively alienated from the tradition that gave his vocation its meaning. "One of the things I've worried about, 'cause I saw it in my own life, and I see it realized in the lives of lots of other priests, [is] that somewhere you reach a point of disillusionment with the church, and you try to carry on your ministry and then you begin to just cut yourself off from all authoritative statements and pronouncements and personnel because you just find it so opprobrious—it's just—it's unbearable, it's paralyzing," as Milwaukee's Father Andrew Nelson, normally articulate, tried rather haltingly to explain. A man could find himself embroiled in the rage and cynicism of late adolescence—"not an acceptable position to be in."[23]

If priests were churchmen, however, they were also pastors. "The arrival of Humanae Vitae caused me a great deal of anguish," in the words of a priest from suburban Chicago. "I was most upset because I knew it would disturb a good many married couples."[24] But how to be simultaneously loyal to the pope and one's troubled parishioners? Could a priest, post-encyclical, still encourage his penitents to decide for themselves with regard to contraception? Given a conservative bishop, was it wholly safe to do so? (The seal of confession does not bind the penitent, who is free to tell anyone she likes about the advice on offer.) If a priest was himself opposed to the logic of *Humanae Vitae,* should he bear public witness to this fact, either as a matter of personal integrity or to reach those many laity who were staying away from confession? Even liberal bishops did not look kindly on public dissent from the encyclical. A dissenting sermon would quickly be news at the local chancery—the result of complaints from conservative hearers, such being the state of polarization by 1968. As for issuing a public statement or signing a manifesto—that was tantamount to flinging a gauntlet at the feet of the local ordinary. In some dioceses, this was risky to do; in others, where a tolerant bishop held sway, it might seem like the rankest disloyalty.

The climate for clerical dissent varied quite widely from one diocese to the next. No bishop—at least none in charge of a diocese—expressed public disagreement with any aspect of *Humanae Vitae,* although 17 percent of the bishops responding to a 1969 poll dissented from some or all of the encyclical's conclusions.[25] A few—Detroit's John Dearden was one—were assumed by many of their clergy to have private doubts about the encyclical. "I have the impression . . . that [Dearden] was as disappointed as we were," as Detroit's Father William Keveney recollects it.[26] Several of my Boston priest informants thought this was true as well of Cardinal Richard Cushing.[27] Prelates like these gave carefully worded endorsement to the encyclical in public, but encouraged their priests to respect individual conscience as necessarily supreme in the matter. "He freed us up an awful lot," Father Lawrence Jackson said of Dearden, citing the small group discussions convened throughout the archdiocese at Dearden's behest, where priests discussed the encyclical among themselves.[28] Father John Blaska agreed: Dearden emphasized "the sacredness of conscience," as he remembers it. "I thought he was a wonderful man and very up to date."[29]

Other bishops took a harder line. Some, like Pittsburgh's John Wright, had never wavered in their conviction that contraception was intrinsically immoral. *Humanae Vitae,* in Wright's eloquent formulation, revealed the pope to be "prophetic in the Old Testament sense, evangelical in the richest sense of the New."[30] Wright's certainty seems to have had an effect, at least among his priests. "You don't hear much about [the encyclical] at all in Pittsburgh from the clergy," a CFM couple reported in October 1968. "Our chaplain is of the opinion that the clergy would not get away with dissent."[31] Other bishops, perhaps no less convinced of the encyclical's wisdom, seemed more immediately worried about shoring up papal authority. "We have arrived at the moment when it must be said that a Catholic follows the Pope," as New York auxiliary John Fearns told an episcopal colleague. "Conscience determines every act but we do not modify our declarations on abortion, racism, murder with the declaration that in spite of the absolute you can follow your conscience. Any such modification will be immediately seized upon as vindication of the proposition that you do what pleases you in spite of the Pope."[32] Some bishops, like Baton Rouge's Robert Tracy and Washington's Patrick O'Boyle, warned their priests that even as confessors, they must not accede to justifications for contraception based on conscience; in O'Boyle's words, the confessor "must teach that objectively contraception is wrong."[33] A good Catholic conscience could not by definition reach conclusions that contradicted an authentic teaching of the Church.[34]

Most bishops who took a hard public line were not eager to enforce it, not even where their priests were concerned. Erie's John Whealon, for example, maintained publicly "that one couldn't be a Catholic and dissent from the encyclical," according to a lay couple from his diocese. "However, he has not taken any steps to discipline the one priest in the diocese who signed the original theologians' [statement] of dissent"—a reference that will be explained shortly. "Nor has he required his priests to sign or take any sort of loyalty oath, though he did send out a strong letter telling them they were not to go against it [*Humanae Vitae*]."[35] Priests in the Archdiocese of Baltimore, where Lawrence Shehan was an earnest defender of the encyclical, evidently trusted their archbishop to tolerate clerical dissent. More than seventy of his priests protested the encyclical publicly—some by means of the above-mentioned theologians' statement, which originated at nearby Catholic University. (Shehan's support of *Humanae Vitae* came despite his having voted with the papal commission's reform majority. His personal affection for Pope Paul, coupled with a strong sense of loyalty to the papacy as an institution, was largely responsible.[36]) Shehan even failed to discipline then-Monsignor Joseph Gallagher, one-time editor of Baltimore's diocesan weekly, who denounced the encyclical at a Roman press conference and surrendered his title of monsignor—"not in anger but simple honesty."[37] Chicago's John Cody, locked by 1968 in acrimonious conflict with his clergy, made no moves to discipline clerical dissenters on the birth control front.[38] "I think he sort of said, 'I'm not going to pick a fight on this if you don't pick a fight on this,'" in the view of Father Tom Ventura.[39]

In the end, there were only two dioceses where priests were punished for dissenting from *Humanae Vitae*. Both episodes involved priests who had signed a statement issued by members of the theology faculty at Catholic University protesting the encyclical's conclusions and asserting the primacy of conscience with regard to marital contraception—an effort spearheaded by Charles Curran. The statement, made precipitously public on 30 July 1968, eventually attracted the signatures of more than six hundred priests and theologians. One of the early signers was Father Thomas Dailey, professor of moral theology at the major seminary for the Diocese of Buffalo. He was soon removed from the seminary faculty by his bishop and, in the words of a local lay couple, "was made pastor of a good parish in Batavia, NY."[40] Another six priest members of the faculty lost their jobs when they protested Dailey's firing and, albeit privately, the doctrine enunciated in *Humanae Vitae*. These events caused excitement locally, spurring the organization of a lay group, tellingly christened "Vox Populi," which was devoted to a broad range of church reforms. But they failed to draw much national attention, perhaps because the second set of firings coincided with the Democratic National Convention in Chicago—an episodically violent affair, as readers of a certain age will surely remember. Then too, none of the priests involved was suspended from the priesthood. All were immediately reassigned to parishes; two were quietly readmitted to the seminary faculty within weeks of their having been dismissed.[41]

Matters were otherwise in Washington, D.C., where Cardinal Patrick O'Boyle suspended some thirty-nine priests for having signed a locally generated protest statement similar to the one originating at Catholic University. (Some had also signed the Catholic University statement.) The suspensions—which for the most part meant that the priest in question could neither preach nor hear confessions—made headlines nationwide and quickly became a cause célèbre among liberal Catholics. Many priests were distressed by what they saw as O'Boyle's high-handedness: the dissenters had been disciplined without adequate due process, most priest sympathizers argued; more fundamentally, their right to conscientious dissent—often analogized to academic freedom—had been egregiously violated. The many laity who were galvanized by the Washington drama certainly sympathized with the dissenters, who took on the status of martyrs for many Catholics. But they could also see that the cardinal's logic was an assault on their own conduct and consciences, since he insisted that dissent from *Humanae Vitae* was not possible for Catholics—not for priests and most decidedly not for the laity. "If we Catholics, who accept the Pope as Peter's successor, are disloyal to the Holy Father—if we dissent from his teaching—we refuse to listen to Christ," O'Boyle told his flock in a post-encyclical pastoral letter.[42]

The Washington dispute dragged on for more than two years, with nineteen of the original group eventually petitioning Rome for redress. Their situation in the interim was for the most part precarious, since the diocesan clergy among them were given no pastoral work and were thus without their accustomed source of income and purpose. (Some of the dissenters were members of religious orders and could, if they chose, be assigned by their superiors to posts outside the Archdiocese of Washington.) Priests who watched from the precincts of safer dioceses sometimes felt cowardly by comparison, at least if they shared the dissenting views of the Washington "martyrs." Others were embittered. "We have been sick at heart at the apparent injustice our fellow priests have experienced," Father Michael O'Connor told Cardinal Dearden, speaking for the Association of Detroit Priests, "and we have been frustrated with our helplessness to come to their aid."[43]

Such emotions were intensified by news that James Shannon, a young auxiliary bishop of St. Paul-Minneapolis, had resigned his episcopal office—or perhaps been demoted, as confused rumors had it—over his doubts about the encyclical. "I cannot believe that God binds man to impossible standards," Shannon told the pope in a letter that was eventually made public, as were Vatican efforts to solve the problem by assigning Shannon—without evident duties—to a post outside the United States.[44] "He is such a symbol of integrity and hope that we cannot afford to lose him," a New Jersey pastor explained. "His letter to the Holy Father has been admirable in its restraint and honesty. It speaks no more than the problems so many of us—bishops, priests, theologians, laity—find in *Humanae Vitae*."[45] Father John Reidy, a well-known Catholic editor and Shannon's contemporary, agreed. Nothing in his priestly life had disturbed him as much as Shannon's resignation, Reidy told Cardinal Dearden in 1969. For Reidy, the treatment of Shannon capped a bad patch of progressive alienation. "The morale of American priests of my age cannot go much lower. By the young, we are told that we are outdated, poorly educated, committed to a concept of the Church which is not theologically sound. By the older Bishops, priests and laity, many of us are told that we are disloyal to the Church, contributing to its destruction and to such phenomena as 'incipient heresy.'"[46]

Humanae Vitae thus had the effect, particularly for younger clergy, of exacerbating an already corrosive crisis of priestly morale and identity. Its aftermath confirmed, at least for the already disaffected, that church leaders were as tarnished a lot as secular politicians—cowardly and dishonest when they were not bullies. The American bishops' pastoral letter in response to the encyclical, issued in November 1968, was a particular irritant, given its compromise character. (It was far more supportive of the pope than the statements of certain national hierarchies in Europe and that of Canada.) "Certain sections of the pastoral represent a symptom of an 'organization episcopacy' where things are done in the machinery and by those who have positions of power and prestige within the machinery," Richard McCormick wrote bluntly, upset in part that Germain Grisez, a minority voice among moralists, was the source of certain of the document's arguments. The bishops had failed to address the widespread rejection of the encyclical or the pastoral problems it had created—not to mention the troubling possibility that the pope might have been wrong.[47] "These paragraphs are probably the strongest things I have ever written," McCormick subsequently acknowledged—a measure of how far he had traveled since his days in the mid-1960s as a theologian frequently consulted by many of the bishops he was now lambasting.[48] What many younger priests perceived as the bishops' evasiveness with regard to the encyclical compounded their resentments over mandatory celibacy—another problem that the bishops were widely believed to be evading.

Men on the brink of leaving the active priesthood—and there were many in this situation—had particular reason to dwell on such grievances and even to exaggerate them. Those who stayed had somehow to make sense of their vocations despite the distrust of authority that *Humanae Vitae* had generated or made worse. A relative few moved from publicly criticizing the encyclical to championing dissent on a range of moral issues—thereby calling into radical question the authority structures of a hierarchical church. "There was nothing more liberating for Catholic people than that document, in the sense that it was so clear that the Church was wrong," as Detroit's Anthony Kosnik firmly maintains with regard to the encyclical. "I felt compelled to speak out. I often talk about that as the moment of my conversion in the sense that it was very clear to me that my responsibility was to respond to God and not the Church."[49] Going this route meant risking one's career. John Dearden was content to have Kosnik teach moral theology in his archdiocese; Dearden's successor was not. No one known (at the Vatican) to have publicly dissented from *Humanae Vitae* would be made a bishop, particularly during the pontificate of John Paul II. The standard form used to vet prospective candidates for the episcopate asks specifically about the candidate's conduct in this regard.[50] Going this route could also make for loneliness, especially in a diocese with a hostile bishop. If one did not become a dangerous man to know—and that could happen— one was apt to be a standing reproach to sympathetic confreres, and a cause of scandal for those who clung to tradition.

Most priests, understandably, opted for private solutions. Those who disagreed with the encyclical continued, as confessors and counselors, to stress the primacy of conscience when it came to marital contraception. A 1969 survey of the American Catholic clergy found that 43 percent described their confessional practice in these terms, while an additional 7 percent claimed that they actively encouraged the "responsible use" of contraceptives when a couple had "adequate reasons." Only 13 percent of the priests who responded, most of them over age fifty-five, were willing to deny absolution to a penitent who refused to try to live according to *Humanae Vitae*. Among the bishops polled, the figure was 42 percent.[51] As these numbers suggest, even priests who agreed with the encyclical did not always try to enforce its norms. What good would it do to deny absolution to someone who had at least come to confession? The probable effect would be to drive him away from the sacrament. And why risk the hostility that would surely be generated by preaching against contraception? Nor was one's bishop apt to encourage such potentially alienating conduct, no matter how firmly he might believe that the pope had been right.

Thus not long after *Humanae Vitae,* a great public silence came to prevail with regard to contraception. The denouement of the Washington case suggests how quickly it happened. The thirty-nine priests whom Cardinal O'Boyle initially suspended had dwindled to nineteen by 1969. A few of the "missing" had reconciled with the cardinal; many more had left the active priesthood. The nineteen remaining decided in 1970 to appeal their case to the pope,[52] since Cardinal O'Boyle had refused all domestic efforts at mediation. In Rome, the case was eventually assigned to the Sacred Congregation for the Clergy, then headed by Cardinal John Wright—former bishop of Pittsburgh and staunch proponent of *Humanae Vitae.* No ruling in the matter was forthcoming until April 1971, when Wright issued a decision that quite masterfully enabled both sides in the dispute to save face. Cardinal O'Boyle, according to Wright, had not violated canon law in his treatment of the dissidents, who were told to be grateful for the Cardinal's "sensitive, forthright leadership." But at the same time, Wright endorsed the dissidents' position on conscience and its rights: "In the final analysis, conscience is inviolable and no man is to be forced to act in a manner contrary to his conscience as the moral tradition of the church attests." He also recommended that O'Boyle revoke the suspension of any priest who declared "his desire to enjoy the full faculties of the Archdiocese." No one should be required—and here Wright rejected a long-standing O'Boyle demand—to sign or accede verbally to any statement of submission or doctrinal orthodoxy.[53] "The Archdiocese of Washington can now rejoin the rest of the Church," in the words of Father Frank Bonnike, president of the National Federation of Priests' Councils, "and live with the ambiguity which is the present state of the whole question of artificial contraception."[54]

Despite what was indisputably a victory for the "Washington 19," Wright's decision caused little stir in the United States—this in a case that had once drawn more than 3,000 Catholics to a Washington rally. This was partly because many of the priests involved had left the active priesthood by 1971. But the lack of interest also reflected the greatly diminished status of contraception as a problem among Catholics. To all appearances, the issue had moved by then to the margins of Catholic consciousness—not just among the laity but the clergy, too. "The whole topic has become tiresome," in the view of moralist John Dedek. "There can be no doubt that there are many good reasons why people should practice birth control."[55] Most laity behaved as if this were indisputably true. And most priests—indeed most bishops—seemed to agree, if only because of their public silence on the question. Many Catholics were aware that the Washington case had taken a heavy toll: priestly careers were ruined, a once-respected cardinal's reputation was in shreds. (O'Boyle had been widely admired by liberals for his characteristically aggressive approach to desegregating the Catholic schools in his archdiocese, an initiative begun in 1949.) Other prelates' reputations suffered, too, perhaps especially among the clergy. "How are we to account for the silence of the American Bishops in the face of a situation which many of them have privately admitted is wrong?" asked Father Joseph Byron, spokesman for the "Washington 19," in 1970.[56] That so painful an episode could so quickly recede from the public consciousness suggests how rapidly the problem of contraception was resolved in the wake of *Humanae Vitae*.

But what, in the broadest sense, did this seeming resolution entail? Conflicting views of Church authority were certainly not reconciled. "The real issue at stake is the *magisterium*," as then-Bishop Joseph Bernardin summed up the dispute between the bishops and dissenting theologians at Catholic University. "The contraception problem is simply the occasion for bringing the much broader problem of the teaching authority of the Church, and specifically the Holy Father, out in the open."[57] Once the pope had spoken, what kind of dissent—if any—was permitted to the faithful? What, in other words, was the nature and function of the magisterium? Those who defended the encyclical often took the position that dissent from its teaching, save for the privately communicated doubts of trained theologians, was simply off-limits to Catholics. The pope's word was final, even if—as was demonstrably the case with *Humanae Vitae*—he failed to consult the world's bishops. Others maintained that dissent, assuming that it was responsible and attentive to tradition, was actually part of the magisterium. "In this light the church's magisterium is seen much more as an ongoing *process* within which the response of the community, while not decisive, can certainly be an important element in the discovery of truth," the Jesuit Richard McCormick explained.[58]

Most Catholic laity, for all their high levels of education, are not trained as theologians. But because contraception is something that touches nearly every adult's life, they have had of necessity to engage in a kind of theologizing around the issue. If the Church forbids the use of so-called artificial birth control, on what grounds can such use be justified? The result in a great many cases has been an essentially dialogic view of Church authority: the pope may propose, but the rest of the Church has something to say as well—a "something" that, contra Richard McCormick, may well be decisive, at least for the individual decision maker. The new mode of thinking was quickly applied to a wide range of issues, many having to do with sex. Was premarital intercourse licit, at least if the couple was in love? Almost 90 percent of twenty-something Catholics, polled in 1992, asserted that it was. "The young people seem to see the morality of premarital sex as depending on situations, not a matter of rules."[59] Even older Catholics by the 1990s were increasingly inclined to see individual conscience as the proper locus of authority with regard to remarriage after divorce. They were somewhat more inclined to vest church leaders with moral authority over abortion. But 52 percent of younger Catholics, those raised after Vatican II, were prepared by the 1990s to say that individual conscience should reign supreme on this issue, which was one in which many bishops were publicly invested. Among devout Catholics, interestingly—as a group these tend to be older—women were much more apt than men to champion the primacy of conscience with regard to sexual morality.[60]

This new mode of moral decision making is certainly congruent with dominant American values. Save for a relatively small population of deeply committed believers and recent immigrants, Catholics today are a culturally mainstream population and presumably grateful for the accompanying sense of belonging fully to America. Many women, moreover, have benefited greatly from the laity's turn toward moral autonomy, as their careers attest. But let us probe more deeply. There are risks inherent in this new mode of moral decision making, to which women are arguably more vulnerable than men, since it is they who get pregnant. Many decisions about sex are made by the young. Nearly all are informed by short-term notions of self-interest. How to ensure, in such circumstances, that the decision maker is in possession of the relevant moral data and knows how to weigh it correctly? It does not help that many Catholics, especially the young, attend church infrequently. Weekly Mass attendance nationwide declined from 71 percent in 1961, on the eve of the Second Vatican Council, to 37 percent in 1999.[61] Nor does it help that younger Catholics are by nearly all measures less theologically literate than their elders. They are no less intelligent and presumably no less committed to the moral life. But many are wholly detached from the assumptions, language, and logic that once defined the interior lives of Catholics and guided their moral choices. On what basis, then, do they form the conscience that now looms so large as an arbiter of morality?

The changes just invoked have much to do with the final collapse of a Catholic subculture in the United States—a development that coincides almost exactly with the Second Vatican Council. But they also have to do with what Richard McCormick has called "the silence since *Humanae Vitae*." Moral theologians by the early 1970s were preoccupied by other issues—abortion, warfare, divorce and remarriage, and, albeit with a certain caution, homosexuality. "The matter of contraception provokes a yawn of public boredom," as McCormick saw matters in 1973. Priests were mostly silent, too, certainly on contraception and often on questions of sex more generally. If one could not speak honestly about birth control, and such was the case for a majority of priests by the 1970s, it was hard to speak about sex at all. Many also lacked the confidence to do so, precisely because of *Humanae Vitae*. "It is likely to be a very long time before the church recaptures any kind of credibility as a teacher of sexual morality," Andrew Greeley asserted in 1972, when he spoke for many of his clerical confreres.[62] The result was a church where sexual ethics were seldom discussed, despite rapid change in the cultural values governing sexual conduct. Retreats and parish missions, once natural venues for talk about sex, have since the late 1960s addressed the issue infrequently. The confessional has been mostly empty, or frequented mainly by older adults. Even parish youth ministries, weaker today than they were in the 1950s, tend to steer away from the topic. "We ought to be saying something to our kids," Detroit's Father Lawrence Jackson admitted, "but I don't know when to say it or what to say. . . . We don't talk much about marriage."[63] As for premarital instruction, it passed almost wholly into lay hands in the 1970s and after. Many priests believed, and still believe, that their celibacy disqualifies them for a role that had once routinely been assigned even to the newly ordained.

Most clergy were troubled by these developments. They watched with dismay as Catholics rushed to join a seemingly anarchic sexual revolution. Divorce rates rose, even among regular churchgoers, as did the practice of premarital cohabitation. Birth and marriage rates declined, in tandem with those of Americans generally. Many Catholics, especially those who came infrequently to Mass, were newly tolerant of abortion. And it was hard for all concerned to avoid the coarsening effects of what was sometimes called a pansexualized culture. Even priests who disagreed vehemently with *Humanae Vitae*'s conclusions nearly always endorsed its placing reverence for life at the heart of sexual morality. "Our human sexuality has a dimension beyond itself," as Father Tom McDevitt puts it. A genuinely Christian marriage, in his view, cannot be one from which children are deliberately excluded.[64] Father Philip Keane, a well-known moral theologian, is of the same mind. "Whether you agree or disagree with the encyclical in terms of its specific dealing with contraception, the underlying notion of child as gift, child as mystery, is a very important theological notion, and I can understand why Paul VI didn't want to lose that."[65] How frustrating, then—and demoralizing, too—to feel bound to public silence when such values were under attack, and with such devastating consequences. Sexual promiscuity, high rates of divorce, and nonmarital childbearing are "part of the whole rejection of any moderation upon sexual appetites that's part of the modern set-up," in the opinion of Msgr. William Sherzer. "It hasn't made for happiness."[66]

On the fifth anniversary of *Humanae Vitae,* Richard McCormick called on the American bishops to "stimulate and support" a "new communal reflection on the meaning of and reasons for the dissent the encyclical provoked." At the very least such an effort would break the prevailing silence and encourage public discussion among Catholics not only of sex but also of authority. Should the bishops choose instead to maintain their silence, largely unbroken since 1968, the effect would almost certainly be "to seriously compromise the credibility of the teaching office of the Church in the long run."[67] McCormick was almost certainly right: the bishops did opt for continued silence, with a handful of heroic exceptions, and experienced what most observers regard as a steady erosion of authority. Their collective authority as a national conference has arguably been damaged by the politics of contraception: when a number of national episcopal conferences—though not that of the United States—responded to *Humanae Vitae* in ambivalent fashion, according to the Jesuit Avery Dulles, the pope was deeply disappointed. "Partly for this reason, the Holy See has tended to question the teaching authority of episcopal conferences and to insist on prior approval of conference statements."[68] The Vatican's insistence that all candidates for the episcopacy be supporters of the encyclical, or at least not public dissenters from it, has arguably resulted in certain mediocre appointments—not venal men, but simply those whose instinct is to duck hard questions. Could such priorities help to explain the dereliction of episcopal duty in too many dioceses in recent decades with regard to clerical sexual abuse?

Most devastating of all has been the pastoral vacuum at the top. Apart from abortion, most bishops have little to say about the many questions of sexual morality that impinge on the lives of their people. Those who do mostly traffic in what theologian Gerard Sloyan has called "prohibitions without adequate reasons."[69] And even on abortion, an issue about which almost every bishop clearly cares, the silence surrounding *Humanae Vitae* has robbed them of credibility. To make matters worse, most lay Catholics—especially the young—are not convinced that the bishops really believe in *Humanae Vitae,* perhaps because so many of today's younger laity find the teaching on contraception so difficult to understand. "It is one thing when people angrily disagree with us, as on many social and economic issues," Saginaw's Bishop Kenneth Untener told his assembled confreres in 1992. "It is quite another when people cynically dismiss us as dissemblers."[70] Even admirers of the current pope, who has written and spoken widely in defense of *Humanae Vitae,* are apt to find their bishops wanting, simply because so many of them cleave to what might charitably be called prudential silence.

And still the silence continues—made infinitely worse today by the flood of dispiriting revelations about clerical sexual abuse and its all-too-frequent cover-up. The "communal reflection" once commended by Richard McCormick has never taken place—not on contraception, not on authority. If anything, the supports for such reflection are weaker today than they were in the early 1970s, when McCormick first called for it. Pope John Paul II has been less tolerant of dissent on this issue than his predecessor Paul, having declared in 1987 that "the Church's teaching on contraception does not belong to the category of matter open to free discussion among theologians."[71] Today's American episcopate harbors few men temperamentally capable of challenging the pope, and—the result of recent developments—no obvious national leaders. Younger clergy today are for the most part papal loyalists and often support the teaching on contraception, at least in the abstract. Older clergy overwhelmingly oppose it, and look with a certain suspicion not only on episcopal authority but their younger colleagues, too. Most priests, regardless of age, suffer at least occasionally from the loneliness and existential doubts created by a steadily worsening priest shortage. As for the laity, most of those in their childbearing years simply cannot grasp the logic behind the teaching, not even when it is presented in the personalist terms that John Paul II speaks so fluently. They speak the language of experience only—a language with vast cultural authority but hardly one, with regard to sex, that most bishops are prepared to hear.

Just as the silence continues, so too do the problems to which it gave rise. What is sex for? What is the nature of marriage? The laity need answers to these questions—authentically Christian answers, grounded in Catholic tradition and consonant with the realities of women's heightened status, a crowded planet, and rapidly evolving technologies of reproduction. Priests, for their part, need to be seen as sources of wisdom in this regard, especially by the young. How can the priestly vocation make sense if priests have nothing convincing to say about the most immediate moral dilemmas faced by their people? These needs are poignantly embodied in that small population of young Catholics who in recent years have unexpectedly embraced *Humanae Vitae* and the various methods of Natural Family Planning, as the rhythm method is now known. Eschewing contraception, for many of them, means rejecting the sexual revolution and the family instability to which it gave such spectacular rise. It is also a way to claim a distinctive Catholic identity and a measure of certitude with regard to the immutability of truth. Most could probably not recapitulate a natural law argument against contraception, or even explain why contraception is always wrong—apart from the pope's having said so. Nor do they invariably stick with the program, once their families have reached a certain size.

Catholics like these are not calling for a return to the 1950s, although many of their older coreligionists—veterans of the birth control wars—accuse them of this. They are products of too individualistic a culture to fit comfortably into that world of confessional triumphalism and gendered life scripts. Nor do most of them really endorse an absolutist approach to contraception, as the passage of time will make clear. But they do want pastoral leadership and high expectations when it comes to personal conduct. They want an existential sense of Catholic identity, too, notwithstanding their simultaneous desire to be unambiguously American. Most of all, they want their lives to bear witness to their faith—something that, with the possible exception of strong-minded saints, requires communal support. They want, in short, what most Catholics want, regardless of age or political orientation. Desires like these ought to form the substance of ongoing communal reflection—of conversations that involve every constituency in the church. How ironic, not to say tragic, that birth control gets in the way.

Notes

Introduction

1. [Name deleted] to Pat and Patty Crowley, undated but ca. 1965, typed copy of original. Archives of the University of Notre Dame (hereafter AUND), Crowley papers—SPCBPC, box 15, folder 1.

2. [Name deleted] to the editor, *Jubilee* magazine, undated but ca. early 1964, typed copy of original. Georgetown University Library Special Collections (hereafter GULSC). Ed Rice papers, box 4, folder 54.

3. Fr. N.N. to Cardinal Lawrence Shehan, 11 June 1966. Archives of the Archdiocese of Baltimore (hereafter AAB). Shehan papers, uncatalogued. Given the confidential nature of the letters in this collection and their relatively recent origin, I have agreed not to reveal the names of correspondents. After having been appointed to the Pontifical Commission for the Study of Population, Family, and Births, Cardinal Shehan asked his priests in the spring of 1966 to advise him by letter of their pastoral experience with regard to the contraception question. Nearly all of them obliged.

4. Fr. N.N. to Cardinal Lawrence Shehan, 20 May 1966. AAB. Shehan papers, uncatalogued.

5. On contraceptive use among Catholics in the mid-1960s, see Norman B. Ryder and Charles F. Westoff, *Reproduction in the United States: 1965* (Princeton, NJ: Princeton University Press, 1971), 185–200.

6. Ronald Freedman, P. K. Whelpton, and Arthur Campbell, *Family Planning, Sterility and Population Growth* (New York: McGraw-Hill, 1959), 281–283; Charles F. Westoff et al., *Family Growth in Metropolitan America* (Princeton, NJ: Princeton University Press, 1961), 194–199; Raymond H. Potvin, Charles F. Westoff, and Norman B. Ryder, "Factors Affecting Catholic Wives' Conformity to Their Church Magisterium's Position on Birth Control," *Journal of Marriage and the Family* 30, no. 2 (May 1968): 264–266; Wilfrid Scanlon, "Orthodoxy? Anomie? Or Pluralism? An Empirical Sociological Analysis of Attitudes of the Catholic Laity in the Archdiocese of Boston toward Contraception" (Ph.D. dissertation, Boston University, 1975), 209–212.

7. Fr. N.N. to Cardinal Lawrence Shehan, 19 May 1966. AAB. Shehan papers, uncatalogued.

8. Fr. Hubert, OSB to Pat and Patty Crowley, 10 May 1965. AUND. Crowley papers—SPCBPC, box 15, folder 3.

9. For responses to a 1965 Gallup Poll, see Leonard Gross, "America's Mood Today," *Look,* 29 June 1965, 17. For results of a 1967 poll, see *Newsweek,* 20 March 1967.

10. Msgr. N.N. to Cardinal Lawrence Shehan, 31 May 1966. AAB. Shehan papers, uncatalogued.

11. Charles F. Westoff and Larry Bumpass, "The Revolution in Birth Control Practices of U.S. Roman Catholics," *Science* 179 (5 Jan. 1973): 41–44.

12. Aidan M. Carr, "Questions Answered," *Homiletic and Pastoral Review* 65, no. 7 (April 1965): 608.

13. Joseph H. Fichter, S.J., *Priest and People* (New York: Sheed and Ward, 1965), 186, whose conclusions are based on a national survey.

14. Avery Dulles, S.J., "*Humanae Vitae* and the Crisis of Dissent," *Origins* 22, no. 45 (April 1993): 776. Fr. Dulles would generally be regarded as a conservative. For liberal agreement with his analysis, see (Rev.) Gerard S. Sloyan, *Catholic Morality Revisited: Origins and Contemporary Challenges* (Mystic, CT: Twenty-Third Publications, 1990), especially pages 98–100 and Bp. Kenneth Untener, "Humanae Vitae: What Has It Done to Us?" *Commonweal* 120 (18 June 1993), 12–14.

15. On the various Protestant denominations and the politics of birth control, see Kathleen Tobin-Schlesinger, "Population and Power: The Religious Debate over Contraception, 1916–1936" (Ph.D. dissertation, University of Chicago, 1994).

16. Alan Graebner, "Birth Control and the Lutherans: The Missouri Synod as a Case Study," in Janet Wilson James, ed., *Women in American Religion* (Philadelphia: University of Pennsylvania Press, 1980), 229–252.

17. Fr. Gaudentius Rossi, C.P., "Some Instructions about the Sermons, Meditations, and Catechisms Delivered by Our Fathers, in Our Missions," ms. dated April 1875. Passionist Provincial Archives: Holy Cross Province, Chicago (hereafter PPA). Sermons of Fr. Gaudentius Rossi, box 250. Joseph Wissel, C.SS.R., *The Redemptorist on the American Missions,* vol. I, 3rd rev. ed. (Norwood, MA: Plimpton Press, 1920), 73–74. The same text is found in the 1885 edition, which is almost identical to that of 1920—save for changes required by the 1917 Code of Canon Law.

18. Fr. Michael Burke, C.SS.R. used this quite typical language in an undated mission instruction "For Married Men." Burke was ordained in 1860 and died in 1891. Redemptorist Archives: Baltimore Province, Brooklyn NY (hereafter RAB). Uncatalogued.

19. On the promulgation, reception, and significance of *Casti Connubii,* see John T. Noonan, *Contraception: A History of Its Treatment by the Catholic Theologians and Canonists,* rev. ed. (Cambridge, MA: Harvard University Press, 1986), 424–432.

20. I have documented this change in sacramental practice for the Archdiocese of Detroit in *Seasons of Grace: A History of the Catholic Archdiocese of Detroit* (Detroit: Wayne State University Press, 1990), 166–174, 403–408. The Archdiocese of Detroit was not atypical in this regard, as a broad literature on American Catholicism indicates.

21. See, for example, Joseph Reiner, S.J. to Wilfrid Parsons, S.J., 2 March 1935. GULSC. Wilfrid Parsons papers, box 8, folder 12.

22. See, for example, Rev. John A. O'Brien, "Moral Causes of Catholic Leakage," *Homiletic and Pastoral Review* 33, no. 7 (April 1933): 693–701.

23. Westoff et al., *Family Growth in Metropolitan America,* especially 78–80; see also Andrew Greeley, "Family Planning among American Catholics," ms. slated for publication in *Chicago Studies* (Spring 1963), undated but ca. 1963, 4. American Catholic History Research Center and University Archives, Catholic University of America (hereafter ACUA), National Catholic Welfare Conference papers (hereafter NCWC), 10/86/5.

24. Fr. N.N. to Cardinal Lawrence Shehan, 2 June 1966. AAB. Shehan papers, uncatalogued.

25. Martin Marty, "What Went Wrong?" *Critic* 34, no. 1 (Fall 1975): 53.

26. Author interview with Msgr. William Sherzer, 18 October 1998, in Ann Arbor MI.

Chapter 1. "The Abominable Crime of Onan"

1. Fr. Gaudentius Rossi, C.P., "Some Instructions about the Sermons, Meditations, and Catechisms Delivered by Our Fathers, in Our Missions," ms. dated April 1875. PPA. Sermons of Fr. Gaudentius Rossi, box 250. Emphasis in original.

2. Kathleen Tobin-Schlesinger, "Population and Power: The Religious Debate over Contraception, 1916–1936" (Ph.D. dissertation, University of Chicago, 1994), 40.

3. Rev. William Stang, *Pastoral Theology,* 2nd rev. ed. (New York: Benziger Brothers, 1897), 171. Father Stang is quoting approvingly from the Jesuit moralist Alphonsus Sabetti. Translated from the original Latin.

4. John R. Gillis, Louise A. Tilly, and David Levine, eds., *The European Experience of Declining Fertility, 1850–1970* (Cambridge, MA and Oxford, UK: Blackwells, 1992), 1–2.

5. Very. Rev. Père Monsabré, O.P., *Marriage Conferences Delivered at Notre Dame, Paris* (New York: Benziger Brothers, English translation, 1890), 115–123. The mode of address employed in these sermons suggests that they were preached only to men. Pierre Toulement, a French Jesuit, argued in 1873 that France's recent defeat by Germany and the terrors of the Paris Commune were divine punishment for the nation's sins of contraception. See Michael S. Teitelbaum and Jay M. Winter, *The Fear of Population Decline* (Orlando, FL: Academic Press, 1985), 18–19. Most of the questions addressed to the Sacred Penitentiary in Rome in the nineteenth century with regard to the treatment of "onanists" in the confessional came from French clergy and bishops. See John T. Noonan, *Contraception: A History of Its Treatment by the Catholic Theologians and Canonists,* rev. ed. (Cambridge, MA: Harvard University Press, 1986), 397–405.

6. *Michigan Catholic,* 23 Nov. 1893, 4:1.

7. Wilson H. Grabill, Clyde V. Kiser, and Pascal K. Whelpton, *The Fertility of American Women* (New York: Wiley, 1958), 107–108; Tamara K. Hareven and Maris A. Vinovskis, "Marital Fertility, Ethnicity, and Occupation in Urban Families: An Analysis of South Boston and the South End in 1880," *Journal of Social History* 8 (Spring 1975): 69–93; Hareven and Vinovskis, "Patterns of Childbearing in Nineteenth-Century America," in *Family and Population in Nineteenth-Century America,* ed., Tamara K. Hareven and Maris A. Vinovskis (Princeton, NJ: Princeton University Press, 1978), 85–125; Avery Guest, "Fertility Variation among the U.S. Foreign Stock Population in 1900," *International Migration Review* 16, no. 3 (Fall 1982): 577–596.

8. John A. Ryan, "Family Limitation," *Ecclesiastical Review* 54, no. 6 (June 1916): 684–685.

9. William Schaefers, "Our Catholic Population," *Homiletic and Pastoral Review* 29, no. 2 (Nov. 1928): 150–151.

10. Hornell Hart, "Differential Fertility in Iowa," *University of Iowa Studies in Child Welfare* 2, no. 2 (1922): 37–39.

11. Orville Griese, *The 'Rhythm' in Marriage and Christian Morality* (Washington, DC: Catholic University of America Press, 1948), 3–4; Leo J. Latz, *The Rhythm of Sterility and Fertility in Women* (Chicago: Dr. Leo J. Latz, 1932), 9; John C. Ford, S.J. and Gerald Kelly, S.J., *Contemporary Moral Theology,* vol. 2: *Marriage Questions* (Westminster, MD: Newman Press, 1963), 384–385.

12. See Janet Farrell Brodie, *Contraception and Abortion in Nineteenth-Century America* (Ithaca, NY: Cornell University Press, 1994), 204–241.

13. Stang, *Pastoral Theology,* 171. Translated from the original Latin.

14. James C. Mohr, *Abortion in America: The Origins and Evolution of National Policy* (New York: Oxford University Press, 1978), 46–85.

15. Joseph Wissel, C.SS.R., *The Redemptorist on the American Missions,* vol. I, 3rd rev. ed. (Norwood, MA: Plimpton Press, 1920), 473.

16. Rev. Louis Cook, C.SS.R. to Bishop Caspar Borgess, 20 Nov. 1885. Archives of the Archdiocese of Detroit (hereafter AAD). Borgess papers, box 2, folder 4.

17. "Race Suiciders," typescript mission sermon, no author given. Undated, but probably—based on its content—ca. 1915. Quote from page 9. PPA. Sermons by unknown authors, file 2–A, box 252. For a later period, see A. McBriarty, C.SS.R., "Parish Missions," *Ecclesiastical Review* 102, no. 3 (March 1940), 201–202.

18. Simon Szreter, *Fertility, Class and Gender in Britain, 1860–1940* (Cambridge: Cambridge University Press, 1996), 389–424.

19. For a perceptive contemporary analysis of the problem, see Rev. Frank A. O'Brien, "Organization and Maintenance of Parish Societies," *Ecclesiastical Review* 14, no. 6 (June 1896): 492–493.

20. Xavier Sutton, C.P, ms. sermon to non-Catholics on "Marriage and Divorce," undated but ca. 1907. PPA. Sermons of Fr. Xavier Sutton, box 770.

21. Rev. Richard T. Donohoe, C.SS.R., "Marriage Instructions," ms. notes, evidently intended as instructions for fellow Redemptorists in hearing premarital confessions and giving premarriage conferences. Undated but probably early twentieth century. RAB. Uncatalogued notebook.

22. Rev. Thomas J. Gerrard, *Marriage and Parenthood: The Catholic Ideal* (New York: Joseph F. Wagner, 1911), 82. When Gerrard's book was reissued in a revised edition in 1937, editor Edgar Schmiedeler, O.S.B., made no changes in the chapter on "Conjugal Restraint."

23. Richard A. Soloway, *Birth Control and the Population Question in England, 1877–1930* (Chapel Hill: University of North Carolina Press, 1982), 98–102, quotes from 99, 100. See also Tobin-Schlesinger, "Population and Power," 49, 53–54.

24. Soloway, *Birth Control and the Population Question,* 241.

25. Joseph Frassinetti, *The New Parish Priests' Practical Manual,* translated by William Hutch, 2nd ed. (London: Burns and Oates, 1885), 220. The book enjoyed a wide circulation in its English translation both in the United States and in the British Isles. Portions of Frassinetti's manual were later incorporated into William Stang's influential *Pastoral Theology.*

26. Alan Graebner, "Birth Control and the Lutherans: The Missouri Synod as a Case Study," in Janet Wilson James, ed., *Women in American Religion* (Philadelphia: University of Pennsylvania Press, 1980), 230–231, 234, 237.

27. J. M. Fleming, O.S.A., "What To Preach," *Ecclesiastical Review* 59, no. 2 (Aug. 1918), 166.

28. Isadore Dwyer, C.P., ms. sermon on "The General Judgment," undated but ca. 1900. PPA. Sermons of Fr. Isadore Dwyer, box 241. The prostitution analogy is at least as old as Augustine and is also found in Thomas Aquinas.

29. "Race Suiciders," 7.

30. For a particularly vigorous statement of the position, see "Practical Hints Concerning the Mission," undated anonymous typescript. PPA. Sermons and papers of Fr. Roch Adamek, C.P., box 240. Adamek was ordained in 1945 and died in 1963; it is possible, however, that he is not the document's author.

31. On the French case, see Noonan, *Contraception,* 397–405; see also A. Vermeersch, S.J. and T. Lincoln Bouscaren, S.J., *What Is Marriage? A Catechism Arranged According to the Encyclical 'Casti Connubii' of Pope Pius XI* (New York: America Press, 1932), 36–38.

32. Ryan, "Family Limitation," 685.

33. The standard work on parish missions in the United States is Jay P. Dolan, *Catholic Revivalism: The American Experience, 1830–1900* (Notre Dame, IN: University of Notre Dame Press, 1978). Frequency of missions is addressed on 55–62.

34. Canon A. Guerra, *The Confessor after the Heart of Jesus* (English-language edition, St. Louis: B. Herder, 1901), 55.

35. Borgess circular letter to the clergy, 4 Aug. 1882. AAD. Borgess papers, box 5, folder 20.

36. This is a concern of long-standing for nearly all manualists. As a typical example, see Caspar E. Schieler, *Theory and Practice of the Confessional: A Guide in the Administration of the Sacrament of Penance,* trans. and ed. by Rev. H. J. Heuser, 2nd ed. (New York: Benziger Brothers, 1906), 384, 609.

37. Frassinetti, *Parish Priest's Practical Manual,* 355.

38. Father Stang's widely used manual urges monthly confession as a norm for all Catholics; see his *Pastoral Theology,* 177.

39. For an account of this process among Michigan Catholics, see L. W. Tentler, *Seasons of*

Grace: A History of the Catholic Archdiocese of Detroit (Detroit: Wayne State University Press, 1990), 166–174.

40. Rossi, "Some Instructions about the Sermons," unpaginated. Wissel, *Redemptorist on the American Missions,* makes the same point, 91.

41. Fr. Xavier Sutton, C.P., ms. record of missions and retreats, 1882–1925. PPA. Papers of Fr. Xavier Sutton. The mission in question was preached at St. Anthony's parish, 1–16 April 1884.

42. Author interview with Fr. Ferdinand De Cneudt, 19 Oct. 1998, in Roseville MI. De Cneudt was born in Belgium; his family emigrated to Detroit in 1920.

43. Fr. John M. Cooper, sermon notes, "Confession—Its Practical Value," 23 Jan. 1916. ACUA. John Montgomery Cooper papers, box 1, folder 1915–1916.

44. This did not keep contemporary anti-Catholic propagandists from asserting that priests routinely and in salacious detail questioned female penitents about sexual sin. For a particularly vivid example by a former Catholic priest, see Rev. Charles Chiniquy, *The Priest, The Woman, and The Confessional* (Chicago: A. Craig & Co., 1880).

45. Stang, *Pastoral Theology,* 171. Translated from the original Latin.

46. The American translator of Caspar Schieler's *Theory and Practice of the Confessional* (1906) apologized for rendering in English passages on certain "most delicate subjects"—the volume, after all, might fall into nonclerical hands. He intimated that many priests' Latin was insufficient for post-seminary refreshment in moral theology, see page 5. The lay author of a handbook for priests on pastoral medicine felt more constrained. Though he devoted almost twenty pages to abortion, he referred his priest reader "to his Latin handbook on Moral Theology" when it came to contraception. Alexander E. Sanford, M.D., *Pastoral Medicine: A Handbook for the Catholic Clergy* (New York: Joseph F. Wagner, 1905), 98.

47. Rt. Rev. Aloysius Roeggl, *The Confessional: or, Admonitions for the Confessional and Penance, according to the gospels for the Sunday and Holydays of the Ecclesiastical Year,* trans. and enlarged by Rev. Augustine Wirth, O.S.B. (Baltimore: John Murphy & Company, 1877), 385–387.

48. Schieler, *Theory and Practice of the Confessional,* 387.

49. Ibid., 599, footnote 553. The latter portion of the sentence is translated from the Latin.

50. Rev. Frederick Schulze, *Manual of Pastoral Theology: A Practical Guide for Ecclesiastical Students and Newly Ordained Priests* (Milwaukee: Diederich-Schaefer Co., 1906), 151. Translated from the original Latin.

51. Joseph McSorley, C.S.P., *Italian Confessions and How to Hear Them: An Easy Method for Busy Priests* (New York: Paulist Press, 1916).

52. Ryan, "Family Limitation," 4.

53. John A. Ryan, moral theology teaching notes, ms. bound volume. Undated but evidently from Ryan's St. Paul years (1902–1915). ACUA, John A. Ryan papers, box 33.

54. Rev. Antony Koch, *A Handbook of Moral Theology,* vol. 2: Sin and the Means of Grace, ad. and ed. by Arthur Preuss, 2nd rev. ed.(St. Louis: B. Herder Book Co., 1919), 163. The Belgian moralist Eduard Genicot went further: "With regard to conjugal onanism: when it happens that a penitent responds that he can't induce a feeling of having sinned mortally for having practiced onanism, when there are grave causes for abstaining from copulation—such as another pregnancy seriously endangering a wife's well-being or causing harm to the children—but he is nonetheless strongly impelled to the marital act, then the confessor, if he judges the man to be otherwise a good Christian, may prudently dissemble" [i.e., not inform the penitent that onanism is in fact a mortal sin]. This passage, from the 1909 (6th) edition of *Institutiones Theologiae Moralis* vol. 2, was later amended to read "it is not possible in these circumstances for the confessor to remain silent." Original Latin quoted in "Studies and Conferences," *American Ecclesiastical Review* 83, no. 6 (Dec. 1930), 633–634.

55. Wissel, *Redemptorist on the American Missions,* vol. 1, 474. Translated from the original Latin.

56. Ibid., 102–103.

57. Franz Xavier Weninger, *Die Heilige Mission* and *Praktische Winke für Missionare* (1885; repr. New York: Arno Press, 1978), 419–450, 452–480. Translated from the original German.

58. Ibid., 430.

59. *The Key of Heaven; or, The Devout Christian's Daily Companion,* no author given (New York: Christian Press Association Publishing Company, undated), 584, 601–604, 613. The imprimatur is that of Cardinal John McCloskey, who received his red hat in 1875 and died in 1885.

60. Rev. A. Konings, C.SS.R., *General Confession Made Easy* (New York: Benziger Brothers, 1879) asks directly about abortion but only obliquely about birth control. Helpful on this subject is Joseph Xavier O'Connor, O.S.A., "A Survey of the Examination of Conscience as Found in Some Popular Prayerbooks" (M.A. thesis, Graduate School of Arts and Sciences, Catholic University of America, 1954).

61. Walter Elliott, C.S.P., *A Manual of Missions* (Washington, DC: Apostolic Mission House, 1922), 34–35.

62. Frassinetti, *Parish Priest's Practical Manual,* 361.

63. Stang, *Pastoral Theology,* 177. He echoes Frassinetti in this regard. Schieler, *Theory and Practice of the Confessional* agrees with Stang, though not in regard to separate confessionals, which would in most instances have been impractical.

64. Schieler, *Theory and Practice of the Confessional,* 387, 612–613, 616–618.

65. The letter's full text appears in the *Michigan Catholic,* 27 Feb. 1890, 1:4–5.

66. Maes's letter stands in contrast to a pastoral on betrothal and marriage issued in 1908 by the bishops of the Cincinnati Province, which makes not even oblique reference to abortion or contraception. *Pastoral Letter on Betrothal and Marriage,* issued by the bishops of the Cincinnati Province, Lent 1908 (New York: Frederick Pustet & Co., 1908).

67. The interview was reprinted in the *Michigan Catholic,* 6 Feb. 1908, 1:6–7.

68. "Race Suiciders," 5.

69. "Conditions Necessary for a Happy Marriage," no author given. *Homiletic Monthly and Catechist* 13, no. 10 (July 1913): 1035.

70. Michael I. Stritch, S.J., "What Menaces the Family," *Catholic Mind* 15, no. 21 (8 Nov. 1917): 502. This is the text of an address delivered to the National Convention of Catholic Societies in Kansas City, August 1917.

71. An Ursuline Religious, "'Movies' and the Young," *Catholic Mind* 18, no. 8 (22 April 1918): 197. This article was distributed by the Catholic Press Association and may have appeared widely in the diocesan press.

72. *Michigan Catholic,* 27 Feb. 1913, 5:1–2. The priest in question was Fr. Henri Blanchot, C.S.Sp., assistant at St. Joachim's church in Detroit. The quote comes from a Lenten sermon. Stang, *Pastoral Theology,* 42.

73. *Michigan Catholic,* 11 July 1907, 1:2. The priest was Fr. Michael Esper, pastor of St. Joseph's church in St. Joseph, Michigan. His sermon made the national press wire.

74. John A. McClory, S.J., *The Brazen Serpent,* 2nd ed. (St. Louis: B. Herder, 1922), 12. The book is a compilation of Lenten sermons preached by Father McClory at SS. Peter and Paul's church in Detroit in 1919.

75. "Race Suiciders," 3.

76. Rev. John Talbot Smith, *The Chaplain's Sermons* (New York: William H. Young & Company, 1896), 239–243. Rev. A. A. Lambing, *Plain Sermons on Mixed Marriages,* 3rd ed. (Newark, NJ: Rev. Augustine Wirth, O.S.B., 1882), makes brief reference to family limitation on pages 49–50, but does so only in the context of a religiously mixed marriage, with the non-Catholic party as the principal sinner. Wirth translated these sermons from the original German.

77. Schulze, *Manual of Pastoral Theology,* 323. Schulze's advice was uniformly dispensed by other manualists. See, for example, Stang, *Pastoral Theology,* 36.

78. The Archdiocese of Chicago instituted the first diocesan sermon outlines in 1918, which also required that priests give doctrinal instructions at all low Masses. Other dioceses, principally in the Midwest, eventually followed suit, though not until the 1930s or even the 1940s. Detroit's Bishop John Foley (1888–1918) prescribed an annual Sunday sermon on marriage, mainly—it seems—for purposes of inveighing against marriage to non-Catholics. But he seemed unsure about how many priests actually complied. A question in this regard appears on the form that Detroit's priests submitted annually on the state of their parishes. Copies are found in the Archives of the Archdiocese of Detroit in any of the parish files from 1889 to 1918.

79. Francis C. Kelley, "About Preaching," *Homiletic and Pastoral Review* 30, no. 1 (Oct. 1929): 9.

80. For an example from early in the period under study, see Cardinal James Gibbons, ms. sermon on "Marriage," delivered in Wilmington, DE, 14 Jan. 1872 and again in Richmond VA, Lent 1875. AAB. Gibbons papers, sermon no. 16. For a later example, see Rt. Rev. Thaddeus Hogan, R.M., "The Sanctity of Christian Marriage," in *Sermons Doctrinal and Moral* (New York: P. J. Kenedy & Sons, 1915), 159–160.

81. John A. Ryan argued in 1904 for seven or eight children per family in "The Small Family and National Decadence," *Ecclesiastical Review* 30 (Feb. 1904): 140–155. Rev. Thomas Gerrard, writing in 1911, thought that fourteen would be better still (*Marriage and Parenthood,* 112). Rev. Charles J. Callan, O.P., reprinted Gerrard's counsel in his *Illustrations for Sermons and Instructions* (New York: Joseph A. Wagner, 1916), 237. A Passionist preacher in 1909 was representative of his generation: "Woe to the parents that have only two or three children when they should have eight or ten!" Reginald Lummer, C.P., ms. sermon on "Marriage—Its End." PPA. Sermons of Father Reginald Lummer, box 247.

82. Rev. J. W. Sullivan, "Christian Marriage," *Homiletic Monthly and Catechist* 8, no. 8 (May 1908): 618.

83. "The Sanctity and Utility of Marriage," no author given, *Homiletic Monthly and Catechist* 13, no. 10 (July 1913): 954.

84. The *Homiletic Monthly and Catechist*—subsequently the *Homiletic and Pastoral Review*—began publication in 1900. The 1924 reference to birth control occurs in an article on mixed marriage.

85. John M. Cooper, ms. notes for a sermon on "Race-Suicide," 4 Feb. 1916. ACUA. John Montgomery Cooper papers, box 1, folder 1916–1917. "Not preached" is in Cooper's hand.

86. Elliott, *Manual of Missions,* 1–2.

87. J. H. Healy, O.P., "The Need of Missions to Parishes," *Homiletic and Pastoral Review* 21, no. 3 (Dec. 1920): 178.

88. This assertion is based on my research in the Paulist Fathers' archives at St. Paul's College, Washington DC.

89. James M. Gillis, C.S.P., ms. sermon on "Scandal," undated but ca. 1907. Archives of the Paulist Fathers (hereafter APF), PPGILLJMO88.

90. Wissel, *Redemptorist on the American Missions,* vol. 1, 73–74. Quote from page 74.

91. This assertion is based on my reading of the sermon manuscripts housed at the Archives of the Redemptorist Fathers of the Baltimore Province, located in Brooklyn.

92. Wissel, *Redemptorist on the American Missions,* vol. 1, 73–74.

93. Ibid., 75–76.

94. Ibid., 474.

95. Ibid., 76.

96. Ibid., 473.

97. Ibid., 474–475.

98. Weninger, *Die Heilige Mission,* 430. Translated from the original German. Weninger's diatribe against family limitation appears on 428–430, 463–466. Weninger, an Austrian, came to the United States in 1848; he preached more than 500 missions in the course of his career.

99. Michael Burke, C.SS.R., "For Married Men," undated. (Burke was ordained in 1860 and

died in 1891.) RAB, uncatalogued. For a slightly later but comparably explicit Redemptorist instruction, see John G. Schneider, C.SS.R., "Duties of Married Men" and "Duties of Married
Women" in volume of ms. sermons titled "State Instructions (Mission)," undated. Schneider was
ordained in 1888 and died in 1914. RAB, uncatalogued.

100. W. M. Brick, C.SS.R., ms. sermon on "The General Judgment," 27 July 1887. RAB, uncatalogued. This sermon and others are found in a bound volume that bears the above date on its
first page.

101. Elliott, *Manual of Missions,* 98.

102. Dwyer, ms. sermon on "The General Judgment."

103. James M. Gillis, C.S.P., ms. sermon on "Judgment," preached at several locations in
1903–1904. APF. PPGILLMOO8.

104. Typescript sermon on "Death," no author given, undated but probably mid-to-late teens.
RAB, uncatalogued.

105. Lummer, "Marriage—Its End."

106. Ms. sermon, "The Death of the Sinner," undated but probably ca. 1900. No author given.
RAB, uncatalogued.

107. Wissel, *Redemptorist on the American Missions,* vol. 1, 95–96.

108. "Race Suiciders," 29.

109. The quote is from Rev. Reynold Kuehnel, "Conferences for the Holy Name Society,"
Homiletic Monthly and Catechist 16, no. 11 (August 1916): 1055.

110. *Michigan Catholic,* 18 May 1916, 4:3.

111. McClory, *Brazen Serpent,* 12.

112. Kuehnel, "Conferences for the Holy Name Society," 1055–1058.

113. Noonan, *Contraception,* 91–94, 98–101, 144, 146, 155, 178, 215–216, 232–237, 360–
365.

114. Ibid., 364–365.

115. Schulze, *Manual of Pastoral Theology,* 280. Rev. J. T. Durward, *A Short Course in Catholic Doctrine for Non-Catholics Intending Marriage with Catholics* (no place of publication,
1909) warns against sinful "prevention" on page 3. Durward was a priest of the Diocese of
LaCrosse; he described his book as a help to priests under increased episcopal pressure to instruct the non-Catholic party in mixed marriages.

116. Donohoe, "Marriage Instructions."

117. Felix M. Kirsch, O.M. Cap., *Sex Education and Training in Chastity* (New York: Benziger Brothers, 1930), 442. Kirsch is quoting from one of the respondents to a questionnaire sent
to some 500 priests engaged in pastoral work.

118. Ryan, "Family Limitation," quote from 690.

119. As examples, see Paul L. Blakely, S.J., "Conscious Birth Restriction," *Catholic Mind* (22
June 1915), reprinted in Benjamin L. Masse, ed., *The Catholic Mind through Fifty Years* (New
York: America Press, 1952); M. P. Dowling, S.J., "Race Suicide," *Catholic Mind* 14, no. 20 (22
Oct. 1916): 519–539; Stritch, "What Menaces the Family."

120. For incisive development of this theme, see John T. McGreevy, *Catholicism and American Freedom: A History* (New York: W.W. Norton, 2003), 153–163.

121. Ryan, "Small Family and National Decadence," 155.

122. John A. Ryan, "Birth Control: An Open Letter," *America* 13, no. 8 (5 June 1915), 200.

123. Ryan, "Family Limitation," 684.

124. Francis P. Sloan to Fr. John Burke, 11 Dec. 1918. ACUA, NCWC papers, 10/22/19.
Burke served as the Council's chairman.

Chapter 2. A Certain Indocility

1. Joseph V. Nevins, S.S., "Education to Catholic Marriage, Part II: Adverse Influences,"
Ecclesiastical Review 79, no. 6 (Dec. 1928): 621–630. Quotes from pages 622, 624, 626.

2. Ibid., 622.

3. Ibid., 625

4. David M. Kennedy, *Freedom From Fear: The American People in Depression and War, 1929–1945* (New York: Oxford University Press, 1999), 28.

5. Kathleen Tobin-Schlesinger, "Population and Power: The Religious Debate over Contraception, 1916–1936" (Ph.D. dissertation, University of Chicago, 1994), 178.

6. Ministello Conversus, "The Non-Catholic Attitude towards Contraceptive Practices," *Acolyte* 1, no. 14 (4 July 1925): 6.

7. Tobin-Schlesinger, "Population and Power," 179–199.

8. Patrick J. Ward, "Memorandum to Father [John] Burke," 18 Feb. 1926. ACUA, NCWC papers, 10/20/4.

9. Charles Bruehl, "Catholics and the Modern Mentality," *Homiletic and Pastoral Review* 28, no. 12 (Sept. 1928): 1268.

10. Henry Woods, S.J. to the editor, *Ecclesiastical Review* 76, no. 5 (Nov. 1929): 523.

11. Minutes of the Administrative Board, National Catholic Welfare Conference, 26 Jan. 1922. ACUA. *Minutes of the Administrative Board, NCWC,* April 25, 1919–Nov. 7, 1929, 26.

12. Bertrand L. Contway, C.S.P., *Birth Control* (New York: Paulist Press, 1924), 5.

13. M. P. Dowling, S.J., *Race-Suicide,* undated but ca. early 1920s, no place of publication given, 8; quote from an anonymous pamphlet, *The Catholic Church and Birth Control,* no date or place of publication but ca. 1927, 17.

14. Dowling, *Race-Suicide,* 8.

15. "Birth Control and the Labor Movement," (Washington, DC: National Catholic Welfare Conference, 1925), single-page leaflet. See also John Montgomery Cooper, *Birth Control* (Washington, DC: National Catholic Welfare Conference, 1923), 58–61.

16. John Burke, C.S.P. to Mrs. Bridget Harrison, 14 Nov. 1927. ACUA, NCWC papers, 10/20/6.

17. Cooper, *Birth Control,* 47.

18. Contway, *Birth Control,* 4.

19. *Catholic Church and Birth Control,* 18.

20. Fulgence Meyer, O.F.M., *Plain Talks on Marriage* (Cincinnati: St. Francis Book Shop, 1927), 78.

21. *Catholic Church and Birth Control,* 13.

22. John A. Ryan to the editor, *Ecclesiastical Review,* 79, no. 4 (Oct. 1928): 411.

23. John Montgomery Cooper to the editor, *Ecclesiastical Review,* 79, no. 5 (Nov. 1928): 529.

24. Cooper, *Birth Control,* 20–23, 77–84. Quotes from 21, 79.

25. John A. Ryan, *Human Sterilization* (Washington, DC: National Catholic Welfare Conference, 1927), 3.

26. For an eloquent statement of the Catholic position, see John Burke to Mary Hawks, 10 Feb. 1926. ACUA, NCWC papers, 10/20/4.

27. Cooper to the editor, *Ecclesiastical Review* (Oct. 1925): 533.

28. Unsigned review of Henry Davis, S.J., *Birth Control Ethics* in *Acolyte* 3, no. 12 (4 June 1927): 10. This periodical, aimed at priests, had only priest contributors in this period.

29. John Montgomery Cooper to Dr. C. P. Ives, 11 March 1930. ACUA. John Montgomery Cooper papers, box 18, folder "American Social Hygiene Association, 1928–1937."

30. Unsigned review of Davis, *Birth Control Ethics,* 10.

31. Copies of these fact-sheets, which address aspects of the topic as varied as overpopulation and the prospects of the labor movement, are found in ACUA, NCWC papers, 10/20/3. Each carries a prominent union label.

32. Vincent McNabb, O.P., "The Catholic Church and Birth Control," *Commonweal* 1, no. 15 (18 Feb. 1925), 396.

33. Tobin-Schlesinger, "Population and Power," 80–101. Quotes from Sanger's editorial in the *Birth Control Review,* Dec. 1921, which is reproduced in part on pages 95–96.

34. "Statement of Admin. Com. NCWC 1/26/22," typescript. ACUA, NCWC papers, 10/20/1.

35. "Notes of Bp. Gibbons, Sept. 1925." ACUA, NCWC papers, 10/20/3.

36. Sara Laughlin to John Burke, 13 Feb. 1921. ACUA, NCWC papers, 10/19/33.

37. Sara Laughlin to John Burke, 24 Feb. 1921. ACUA, NCWC papers, 10/19/33.

38. Sara Laughlin to John Burke, 13 Feb. 1921. ACUA, NCWC papers, 10/19/33.

39. David M. Kennedy, *Birth Control in America: The Career of Margaret Sanger* (New Haven: Yale University Press, 1970), 219–224.

40. Minutes of the Administrative Board, National Catholic Welfare Conference, 13 April 1926. ACUA. *Minutes of the Administrative Board, NCWC,* April 25, 1919–Nov. 7, 1929, 103.

41. Perry Patterson to Archbishop Mundelein, 16 Jan. 1924. Archives of the Archdiocese of Chicago (hereafter AAC). Mundelein Chancery correspondence, 8 1924 M 14. Not every bishop was equally aggressive. Baltimore's Michael Curley apparently took no action when a birth control clinic was established at Johns Hopkins University in the late 1920s. Patrick Ward to Fr. John Burke, 30 June 1931. ACUA, NCWC papers, 10/20/16.

42. Rev. Alexis L. Hopkins to Rev. James H. Ryan, undated but 1924. ACUA, NCWC papers, 10/20/3.

43. Patrick J. Ward to John Burke, 19 March 1927. ACUA, NCWC papers, 10/20/6.

44. The "women's statement" appears in the in the National Catholic Welfare Council *Bulletin,* 2, no. 1 (Jan. 1921): 21; Ryan published the text as his own in the Dec. 1920 issue of the *Catholic Charities Review.*

45. John Burke to Sara Laughlin, 26 Oct. 1928. ACUA, NCWC papers, 10/20/7.

46. Sara Laughlin to John Burke, 16 Jan. 1921. ACUA, NCWC papers, 10/19/33.

47. John Burke to Father Robert E. Lucey, 10 June 1925. ACUA, NCWC papers, 10/20/3.

48. John Burke to Bp. Francis J. Thief, 28 May 1925. ACUA, NCWC papers, 10/20/3.

49. Felix M. Kirsch, O.M. Cap., *Sex Education and Training in Chastity* (New York: Benziger Brothers, 1930), 431.

50. Nevins, "Education to Catholic Marriage," Part II, 624, 631.

51. Joseph V. Nevins, S.S., "Education to Catholic Marriage," Part 1, *Ecclesiastical Review* 79, no. 3 (Sept. 1928): 249.

52. Mrs. Dorothy G. Fisher to Wilfrid Parsons, S.J., undated but probably Jan. 1927. GULSC. America Magazine Archives, box 1, folder 17.

53. A.C.L. to Fr. John Burke, 9 Feb. 1931. ACUA, NCWC papers, 10/20/9.

54. Nevins, "Education to Catholic Marriage," Part II, 630.

55. Mary F. Coughlin to the editor, *America* 36, no. 26 (April 1927), 630.

56. Rev. Charles Bruehl, "Pastoralia: Readjustments to Relieve Excessive Crowding at the Confessional," *Homiletic and Pastoral Review* 24, no. 8 (May 1924): 786.

57. Bp. J. F. Noll, "How to Help the Penitent," *Acolyte* 3, no. 23 (5 Nov. 1927): 5.

58. Fr. Stanislaus Woywod, O.F.M., "Answers to Questions: Frequent Confession and Holy Communion Best Remedy to Break Sinful Habits," *Homiletic Monthly and Pastoral Review* 20, no. 12 (Sept. 1920): 1162.

59. P.H.D., "Practical Psychology for Parish Priests: The Mental Attitude towards Birth Control," *Acolyte* 2, no. 16 (31 July 1926): 11.

60. Coughlin to the editor, *America* (9 April 1927), 630.

61. Unsigned review of *Plain Talks on Marriage* by Rev. Fulgence Meyer, O.F.M., *Acolyte* 3, No. 6 (12 March 1927): 5.

62. Francis Lucidi, "De Vaginalibus Lotionibus," *Homiletic and Pastoral Review* 25, no. 10 (July 1925): 1096–1099.

63. Stanislaus Woywod, O.F.M., "Answers to Questions: Is It a Reserved Case to Have Ovariotomy Performed?" *Homiletic and Pastoral Review* 26, no. 5 (Feb. 1926): 507–508.

64. Stanislaus Woywod, O.F.M., "Answers to Questions: Birth Control the Crux of the Confessor," *Homiletic and Pastoral Review* 29, no. 1 (Oct. 1928): 74.

65. Kirsch, *Sex Education and Training in Chastity,* 431, 433, 434.

66. Joseph Turner, C.SS.R., "State Instruction—Married Women," undated. This text is certainly post-1918 and probably early 1920s. Quote from page 5. RAB. Text in bound volume titled "Missions—Renewals," undated and otherwise uncatalogued.

67. Meyer, *Plain Talks on Marriage,* 73–74.

68. Edward F. Garesche, S.J., *Modern Parish Problems* (New York: Joseph F. Wagner, 1928), 228. The copy in the library of the Catholic University of America was once the property of Washington's Cardinal Patrick O'Boyle, who played a dramatic role in 1968 in support of *Humanae Vitae.*

69. Woods to the editor, *Ecclesiastical Review,* 523.

70. P.H.D., "Practical Psychology for Parish Priests," 11.

71. Fr. Joseph Selinger to the editor, *Ecclesiastical Review* 81, no. 3 (Sept. 1929): 318.

72. Francis C. Kelley, "About Preaching," *Homiletic and Pastoral Review* 30, no. 1 (Oct. 1929): 9–16.

73. "Prenuptial Agreements," *Ecclesiastical Review* 79, no. 4 (Oct. 1928): 407.

74. Rev. J. F. Kelly, "Duties of Parents," *Homiletic and Pastoral Review* 20, no. 5 (Feb. 1920): 478.

75. Rev. V. Simeon, "Sermons I Have Not Preached," *Acolyte* 6, no. 2 (25 Jan. 1930): 3–4.

76. "The Sin of Birth Control: Pastoral Letter of His Grace Archbishop Hayes," *Catholic Mind* 20, no. 2 (22 Jan. 1922): 34. The letter appeared as well in the *New York Times,* 18 Dec. 1921, and subsequently as a pamphlet. Hayes's pastoral contrasts sharply with that of Covington's Bishop Ferdinand Brossart, which was also issued in 1921 and dealt with marriage. Brossart said nothing about either birth control or abortion. His reticence was almost certainly more typical of his episcopal contemporaries. Rt. Rev. Ferdinand Brossart, *Pastoral Letter of the Rt. Rev. Bishop of Covington: Marriage and Divorce* (no place or date of publication given.).

77. "Hopeful" to the editor, *Acolyte,* 6, no. 5 (8 March 1930): 8.

78. Meyer, *Plain Talks on Marriage,* 63.

79. Walter Elliott, C.S.P., *A Manual of Missions* (Washington, DC: Apostolic Mission House, 1922), 81.

80. Rev. Alfred Menth, C.SS.R., mission instruction to "Married Men," undated but probably early-to-mid 1920s. RAB, uncatalogued.

81. Joseph Turner, C.SS.R., "State Instruction—Married Women," 5.

82. Meyer, *Plain Talks on Marriage,* 81.

83. Fr. Theophane Gescavitz, C.P., sermon on "The General Judgment," 19 March 1930. PPA. Sermons of Fr. Theophane Gescavitz, box 243.

84. Joseph Turner, C.SS.R., "The Knight of Columbus and His Home Relations," undated but probably 1920s. RAB, uncatalogued.

85. Joseph Turner, C.SS.R., "State Instruction—Married Women," 5.

86. William A. Thumel, C.SS.R., "General Judgment," undated but probably 1920s. RAB. Bound volumes of Thumel's sermons, unnumbered.

87. William A. Thumel, C.SS.R., "Death," undated but probably 1920s. RAB. Bound volumes of Thumel's sermons, unnumbered.

88. Anon., undated account of a Lenten sermon by David W. Kennedy, C.S.P. Internal evidence suggests that it was preached in the 1920s. (Kennedy died in 1934.) The account appears to be either a press release or the draft of a contribution to the Paulist-edited *Catholic World.* It quotes Kennedy extensively and—given the apparent nature of the document—I assume accurately. APF. Folder labeled David W. Kennedy.

89. See, for example, Joseph Turner, C.SS.R., "State Instruction—Married Women," 5; Alfred Menth, C.SS.R., mission sermon on the "General Judgment," undated but probably early 1920s. RAB. Binder of Menth sermons; William Thumel, C.SS.R., mission sermons on "Mortal Sin" and the "General Judgment," undated but probably early 1920s. RAB, in one of five unnumbered volumes of Thumel's sermons; Vincent Ehinger, C.P., mission sermon on "The Last

Judgment," 28 March 1924, PPA. Sermons of Fr. Vincent Ehinger, box 242; Gescavitz, "General Judgment."

90. Meyer, *Plain Talks on Marriage,* 68.

91. Alfred Menth, C.SS.R., "Particular Judgment," undated but probably early 1920s. RAB. Binder of Menth sermons. See also Menth sermons on "Effects of Mortal Sin" and "Relapse."

92. William I. Lonergan, S.J., *Campaigning with Christ's Church: A Course of Sermons for Lent with a Sermon for Easter* (New York: Joseph F. Wagner, 1927), 45. The various sermons, according to the author, had been repeatedly preached at various locales throughout the country.

93. See, for example, an anon. sermon on "The General Judgment," undated but ca. 1920s. RAB, housed in metal box labeled "Sermons of Fr. Joseph Turner," which includes texts by other men as well.

94. Turner, "State Instruction—Married Women," 5.

95. William A. Thumel, C.SS.R., sermon on "Mortal Sin," undated but probably early 1920s. RAB. Bound volumes of Thumel sermons, unnumbered.

96. Gescavitz, "General Judgment."

97. John J. Burke, C.S.P., ms. sermon for Christmas Eve, 1928. APF. John J. Burke papers, sermons PPBURKJJ032, folder FF02.

98. F.M.A. to the editor, *America,* 31, no. 7 (31 May 1924), 158.

99. William A. Thumel, C.SS.R., mission instructions to married men, undated but probably early 1920s. RAB, in one of five unnumbered volumes of Thumel's sermons.

100. Fulgence Meyer, O.F.M., *Back to God: A Treatise on Confession, or the Sacrament of Penance* (Cincinnati: St. Francis Book Shop, 1928), 327.

101. Ferdinand Heckmann, O.F.M., "The Family and the Holy Eucharist" [a sermon for the first Sunday after Epiphany], *Homiletic and Pastoral Review* 30, no. 3 (Dec. 1929): 315.

102. Leo J. Latz, *The Rhythm of Sterility and Fertility in Women* (Chicago: Dr. Leo J. Latz, 1932), 103–104. Latz has reference to "Abortion in Relation to Fetal and Maternal Welfare," prepared for a 1928 White House Conference.

103. Alice Hamilton, M.D., *Poverty and Birth Control* (New York: American Birth Control League, undated), unpaginated. This pamphlet was almost certainly published in the 1920s. A copy was sent to Philadelphia's Cardinal Dennis Dougherty, presumably by Sara Laughlin, in March 1928.

104. Ibid.

105. Marie E. Kopp, *Birth Control in Practice: Analysis of Ten Thousand Case Histories of the Birth Control Clinical Research Bureau* (New York: Robert M. McBride & Company, 1934), 55, 216.

106. Turner, "State Instruction—Married Women," 4.

107. Rev. W. J. Flanagan to Rev. Francis P. Le Buffe, S.J., 26 Sept. 1927. GULSC. America Magazine Archives, box 1, folder 17. Father Flanagan wrote from Hubbardstown MI.

108. Wilfrid Parsons, S.J. to Rev. W. J. Flanagan, 20 Oct. 1927. GULSC. America Magazine Archives, box 1, folder 17.

109. Mary Gordon, "The Woman's Side of It," *America* 35, no. 23 (18 Sept. 1926), 537, 538.

110. Margaret Hughes, "The Woman's Side of It, Continued," *America* 36, no. 17 (5 Feb. 1927), 402, 404.

111. Mary H. Kennedy, "For We Have Ideals," and Jo Nichol, "Still Another Woman's Viewpoint," both in *America* 36, no. 21 (5 March 1927), 499–501; Edna N. Dealy to the editor, *America* 36, no. 21 (5 March 1927), 509; Mary L. Cox to the editor, *America* 36, no. 22 (12 March 1927), 534; (Mrs.) Helen Reynolds to the editor, *America* 36, no. 24 (26 March 1927), 581–582; Joseph H. Wels, S.J. to the editor, *America* 37, no. 5 (14 May 1927), 119; J.F.S. to the editor, *America* 37, no. 10 (18 June 1927), 239.

112. Nevins, "Education to Catholic Marriage," Part I, 252–253.

113. On the Catholic debate over the marital debt, see John T. Noonan, *Contraception: A His-*

tory of Its Treatment by the Catholic Theologians and Canonists, rev. ed. (Cambridge, MA: Harvard University Press, 1986), 42, 52, 130–131, 283–285, 330–336.

114. Meyer, *Plain Talks on Marriage,* 82.

115. Minutes, General Meeting of the Bishops, afternoon session of the first day, 6 Nov. 1929. ACUA. *Minutes of the Annual Meetings of the Bishops of the United States,* 1919–1935, 7.

116. Nevins, "Education to Catholic Marriage," Part II, 624.

117. Turner, "State Instruction—Married Women," 4.

118. Quoted in Noonan, *Contraception,* 427, 431.

Chapter 3. "No Longer a Time for Reticence"

1. Kathleen Tobin-Schlesinger, "Population and Power: The Religious Debate over Contraception, 1916–1936" (Ph.D. dissertation, University of Chicago, 1994), 211–216.

2. Richard A. Soloway, *Birth Control and the Population Question in England, 1877–1930* (Chapel Hill: University of North Carolina Press, 1982), 251–255.

3. Quoted in John T. Noonan, *Contraception: A History of Its Treatment by the Catholic Theologians and Canonists, rev. ed.* (Cambridge, MA: Harvard University Press, 1986), 427.

4. "Rome Has Spoken," *Commonweal* 13, no. 12 (21 Jan. 1931), 309–310.

5. See, for example, Arnaldo Cortesi, "Pope Pius XI, in Encyclical, Condemns Trial Marriage, Divorce, and Birth Control," *New York Times,* 9 Jan. 1931, 16:1–3 and especially the editorial "Roma Dixit," *New York Times,* 10 Jan. 1931, 14:4. Like a number of other U.S. papers, the *Times* reprinted the full text of *Casti Connubii.*

6. P.J.C., "The Latest Encyclical," *Ave Maria* 33 (7 Feb. 1931), 181.

7. Noonan, *Contraception,* 431. The pope's instruction to priests in the encyclical apparently reflected most immediately his worry about dissenting views on contraception in Germany and Belgium. Ibid., 425–426. But the doctrine of "good faith" ignorance informed pastoral practice in other countries, too.

8. A. Vermeersch, S.J. and T. Lincoln Bouscaren, S.J., *What Is Marriage? A Catechism Arranged According to the Encyclical 'Casti Connubii' of Pope Pius XI* (New York: America Press, 1932), 33–34.

9. Valentine Schaaf, O.F.M., "Canonical Notes on the Encyclical Letter on Christian Marriage," *Ecclesiastical Review* 84, no. 3 (March 1931): 272.

10. John J. Burke, C.S.P., "Our Blessed Lady," typescript sermon to a women's retreat, dated March 28 with no year given. I would guess that it dates from the late 1920s or early 1930s. Burke was by then a veteran of the Washington birth control wars and well accustomed to such talk. Nonetheless, his words seem to come from the heart. APF. PPBURKJJO33, folder FF05.

11. William J. Bergin, C.S.V., "Conjugal Chastity and Periodic Abstention: Personal Opinions vs. Principles and Facts," *Homiletic and Pastoral Review* 35, no. 3 (Dec. 1934): 273–274.

12. See, for example, Raymond Pearl, "Contraception and Fertility in 4945 Married Women: A Second Report on a Study of Family Limitation," *Human Biology* 6 (1934): 384–386. See also Andrea Tone, "Contraceptive Consumers: Gender and the Political Economy of Birth Control in the 1930s," *Journal of Social History* 29, no. 3 (Spring 1996): 485–506.

13. John Winchell Riley and Matilda White, "The Uses of Various Methods of Contraception," *American Sociological Review* 5, no. 6 (Dec. 1940): 895, 897–898.

14. Ibid., 895.

15. Samuel A. Stouffer, "Trends in the Fertility of Catholics and Non-Catholics," *American Journal of Sociology* 41, no. 2 (Sept. 1935): 143–166.

16. About 26 percent of the patients seen at the Sanger clinic in New York from 1925 through 1930 identified themselves as Catholics. Marie E. Kopp, *Birth Control in Practice: Analysis of Ten Thousand Case Histories of the Birth Control Clinical Research Bureau* (New York: Robert M. McBride & Company, 1934), 52. See also P.H.D., "Getting Away With Murder," *Acolyte* 9,

no. 9 (29 April 1933): 8; Rev. John A. O'Brien, "Private Judgment and Family Limitation," *Homiletic and Pastoral Review* 33, no. 9 (June 1933): 917–918; Emily C. Hartung, "Notes Taken at the Fifteenth Annual Meeting of the American Birth Control League," 22 Jan. 1936. ACUA, NCWC papers, 10/21/13.

17. Alla Nekrassova, M.D., "Birth Control for Isolated Social Groups," undated but ca. mid-1930s, no place of publication given. The pamphlet was evidently intended for birth control professionals; Nekrassova was affiliated with the Pennsylvania Birth Control Federation.

18. Rev. Ambrose Adams, "The Handwriting on the Wall," *Acolyte* 7, no. 19 (5 Sept. 1931): 5.

19. H. A. Seifert, C.SS.R., "Marriage Instruction Regarding Birth Control," *Ecclesiastical Review* 91, no. 4 (April 1937): 401.

20. J.F.M. to the editor, *Catholic Transcript,* 29 Jan. 1931. Clipping in ACUA, NCWC papers, 10/20, folder 9.

21. Pearl, "Contraception and Fertility in 4945 Married Women," 363, 364–366, 371.

22. Nekrassova, "Birth Control for Isolated Social Groups," unpaginated.

23. See, for example, figures quoted in James J. Walsh, "Are We Due to Disappear?" *Commonweal* 12, no. 22 (1 Oct. 1930), 548–550 and in Edgar Schmiedeler, O.S.B., *The Sacred Bond: Happiness with Holiness in Family Life* (New York: P.J. Kenedy and Sons, 1940), 39.

24. See Victoria De Grazia, *How Fascism Ruled Women: Italy, 1922–1945* (Berkeley and Los Angeles: University of California Press, 1993), 88–94; Richard A. Soloway, *Demography and Degeneration: Eugenics and the Declining Birthrate in Twentieth Century Britain* (Chapel Hill: University of North Carolina Press, 1995), 259–282.

25. Rt. Rev. John A. Ryan to the editor, *Commonweal* 19, no. 14 (2. Feb. 1934), 384.

26. Alexander Wyse, O.F.M., *Shall Heaven Be Filled?* (Paterson, NJ: St. Anthony's Guild, 1940), 22.

27. Frank A. Smothers, "New Light on Birth Control," *Commonweal* 17, no. 19 (8 March 1933), 513.

28. Quoted in Noonan, *Contraception,* 431.

29. John A. McHugh, O.P. and Charles J. Callan, O.P., *Moral Theology: A Complete Course,* vol. 2 (New York: Joseph F. Wagner, Inc., 1930), 605–606. Translated from the original Latin. The same Latin passage appears in the revised and enlarged edition of 1959.

30. Ibid., 510.

31. Ibid., 601. "Contraception seems to rank next in enormity [to murder], since it prevents human life from coming into existence."

32. Msgr. John L. Belford, "Neglect of the Holy Year," *Homiletic and Pastoral Review* 34, no. 5 (Feb. 1934): 471.

33. Fr. Edward S. Schwegler, "The Other Side of the Grille," *Sign* 14, no. 11 (June 1935), 684. See also P.H.D., "Infantilism in the Confessional," *Acolyte* 9, no. 2 (21 Jan. 1933): 6–7.

34. M. V. Kelly, O.S.B., "A Wolf in Sheep's Clothing—Perhaps," *Acolyte* 16, no. 1 (Jan. 1940): 18–19.

35. Julester Shrady Post, "Confessors," *Sign* 14, no. 2 (Sept. 1934), 106.

36. Rev. A. Verhoven to the editors, *Homiletic and Pastoral Review* 34, no. 6 (March 1934): 659.

37. Msgr. Reynold Hillenbrand, notes for a sermon on confession, undated but probably mid-to-late 1930s. AUND. Reynold Hillenbrand papers, CMRH, box 4, folder 4.

38. Msgr. Reynold Hillenbrand, notes for a "morning talk" on confession, undated but probably mid-to-late 1930s. AUND. Reynold Hillenbrand papers, CMRH, box 4, folder 4.

39. Cardinal George Mundelein to Rita McGoldrick, 18 July 1932. AAC. Mundelein Chancery correspondence, box 13 [1932M-N], folder 11.

40. Cardinal George Mundelein, notes for a sermon to his priests, undated but 1932. AAC. Mundelein personal papers, box 8, folder 3.

41. Mundelein to McGoldrick, 18 July 1932. By way of contrast, a pamphlet published in

1931 for the use of priests counseling couples prior to a religiously mixed marriage contains no direct references to contraception. Rt. Rev. Joseph Selinger, D.D., *A Catechism on the Pledges Required for Dispensation for a Mixed Marriage* (St. Louis: Central Bureau, Catholic Central Verein of America, 1931.)

42. Mundelein to McGoldrick, 18 June 1932.

43. Minutes, General Meeting of the Bishops, morning session of the second day, 14 Nov. 1935, 25. ACUA. *Minutes of the Annual Meetings of the Bishops of the United States, 1919–1935.*

44. Msgr. Kiefer, *Instructio Pro Confessariis* (Milwaukee: Bruce Publishing Co., 1950, expansion and translation of the 1931 German-language edition), 37. The quote is from translator-editor Fr. Clarence Liederbach's preface.

45. Mundelein to McGoldrick, 18 July 1932.

46. Joseph Reiner, S.J. to Wilfrid Parsons, S.J., 2 March 1933. GULSC. Wilfrid Parsons papers, box 8, folder 12.

47. Author interview with Msgr. John Egan, 9 Sept. 1998, Chicago.

48. Fr. Andrew McDonough, a classmate of Egan's, recalls being taught to question every penitent who had not confessed for three, rather than six, months. Otherwise his recollections square with Egan's. Author interview with McDonough, 10 Nov. 1998, Chicago.

49. Seifert, "Marriage Instructions Regarding Birth Control," 402.

50. Ibid., 403.

51. T. F. to the editor, *Sign* 13, no. 11 (June 1934), 663.

52. "Studies and Conferences," *Ecclesiastical Review* 83, no. 3 (Sept. 1930): 278.

53. "Studies and Conferences," *Ecclesiastical Review* 93, no. 4 (Oct. 1935): 413–414.

54. Stanislaus Woywod, O.F.M., "Marital Relations Forced by Drunken Husband and Use of Contraceptives by Wife," *Homiletic and Pastoral Review* 33, no. 3 (Dec. 1932): 293–294.

55. Stanislaus Woywod, O.F.M., "Wrong Advice in Confession May Become Solicitation," *Homiletic and Pastoral Review* 33, no. 5 (Feb. 1933): 524–525.

56. Joseph P. Donovan, C.M., "At What Moment is the Soul Infused Into the Fetus?" *Homiletic and Pastoral Review* 41, no. 11 (Aug. 1941): 1132, 1134.

57. Stanislaus Woywod, O.F.M., "Use of Contraceptives and Sacramental Absolution," *Homiletic and Pastoral Review* 31, no. 6 (March 1931): 628–630; "Co-operation in the Use of Contraceptives," *Ecclesiastical Review* 104, no. 1 (Jan. 1941): 77.

58. Joseph P. Donovan, C.M., "Fornication [*sic*] Couples with Use of Contraceptives," *Homiletic and Pastoral Review* 41, no. 11 (Aug. 1941): 1132.

59. Stanislaus Woywod, O.F.M., "Absolution of Persons Living in an Occasion of Sin and Frequently Falling into the Same Sin," *Homiletic and Pastoral Review* 39, no. 6 (March 1939): 618–619; Woywod, "What Is the Confessor to Do When the Penitent Says that He Cannot Stop Some Sin?" *Homiletic and Pastoral Review* 40, no. 1 (Oct. 1939): 70–72.

60. Eugene A. Dooley, O.M.I., "Sex Sins in the Confessional," *Ecclesiastical Review* 106, no. 4 (April 1941): 298.

61. Seifert, "Marriage Instructions Regarding Birth Control," 404.

62. John A. Ryan, "The Moral Teaching of the Encyclical," *Ecclesiastical Review* 84, no. 3 (March 1931): 266.

63. Woywod, "Marital Relations Forced by Drunken Husband," 293.

64. Mundelein, notes for a sermon to his priests, undated but 1932.

65. Rev. John K. Sharp, *Spoken in the Market Place: A Year's Instructions and Sermons on the Creed and the Sacraments* (New York: Joseph F. Wagner, 1939), 213. The sermons were originally published "some years ago," but certainly post-*Casti Connubii.*

66. James H. Kearney, S.J., "Studies and Conferences," *Ecclesiastical Review* 86, no. 5 (May 1931): 503; Franklyn J. Kennedy, "A Neglected Part of 'Casti Connubii,'" *Homiletic and Pastoral Review* 31, no. 10 (July 1931): 1084; Rev. Ambrose Reger, O.S.B., "Extracts from a Lenten Diary," *Acolyte,* 9, no. 5 (4 March 1933): 7; Rt. Rev. Msgr. William M. Farrell, *Radio Talks on*

Christian Marriage (Wichita, KA: Catholic Action Committee of the Knights of Columbus, Council 691, May 1935), 35. Nashville's Bishop Alphonse J. Smith spoke forcefully against birth control in a pastoral letter issued prior to *Casti Connubii*. Such a pastoral letter would almost certainly have been read from every pulpit in the diocese. See Smith, *The Catholic Ideal of Marriage* (no place or date of publication given, but issued 1 March 1930), 25–28.

67. Rev. Robert F. Kaiser, C.PP.S., "Inculcating Chastity," *Acolyte* 9, no. 22 (28 October 1933): 8.

68. Mundelein to McGoldrick, 18 July 1932.

69. Archdiocese of Chicago, *Program of Instruction for the Ecclesiastical Year 1935–1936* (Chicago: Archdiocese of Chicago, 1935). The sermons in question were preached on the 20th and 21st Sundays after Pentecost.

70. Msgr. Reynold Hillenbrand, teaching notes with regard to birth control in preaching and confession, undated but ca. mid-to-late 1930s. Hillenbrand was rector at Chicago's major seminary from 1935 to 1944. AUND. Reynold Hillenbrand papers, CMRH, box 4, folder 2.

71. Right Rev. Msgr. H. T. Henry, "Preaching on Purity," *Homiletic and Pastoral Review,* 32, no. 1 (Oct. 1931): 13.

72. Rev. Joseph B. Collins, "Why the Church Stands Out Alone," *Homiletic and Pastoral Review* 32, no. 7 (April 1932): 768.

73. Anon., "Sermon for the feast of the Holy Family," *Acolyte* 13, no. 1 (Jan. 1937): 21.

74. Rev. John A. O'Brien, "Is Preaching Dying in America?" *Homiletic and Pastoral Review* 33, no. 5 (Feb. 1933): 486.

75. Rev. John A. O'Brien, "Moral Causes of Catholic Leakage," *Homiletic and Pastoral Review* 33, no. 7 (April 1933): 698.

76. Rev. Thomas A. Fox, C.S.P., "Musings of a Parish Missioner," *Ecclesiastical Review* 103, no. 6 (Dec. 1940): 518.

77. Author interview with Father Daniel Budzynski, 20 November 1998, Milwaukee WI.

78. Seifert, "Marriage Instructions Regarding Birth Control," 401.

79. Results of this survey, with sample letters, appeared in *Acolyte* 13, no. 10 (Oct. 1937): 3–5. Quote from 3.

80. Rev. Leo A. Pursley, "Sermon for the Sunday within the Octave of Corpus Christi," *Acolyte* 15, no. 6 (June 1939): 22.

81. Anon., "Sermon for the Nineteenth Sunday after Pentecost," *Acolyte* 12, no. 10 (Oct. 1936): 4.

82. C. C. Martindale, S.J., "Contraception," *Homiletic and Pastoral Review* 38, no. 9 (June 1938): 986. Emphasis in original.

83. Anon. to the editor, *Acolyte* 15, no. 6 (June 1939): 29.

84. Cardinal George Mundelein "To the Clergy and Faithful of the Archdiocese of Chicago," 6 Sept., 1933. AAC. Mundelein personal papers, box 10, folder 42.

85. Francis P. Lyons, C.S.P., transcript of a mission preached at the church of St. Elizabeth, Minneapolis, 18 Nov.–2 Dec. 1934. Quote from the evening sermon for 20 Nov. APF. Rev. Francis P. Lyons papers, uncatalogued.

86. Alfred Menth, C.SS.R., typescript sermon on the "General Judgment," undated but early-to-mid 1930s. RAB, uncatalogued.

87. Albert H. Dolan, O. Carm., *A Modern Messenger of Purity: Sermons Concerning the Sixth Commandment* (Chicago: Carmelite Press, 1932), 43.

88. The adjectives, though common to many preached texts, are taken from Rev. Alfred Menth, C.SS.R., "State Instruction (Married)," undated but early to mid 1930s, 42. RAB, uncataloqued; and from Jones I. Corrigan, S.J., *Companionate Marriage* (New York: America Press, 1931), 2. The text of this pamphlet was initially a sermon.

89. Anon., "Redemptorist Mission Sermons: State Instruction to the Married," undated but ca. early 1940s. This was meant to update and supplement the older guide by Father Wissel. RAB, uncatalogued.

90. A. McBriarty, C.SS.R., "Parish Mission," *Ecclesiastical Review* 102, no. 3 (March 1940): 202.

91. John A. Ryan, "The Moral Aspects of Periodical Continence," *Ecclesiastical Review* 84, no. 1 (July 1933): 31–32.

92. See, for example, Alfred Menth, C.SS.R., "State Instruction (Married)," 42; Anon., "Redemptorist Mission Sermons."

93. Msgr. Reynold Hillenbrand, "Quod Deus junxit, nemo separet," undated but ca. mid-1930s. AUND. Reynold Hillenbrand papers—CMRH, box 4, folder 2. Hillenbrand was named head of the archdiocesan "mission band" in 1933, the year that the band was established by Cardinal George Mundelein. According to one of my Chicago priest informants, the mission band was discontinued in 1965.

94. Msgr. Reynold Hillenbrand, sermon notes on birth control, undated but ca. 1930s. AUND. Reynold Hillenbrand papers—CMRH, box 4, folder 2.

95. Fr. Mel Schneider, C.P., "Instructions on the Decalogue," 1939. PPA. Sermons of Fr. Mel Schneider, box 250.

96. Anon., "Sermon for the Feast of the Holy Family," *Acolyte* 6, no. 26 (27 Dec. 1930): 4.

97. As a sign of the times in this regard, see Rev. Stanley Bertke, *The Possibility of Invincible Ignorance of the Natural Law* (Washington, DC: Catholic University of America, Studies in Sacred Theology No. 58, 1941). Father Bertke cited widespread public acceptance of contraception as the most obvious example of such "invincible ignorance."

98. Albert H. Dolan, O. Carm., *Happiness in Marriage* (Englewood, NJ: Carmelite Press, 1940), 15–16. The pamphlet's contents were originally preached as sermons.

99. Anon., "My Conscience" [sermon notes for the third Sunday in Lent], *Acolyte* 16, no. 2 (Feb. 1940): 29.

100. Anon., "Thoughts for the Lenten Season," *Acolyte* 16, no. 2 (Feb. 1940): 11.

101. Richard A. Malloy, C.S.P., mission sermon on "Death," undated but ca. 1940. APF. Richard Aloysius Malloy papers, uncatalogued.

102. Richard A. Malloy, C.S.P., mission sermon on "Particular Judgment," undated but probably late 1930s. APF. Richard Aloysius Malloy papers, uncatalogued.

103. Sermon for the second Sunday in Advent, *Acolyte* 6, no. 23 (15 Nov. 1930): 4.

104. Rev. Ralph Brisk, C.P., sermon on "Mary, the Mother of God," 3 March 1932. PPA. Sermons of Fr. Ralph Brisk, box 241.

105. Fulgence Meyer, O.F.M., *Conferences for Married Men* (St. Louis: B. Herder, 1936), vii, 23, 24–25, 134.

106. Card. George Mundelein, text of talk at Mundelein College, June 1932. AAC, Mundelein Chancery Correspondence, box 13, folder 17.

107. Adams, "The Handwriting on the Wall," 5.

108. Daniel Lord, S.J., *What Birth Control Is Doing to the United States* (St. Louis: Queen's Work, 1936), 22.

109. Wilfrid Avery, C.P., ms. sermon on Mary, undated but probably early 1930s. PPA. Sermons of Fr. Roch Adamek, box 240. Fr. Adamek may have appropriated this text from Fr. Avery upon the latter's death in 1934.

110. Menth, "State Instruction (Married)."

111. Reginald Lummer, C.P., sermon notes on "Conscience," undated but ca. 1930s. PPA. Sermons of Fr. Reginald Lummer, box 247.

112. Gilbert Kroger, C.P., "The Catholic Home," mission and retreat sermon preached variously between 1932 and 1957. PPA. Sermons of Fr. Gilbert Kroger, box 246.

113. Richard A. Malloy, C.S.P., sermon on "The Dignity and Position of Woman," undated but ca. 1940. APF. Richard Aloysius Malloy papers, uncatalogued.

114. Ibid.

115. Felix M. Kirsch, O.F.M.Cap. "The Challenge of the Sex Problem," *Homiletic and Pastoral Review* 38, no. 8 (May 1938): 805.

116. Rev. F. J. Rembler, C.M., "The Cause of Catholic Leakage," *Acolyte* 12, no. 12 (Dec. 1936): 19.

117. Malloy, "Dignity and Position of Woman."

118. Dolan, *Modern Messenger of Purity.*

119. Reynold Hillenbrand, notes for an untitled mission sermon on purity, undated but ca. mid-1930s; notes for a sermons on mixed marriage, intended for high schoolers, undated but mid-1930s. AUND. Reynold Hillenbrand papers—CMRH, box 4, folder 2.

120. Rev. Alfred Menth, C.SS.R., "State Instruction (Single)," undated but early-to-mid 1930s. RAB, uncatalogued. Emphasis in original.

121. Dolan, *Modern Messenger of Purity,* 180, 56–57.

122. Rev. Fulton J. Sheen, "The Church and the Times," delivered 6 March 1932; "The Crucifixion," delivered 13 March 1932, both on the *Catholic Hour.* Printed copies of both texts are found in the Archives of the Archdiocese of Philadelphia (hereafter AAPhi), RC 58, 1–8. In the later 1930s and early 1940s, the *Catholic Hour* apparently avoided the subject of contraception—on the unwritten proviso that NBC would refrain from carrying talks endorsing it. See Edward J. Heffron to Thomas D. Rishworth, 11 Feb. 1942. ACUA, NCWC papers, 10/110/15.

123. Corrigan, "Companionate Marriage."

124. Ignatius W. Cox, S.J., *Birth Control, Birth Controllers and Perversion of Logic* (New York: Paulist Press, 1936), 10. The text is a sermon preached on New York's station WLWL on 6 Dec. 1935.

125. Ibid.

126. My account of the *Rosary Hour* is based on the research of Fr. Stanislaw Hajkowski, a doctoral student at the Catholic University of America. My deepest gratitude to Fr. Stan for providing me with the relevant documents and assisting in translation.

127. *Mowy Radjowe Przwe. Ojca Justyna,* vol. 2, 1933–1934 (Milwaukee: Drukiem Nowin Polskich), 97.

128. *Mowy Radjowe Przewieldbnego Ojca Justyna,* vol. 2, 1936–1937 (Milwaukee: Drukiem Nowin Polskich), 17. The programs dealing with abortion were broadcast on Feb. 7, 14, and 21, 1937.

129. *Mowy Radjowe Przew. Ojca Justyna,* vol. 1, 1935–1936 (Milwaukee: Drukiem Nowin Polskich), 157.

130. Fr. Apollinarius, O.F.M. Cap., *Another Baby?* (Yonkers, NY: Mission Almanac, 1933), 8, 14.

131. Quotes from Daniel A. Lord, S.J., *Speaking of Birth Control* (St. Louis: Queen's Work, 1945), 4, 3, 2. The 1945 edition was the twentieth printing; it is almost unchanged from the 1930 original.

132. Ibid., 27.

133. Mundelein, notes for a sermon to his priests, undated but 1932. For similar logic from a prominent Catholic preacher and pamphleteer see the Paulist James Gillis's introduction to William Thomas Walsh, *Babies—Not Bullets!* (New York: Paulist Press, undated but ca. 1940).

134. Lord, *Speaking of Birth Control,* 2, 7, 10, 8. That contraceptive sex caused husbands to lose "love and respect" for their wives was a common theme in period Catholic pamphlets. See, for example, Wilfrid G. Hurley, C.S.P., *Marriage Is a Sacrament* (New York: Paulist Press, 1935), 8–9.

135. Bp. Robert E. Lucey, *Artificial Birth Control* (Brooklyn, NY: International Catholic Truth Society, 1935), 9. Lucey was the bishop of Amarillo, Texas, and a longtime advocate of social justice, especially for migrant farm workers.

136. Joseph Reiner, S.J. to Terence Ahearn, S.J., 11 Aug. 1934, Loyola University of Chicago Archives (hereafter Loyola), biographical folder for Leo Latz, M.D.

137. The dominant medical opinion in the late 1920s assumed that ovulation occurred most frequently at the middle of the menstrual cycle, though it might occur at other times. Since most physicians also assumed a long period of survival for the non-fertilized ovule, they believed that pregnancy was possible throughout the cycle. R. De Guchteneere, M.D., "The Scientific Value

of Knaus-Ogino Theory," *Homiletic and Pastoral Review* 31, no. 1 (Oct. 1933): 24–25. See also Leo J. Latz, *The Rhythm of Sterility and Fertility in Women* (Chicago: Dr. Leo J. Latz, 1932), 9.

138. McHugh and Callan, *Moral Theology,* vol. 2, 509.

139. On this debate, see Noonan, *Contraception,* 438–442.

140. Fulgence Meyer, O.F.M., *Plain Talks on Marriage* (Cincinnati: St. Francis Book Shop, 1927), 90.

141. Ryan, "Moral Aspects of Periodic Continence," 29.

142. De Guchteneere, "Scientific Value of Knaus-Ogino," 25–29. On calculation of the safe period, see, among many others, Latz, *The Rhythm,* 46–60; John A. O'Brien, *Legitimate Birth Control* (Huntington, IN: Our Sunday Visitor Press, 1934), 63–70.

143. Vermeersch and Bouscaren, *What Is Marriage?* 40; Noonan, *Contraception,* 443. The Catholic moralist Ludwig Ruland discussed Knaus's findings in his authoritative *Pastoral Medicine,* published in Germany in 1929. He recounts his pioneering role in the first English-language edition of the book, published in 1934 (St. Louis: B. Herder, 14). The single most important publication in rhythm's German popularization was J. N. J. Smulders, *Periodische Enthaltung in der Ehe. Method: Ogino-Knaus* (Regensburg, 1932). It played the role of Latz's *The Rhythm* in the United States, and bore an imprimatur from the Bishop of Regensburg.

144. Leo J. Latz to Msgr. R. C. Maguire, 22 Oct. 1932. AAC. Mundelein Chancery Correspondence, box 13, folder 6; Joseph Reiner, S.J. to Samuel Wilson, S.J., 27 August 1934. Loyola. Office of the President: Papers of Samuel Knox Wilson, S.J., box 20, folder 4.

145. Very Rev. Canon Valère J. Coucke and James J. Walsh, M.D., *The Sterile Period in Family Life* (New York: Joseph F. Wagner, 1932), 32.

146. O'Brien, *Legitimate Birth Control,* 54–55. See also Latz, *The Rhythm,* 65–66.

147. This pre-publication advertisement first appeared in the *Acolyte,* a journal for priests, in the 23 Dec. 1933 edition.

148. Latz, *The Rhythm,* 162.

149. O'Brien, *Legitimate Birth Control,* 37.

150. Dietrich von Hildebrand, *In Defense of Purity: An Analysis of the Catholic Ideals of Purity and Virginity* (Baltimore: Helicon Press, 1962), 13. Von Hildebrand's book originated as lectures delivered in 1925 at a meeting of the Federation of Catholic Students' Unions at Innsbruck.

151. Noonan, *Contraception,* 495.

152. Ibid., 441–442.

153. Ryan, "Moral Aspects of Periodic Continence," 37.

154. Leo Latz, M.D. to Samuel K. Wilson, S.J., 19 Nov. 1935. Loyola. Biographical folder, Leo Latz, M.D. Latz claims in this letter that "almost 100,000" copies had been sold.

155. The pamphlet was advertised in the *Acolyte* on 15 April 1933, which also carried ads for the *Rhythm* on 24 June and 22 July 1933. An advertisement for a second Latz pamphlet appeared in the *Acolyte* for 17 March and 31 March 1934. Of the three leading Catholic clerical journals, the *Acolyte* alone carried advertising.

156. Patrick Masterson, S.J. to "Your Excellency," 29 March 1934. Loyola. Office of the President: Papers of Samuel Knox Wilson, S.J., box 20, folder 4.

157. The ad for "Control of Family through Natural Laws" was carried in the *Acolyte* on 28 Oct. 1933.

158. Bergin, "Conjugal Chastity and Periodic Abstention," 270.

159. The ad appeared in the *Acolyte* for 23 Dec. 1933, 6 Jan. and 20 Jan. 1934.

160. "Moral Birth Control Versus Contraception," *Michigan Catholic,* 22 Dec. 1932, 4:1; see also brief inserts in the editions for 29 Dec. 1932, 4:2 and 19 Jan. 1933, 6:2.

161. "Be Certain of Your Cycle Calendar," found in AUND. John A. O'Brien papers—COBR, box 6, folder 13. The reference is to a study reported in the April 1938 issue of *Surgery, Gynecology and Obstetrics.* The promotional material for "Natural Birth Control" is also found in the O'Brien papers.

162. Kathleen McLaughlin, "Science in Birth Control Quest Favors Natural Law," *Chicago*

Sunday Tribune, 4 Nov. 1934, 3. The method also found favor with certain secular proponents of family limitation. See, for example, Charles A. Clinton, M.D., *New Birth Control Facts* (New York: Pioneer Publications, 1935).

163. John C. Ford, S.J., teaching notes on periodic continence, undated but probably late 1930s. Archives of the New England Province of the Society of Jesus [hereafter NESJ]. John C. Ford, S.J. papers, box 10 (preliminary cataloguing).

164. Letter from "Mrs. M.G.," quoted in Katherine Burton, "Woman to Woman," *Sign* (Jan. 1935), 364.

165. (Mrs.) M.G. to Cardinal Lawrence Shehan, 30 June 1964. AAB. Shehan papers, uncatalogued. The letter urged archdiocesan officials to open a "rhythm clinic."

166. O'Brien, *Legitimate Birth Control,* 9, 11.

167. Daniel A. Lord, S.J., *What of Lawful Birth Control?* (St. Louis: Queen's Work, 1935), 11.

168. Reiner to Terence Ahearn, S.J., 11 Aug. 1934.

169. John O'Connell, C.S.C., "Birth Control Clinics Needed," *Ecclesiastical Review* 101, no. 3 (Sept. 1939): 250–252. A conservative Franciscan moralist, who shared none of O'Connell's critical views, was still sufficiently worried about contraceptive practice among Catholics to give public endorsement to O'Connell's clinic proposal. See Stanislaus Woywood, O.F.M., "Answers to Questions," *Homiletic and Pastoral Review* 40, no. 7 (April 1940): 780.

170. See, for example, Valentine Schaaf, O.F.M. in the "Studies and Conferences" section of the *Ecclesiastical Review* 91, no. 6 (Dec. 1934): 624–625.

171. See, for example, C. J. Wollen, "The Problem of Population," *Homiletic and Pastoral Review* 41, no. 1 (Oct. 1940): 38–39.

172. James A. Costin to Wilfrid Parsons, S.J., 23 March 1933. GULSC. Wilfrid Parsons, S.J. papers, box 8, folder 12.

173. Fr. Apollinaris, O.F.M.Cap., *Birth Control Methods—The Right Way* (Yonkers, NY: Mission Almanac, 1933), 9.

174. Cox, *Birth Control, Birth Controllers, and Perversion of Logic,* 19. The sermon was broadcast over New York's station WLWL on 13 Dec. 1935.

175. Lord, *What of Lawful Birth Control?,* 20, 35.

176. Ford, teaching notes on periodic continence.

177. Valère J. Coucke, "Birth Control and the Tempus Ageneseos: The Moral Aspect of the Question," *Homiletic and Pastoral Review* 33, no. 1 (Oct. 1932): 23.

178. Anon., "Non-Catholic Reactions to Theories of 'Periodic Abstinence,'" *Acolyte* 11, no. 3 (2 Feb. 1935): 10.

179. Rev. William Granger Ryan to the editor, *Ecclesiastical Review* 92, no. 3 (March 1935): 282.

180. Daniel Lord, S.J., *What Birth Control Is Doing to the United States* (St. Louis: Queen's Work, 1936), 37.

181. John Montgomery Cooper to Edgar Schmiedeler, 26 Nov. 1932. ACUA. John M. Cooper papers, box 13, "Schmiedeler" folder.

182. Wilfrid Parsons, S.J. to Joseph Reiner, S.J., 20 March 1934. GULSC. America Magazine Archives, box 3, folder 23.

183. Guy Irving Burch, "Catholics on Birth Control," *New Republic* 77 (5 Sept. 1934), 98.

184. Dorothy Dunbar Bromley, "Birth Control and the Depression," *Harper's Magazine* 147, no. 8 (Oct. 1934), 571. The article was subsequently published as a pro-birth control pamphlet.

185. Burch, "Catholics on Birth Control," 98.

186. Dr. Edward J. Morris to Dr. Alice Hamilton, 8 Jan. 1935. GULSC. Wilfrid Parsons, S.J. papers, box 5, folder 27. Morris quotes in this letter from a Hamilton book review that appeared in the *Herald-Tribune* on 6 Jan. 1935.

187. Log of activities, 28–29 April 1934. The anonymous author was almost certainly John Burke, C.S.P., longtime executive secretary of the National Catholic Welfare Conference. ACUA, NCWC papers, 10/20/11.

188. Bp. Joseph Rummel to John J. Burke, C.S.P., 27 Nov. 1934. ACUA, NCWC papers, 10/20/11.

189. Wilfrid Parsons, S.J., "Is This 'Catholic' Birth Control?" *America* 48, no. 21 (25 Feb. 1933), 496.

190. Ignatius Cox, S.J. to Wilfrid Parsons, S.J., undated but received 2 Oct. 1933. GULSC. Wilfrid Parsons papers, box 4, folder 8.

191. T. H. Ahearn, S.J. to Leo L. Latz, M.D., 1 August 1934. Loyola. Office of the President: Papers of Samuel Knox Wilson, S.J., box 20, folder 4. This terse letter gives no reason for Latz's firing but instructs him to "respect this information in future editions of your works."

192. Leo J. Latz, M.D. to Samuel M. Wilson, S.J., 24 August 1934. Loyola. Biographical folder for Leo Latz, M.D.

193. T. H. Ahearn, S.J. to Samuel M. Wilson, S.J., Oct. 3 1934. Loyola. Office of the President: Papers of Samuel Knox Wilson, S.J., box 20, folder 4.

194. Joseph Reiner, S.J. to Terence Ahearn, S.J., 11 August 1934; Reiner to Samuel Knox Wilson, S.J., 27 August 1934. Loyola. Biographical folder on Leo Latz, M.D.

195. Leo J. Latz to Samuel K. Wilson, S.J., 19 Nov. 1935. Loyola. Biographical folder, Leo Latz, M.D.

196. Francis J. Connell, C.SS.R. to Wilfrid Parsons, S.J., 3 March 1933. GULSC. Wilfrid Parsons, S.J. papers, box 8, folder 12. Connell wrote from the Redemptorist house at Mt. St. Alphonsus, Esopus NY.

197. Bishop John Francis Noll to Rev. M. A. Chapman, S.J., 24 Aug. 1934; Noll to John A. O'Brien, 24 Nov. 1934; Noll to John J. Burke, C.S.P., 1 Dec. 1934. ACUA, NCWC papers, 10/20/11.

198. Noll spoke of his numerous family in the dedication to *The Catholic Church vs the Federal Council [of] Churches of Christ in America* (Huntington, IN: Our Sunday Visitor Press, undated but ca. 1933), 2. Noll authored this pamphlet semi-pseudonymously as "J.F.N."

199. Noll to Chapman, 24 Aug. 1934.

200. Minutes, meeting of the Administrative Board, NCWC, 13 Nov. 1934. ACUA. *Minutes of the Administrative Board, NCWC,* 29 April 1930–17 Nov. 1939, 284.

201. Archbishop Edward J. Hanna [San Francisco] to "Your Excellency," 22 Dec. 1934. ACUA, NCWC papers, 10/20/11. Burke's initial draft is found at this same location. Hanna was chairman in 1934 of the Administrative Committee.

202. Bishop John Peterson to John J. Burke, C.S.P., 24 Nov. 1934. ACUA, NCWC papers, 10/20/11. Peterson was bishop of Manchester.

203. Cardinal Patrick Hayes, "Official Monitum," 8 Sept. 1936, *Conference Bulletin of the Archdiocese of New York* 14, no. 2 (Sept. 1936), 78.

204. Minutes, General Meeting of the Bishops, morning session, 14 Nov. 1935.

205. Editorial preface to Albert Kaiser, C.PP.S., "The Objective Morality of Natural Birth-Control," *Acolyte* 10, no. 23 (10 Nov. 1934): 8. Kaiser's article was the last to appear on the subject.

206. Bishop Gerald Shaunessy, S.M. to Rev. John Burke, C.S.P., 20 Dec. 1934, 13 Feb. 1935, 14 Feb. 1935, 27 Feb. 1935. Quote from letter of 27 Feb. Burke to Shaunessy, 21 Feb. 1935. All in ACUA, NCWC papers, 10/20/11–12. Burke wrote to Harry Hopkins, then head of the Federal Emergency Relief Administration, to whom Shaunessy feared—apparently erroneously—that the pamphlet might be peddled and to Benziger Brothers Publishing Company, which Shaunessy correctly assumed would be approached on the matter of national distribution. John J. Burke, C.S.P. to Harry Hopkins, 18 Feb. 1935; Alfred Benziger to John J. Burke, C.S.P., 25 Feb. 1935; Aubrey Williams to Burke, 27 Feb. 1935. All in ACUA, NCWC papers, 10/20/12. The priest, Monsignor Theodore Ryan, published his pamphlet anonymously but made clear that the author was indeed a priest.

207. Amleto Cicgognani to "Your Excellency," 23 May 1936. ACUA, NCWC papers, Social Action: Family Life Bureau: Birth Control, 1930–1944. A copy in the John Ford, S.J. papers is addressed to "Bishop Johannes," who is not further identified.

208. Ford, teaching notes on periodic continence.

209. Hillenbrand, teaching notes with regard to birth control in preaching and confession.

210. Emmett J. Culligan, "The Deception of Contraception," *Acolyte* 10, no. 15 (21 July 1934): 9. This article is taken verbatim from Culligan's book.

211. William Thomas Walsh, "Babies, Not Bullets, Will Conquer the World," *Catholic World* 149 (August 1939), 549.

212. Wyse, *Shall Heaven Be Filled?,* 29–30.

213. Dominic Pruemmer, O.P., "The Ethics of Birth Control," *Homiletic and Pastoral Review* 31, no. 7 (April 1931): 709. Rev. Edward Roberts Moore, *The Case Against Birth Control* (New York: Century Company, 1931), warned that "habitual excess in coitus . . . may result in neurological disturbances, and sometimes in virtual impotency," 30–31.

214. Stanislaus Woywod, O.F.M., "Answers to Questions: Advisability of Speaking Publicly of Rhythm of Sterile Period or Any Other Natural Way for Prevention of Pregnancy," *Homiletic and Pastoral Review* 37, no. 10 (July 1937): 1080–1081.

215. Ignatius W. Cox, S.J., *Birth Control Is Wrong!* (New York: America Press, 1930), 7. The pamphlet is the text of a radio address given over station WLWL, 30 May 1930.

216. For a perceptive discussion of Protestant views on the family, sexuality, and birth control in the 1930s, see David M. Kennedy, *Birth Control in America: The Career of Margaret Sanger* (New Haven: Yale University Press, 1970), 153–171.

217. Rt. Rev. Louis Nau, "Conjugal Chastity and Periodic Abstention," *Acolyte* 10, no. 16 (4 Aug. 1934): 6.

218. Kennedy, *Birth Control in America,* 245–255.

219. A note to this effect by the NCWC's Msgr. Michael Ready, dated 17 Jan. 1937, is found in ACUA, NCWC papers, 10/20/13.

220. Kennedy, *Birth Control in America,* 214–216, 257–260. Quote from 216.

221. Charleston's Bishop Emmet Walsh complained about this at the 2 April 1940 meeting of the NCWC's Administrative Board. He was "convinced that many such clinics in South Carolina, at least, are operated with tax funds, although it is exceedingly difficult to obtain proof and state authorities deny the allegation." ACUA. *Minutes of the Administrative Board, NCWC,* 1 April 1940–16 Nov. 1945, 433. The motivation for state support, in South Carolina as elsewhere, had mostly to do with white fears about the still-high birthrate among African Americans.

222. A nice example of Catholic influence is found in the minutes of the Administrative Board of the NCWC for 15 Nov. 1934. "The General Secretary [of the NCWC] reported that when the first newspaper reached him that the United States Rehabilitation Programme for Puerto Rico would include a recommendation of Birth Control, he personally went to the President and asked the President that no such recommendation be allowed to appear in the report. The President answered him that it would not." ACUA. *Minutes of the Administrative Board, NCWC,* 29 April 1930–17 Nov. 1939, 290.

223. John J. Burke to Bishop John F. Noll, 20 Feb, 1931. ACUA, NCWC papers, 10/20/18.

224. Ignatius Cox to Msgr. Michael Ready, 15 Feb. 1935. ACUA, NCWC papers, 10/20/21.

225. Edward J. Heffron to Msgr. Michael Ready, 14 Dec. 1936. ACUA, NCWC papers, 10/20/13.

226. Ignatius Cox, S.J. to Fr. Michael Ready, 20 Jan. 1934. ACUA, NCWC papers, 10/20/11.

227. Archbishop Samuel Stritch to Bishop James A. Griffin, 20 May 1940. ACUA, NCWC papers, 10/20/15. Stritch succeeded Cardinal George Mundelein early in 1940.

228. Ignatius Cox, S.J. to Wilfrid Parsons, S.J., 28 Jan. 1932. GULSC, Wilfrid Parsons, S.J. papers, box 4, folder 8. Emphasis in the original.

229. Burke to Noll, 20 Feb. 1931.

230. "The Position of the National Catholic Alumni Federation and Its Associations," undated but ca. 1934. GULSC. Wilfrid Parsons, S.J. papers, box 10, folder 24.

231. The text of Cardinal Hayes's sermon appeared in the *New York Times* on 9 Dec. 1935

and in the *Catholic Mind* 34, no. 1 (8 Jan. 1936): 1–6. The NCWC's John Burke sent fulsome congratulations to Hayes on 10 Dec. 1935: "You will hardly realize all the effective good that sermon, courageous, manly, unanswerable, will do here in Washington, and indeed throughout the country. I plan to have it printed, to send it to all members of Congress; to publicize it in 'Catholic Action'; to have it distributed through N[ational] C[ouncil of] C[atholic] M[en] and N[ational] C[ouncil of] C[atholic] W[omen]." ACUA, NCWC papers, 10/85/22.

232. Administrative Committee of the National Catholic Welfare Conference, "A Statement on the Present Crisis," 12–13, 23–24. The statement was authorized by the nation's bishops at their annual meeting in Nov. 1932. AAC. Mundelein personal papers, box 1, folder 9.

233. Anna Dill Gamble, *Open Letter to Mrs. John M. Phillips, President of the State Federation of Pennsylvania Women* (Philadelphia: Dolphin Press, undated but ca. 1935.), 12. Mrs. Phillips's speech endorsing birth control was delivered in November 1934.

234. Moore, *Case Against Birth Control,* 19–20.

235. Patrick Scanlon to John J. Burke, C.S.P., 2 Feb. 1933. ACUA, NCWC papers, 10/20/20; Scanlon to Wilfrid Parsons, S.J., 4 Feb. 1933. GULSC. Wilfrid Parsons, S.J. papers, box 5, folder 25.

236. Bp. J. F. Noll, "A Bishop's New Year Word to His Priests," *Acolyte* 16, no. 2 (Feb. 1940): 9.

237. "Birth Control Ban Issued by Archbishop," *New York Times,* 18 Aug. 1935, 3:6.

238. Minutes of the Administrative Board, NCWC, 11 Nov. 1935. *Minutes of the Administrative Board, NCWC,* 29 April 1930–17 Nov. 1939, 316. Minutes of the annual meeting of the U.S. bishops, 13 Nov. 1935. *Minutes of the Annual Meetings of the Bishops of the United States, 1919–1935.* Both in ACUA.

239. Lord, *What Birth Control Is Doing,* 7.

240. See, for example, Grace H. Sherwood, "The Church and the Dignity of Woman," in *Christian Marriage and the Family* (Washington, DC: Family Life Section, Social Action Department, NCWC, 1932). The anonymously edited pamphlet consists of nine articles taken from the Jan. 1932 and July 1932 issues of *Catholic Action* magazine.

241. Cardinal George Mundelein, draft of a speech on the endowment of the Lewis Memorial Maternity Hospital, undated but probably 1931. The speech was apparently intended for a clerical audience. AAC. Mundelein personal papers, box 8, folder 7.

242. John Robert Gavin, O.S.A., "A Study of the Catholic Maternity Guild Apostolate," (Master's Thesis, School of Social Science, Catholic University of America, 1950), 33.

243. Dorothy Weston, "Why Maternity Guilds?" *Catholic Mind* 33, no. 16 (22 Aug. 1935): 316. Ellipses in original. Weston's article was a reprint of a speech she gave at the Catholic Women's Union in New York and originally appeared in the June 1935 edition of the *Catholic Worker.*

244. Gavin, "Catholic Maternity Guild Apostolate," 34.

245. John J. Burke, C.S.P. to Bishop Edward Mooney, 7 July 1937. ACUA, NCWC papers, 10/85/22.

246. Bishop Edward Mooney to Msgr. Michael Ready, 22 July 1937. ACUA, NCWC, 10/85/22. Mooney was soon to become Archbishop of Detroit.

247. Rev. Augustine Student, O.S.B., "Annual Renovation of the Marriage Vows," *Acolyte* 14, no. 3 (March 1938): 9.

248. Bp. Duane G. Hunt to Archbishop Edward Mooney, 21 Jan. 1941. ACUA, NCWC papers, 10/20/15.

249. Msgr. Michael Ready to Bishop Duane G. Hunt, 21 July 1941. ACUA, NCWC papers, 10/20/15. Ready actually referred to the Birth Control League, though the group had abandoned this name upon reorganization in 1937.

250. Archbishop Edward Mooney to Bishop Duane G. Hunt, 27 Jan. 1941. ACUA, NCWC papers, 10/20/15.

251. Ready to Hunt, 21 July 1941.

Chapter 4. "Life is a Warfare"

1. J. F. Powers, *Morte D'Urban* (1962; repr. New York: Vintage Books, 1979), 75.
2. Andrew M. Greeley, *The American Catholic: A Social Portrait* (New York: Basic Books, 1977), 57–62.
3. John J. Lynch, S.J., "Notes on Moral Theology," *Theological Studies* 18, no. 2 (June 1957): 247.
4. "Being a Catholic," unsigned editorial from *Today* 2, no. 3 (Nov. 1946), 2. *Today* was published by Chicago Inter-Student Catholic Action, an organization of Catholic college students. This same editorial challenged Catholics to do battle against racism and political corruption.
5. "Big Family," *Jubilee* 1, no. 3 (July 1953), 29. No author given.
6. D. F. Miller, C.SS.R., "For Victims of Birth Control," *Liguorian* 39, no. 5 (May 1951), 258, 261.
7. Ibid., 259.
8. Andrew Greeley, "Family Planning among American Catholics," ms. slated for publication in *Chicago Studies* (Spring 1963), undated but ca. 1963, 5. ACUA, NCWC, box 86, folder 5; Gavin Jones and Dorothy Nortman, "Roman Catholic Fertility and Family Planning: A Comparative Review of the Research Literature," *Studies in Family Planning: A Publication of the Population Research Council* 34 (Oct. 1968), 5.
9. Charles F. Westoff and Raymond E. Potvin, *College Women and Fertility Values* (Princeton, NJ: Princeton University Press, 1967), 48.
10. Charles F. Westoff, Robert G. Potter, and Philip G. Sagi, *The Third Child: A Study in the Prediction of Fertility* (Princeton, NJ: Princeton University Press, 1963), 99.
11. Charles F. Westoff and Norman B. Ryder, *The Contraceptive Revolution* (Princeton, NJ: Princeton University Press, 1977), 25.
12. Norman B. Ryder and Charles F. Westoff, *Reproduction in the United States: 1965* (Princeton, NJ: Princeton University Press, 1971), 186.
13. Charles F. Westoff et al., *Family Growth in Metropolitan America* (Princeton, NJ: Princeton University Press, 1961), 79–80.
14. For a discussion of the phenomenon, see Lee Rainwater, *Family Design: Marital Sexuality, Family Size, and Contraception* (Chicago: Aldine Publishing Company, 1965), 202–203, 207.
15. George A. Kelly, "Catholics and the Practice of the Faith," (Ph.D. dissertation, School of Social Science, Catholic University of America, 1946), 58–59, 61–63; Joseph H. Fichter, S.J., *Social Relations in the Urban Parish* (Chicago: University of Chicago Press, 1954), 83, 87–88; Joseph B. Schuyler, S.J., *Northern Parish: A Sociological and Pastoral Study* (Chicago: Loyola University Press, 1960), 218–220.
16. See Pascal K. Whelpton, Arthur A. Campbell, and John E. Patterson, *Fertility and Family Planning in the United States* (Princeton, NJ: Princeton University Press, 1966), 34, for a summary of public opinion research on ideal family size, 1941–1960.
17. Even in 1940, George Gallup was finding large majorities in favor of liberalized access to contraceptive information for the married. "Regardless of the manner in which the issue was stated, all of the institute's studies have found sentiment running between 70 and 80 per cent favorable to the birth control program." *New York Times,* 24 Jan. 1940, 22:4.
18. On the early history of the "population lobby," see Donald T. Critchlow, *Intended Consequences: Birth Control, Abortion, and the Federal Government in Modern America* (New York: Oxford University Press, 1999), 13–33.
19. Karl Sax, *Standing Room Only: The Challenge of Overpopulation* (Boston: Beacon Press, 1955). For an irate Catholic response to the book, see Catherine Schaefer to Martin Work, 29 August 1955. ACUA, NCWC papers, 10/85/23.

20. Heinz Von Foerster, Patricia M. Mora, Lawrence W. Amiot, "Doomsday: Friday, 13 November, A.D. 2026," *Science* 132 (Nov. 1960): 1291–1295.

21. Westoff and Ryder, *Contraceptive Revolution,* 27–29.

22. John T. Noonan, *Contraception: A History of Its Treatment by the Catholic Theologians and Canonists,* rev. ed. (Cambridge, MA: Harvard University Press, 1986), 472.

23. Clement S. Mihanovich, Ph.D., *Wither Birth Control? The Death of a Nation* (St. Louis: Queen's Work, 1947), 36, provides a dramatic example. "The birth controllers do not publish the figures that show that from 30 per cent to 60 per cent of the women in many of our mental hospitals are there because they practiced birth control."

24. Daniel Lord, S.J., *A Mother Looks at Birth Control: A Letter from a Mother to a Priest* (St. Louis: Queen's Work, 1947), 9. The letter in question, from which the quote comes, is by one Margaret Theresa Boylan, the very young mother of three children—born in as many years. Whether Lord edited Boylan's letter—or even manufactured it whole cloth—cannot be known.

25. Anon., *A Holy War Against the Enemies of the Home and the Nation* (Washington, DC: Family Life Bureau, National Catholic Welfare Conference, 1942), 29. The anonymous author was probably Edgar Schmiedeler, O.S.B., then head of the Bureau. He repeated the above-quoted language as his own in a book that came out in 1943.

26. Philip Christopher M. Kelly, C.S.C., *The Catholic Book of Marriage: The Marriage Ceremony and Counsels for Success and Happiness in Married Life* (New York: Farrar, Straus and Young, 1951), 86, speaks of "a kind of murderous intention" on the part of those who practice contraception. See also Joseph A. Breig, *A Father Talks to Anti-Lifers* (Oconomowoc, WI: Liguorian Pamphlet Office, 1944), 5–6.

27. See, for example, the various essays in *Sanctity and Success in Marriage: Selected Papers from the 1956 Proceedings of the National Catholic Conference on Family Life,* eds., Rt Rev. Msgr. Irving A. DeBlanc and Norma L. Schavilla (Washington, DC: Family Life Bureau, National Catholic Welfare Conference, 1956).

28. Clarenge [*sic*] Engler, Ph.D., "Cana Clubs," undated typescript but early 1950s. Engler wrote on the back of letterhead from the U.S. Department of Agriculture and was evidently an enthusiastic member of a Washington-area Cana Club. ACUA. Alphonse H. Clemens papers (collection 81), box 2, folder "Cana Clubs." This collection has not been definitively processed.

29. Arthur Tonne, O.F.M., *Talks on the Sacraments: Sermons on the Seven Sacraments for Every Sunday and Feast of Obligation* (Emporia, KS: Didde Printing Company, 1947), 64–65.

30. See, for example, John Sheerin, C.S.P., "Confession and Psychiatry," *Homiletic and Pastoral Review* 50, no. 3 (Dec. 1949): 215–219.

31. Author interview with Fr. Robert Ferrigan, 16 Nov. 1998, Winnetka IL.

32. *The Common Rule of Saint John's Seminary* (Brighton, MA, 1946), 73, no author or publisher given.

33. Edward Leen, *Progress through Mental Prayer* (New York: Sheed and Ward, 1940), 244.

34. Author interview with Msgr. Vincent Horkan, 3 Nov. 1998, in Livonia MI. Horkan, who did his major seminary courses at Catholic University, was ordained in 1941.

35. Author interview with Msgr. Vincent Howard, 27 Oct. 1998, in Chelsea MI.

36. Author interview with Fr. Leo Mahon, 17 Nov. 1998, in Chicago.

37. Author interview with Fr. Joseph Ryder, 18 Jan. 1999, in West Bloomfield MI.

38. The large-family pattern was still evident in the mid-1960s. See Raymond H. Potvin and Antanas Suziedelis, *Seminarians of the Sixties: A National Survey* (Washington, DC: Center for Applied Research in the Apostolate, 1969), 25.

39. Author interview with Fr. Daniel Budzynski, 20 Nov. 1998, in Milwaukee.

40. Author interview with Fr. Edward Prus, 16 Oct. 1998, in Garden City MI. Prus was ordained in 1961.

41. Author interview with Fr. Clifford Ruskowski, 2 Oct. 1998, in Clinton Twp. MI.

42. Author interview with Fr. Anthony Kosnik, 27 May 1998, in Detroit.

43. Author interview with Fr. John Blaska, 6 Nov. 1998, in Troy MI. Blaska was ordained in 1953.

44. Prus interview.

45. M. Eugene Boylan, O. Cist. R., "The Kind Confessor," *Priest* 4, no. 1 (Jan. 1948): 29.

46. Anonymous letter to the editor, *Priest* 7, no. 2 (Feb. 1951): 149.

47. Theodore C. P. Vermilye, "Thoughts of a Penitent," *Homiletic and Pastoral Review* 59, no. 8 (May 1959): 732, 733.

48. Author interview with Fr. Joseph Gallagher, 3 Feb. 1999, in Baltimore. Gallagher was ordained in 1955.

49. Schuyler, *Northern Parish,* 190. The parish had about 10,000 members; it was also located adjacent to a busy shopping center, which increased traffic in the confessionals. Four assistants and an "auxiliary curate" did most of the work.

50. Boylan, "Kind Confessor," 29.

51. Ryder interview.

52. Fr. Edward Vitti, C.P., "The Good Priest," undated but probably 1950s. This sermon was preached at priests' retreats in Sierra Madre CA and Boise and perhaps elsewhere. PPA. Sermons of Fr. Edward Vitti, box 251.

53. Author interview with Fr. Edward Scheuerman, 15 July 1998, in Livonia MI.

54. Author interview with Fr. Richard McCormick, S.J., 12 Nov. 1998, at the University of Notre Dame.

55. Francis J. Connell, C.SS.R., *Spiritual and Pastoral Conferences to Priests* (Westminster, MD: Newman Press, 1962), 124. The various chapters in this volume were presented to semiannual clergy conferences in the Dioceses of Harrisburg PA and Covington KY between 1943 and 1962 in the former locale and 1949–1960 in the latter.

56. John B. Sheerin, C.S.P. and Joseph McSorley, C.S.P., *Spanish Confessions: How to Hear Them* (St. Louis: B. Herder, 1942), 31–32. Interestingly, the book contains no questions about abortion.

57. Gerald Kelly, S.J., "Notes on Moral Theology, 1952," *Theological Studies* 14, no. 1 (March 1953): 71–72; Noonan, *Contraception,* 504–505.

58. Gerald A. Kelly, *The Good Confessor (New York: Sentinel Press, 1951),* 39–40.

59. Msgr. John L. Linsenmeyer, "Artificial Birth Control: A Few Suggestions as to the Practical Nature of Dealing with Penitents," a paper delivered at a clergy conference in the Archdiocese of Detroit, 11–12 June 1945. Michigan Historical Collections, Bentley Historical Library. St. Mary's Student Chapel papers, box 2.

60. John J. Lynch, S.J., "Notes on Moral Theology," *Theological Studies* 17, no. 2 (June 1956): 192.

61. Scheuerman interview.

62. Kelly, *Good Confessor,* 65.

63. Mahon interview.

64. Author interview with Fr. William Pettit, 10 Dec. 1998, in Livonia MI.

65. Author interview with Msgr. William Sherzer, 18 October 1998, in Ann Arbor MI.

66. Connell, *Spiritual and Pastoral Conferences,* 123.

67. Mahan interview. Fr. Matthew Gottschalk, O.F.M. Cap., ordained in 1953, cannot remember contraception being discussed at any of the many meetings he attended of the Midwest Clergy Conference for Negro Welfare. Author interview with Fr. Gottschalk, 7 Oct. 1998, in Milwaukee.

68. Author interview with Msgr. Gerald Martin, 29 Sept. 1998, in Detroit. Martin was ordained in 1954. See also Budzynski interview.

69. William F. Allen, "Quid in Casu?" *Pastoral Life* 7, no. 1 (Jan.–Feb. 1959): 34.

70. Francis J. Connell, "How Must the Confessor Deal with an Onanist?" *Ecclesiastical Review* 107, no. 1 (July 1942): 58.

71. John C. Ford, S.J., teaching notes, moral philosophy, on abortion, undated manuscript. NESJ. Papers of John C. Ford, S.J., box 1 (preliminary cataloguing). No pagination.

72. John J. Danagher, "Questions Answered: Conditional Absolution and Onanists," *Homiletic and Pastoral Review* 52, no. 12 (Sept. 1952): 1116.

73. Kelly, *Good Confessor,* 96. See also Linsenmeyer, "Artificial Birth Control," 2; H. Martindale, "Are We Lions in the Pulpit and Lambs in the Confessional?" *Homiletic and Pastoral Review* 54, no. 9 (June 1954): 800 and Connell, *Spiritual and Pastoral Conferences,* 123.

74. Author interview with Fr. Lawrence Jackson, 15 Oct. 1998, in Sterling Heights MI. Jackson was ordained in 1960.

75. Sherzer interview.

76. John J. Danagher, C.M., "Questions Answered: Is a Promise to Try Sufficient?" *Homiletic and Pastoral Review* 54, no. 2 (Nov. 1953): 170.

77. Connell, *Spiritual and Pastoral Conferences,* 124. See also Eugene A. Dooley, O.M.I., "Sex Sins in the Confessional," *Ecclesiastical Review* 106, no. 4 (April 1941): 298–300; Rev. Raymond Francis O'Brien, C.M., "The Absolution of Recidivists in the Sacrament of Penance," (Ph.D. dissertation, School of Sacred Theology of the Catholic University of America, 1943), 150–153; Msgr. Kiefer, *Instructio Pro Confessariis* (Milwaukee: Bruce Publishing Co., 1950, expansion and translation of the 1931 German-language edition by Rev. Clarence A. Liederbach), 57–58; Rev. David Warham, "How Lenient Can You Be?" *Priest* 12, no. 12 (Dec. 1956): 1042–1043.

78. Author interview with Msgr. Edward Sviokla, 24 April 1999, in Everett MA. Sviokla was ordained in 1951.

79. Horkan interview.

80. J. McCarthy, "The Recidivist," *Priest* 6, no. 5 (May 1950): 352.

81. Ruskowski interview.

82. Warham, "How Lenient Can You Be?," 1043.

83. Author interview with Fr. John Michael Murphy, 9 Oct. 1998, in Milwaukee.

84. Author interview with Fr. Thomas Ventura, 17 Nov. 1998, in Winnetka IL.

85. Martin interview.

86. Lucille Halsey, "Feelings Don't Count," *Priest* 6, no. 12 (Dec. 1950): 913, 915.

87. An interesting look at confession from the perspective of highly educated and devout Catholic women can be found in Sally Cunneen, *Sex: Female, Religion: Catholic* (New York: Holt, Rinehart and Winston, 1968), 58–71. It is based on polling and small-group research done in the mid-1960s.

88. Sherzer interview.

89. Connell, "How Must the Confessor Deal with an Onanist?," 58–59. Connell was actually a relative liberal on the question. See Joseph Comyns, C.SS.R. and Francis J. Connell, C.SS.R., "Two Views on the Obligations of a Wife Whose Husband is Addicted to Condomistic Intercourse," *American Ecclesiastical Review* 112, no. 4 (April 1945): 264–286.

90. Anon., "A Husband's Rights," *American Ecclesiastical Review* 123, no. 6 (Dec. 1950): 460. Many moralists disputed this position. But it was still widely recognized as "probable"— which meant that confessors ought as a matter of right to apply it to relevant situations.

91. Gerald Kelly, S.J., "Notes on Moral Theology, 1951," *Theological Studies* 13, no. 1 (March 1952): 80.

92. John R. Connery, S.J., "Notes on Moral Theology," *Theological Studies* 17, no. 4 (Dec. 1956): 554. Connery is paraphrasing the argument of Canon Jacques LeClercq, whose 1949 *L'Enseignement de la morale chrétienne* was withdrawn from circulation by papal order in 1956.

93. John J. Lynch, S.J., "Notes on Moral Theology," *Theological Studies* 19, no. 2 (June 1958): 165.

94. John C. Ford, S.J. and Gerald Kelly, "Notes on Moral Theology, 1953," *Theological Studies* 15, no. 1 (March 1954): 60. Oraison's *Vie chrétienne et problèmes de la sexualité* was published in 1952 and placed on the Index of Forbidden Books in Jan. 1955.

95. For a good summary of this approach, despite its having been produced by highly critical authors, see Edouard Gagnon, S.S. and Aidan Carr, O.F.M. Conv., "A New Conjugal Morality?" *American Ecclesiastical Review* 127, no. 3 (Sept. 1952): 173–181.

96. John R. Connery, S.J., "Notes on Moral Theology," *Theological Studies* 18, no. 4 (Dec. 1957): 566.

97. Author interview with Msgr. John Egan, 9 Sept. 1998, Chicago.

98. Howard interview.

99. Dom Desmond Schlegel, *Hearing Confessions* (Westminster, MD: Newman Press, 1960), 21, 20, 5. Schelgel's book was initially published in Great Britain.

100. McCormick interview.

101. Howard interview.

102. Author interview with Fr. William Carolin, 28 Oct. 1998, in Brighton MI. Carolin was ordained for the Archdiocese of Detroit in 1945.

103. *Sermon Outlines for the Ecclesiastical Year, Part Two: The Commandments of God, for Use in the Archdiocese of Detroit, 1955–1956* (Ann Arbor, MI: Edwards Brothers, n.d. but 1955), unpaginated. The Detroit outlines listed no authors, though several of my informants claimed that these included Msgr. Archibald Stritt.

104. *Pastors Look at the Family* (Washington, DC: The Family Life Bureau, National Catholic Welfare Conference, n.d.), 21–22. Quote from 22. No author given. Internal evidence suggests that the survey was done in the latter stages of the Second World War.

105. "Birth Control is *Still* Against God's Law," sent to all priests in the Archdiocese of Boston with a cover letter from Archbishop Richard Cushing to "Reverend and Dear Father," 13 Oct. 1948. Archives of the Archdiocese of Boston (hereafter AABo). Record Group III.G.2 [Chancellor's Office: Birth Control and Abortion], box 21.

106. John C. Ford, S.J., "Notes for Fourth Year Fathers on Birth Control Amendment," undated typescript but 1942, 6. NESJ, Papers of John C. Ford, S.J., box 7 (preliminary cataloguing).

107. See, for example, *Sermon Outlines for the Sundays of the Ecclesiastical Year, Part Two— The Commandments of God, for use in the Archdiocese of Detroit, 1961–62* (Ann Arbor, MI: Edwards Brothers, undated), unpaginated; Archdiocese of Milwaukee, *Program of Instruction on the Christian Family for the Ecclesiastical Year 1958–59* (Milwaukee: Archdiocese of Milwaukee, 1958), 32, sermon for the second Sunday after Easter. The latter publication was issued with the approval of Archbishop Albert Meyer, himself trained as a Biblical scholar.

108. Fr. Cyprian Omerek, "Birth Control," undated typescript but ca. 1946, 1. Archives of the Franciscans of the Assumption Province, Pulaski WI (hereafter AFAP). Fr. Cyprian Omerek personal file. My thanks for this cite to Fr. Stanislaus Hajkowski.

109. "Lenten Course on Marriage," anonymous, undated typescript, but almost certainly authored by Albert Meyer, who served as bishop of Superior from 1946 to 1953. Handwritten insertions on the document are in Meyer's hand. Quote from the first of six sermons, "God the Creator of Human Marriage," unpaginated. AAC. Meyer papers, box 43829.03. Collection not fully processed at the time of my use.

110. Archdiocese of Milwaukee, *Program of Instructions for the Ecclesiastical Year 1948– 49* (Milwaukee: Archdiocese of Milwaukee, 1948), 85.

111. Quoted in Edgar Schmiedeler, *Twenty-Five Years of Uncontrol* (Huntington IN: Our Sunday Visitor Press, 1943), 144.

112. Ford, "Notes for Fourth Year Fathers," 6.

113. Rev. Hugh Calkins, "Keep Your Place in Marriage," text of a 25 August 1946 broadcast on the "Hour of Faith," a nationwide program sponsored by the National Council of Catholic Men. Copy in PPA. Sermons of Fr. Gilbert Kroger, box 246.

114. "Lenten Course on Marriage." Quote from the fourth of six sermons, "The Campaign Against Marriage."

115. Archdiocese of Milwaukee, *Program of Instruction for the Ecclesiastical Year 1948–49*, 85.

116. Rev. L. E. Lover, C.SS.R., "Holiness of Marriage," undated typescript but ca. early 1950s. RAB. Cardboard folder entitled "Sunday Sermons, L. E. Lover, C.SS.R."

117. Fr. Flannon Gannon, C.P., "Family Life," undated but during the Second World War. This sermon was evidently preached to congregations of both sexes and all ages. PPA. Sermons of Fr. Flannon Gannon, box 243.

118. Archdiocese of Chicago, *Program of Instructions for the Sunday Masses throughout the Year: Christ in the Church, in the State, and in the Home, 1950–51* (no place or date of publication), 91.

119. Howard interview.

120. Sviokla interview.

121. Joseph H. Fichter, *Southern Parish,* vol. 1 (Chicago: University of Chicago Press, 1951), 203.

122. Thomas R. Costello to the editor, *Priest* 10, no. 12 (Dec. 1954): 1118, 1119.

123. [Rev.] Thomas Regis Murphy, *A Priest Must Preach* (Milwaukee: Bruce Publishing, 1945), 146, 213–214.

124. Ibid., 145.

125. Kosnik interview.

126. "Catholic Mother of the Year and Family," *Family Apostolate* 2, no. 7 (Fall 1952), 3.

127. "Our Model? She's the Mother of Many!" *Chicago Tribune,* Sunday, 24 March 1963, 5:5. My thanks to Ellen Skerrett for this source.

128. Edwin J. Rowan, C.P., "In Defense of the Old Parish Mission," *Homiletic and Pastoral Review* 61, no. 6 (March 1961): 563.

129. The same criticisms had surfaced in Great Britain and western Europe, too. See P. J. Hanrahan, "Mission Preaching," in Ronan Drury, ed., *Preaching* (New York: Sheed and Ward, 1962), 66–71.

130. April Oursler Armstrong, "A Hard Look at the Parish Mission," *Priest* 15, no. 6 (June 1959): 475.

131. Ibid., 475. See also Rev. Nicholas E. Walsh, "An Investigation into the Content Matter of Missions and Retreats," (MA dissertation, Graduate School of Arts and Sciences, the Catholic University of America, June 1947).

132. L. C. Miller, "Are Missions Outdated?" *Homiletic and Pastoral Review* 49, no. 7 (April 1949): 555. See also M. H. Pathe, C.SS.R., "Why I Preach on Hell," *Liguorian* 41, no. 6 (June 1953), 334; D. F. Miller, C.SS.R., "I Preach Missions," *Liguorian* 40, no. 10 (Oct. 1952), 579–580; M. H. Pathe, C.SS.R., "'I Hate Missions,'" *Liguorian* 39, no. 4 (June 1939), 343–345.

133. Gannon, "Family Life."

134. Fr. Wilfrid Flanery, C.P., "Mortal Sin," undated but 1940s–1950s. Flanery was ordained in 1940. PPA. Sermons of Fr. Wilfrid Flanery, box 243.

135. Fr. Gilbert Kroger, C.P., "Sacrament of Matrimony," undated typescript preached variously between 1942 and 1956, 4. PPA. Sermons of Fr. Gilbert Kroger.

136. Fichter, *Southern Parish,* 216.

137. Fr. Flannon Gannon, C.P., "Salvation," undated typescript but probably 1940s. PPA. Sermons of Fr. Flannon Gannon, box 243.

138. Omerek, "Birth Control," 2.

139. Anthony McBriarty, C.SS.R., "Preaching the Eternal Truths: What About Hell?" *American Ecclesiastical Review* 121, no. 5 (Nov. 1949): 406–410; Pathe, "'I Hate Missions,'" 344. This analysis is also based on sermon texts from the 1940s and 1950s found in the Passionist, Paulist, and Redemptorist archives and various printed mission sermons.

140. Kilian J. Hennrich, O.F.M. Cap., "Concerning Parish Missions," *Homiletic and Pastoral Review* 42, no. 2 (Nov. 1941): 183.

141. Fr. Mel Schneider, C.P., "Home—the Goal of Marriage," typescript dated May 1943 and preached variously between 1943 and 1952. This sermon was written for a "mixed" congregation of men and women. PPA. Sermons of Fr. Mel Schneider, C.P., box 250.

142. Venantius Buessing, O.F.M. Cap., *My Dear People: Occasional Sermons After Old Capuchin Fashion* (New York: Joseph F. Wagner, 1957), 101.

143. Author interview with Fr. Donald Dacey, 27 April 1999, in Dearborn MI.

144. Memorandum, "Use of Public Funds by Public Health Departments in Giving Contraceptive Advice," (Mr.) William F. Montavon to Msgr. Michael Ready, 2 July 1941. ACUA, NCWC papers, 10/20/15.

145. Memorandum, "Correspondence re Installation of Contraceptive Vending Machines in Camp Barber Shops," undated but 1941. AAD. Cardinal Edward Mooney papers, uncatalogued.

146. Bp. Edward D. Howard [Portland OR] to Msgr. Michael Ready, 14 Oct. 1942; R. S. Vonderlehr [Assistant U.S. Surgeon General] to Msgr. Michael Ready, 13 Jan. 1943. Both in ACUA, NCWC papers, 10/20/26.

147. Quoted in "Of Note—Controversy in New York," *Commonweal* 69 (17 Oct. 1958), 76.

148. "Of Note: Birth Control and Public Policy," *Commonweal* 72 (5 Aug. 1960), 399. The editors were quoting approvingly from a report by Norman St. John-Stevas. See also James O'Gara, "All Things Considered: Birth Control Laws Again," *Commonweal* 75 (26 Jan. 1962), 450.

149. Msgr. John S. Kennedy, "Not Peter's Rock," *Our Sunday Visitor,* 19 May 1963, 11.

150. Bp. Aloysius J. Muensch, "Sermon Outlines for Five Sundays," *Acolyte* 19, no. 5 (May 1943), 28. The outlines were based on Muensch's pastoral letter.

151. J. J. Clifford, S.J. to Archbishop S. A. Stritch, 14 Sept. 1943. AAD. Cardinal Edward Mooney papers, uncatalogued.

152. Msgr. Michael Ready [General Secretary, NCWC] to Hon. Frank Knox, 26 September 1941. AAD. Cardinal Edward Mooney papers, uncatalogued. The same letter was apparently sent to Henry Stimson, then Secretary of War.

153. Archbishop Edward Mooney to Franklin Roosevelt, 8 June 1943. AAD. Cardinal Edward Mooney papers, uncatalogued.

154. Administrative Committee, NCWC to Paul McNutt [Administrator, Federal Security Agency, U.S. Public Health Service], draft statement on the pamphlet "It Doesn't Pay," 11 Nov. 1942. ACUA, NCWC papers, 10/20/26.

155. Henry Stimson to Msgr. Michael Ready, 31 Oct. 1941. AAD. Cardinal Edward Mooney papers, uncatalogued.

156. Alphonse M. Schwitalla, S.J. to Msgr. Michael J. Ready, 17 April 1943 discusses the group's first meeting. ACUA, NCWC papers, 10/20/26. Other letters in the file describe in detail his negotiations with committee colleagues and the compromises he was able at times to secure. Msgr. Howard Carroll, Assistant General Secretary of the NCWC, was later appointed to another such advisory committee. See Paul V. McNutt to Msgr. Howard J. Carroll, 1 March, 1944. ACUA, NCWC papers, 10/20/27.

157. Alphonse M. Schwitalla, S.J. to Msgr. Howard Carroll, 30 June 1944. ACUA, NCWC papers, 10/20/27.

158. Bp. Bartholemew Eustace [Camden NJ] to Msgr. Michael Ready, 2 March 1943. See also Bp. J. Francis A. McIntyre [auxiliary, NY] to Ready, 17 Feb. 1943 and Bp. John O'Hara [Military Ordinariate] to Ready, 17 Feb. 1943. All in ACUA, NCWC papers, 10/20/26.

159. "Minutes of the Meeting of the Joint Committee on Prophylaxis of the United States Public Health Service and the American Social Hygiene Association, January 27, 1943," 5. ACUA, NCWC papers, 10/20/26.

160. Memo, 17 Jan. 1946, no author or recipient given. ACUA, NCWC papers, 10/85/23. See also Bp. Karl Alter, "The Conference of Bishops' Representatives: Bishop Alter's Report on Certain Moral Problems Involving Public Policy", undated but Dec. 1947. ACUA, NCWC papers, 10/85/23.

161. Minutes, meeting of the Administrative Board, NCWC, 11 Nov. 1947. ACUA. *Minutes of the Administrative Board, NCWC,* April 30, 1946–Nov. 18, 1955, 756.

162. Quoted in Aidan M. Carr, "Logic: R.I.P.," *Homiletic and Pastoral Review* 58, no. 11 (Aug. 1958): 1196.

163. Fr. Thomas Donnellan [Chancellor of the Archdiocese of New York] to Msgr. Cletus O'Donnell, 26 July 1960 provides an excellent overview of the controversy and also the quote. AAC. Cardinal Albert Meyer papers, box 43785.02, folder "CBC General Correspondence: Birth Control." On NCWC involvement in the New York controversy see F.T.H. to Msgr. Paul Tanner, 28 June 1958. ACUA, NCWC papers, 10/85/25.

164. "Memorandum on Proposed Planned Parenthood Clinic at Cook County Hospital," 5 Feb. 1962, no author or recipient listed, 2. ACUA, NCWC papers, 10/86/3.

165. Quoted in Ibid., 4.

166. On the internal workings of the Committee to Study the United States Military Assistance Programs, headed by General William H. Draper, and on the reception of its report, see Critchlow, *Intended Consequences,* 42–45.

167. Memo, Harmon Burns, Jr. to Msgr. Paul Tanner, 27 Sept. 1961. ACUA, NCWC papers, 10/86/3.

168. Boston *Pilot,* 5 Sept. 1942, 4:1–2.

169. Ford, "Notes for Fourth Year Fathers," especially page 2.

170. Almost no records survive of the 1942 campaign, at least in the Archives of the Archdiocese of Boston. The John Ford, S.J. papers, however, contain information about the campaign and a few samples of anti-amendment literature. The "dramalogue" referred to below was certainly broadcast in 1948; I do not know whether this was true in 1942, although I suspect that it was. See NESJ. Papers of John C. Ford, S.J., box 7 (preliminary cataloguing).

171. John T. Noonan, *The Lustre of Our Country: The American Experience of Religious Freedom* (Berkeley and Los Angeles: University of California Press, 1998), 21.

172. D. C. Rakes, "Election Day: A Dramalogue on Birth Control," *Catholic Mirror,* Oct. 1942, 7–8.

173. James M. O'Toole, "Prelates and Politicos: Catholics and Politics in Massachusetts, 1900–1970," in Robert E. Sullivan and James M. O'Toole, editors, *Catholic Boston: Studies in Religion and Community, 1870–1970* (Boston: Roman Catholic Archdiocese of Boston, 1985), 32–35.

174. Archbishop Richard Cushing to "Reverend and Dear Father," 22 July 1948, marked *STRICTLY CONFIDENTIAL.* AABo. Record Group III.C.2 [Chancellor's Office—Birth Control and Abortion], box 21.

175. Archdiocese of Boston, Office of the Chancellor, reporting form sent to all pastors "to be returned to the Chancellor's Office no later than *September 1, 1948.*" AABo. Record Group III.C.2 [Chancellor's Office—Birth Control and Abortion], box 21.

176. Bp. James E. Cassidy [Fall River] to "Reverend and Dear Father," 6 Oct. 1948 explains the parish-based distribution of propaganda. AABo. Record Group III.C.2 [Chancellor's Office, Birth Control and Abortion], box 21. For discussion of the radio campaign, see O'Toole, "Prelates and Politicos," 52. Texts of certain radio features are found in AABo as cited immediately above. The campaign in the Archdiocese of Boston also included billboards and ads on the subways and trolleys.

177. Committee Opposing Adoption of Referendum Number Four, minutes of meeting of Sept. 22, 1948. The various sermons were delivered on Oct. 3, 17, and 31. AABo. Record Group III.C.2 [Chancellor's Office—Birth Control and Abortion], box 21.

178. O'Toole, "Prelates and Politicos," 55.

179. Daniel F. Sullivan Co., Boston, transcript for radio spot #1, undated but 1948. Ellipses in original. AABo. Record Group III.C.2 [Chancellor's Office—Birth Control and Abortion], box 21.

180. Language like this is found in two *Pilot* editorials in 1942, but not in other surviving examples of propaganda. Since so little survives by way of evidence from the 1942 campaign, it is possible that such rhetoric was as widely used in 1942 as it was in 1948.

181. The emphasis is evident both in the various radio spots and especially in the radio minidramas. Transcripts are housed in AABo. Record Group III.C.2 [Chancellor's Office—Birth Control and Abortion], box 21.

182. Script for a five-minute radio broadcast, undated but 1948. AABo. Record Group III.C.2 [Chancellor's Office—Birth Control and Abortion], box 21.

183. *Catholic Mirror* 28, no. 12 (Oct. 1948). The full-page illustration was carried on the back cover.

184. Nathaniel W. Faxon, M.D. to "Dear Doctor," 26 May 1950. Faxon was chairman of the Physicians' Committee for Planned Parenthood. AABo. Record Group III.C.2 [Chancellor's Office—Birth Control and Abortion], box 21.

185. Archbishop Richard J. Cushing to Frederick W. Mansfield, 27 March 1952. AABo. Record Group III.C.2 [Chancellor's Office—Birth Control and Abortion], box 21.

186. Assistant General Secretary, Family Life Bureau, NCWC to Father [Edgar] Schmiedeler, 2 Dec. 1948 puts the gain in votes at 200,000. ACUA, NCWC papers, 10/85/23.

187. Negotiations over an amendment seem to have begun in 1964. See Fr. James A. O'Donohoe to Cardinal Richard Cushing, 27 Nov. 1964 and the appended "Report on Meeting Held to Propose a Change in Birth Control Legislation in the Commonwealth," 27 Nov. 1964. AABo. Record Group III.C.2 [Chancellor's Office—Birth Control and Abortion], box 21.

188. "A Statement of Richard Cardinal Cushing, Archbishop of Boston, to be read by Henry M. Lean, Esq. At the public hearing concerning House Bill #1401 on March 2, 1965." The role of Lally and Murray is outlined in Msgr. Francis J. Lally to Msgr. Francis J. Sexton, 26 Feb. 1965. Both in AABo. Record Group III.C.2 [Chancellor's Office—Birth Control and Abortion], box 21. See also John Courtney Murray to Cardinal Richard Cushing, undated but ca. 1965. GULSC, John Courtney Murray papers, box 1, folder 43.

189. John C. Ford, S.J. to Joseph Dorsey, M.D., undated but Dec. 1964. NESJ. John C. Ford, S.J. papers, box 7 (preliminary cataloguing).

190. Bernard Asbell, *The Pill: A Biography of the Drug That Changed the World* (New York: Random House, 1995), 242.

Chapter 5. "It Isn't Easy to Be a Catholic"

1. Peter Michaels, "Sins of Flesh and Commerce," *Integrity* 1, no. 8 (May 1947), 33.

2. Unsigned editorial, *Today* 2, no. 3 (Nov. 1946), 2. *Today* was published by Chicago Inter-Student Catholic Action.

3. "N.N." to "Dear Father," *Liguorian* 43, no. 3 (March 1955), 148–149.

4. Ibid., 149.

5. The advertisement appeared in the late 1940s in both *Candid Confessions* and *Greatest Detective Cases.* Clippings in AUND. John A. O'Brien papers—COBR, box 1, folder 5.

6. Unsigned editorial, *Integrity* 2, no. 9 (June 1948), 1.

7. Msgr. John L. Linsenmeyer, "Artificial Birth Control: A Few Suggestions as to the Practical Manner of Dealing with Penitents," delivered to a clergy conference, Archdiocese of Detroit, 11–12 June 1945. Michigan Historical Collections, Bentley Historical Library. St. Mary's Student Chapel papers, box 2.

8. Anon., "Redemptorist Mission Sermons: State Instruction to the Married," undated typescript but ca. 1940s. RAB. Box temporarily labeled "Hanley."

9. Rev. P. J. Lydon, "Questions in Moral Theology," *Priest* 1, no. 2 (Feb. 1945): 36, 38.

10. As conservative a moralist as Joseph Connell thought it right to speak about rhythm in each of these venues. See his replies to priest questioners in *American Ecclesiastical Review* 121, no. 2 (August 1949): 153 and 121, no. 4 (Oct. 1949): 342.

11. Hugh Calkins, O.S.A., "Rhythm—The Unhappy Compromise," *Integrity* 2, no. 9 (June 1948), 7.

12. Bro. Gerald J. Schnepp, S.M. and Joseph Mundi, "What Doctors Think of the Rhythm Method," *American Ecclesiastical Review* 123, no. 2 (Aug. 1950): 113, 114.

13. Fr. Valentine Leitsch, C.P., "Confession," undated typescript but approved by the Passionist superior in 1951. It was probably also preached prior to that date, however, as well as after. PPA. Sermons of Fr. Valentine Leitsch, box 247.

14. Charles F. Westoff et al., *Family Growth in Metropolitan America* (Princeton, NJ: Princeton University Press, 1961), 78.

15. Pascal K. Whelpton, Arthur A. Campbell, and John E. Patterson, *Fertility and Family Planning in the United States* (Princeton, NJ: Princeton University Press, 1966), 281.

16. Ibid., 283.

17. Ibid.,283.

18. G.L. to John C. Ford, S.J., 13 Sept. 1956. NESJ. John C. Ford, S.J. papers, box 10 [preliminary cataloguing].

19. Edwin Healy, S.J. speaks of the basal temperature method in *Marriage Guidance: A Study of the Problems of the Married and of Those Contemplating Marriage* (Chicago: Loyola University Press, 1948), 162–163. The book was meant mainly for Catholic college students and young adult study groups. See also Robert Latou Dickinson, M.D., *Techniques of Conception Control* (Baltimore: Williams & Wilkin Company for the Planned Parenthood Federation, 1950), 39–40.

20. "The Rhythm Method Based on Body Temperature," (Chicago: Catholic Family Information, Cana Conference of Chicago,) undated but probably early 1960s. Unpaginated.

21. Fr. John Dietzen and Frank Ewers, M.D., "Fertile or Sterile?" *Priest* 17, no. 10 (Oct. 1961): 834–836. See also John Rock, M.D., *The Time Has Come: A Catholic Doctor's Proposals to End the Battle over Birth Control* (New York: Alfred A. Knopf, 1963), 188.

22. "Mother of Three, Jamaica, N.Y.," to the editor, *Jubilee,* typed copy of original, undated but early 1964. GULSC. Ed Rice papers, box 4, folder 58.

23. Fred Benjamin, M.D., "Basal Body Temperature Recordings in Gynaecology and Obstetrics," excerpted from *The Journal of Obstetrics and Gynaecology of the British Empire* 67 (Dec. 1960): 177–187 for a one-page handout, probably by the Catholic Marriage Advisory Council in Great Britain.

24. David Lodge, *Souls and Bodies* (New York: Penguin Books, U.S.A., 1990), 117. The novel was originally published in 1980.

25. John Ford, S.J. to Frank McQuaid, S.J., 8 Feb. 1959. NESJ. John C. Ford, S.J. papers, box 10 [preliminary cataloguing].

26. Hugh J. O'Connell, C.SS.R., "Does Rhythm Really Work?" *Liguorian* 49, no. 11 (Nov. 1961), 16.

27. John L. Thomas, S.J., *Marriage and Rhythm* (Westminster, MD: Newman Press, 1957), 117.

28. Fr. Flannon Gannon, C.P., "Faith: Its Nature," undated typescript but probably preached in the 1940s and '50s. PPA. Sermons of Fr. Flannon Gannon, C.P., box 243.

29. Orville Griese, *The 'Rhythm' in Marriage and Christian Morality* (Washington, DC: Catholic University of America Press, 1948), 85, 82, 58, 94.

30. Hugh J. O'Connell, C.SS.R., "Is 'Rhythm' Per Se Illicit?" *American Ecclesiastical Review* 119, no. 5 (Nov. 1948): 339.

31. Calkins, "Rhythm—the Unhappy Compromise," 6–7, 8, 9, 10.

32. Joseph P. Donovan, C.M., "Rhythm and the Archangel Raphael," *Priest* 6, no. 4 (April 1950): 264.

33. Bill Morgan, "Six Isn't Enough!" *Integrity* 2, no. 9 (June 1948), 12–18.

34. Michaels, "Sins of Flesh and Commerce," 33.

35. John T. Noonan, *Contraception: A History of Its Treatment by the Catholic Theologians and Canonists,* rev. ed. (Cambridge, MA: Harvard University Press, 1986), 445–447. All quotes from 446.

36. Calkins, "Rhythm—the Unhappy Compromise," 4–5.

37. John C. Ford, S.J. and Gerald Kelly, S.J., *Contemporary Moral Theology,* vol. 2: *Marriage Questions* (Westminster, MD: Newman Press, 1963), 400–402.

38. Francis J. Connell, C.SS.R., "Answers to Questions: The Use of 'Rhythm,'" *American Ecclesiastical Review* 126, no. 1 (Jan. 1952): 66.

39. Gerald Kelly, S.J., "Notes on Moral Theology, 1951," *Theological Studies* 13, no. 1

(March 1952), 82–83; Ford and Kelly, *Contemporary Moral Theology,* vol. 2: *Marriage Questions,* 401.

40. Fr. John C. Ford, S.J., undated teaching notes, but cumulative from the 1940s and '50s. Ford has written "omit" in the margins next to his caution on rhythm publicity. NESJ. Papers of John C. Ford, S.J., box 7 (preliminary cataloguing).

41. Thomas, *Marriage and Rhythm,* 159–160.

42. John C. Ford, S.J., teaching notes for moral theology, undated but ca. mid-1950s. NESJ. Papers of John C. Ford, S.J., box 10 (preliminary cataloguing); Thomas, *Marriage and Rhythm,* 164; Rev. George A. Kelly, *The Catholic Marriage Manual* (New York: Random House, 1958), 61.

43. Paul Hilsdale, "Birth Control or Rhythm?" *America* 102, no. 8 (21 Nov. 1959), 236.

44. Msgr. Lawrence J. Riley, "Moral Aspects of the Practice of Periodic Continence," *Homiletic and Pastoral Review* 57, no. 9 (June 1957): 825.

45. John C. Ford, S.J., "Casus: de Continentes Periodica," undated typescript but ca. late 1950s, makes reference to the problem of confessors refusing absolution. NESJ. Papers of John C. Ford, S.J., box 10 (preliminary cataloguing).

46. John C. Ford, S.J., teaching notes for moral theology; see also John A. Goodwine, "The Problem of Periodic Continence," *American Ecclesiastical Review* 137, no. 3 (Sept. 1957): 156–157; Cecil Parres, C.M., "Questions Answered: Rhythm Without Sufficient Reason," *Homiletic and Pastoral Review* 60, no. 1 (Oct. 1959): 177–178; "Quid in Casu?" *Pastoral Life* 8, no. 2 (March–April 1960): 39–40.

47. "Answers to Questions: The Confessor Suggesting Rhythm," *American Ecclesiastical Review* 141, no. 1 (July 1959): 59. No author given.

48. Thomas, *Marriage and Rhythm,* 160.

49. "For just reasons you can practice the rhythm theory, following your calendar and the changes of temperature of the woman, according to the advice of some good doctor who is Catholic or an honorable man. He will tell you the days of your monthly cycle in which you may have relations without always becoming pregnant." Arthur D. Spearman, S.J., *The Spanish-English Confessor's Guide,* rev. ed. (Paterson, NJ: St. Anthony Guild Press, 1960), 69, 71.

50. H.J. to the editors, *Liguorian* 50, no. 2 (Feb. 1962), 31.

51. Mrs. N.N. to the editors, *Liguorian* 45, no. 4 (April 1957), 39.

52. Mrs. D.M. to the editor, *Marriage* 42, no. 12 (Dec. 1960).

53. Gerald Kelly, S.J., *Rhythm in Marriage: Duty and Idealism* (America Press, 1957), 5–6. The pamphlet reprints Kelly's original article, which appeared in *America* on 3 May 1952.

54. Ford and Kelly, *Contemporary Moral Theology,* vol. 2, 420–421, 423.

55. Fr. Maurice Geary to John C. Ford, S.C., 8 Jan. 1960, in which Geary summarizes the argument of a letter recently received from Ford. NESJ. Papers of John C. Ford, S.J., box 10 (preliminary cataloguing). See also John A. McHugh O.P. and Charles J. Callan, O.P., *Moral Theology: A Complete Course,* vol. 2 (New York: Joseph F. Wagner, 1958 edition, revised and enlarged by Edward P. Farrell, O.P.), 621–622. This exceedingly cautious text confirms the probable status of Kelly's approach. For an argument contra Kelly, see Francis J. Connell, C.SS.R., "Answers to Questions: The Lawful Use of Rhythm," *American Ecclesiastical Review* 127, no. 2 (Aug. 1952): 136–141.

56. Kelly, *Catholic Marriage Manual,* 60–61. Many other publications from the 1950s and early 1960s make almost identical arguments. See, for example, Rev. William F. McManus, *Marriage Guide for Engaged Catholics* (New York: Paulist Press, 1962), 86–87.

57. Kelly, *Catholic Marriage Manual,* 61.

58. Rev. Laurence G. Lovaski, S.V.D., *The Rhythm Practice* (Techny, IL: Divine Word Publications, 1962), 14.

59. Shirley de Leon, "The Buffalo Family Clinic," *Marriage* 46, no. 10 (Oct. 1964): 16–19; *The Cana Newsletter* [Archdiocese of Chicago], 9, no. 3 (June–July 1963) and 9, no. 4 (Sept.–Oct. 1963); Memo to Catholic Family Information Personnel from the Cana Conference, Arch-

diocese of Chicago, May 1964. AAC. Cardinal Albert Meyer papers, box 43827.01 (temporary cataloguing).

60. "Memorandum re: *RHYTHM CLINICS*," NCWC Family Life Bureau, 4 Aug. 1965. AAB. Lawrence Shehan papers, uncatalogued.

61. "Excerpt from 'Population in a Changing World,' by Louis McKernan, C.S.P.," undated typescript. The McKernan article appeared in the *Catholic World* in Feb. 1960. Clipping in AUND. John A. O'Brien papers—COBR, box 6, folder 13. See also, John Maguire, C.S.C., "Once More—On Birth Control," *Ave Maria* 94, no. 5 (29 July 1961), 18.

62. Undated typescript in question-and-answer form, evidently relating to the 10 May 1962 broadcast of "CBS Reports—Birth Control and the Law." O'Brien's call for federal funding may have been cut from the program, though his endorsement of rhythm was not. AUND. John A. O'Brien papers—COBR, box 6, folder 10.

63. Msgr. John C. Knott, "Memorandum: Latest Developments concerning Methods of Birth Control," 30 Oct. 1964. Knott made the same claim in his column, widely syndicated in the Catholic press. ACUA, NCWC papers, 10/86/6.

64. John C. Ford, S.J. to "Dear Gerry," 11 Sept. 1962. NESJ. Papers of John C. Ford, S.J., box 9 (preliminary cataloguing). Ford's and Kelly's *Contemporary Moral Theology*, vol. 2: *Marriage Questions* asserted that no priest "may legitimately impose a grave obligation on the consciences of the faithful to fulfill an affirmative obligation to procreate," 428–429.

65. Transcript of "David Brinkley Journal Special: Birth Control How?," broadcast 12 Jan. 1964. AUND. John A O'Brien papers—COBR, box 6, folder 13.

66. William J. Gibbons and Thomas K. Burch, "Physiologic Control of Fertility: Process and Morality," *American Ecclesiastical Review* 138, no. 4 (April 1958): 265–266; John R. Connery, S.J., "Notes on Moral Theology," *Theological Studies* 19, no. 4 (Dec. 1958): 550.

67. Transcript, "David Brinkley Journal."

68. Quoted in Noonan, *Contraception,* 465.

69. John C. Ford, S.J. to Msgr. Irving A. DeBlanc, 18 May 1961. ACUA, NCWC papers, 10/86/3; John J. Lynch, S.J., "Notes on Moral Theology," *Theological Studies* 23, no. 2 (June 1962): 243–247.

70. Symptomatic of the new situation was a brochure issued, "with ecclesiastical approval," by Chicago's Cana Conference in May 1962. Called "What About the Pill?," the brochure endorsed use of the Pill for purpose of achieving a sufficiently regular menstrual cycle to enable a woman to practice rhythm.

71. T.B. to Cardinal Lawrence Shehan, 12 June 1966, reflecting on the recent past. AAB. Lawrence Shehan papers, uncatalogued.

72. *Marriage as a Career: Report of a Brooklyn Project,* no author, date, or place of publication listed. Unpaginated. The program described began in May 1945 and was cosponsored by the Youth Committee of the Diocesan Council of Catholic Women, the Sodality of Our Lady, and the diocesan Catholic Youth Organization.

73. Martin Stevens, "Headstart on Marriage," *Priest* 5, no. 12 (Dec. 1949): 929.

74. R.C. Maguire [Chancellor, Archdiocese of Chicago] to "Reverend and dear Father," 12 July 1932. AAC. Mundelein Chancery Correspondence, box 13 (1932 M-N), folder 4. See also Cardinal George Mundelein to Rita McGoldrick, 18 June 1932, same cite but folder 6.

75. Bp. J. F. Noll, "Sermon Outlines for Four Sundays: Marriage," *Acolyte* 19, no. 4 (April 1943): 25, assumes that such promises are generally required in mixed marriages. Canon E. J. Mahoney, *Marriage Preliminaries: The Instruction 'Sacrosanctum' 19 June 1941, with a Commentary* (Westminster, MD: Newman Press, 1949), 35, 51, 72, discusses their increasingly widespread use in marriages between Catholics.

76. "Answers to Questions: A Problem on the Pre-Marital Questionnaire," *American Ecclesiastical Review* 117, no. 6 (Dec. 1947): 469.

77. Most Rev. Joseph H. Schlarman, *Why Six Instructions? Arranging for a Mixed Marriage* (St. Louis: B. Herder Book Company, 1944), 54. The booklet was first published in 1939.

78. Joseph H. Fichter, *Southern Parish,* vol. 1 (Chicago: University of Chicago Press, 1951), 99.

79. Mahoney, *Marriage Preliminaries,* 35. Swearing on the Bible may have been a common practice: couples in the Archdiocese of Chicago filled out the premarital questionnaire "under oath, touching the Holy Gospels." *The Basic Cana Manual,* ed., Rev. Walter J. Imbiorski (1957; repr. Chicago: Cana Conference of Chicago, 1963), 111.

80. Mahoney, *Marriage Preliminaries,* 72–73; J. F. Marbach, "Code and Cult," *Priest* 9, no. 2 (Feb. 1953): 132–138; John J. Danagher, C.M., "Questions Answered: Marriage Validation and Birth Prevention," *Homiletic and Pastoral Review* 56, no. 4 (Jan. 1956): 426, 428–430; William Allen, "Quid in Casu?" *Pastoral Life* 10, no. 4 (July–Aug. 1962): 47. For a dissenting view, almost certainly by Joseph Connell, see "Answers to Questions: A Problem of the Pre-marital Questionnaire," *American Ecclesiastical Review,* 469–470.

81. My thanks to Saginaw's Bishop Kenneth Untener for the Saginaw form. This particular copy was dated 1960 (the relevant personal information had been removed); I have no idea—nor did the bishop—how long this version was in use. It seems likely that Saginaw would have used a form common to all the dioceses of the Michigan Province. One of my Detroit informants, ordained in 1954, recalled the prenuptial form in use in that archdiocese—whose bishop was head of the Michigan Province—as including a promise not to use what the form called "sinful birth control." This question, he said, had been introduced shortly after his ordination and was changed at a later date, though he did not remember precisely when. This particular interviewee asked to remain anonymous. The interview took place on 3 May 1999.

82. Fichter, *Southern Parish,* 99.

83. Author interview with Msgr. Vincent Howard, 27 Oct. 1998, in Chelsea MI.

84. *Happiness in Marriage: An Ethico-Medical Interpretation,* no author, place or date of publication given, quotes from 7, 57–58. Birth control is discussed on 35–42.

85. Author interview with Fr. William Carolin, 28 Oct. 1998, in Brighton MI. Howard interview.

86. Quoted in "Answers to Questions: Instruction in Sex Matters," *American Ecclesiastical Review* 127, no. 2 (Aug. 1952): 136.

87. Reminiscences of Fr. John Wittstock, in *Recollections of Vocation and Priestly Ministry,* ed., Rev. Edward L. Scheuerman (privately printed, 1998), 229. My thanks to Fr. Scheuerman for lending me his manuscript copy.

88. Fred J. Mann, C.SS.R., "Content and Techniques of Cana Conference Program," prepared for the First Annual Meeting of Cana Conference Priests, Catholic University, Aug. 1947. AAC. Cardinal Albert Meyer papers, box 43829.03, folder "Marriage and family planning."

89. Dr. A. H. Clemens, *The Cana Movement in the United States* (Washington, DC: Catholic University of America Press, 1953), 14.

90. Rev. Matthias Fischer, "Approach and Content in the Pre-Cana Conference," in *The Cana Conference: Proceedings of the Chicago Archdiocesan Study Week on the Cana Conference, December 27–28–29, 1950,* vol. II (Chicago: Cana Conference of Chicago, 1951), 50.

91. *Basic Cana Manual,* ed, Imbiorski, 70, 74.

92. Ibid., 80.

93. Ibid., 69, 67. The same themes appear in Rev. John C. Knott, "Director's Outline, Pre-Cana Conference, Archdiocese of Hartford," typescript dated Jan. 1956, 11–12. ACUA. Alphonse Clemens papers, 81.2, folder "Cana Clubs" and in Milwaukee Archdiocesan Family Life Program, Marriage Preparation Course, Priest's Talk, Lecture III, undated typescript but 1962, 3–5. Archives of the Archdiocese of Milwaukee (hereafter AAM). AS 36, box 1, folder 9.

94. *Basic Cana Manual,* ed., Imbiorski, 61.

95. Ibid., 70.

96. Ibid., 75, 84, 104–105.

97. Ibid., 81–82.

98. Kathryn A. Johnson, "A Question of Authority: Friction in the Catholic Family Life Movement, 1948–1962," *The Catholic Historical Review* 86, no. 2 (April 2000): 227–228.

99. Letter [signature deleted] to Pat and Patty Crowley, 1 June 1965. Emphasis in original. The letter writer had gone on the Pill by 1965, by then the mother of eleven children. AUND. Patty Crowley papers—SPCBPC, box 15, folder 5. My thanks to Patty Crowley for permission to use this invaluable collection.

100. Fr. Frederick Mann, C.SS.R. to Dr. Alphonse Clemens, 11 Feb. 1948. ACUA. Alphonse Clemens papers, box 2, folder "Cana Institute."

101. Letter, no author or date, but evidently to Pat and Patty Crowley, ca. 1965. AUND. Crowley papers—SPCBPC, box 15, folder 1.

102. Clarence and Kathleen Enzler, "Sanctity in Marriage: It's the Same Difference," in *Sanctity and Success in Marriage: Selected Papers from the 1956 Proceedings of the National Catholic Conference on Family Life,* eds., Msgr. Irving A. LeBlanc and Norma L. Schavilla (Washington, DC: Family Life Bureau, National Catholic Welfare Conference, 1956), 82.

103. *Basic Cana Manual,* ed. Imbiorski, 124.

104. Conleth Overman, C.P., "Notes for Chicago Cana Conference, Second Conference: Physical Union," undated but ca. 1950. PPA. Sermons of Fr. Conleth Overman, C.P., box 250.

105. "Widow, Ottawa, Canada" to the editor, *Jubilee,* 21 Jan. 1964. Typed version of original. GULSC. Ed Rice papers, box 4, folder 55.

106. "Professor of English at a Catholic College, New England" to the editor, *Jubilee,* dated 3 Dec. 1958 but almost certainly erroneously. The correct date is probably 1963. Typed version of original. GULSC. Ed Rice papers, box 4, folder 55.

107. Mrs. James A. Kenny to the editor, *America* 110, no. 9 (20 Feb. 1964), 270.

108. Letter, signature deleted, to Pat and Patty Crowley, undated but probably 1965. AUND. Patty Crowley papers—SPCBPC, box 15, folder 5.

109. John Michael Murphy interview.

110. J. E. Manson, C.SS.R. to Alphonse H. Clemens, 25 Feb. 1948. ACUA. Alphonse H. Clemens papers, 81.2, folder "Cana Institute." The conference in question took place at the Catholic University in Washington DC.

111. "Woman's Place in the Home," typescript Cana Club discussion outline, undated but ca. 1950. ACUA. Alphonse Clemens papers, 81.2, folder "Cana Clubs."

112. Msgr. George W. Casey, "The Pastoral Crisis," *Commonweal* 80, no. 11 (5 June 1964), 318.

113. Letter, signature deleted, to Pat and Patty Crowley, 3 June 1965. AUND. Crowley papers—SPCBPC, box 15, folder 10.

114. Michael Novak, "Marriage: The Lay View," *Commonweal* 79, no. 20 (14 Feb. 1964), 590.

115. William J. Nagle, "Failures—Lay and Clerical," *Commonweal* 76 (27 July 1962), 424.

116. Mrs. Virgil M. Sweet to the editor, *Sign* 79 (July 1950), 72.

117. (Mrs.) Doris Mathisen to the editor, *Sign* 79 (July 1950), 72.

118. Fr. Paul Brussard to Archbishop John F. O'Hara, C.S.C., 31 March 1953. AAPhi. Cardinal John O'Hara papers, 90.150. Results from the poll—minus the offending data—were published in the *Catholic Digest* beginning in Nov. 1952 and continuing until May 1954.

119. Daniel Callahan, "Authority and the Theologian," *Commonweal* 80, no. 11 (5 June 1964), 320.

120. "Sideglances: Dialogue between Liguorian Editors and Readers," *Liguorian* 51, no. 3 (March 1963), 30.

121. Mrs. B.P.M. to the editors, *Liguorian* 46, no. 7 (July 1958), 40.

122. Mrs. A.G.B. to the editor, *Liguorian* 45, no. 10 (Oct. 1957), 41.

123. J.H.L. to the editor, *Liguorian* 46, no. 6 (June 1958), 42.

124. Anon., California to the editors, *Liguorian* 47, no. 12 (Dec. 1959), 37.

125. N.N. to the editor, *Liguorian* 45, no. 10 (Oct. 1957), 30.

126. Mrs. M.L. O'D. to the editor, *Liguorian* 43, no. 7 (July 1955), 415.

127. Anon. to the editor *Liguorian* 48, no. 10 (Oct. 1960), 39.

128. Mrs. C.L. to the editor, *Liguorian* 46, no. 6 (June 1958), 41–42.

129. N.N. to the editor, *Liguorian* (Mar. 1955), 148.

130. N.N. to the editor, *Liguorian* (Oct. 1957), 29.

131. Donald F. Miller, C.SS.R., "For Wives and Husbands Only: Birth Prevention or Peace?" *Liguorian* 48, no. 1 (Jan. 1960), 36. The letter appears at the head of this regular feature.

132. Ibid., 36–37.

133. Mrs. Alice O'Connell, "Feature 'X'," *America* 93 (9 April 1955), 43.

Chapter 6.   The Church's First Duty Is Charity

1. N.N. to Archbp. Lawrence Shehan, 24 May 1966. AAB. Shehan papers, uncatalogued.

2. Quoted in Xavier Rynne, *Vatican Council II* (Maryknoll, NY: Orbis Book, 1999), 80. Bea was addressing the Council with regard to the proposed Schema on Revelation.

3. James Burtchaell, C.S.C., "Human Life and Human Love," undated typescript, but ca. Aug. 1968. AUND. John A. O'Brien papers, box 6, folder 1.

4. Quoted in Rynne, *Vatican Council II,* 576. The Holy Office is now known as the Congregation for the Doctrine of the Faith.

5. Lois R. Chevalier, "The Secret Drama Behind the Pope's Momentous Decision on Birth Control," *Ladies' Home Journal* 83, no. 3 (March 1966), 88.

6. Robert McClory, *Turning Point* (New York: Crossroad, 1995), 2, 38–43 and passim; for the text of the Commission's report, see 171–183.

7. Adrienne Rich, "Compulsory Heterosexuality and Lesbian Existence," *Signs* 5, no. 4 (Summer 1980): 631–660.

8. Gallup polls done in 1968 and 1974 measured declines of 30 percent among Catholics who regarded four or more children as ideal, and 26 percent among female respondents. In 1968, fully 50 percent of the Catholics sampled endorsed an ideal of four or more children, though their actual fertility by this date was certainly less. Quoted in Wilfrid Scanlon, "Orthodoxy? Anomie? Or Pluralism? An Empirical Sociological Analysis of Attitudes of the Catholic Laity in the Archdiocese of Boston toward Contraception" (Ph.D. dissertation, Boston University, 1975), 78.

9. Letter [signature deleted] to Fr. Walter Imbiorski, undated but probably 1965. The writer is responding to an Imbiorski questionnaire, published in the July 1965 issue of ACT, the newsletter of Chicago CFM. AUND. Crowley papers—SPCBPC, box 15, folder 5.

10. "Adult Obedience," in Michael Novak, *A Time to Build* (New York: Macmillan, 1967), 158. The article appeared originally in a 1967 issue of *Marriage.*

11. N.N. to Cardinal Lawrence Shehan, 7 June 1966. AAB. Shehan papers, uncatalogued.

12. James Patrick Shannon tells his story in *Reluctant Dissenter: An Autobiography* (New York: Crossroad, 1998). He subsequently left the priesthood to marry.

13. John Rock, *The Time Has Come: A Catholic Doctor's Proposals to End the Battle over Birth Control* (New York: Knopf, 1963), 159–178 and passim; quote from 169–170.

14. "Dr. Rock's Book," *Commonweal* 78 (17 May 1963), 214.

15. "The Good and Bad of Dr. Rock's Book," *Michigan Catholic,* 6 June 1963, 8:1–6. O'Leary taught philosophy at Sacred Heart Seminary in Detroit.

16. George Barrett, "Catholics and Birth Control: Growing Debate," *New York Times,* 5 Aug. 1963, 1:3–6, 12:1–8. Three subsequent articles by Barrett appeared on 6, 7, and 8 August.

17. Hugh J. O'Connell, C.SS.R., "Contraception and Confusion," *Liguorian* 52, no. 2 (Feb. 1964), 12, 8.

18. Hugh J. O'Connell, C.SS.R., "Contraception and More Confusion," *Liguorian* 52, no. 6 (June 1964), 26.

19. Bruce Cooper, "An English Father Hopes the Council Will Act," *Jubilee* 11 (Dec. 1963), 20–21.

20. Rosemary Reuther, "Marriage, Love, Children," *Jubilee* 11 (Dec. 1963), 20.

21. "Priest, California" to the editor, *Jubilee* 12 (June 1964), 28. No names were attached to any of the printed letters.

22. "Mother of nine, Syracuse, New York" to the editor, *Jubilee,* undated but late 1963 or early 1964. GULSC. Ed Rice papers, box 5, folder 54. This collection includes letters that were not printed in the magazine. The unpublished letters typically make similar arguments to the published ones.

23. "Mother of nine, Indiana" to the editor, *Jubilee* 12 (June 1964), 19.

24. "Father of four, Midwest" to the editor, *Jubilee* 12 (June 1964), 28.

25. "Missionary priest in Africa" to the editor, *Jubilee* 12 (June 1964), 28.

26. "Mother of six, East Coast" to the editor, *Jubilee* 12 (June 1964), 23.

27. "Priest, New Jersey" to the editor, *Jubilee* 12 (June 1964), 20.

28. "Mother of five, Philadelphia" to the editor, *Jubilee* 12 (June 1964), 22.

29. "Mother of six, Arizona" to the editor, *Jubilee* 12 (June 1964), 26.

30. "Mother of six, Canada" to the editor, *Jubilee* 12 (June 1964), 27.

31. "Rancher, California" to the editor, *Jubilee* 12 (June 1964), 18.

32. "Mother of three, Jamaica, NY" to the editor, *Jubilee,* undated but late 1963 or early 1964. GULSC. Ed Rice papers, box 4, folder 58.

33. "Physician, father of six, New Orleans" to the editor, *Jubilee,* 10 Jan. 1964. GULSC. Ed Rice papers, box 4, folder 55.

34. "Mother of six, East Coast," 25.

35. "Mother of four, West Islip, NY" to the editor, *Jubilee* 12 (June 1964), 30.

36. Mrs. K. B. Lake to the editor, *Jubilee,* 11 Dec. 1963. GULSC. Ed Rice papers, box 4, folder 55.

37. "Mother of three, Jamaica, N.Y."

38. Ibid.

39. Sylvia Bangert to the editor, *Jubilee,* 6 Jan. 1964. GULSC. Ed Rice papers, box 4, folder 55.

40. "Physician's wife, mother of four, Virginia" to the editor, *Jubilee,* undated but late 1963 or early 1964. GULSC. Ed Rice papers, box 4, folder 54.

41. "Professor of English at a Catholic College, New England" to the editor, *Jubilee,* dated 3 Dec. 1958 but almost certainly erroneously. The correct date is probably 1963. Typed version of original. GULSC. Ed Rice papers, box 4, folder 55.

42. "Father of four, Illinois" to the editor, *Jubilee,* 1 July 1964. GULSC. Ed Rice papers, box 4, folder 56.

43. "Responsible Parenthood," *Commonweal* 80, no. 11 (5 June 1964), 312. The editor at this juncture was Edward Skillin.

44. Quoted in Bernard Asbell, *The Pill: A Biography of the Drug That Changed the World* (New York: Random House, 1995), 229. The issue in question appeared in Sept. 1964.

45. John A. O'Brien, "Help in Regulating Births," *Priest* 20, no. 4 (April 1964): 317.

46. Michael Novak, ed., *The Experience of Marriage* (New York: Macmillan, 1964); William Birmingham, ed., *What Modern Catholics Think About Birth Control* (New York: Signet Books, 1964).

47. Charles Curran, review of Michael Novak, ed., *The Experience of Marriage, Sign* 44, no. 3 (Oct. 1964), 59, 61–62.

48. William G. Keane to the editor, *Commonweal* 79, no. 25 (20 March 1964), 752.

49. Novak, *Experience of Marriage,* 160. All contributors to the Novak anthology were anonymous.

50. Sally Sullivan, "Woman: Mother or Person?" in Birmingham, ed., What *Modern Catholics Think,* 205, 213.

51. Anne Martin, "Time to Grow in Love," in Birmingham, ed., What *Modern Catholics Think,* 198.

52. Novak, *Experience of Marriage,* 124.

53. Raymond H. Potvin, Charles F. Westoff, and Norman B. Ryder, "Factors Affecting Catholic Wives' Conformity to Their Church Magisterium's Position on Birth Control," *Journal of Marriage and the Family* 30, no. 2 (May 1968): 263–272. Quote from 272.

54. Charles F. Westoff and Larry Bumpass, "The Revolution in Birth Control Practices of U.S. Roman Catholics," *Science* 179 (5 Jan. 1973): 41.

55. Unsigned, undated questionnaire, ca. 1965. AUND. Crowley papers—SPCBPC, box 13, folder 1.

56. "Majority of Catholics Think Church Will Change Stand on Birth Control," 19 Aug. 1965. The document was apparently a press release from the Gallup polling organization. Copy in ACUA. NCWC papers, 10/86/8.

57. Francis R. McGovern to "Father Blaise," *Marriage* 47, no. 2 (Feb. 1965), 59.

58. The Crowleys' experience on the commission is chronicled in McClory, *Turning Point.*

59. Pat and Patty Crowley to "Dear Barbara," 2 July 1965. AUND. Crowley papers—SPCBPC, box 15, folder 13.

60. Pat and Patty Crowley to Mr. and Mrs. Gerald Xaver, 7 April 1966. AUND. Crowley papers—SPCBPC, box 5, folder 13.

61. Statement of Cardinal John Heenan, 22 June [1966], typescript. Copy in NESJ. John C. Ford papers, box 9 (preliminary cataloguing). Emphasis in original.

62. Letter, signature deleted, to Pat and Patty Crowley, undated but ca. 1965. AUND. Crowley papers—SPCBPC, box 15, folder 1.

63. Letter, signature deleted, to Pat and Patty Crowley, undated but ca. 1965. AUND. Crowley papers—SPCBPC, box 15, folder 5.

64. Questionnaire form, unsigned and undated, but ca. 1965. AUND. Crowley papers—SPCBPC, box 3, folder 2.

65. Letter, signature deleted, to Pat and Patty Crowley, 24 May 1965. AUND. Crowley papers—SPCBPC, box 15, folder 10.

66. Letter, signature deleted, to Pat and Patty Crowley, 18 May 1965. AUND. Crowley papers—SPCBPC, box 15, folder 5.

67. Unsigned, undated questionnaire with comments added, ca. 1965. AUND. Crowley papers—SPCBPC, box 15, folder 3.

68. Letter, signature deleted, to Pat and Patty Crowley, undated but ca. 1965. AUND. Crowley papers—SPCBPC, box 15, folder 5.

69. Letter, signature deleted, to Pat and Patty Crowley, undated but ca. 1965. AUND. Crowley papers—SPCBPC, box 15, folder 4.

70. Letter, signature deleted, to Pat and Patty Crowley, undated but ca. 1965. AUND. Crowley papers—SPCBPC, box 15, folder 11.

71. Letter, signature deleted, to Pat and Patty Crowley, 3 June 1965. AUND. Crowley papers—SPCBPC, box 15, folder 11.

72. Questionnaire form, unsigned and undated, but ca. 1965. AUND. Crowley papers—SPCBPC, box 3, folder 2.

73. McClory, *Turning Point,* 96–97.

74. John C. Ford, typescript diary for Nov.–Dec. 1965. The diary was mainly devoted to Ford's behind-the-scenes work to amend the Council's schema on marriage. It was apparently assembled after the fact, based on notes taken at the time of the events described. NESJ. John C. Ford papers, box 9, preliminary cataloguing.

75. Quoted in McClory, *Turning Point,* 103.

76. Statement of Patty Crowley to the Papal Commission, May 1966. NESJ. John C. Ford papers, box 8, preliminary cataloguing. This document differs in some respects from the statement quoted in McClory, *Turning Point.* I cannot explain the discrepancies but would add that the substance of the two documents is similar.

77. "Statement of Patty Crowley," 1.

78. Ibid., 3.

79. "Statement of Mme. Potvin to the papal commission," May 1966. NESJ. John C. Ford papers, box 8, preliminary cataloguing. Translated from the original French.

80. McClory, *Turning Point,* 106.

81. "Statement of Mme. Potvin," 1.

82. Ibid., 1.

83. Quoted in McClory, *Turning Point,* 113.

84. Ibid., 113.

85. John C. Ford, S.J., "Statement of Position," 25 May 1966. NESJ. John C. Ford papers, box 9, preliminary cataloguing. This was delivered orally at a meeting of the papal commission. Emphasis in original.

86. "Minority Papal Commission Report," in Daniel Callahan, ed., *The Catholic Case for Contraception* (New York: Macmillan, 1969), 184.

87. Ford, "Statement of Position."

88. Msgr. Francis X. Canfield to Msgr. Arthur L. Valade, 20 Jan. 1967. Archives of the Diocese of Lansing MI (hereafter ADL). Alexander Zaleski papers, folder "NCCB Committee on Doctrine: Bishops' Response to Cardinal Ottaviani's Letter, 1967."

89. Bp. Alexander Zaleski to Archbishop Terence J. Cooke, 1 July 1968. ADL. Alexander Zaleski papers, folder "NCCB Committee on Doctrine: Inquiry re Fr. Flynn's Statement on Fertility Control, May–July 1968."

90. Msgr. William J. Sherzer to Msgr. Arthur Valade, 21 Jan. 1967. ADL. Alexander Zaleski papers, folder "NCCB Committee on Doctrine: Bishops' Response to Cardinal Ottaviani's Letter, 1967."

91. The event is covered in Robert Blair Kaiser, *The Politics of Sex and Religion: A Case History in the Development of Doctrine, 1962–1984* (Kansas City, MO: Leaven Press, 1985), 185.

92. Westoff and Bumpass, "Revolution in Birth Control Practices," 41.

93. Rev. James E. Kraus to Bp. John J. Carberry, undated but ca. Feb. 1967. ADL. Alexander Zaleski papers, folder "NCCB Committee on Doctrine: Bishops' Responses to Cardinal Ottaviani's Letter."

94. Sally Cunneen, *Sex: Female, Religion: Catholic* (New York: Holt, Rinehart and Winston, 1968), 62. The question of clerical celibacy and its negative effects in confession is addressed on page 66.

95. Quoted in Maurice J. Moore, "Death of a Dogma? The American Catholic Clergy's Views of Contraception" (Ph.D. dissertation, Department of Sociology, University of Chicago, 1972), 3.

96. Andrew Greeley, "Is Catholic Sexual Teaching Coming Apart?" *Critic* 30, no. 4 (March–April 1972): 32.

97. P.J. to Cardinal Lawrence Shehan, 7 Sept. 1968. AAB. Lawrence Shehan papers, uncatalogued. As with all quite recent private correspondence, I have not used the writer's full name.

98. C.P. to Cardinal Lawrence Shehan, 14 Aug. 1968. AAB. Lawrence Shehan papers, uncatalogued.

99. M.J.P.A. to Pope Paul VI, with copies of various members of the U.S. hierarchy, including Cardinal Lawrence Shehan, 23 Sept. 1968. AAB. Lawrence Shehan papers, uncatalogued.

100. Novak, "Adult Obedience," 158.

101. Hazel F. Firstman et al., "Beyond Birth Control," draft report of a study sponsored by the Marriage and Family Research Project, under the auspices of the St. Thomas More Marriage and Family Clinics of Los Angeles, undated and unpaginated. Copy in AUND. Crowley papers—SPCBPC, box 8, folder 6.

102. David P. O'Neill, *The Priest in Crisis: A Study in Role Change* (Dayton, OH: Pflaum Press, 1968), 62, 78.

103. Summary notes of a priests' meeting in Chicago, in preparation for an upcoming archdiocesan synod, 3 Dec. 1963. AAC. Catholic Action Federations papers, box 2, folder 48.

104. "Religious priest" to the editor, *Liguorian* 52, no. 4 (April 1964), 30.

105. Author interview with Fr. Joseph Gallagher, 3 Feb. 1999, in Baltimore. Gallagher was ordained in 1955.

106. Timothy McCarthy, O.P., "The Role of the Priest," *Pastoral Life* 14, no. 12 (Dec. 1966): 657.

107. Cardinal Lawrence Shehan to Bp. Alexander Zaleski, 19 Jan. 1967. ADL. Alexander Zaleski papers, folder "NCCB Committee on Doctrine: Bishop's Responses to Cardinal Ottaviani's Latter, 1967." Emphases in original.

108. For a good discussion of period literature on celibacy, see Richard A. McCormick, S.J., *Notes on Moral Theology, 1965 through 1980* (Washington, DC: University Press of America, 1981), 144–153.

109. Rev. L. J. McCloskey, "The Case for Optional Celibacy," in *Study and Discussion Papers Prepared for National Federation of Priests' Councils,* undated but 1968. This unpublished collection was used as a basis for discussion at regional meetings of the National Federation of Priests' Councils, fall 1968. AAC. Catholic Action Federations papers, box 2, folder 3.

110. Rev. Eugene C. Kennedy, M.M. to Archbishop John Dearden, 3 Sept. 1968. AUND. John Dearden papers—CDRD, 34/11.

111. Joseph H. Fichter, *America's Forgotten Priests: What They Are Saying* (New York: Harper and Row, 1968) 163, and Andrew M. Greeley, *The Catholic Priest in the United States: Sociological Investigations* (Washington, DC: United States Catholic Conference, 1972), 234–235. See also Richard A. Schoenherr, edited with an introduction by David Yamane, *Goodbye Father: The Celibate Male Priesthood and the Future of the Catholic Church* (New York: Oxford University Press, 2002), 15–28. Fichter's 1966 survey was weighted in favor of younger respondents, which accounts for its inflated majority in favor of optional celibacy.

112. McCormick, *Notes on Moral Theology,* 151–152.

113. *Commonweal* 86, no. 16 (14 July 1967), 436. In fairness to the editors, the phrase comes from a well-known intervention at the Second Vatican Council by Melkite Patriarch Maximos IV Saigh, who was speaking critically about Church teaching on contraception. Rynne, *Vatican Council II,* 368.

114. O'Neill, *Priest in Crisis,* 174.

115. "A Report on the Condition of Priestly Ministry and Celibacy in the United States Made to the Canon Law Society of America," no author or date, but 1971. This was evidently the product of a symposium on celibacy held at Cathedral College, Douglaston NY, 19–22 Aug. 1971. AUND. Association of Chicago Priests' papers—CACP, 2/15.

116. "Role of the Priest Committee," in *Position Papers Prepared by the Standing Committees of the Association of Chicago Priests for the Second Plenary Session, May 8, 1967,* no author given. AAC. Catholic Action Federations papers, box 2, folder 5.

117. Marty Marty, "What Went Wrong?" *Critic* 34, no. 1 (Fall 1975): 53.

118. O'Neill, *Priest in Crisis,* 10.

119. Father Charles Irvin is paraphrased in Archdiocese of Detroit, Priests' Senate, minutes for 15 Dec. 1970. Copy in AUND. Association of Chicago Priests papers—CACP 9/43.

120. John A. O'Brien to Harold W. Bostrom, 19 Sept. 1969. AUND. John A. O'Brien papers—COBR, box 1, folder 3.

121. On this sensitive topic, see Thomas P. Rausch, S.J., *Priesthood Today: An Appraisal* (New York: Paulist Press, 1992), 66–67.

122. O'Neill, *Priest in Crisis,* 60.

123. N.N. to Cardinal Lawrence Shehan, 2 June 1966. The priest in question belonged to the Archdiocese of Baltimore. AAB. Lawrence Shehan papers, uncatalogued.

124. N.N. to Cardinal Lawrence Shehan, undated but ca. June 1966. AAB. Lawrence Shehan papers, uncatalogued.

125. O'Neill, *Priest in Crisis,* 62.

126. Author interview with Bp. Kenneth Untener, 21 Dec. 1998, in Saginaw MI.

127. Author interview with Fr. Robert Ferrigan, 16 Nov. 1998, in Winnetka IL.

128. Gallagher interview.

129. David Clark to "Moe," 2 May 1964. My thanks to Elaine G. Clark for a copy of this letter.

130. N.N. to Cardinal Lawrence Shehan, 10 June 1966. AAB. Lawrence Shehan papers, un-catalogued. The priest in question was ordained in 1962.

131. John T. Noonan, *Contraception: A History of Its Treatment by the Catholic Theologians and Canonists,* rev. ed. (Cambridge, MA: Harvard University Press, 1986), 469.

132. Francis Canavan, S.J. to Arthur W. Kane, S.J., 8 April 1964. NESJ. Papers of John C. Ford, S.J., box 10 (preliminary cataloguing). For the relevant copy in *Marriage Questions,* see John C. Ford, S.J. and Gerald Kelly, S.J., *Contemporary Moral Theology,* vol. 2: *Marriage Questions* (Westminster, MD: Newman Press, 1963), 271–272.

133. "Priest, New Jersey" to the editor, *Jubilee.*

134. Joseph Fitzmeyer, S.J. to John C. Ford, S.J., 2 April 1966. NESJ. Papers of John C. Ford, S.J., box 8 (preliminary cataloguing).

135. The Chicago reference occurs in the outline for Feb. 10, 1963: "The Christian Family in Modern Society." Archdiocese of Chicago, *The Love of Neighbor: Program of Instructions for the Church Year 1962–63,* 33.

136. For a survey of the problem, see Niels J. Anderson, S.J., "What's Killing Parish Missions?" *Pastoral Life* 12, no. 10 (Oct. 1964): 10–13.

137. Rian Clancy, C.P. to the editor, *Priest* 20, no. 2 (Feb. 1964): 169.

138. Donald F. Miller, C.SS.R., "Why Parish Missions Are Necessary," *Liguorian* 56, no. 6 (June 1968), 26.

139. Fr. Tom Clancy, S.J., "Preachers: Jesuits on the Mission Band," *Company: A Magazine of the American Jesuits* 15, no. 4 (Summer 1998), 21.

140. Richard A. Malloy, C.S.P., "A Kerygmatic Parish Mission," *Priest* 20, no. 10 (Oct. 1964): 862.

141. Clancy to the editor, *Priest.* See also Paul J. Frank, "New Format for the Parish Mission," *Pastoral Psychology* 14, no. 2 (Feb. 1966): 80.

142. Malloy, "Kerygmatic Parish Mission."

143. Archdiocese of Milwaukee, Catholic Family Life Program, "Newsnotes," 10, no. 4 (July 1965), 2.

144. See, for example, Milwaukee Archdiocesan Family Life Program, "Marriage Preparation Course," lecture 5, revised version, 1966, 8–9. AAM. Catholic Family Life Programs, box 1, folder 10, and "Pre-Cana Manual, Diocese of Lincoln," typescript, 30 Sept. 1965, 4a–4b. ACUA. Alphonse Clemens papers—81, box 2.

145. "Bernard" to Dr. Alphonse Clemens, 12 Nov. 1969. ACUA. Alphonse Clemens papers—81, box 1. Emphasis in original.

146. Author interview with Fr. Anthony Kosnik, 27 May 1998, in Detroit.

147. "Priest, Boston, Mass.," to the editor, *Jubilee* 12 (June 1964), 27.

148. Rev. Michael O'Leary, "Some Thoughts About the Oral-Steroid Pill," *Jubilee* 11, no. 11 (March 1964), 44–46; Joseph W. Oppitz, C.SS.R., "Marital Contraception: Licit?" *Priest* 21, no. 8 (Aug. 1965): 668–673.

149. William Allen, C.J.D., "Quid in Casu?" *Pastoral Life* 11, no. 12 (Dec. 1963): 48. The clerical questioner was not identified.

150. "Christian Marriage and Family Planning: Father John A. O'Brien Interviews Father Bernard Haring," in Donald N. Barrett, *The Problem of Population: Moral and Theological Considerations* (Notre Dame, IN: Notre Dame University Press, 1964), 18–19.

151. Fr. Edwin Faltaisek, S.J., transcript of a lecture to the students in moral theology at St. Mary's College, St. Mary's, KS, May 1965. NESJ. John C. Ford, S.J. papers, box 7 (preliminary cataloguing).

152. Joseph T. Mangan, "Questions on 'The Pill' and the Practice of Artificial Birth Control," *Chicago Studies* 5, no. 2 (Summer 1966): 198–199. This article reprints the "norms for confessors" given to newly ordained priests in April 1966.

153. Fr. Bernard Häring, C.SS.R., "Questions and Answers," in *The Priest: Teacher of Morality* (Detroit: Midwestern Institute of Pastoral Theology, 1965), 145.

154. N.N. to Cardinal Lawrence Shehan, 20 May 1966. AAB. Lawrence Shehan papers, uncatalogued.

155. Francis J. Connell, "Answers to Questions: Supremacy of Conscience," *American Ecclesiastical Review* 151, no. 5 (Nov. 1964): 344.

156. Faltaisek, lecture transcript.

157. Lawrence Shehan to "Reverend and Dear Father," 14 June 1965. AAB. Shehan papers, uncatalogued. See also, for the Diocese of Cleveland: Bp. Clarence G. Issermann to Bp. Alexander Zaleski, 28 Dec. 1966. ADL. Alexander Zaleski papers, folder "NCCB Committee on Doctrine: Bishops' Response to Cardinal Ottaviani's Letter, 1967"; for the Diocese of Joliet, see "Chancellor" to "Dear Fathers," 27 June 1968, which makes reference to Bp. Romeo Blanchette's 1965 instruction to his clergy. Also in Zaleski papers, folder "personal correspondence, 1968"; for the Diocese of Wilmington, see "Draft of Bishop Hyle's Statement," undated but ca. Mar. 1966. NESJ. John C. Ford, S.J. papers, box 9 (preliminary cataloguing); for the Archdiocese of Los Angeles, see National Catholic News Service press release, 26 June 1968. Copy in AAB. Lawrence Shehan papers, uncatalogued.

158. McCormick, *Notes on Moral Theology,* 168. McCormick was evincing great sympathy for the "probabilist" position even in 1966.

159. Bp. John Fearns to Bp. Alexander Zaleski, 24 July 1968. ADL. Alexander Zaleski papers, folder "NCCB Committee on Doctrine: Inquiry re Fr. Flynn's Statement on Fertility Control, May–July 1968."

160. N.N. to Cardinal Lawrence Shehan, 9 June 1966. AAB. Shehan papers, uncatalogued.

161. N.N. to Cardinal Lawrence Shehan, 19 June 1966. AAB. Shehan papers, uncatalogued.

162. When Cardinal Lawrence Shehan polled his priests in spring 1966, he seems to have received responses from the great majority. While some responses are hard to classify, close to 80 percent appear to have endorsed a change in the teaching on contraception.

163. N.N. to Cardinal Lawrence Shehan, 6 June 1966. AAB. Lawrence Shehan papers, uncatalogued. Emphasis in original. This particular correspondent does not fit the "conservative as older man" generalization, having been ordained in 1956.

164. Author interview with Fr. Louis Grandpre, 27 April 1999, in Clinton Township MI.

165. Author interview with Msgr. Dennis Harrity, 5 Nov. 1998, in St. Clair Shores MI. Msgr. Harrity was ordained for Detroit in 1960.

166. Author interview with Fr. William John Murphy, 16 April 1999, in Orchard Lake MI. Fr. Murphy was ordained in 1957.

167. Author interview with Fr. Ralph Kowalski, 26 June 1998 in Livonia MI. Kowalski was ordained for Detroit in 1942.

168. John C. Ford, "Commentary on 'The Projected Pastoral Instruction'," undated but 1965. NESJ. John C. Ford, S.J. papers, box 8 (preliminary cataloguing). Ford was commenting on a document submitted by a group from the papal commission to the Holy See proposing new norms for confessors with regard to birth control. The document was eventually rejected by Pope Paul VI.

169. Letter, signature deleted, to Pat and Patty Crowley, 15 Dec. 1965. AUND. Crowley papers—SPCBPC, box 15, folder 13.

170. Rev. Anthony Kosnik, *Penance* (Detroit: Archdiocese of Detroit, Institute of Continuing Education, 1969), 1.

171. Joseph M. Champlin, "Sex and Confession," part one, *Pastoral Life* 16, no. 5 (May 1968): 272.

172. Lawrence A. Castagnola, S.J., "Pastoral Reflections: Wanted: Confessors with Time," *Pastoral Life* 13, no. 12 (Dec. 1965): 687.

173. Author interview with Fr. Kevin O'Brien, 28 April 1999, in Farmington MI. O'Brien was ordained for Detroit in 1954.

174. Author interview with Fr. Jerome Krieg, 19 Jan. 1999, in Waterford MI.

175. McCarthy, "The Role of the Priest," 659.

176. "Thoughts of Dorothy & John Drish after the last Executive meeting," undated but ca. 1966. AAM. Catholic Family Life Program, box 8, folder 11.

177. Author interview with Fr. Francis Delaney, 24 April 1999, in Peabody MA. Delaney was ordained in 1952.

178. Marty, "What Went Wrong?" 51.

179. O'Neill, *Priest in Crisis,* 9.

180. Joseph A. Komonchak, "What They Said Before the Council: How the US Bishops Envisioned Vatican II," *Commonweal* 117, no. 21 (7 Dec. 1990), 714–717.

181. Rynne, *Vatican Council II,* 39.

182. "U.S. Bishop's Plea for Unity Is Hailed in Council," *New York Times,* 27 Nov. 1963, 2:3–6. Leven was an auxiliary bishop of San Antonio.

183. Author interview with Msgr. John Egan, 9 Sept. 1998, Chicago.

184. Egidio Vagnozzi to Most Rev. Patrick A. O'Boyle, 20 Feb. 1964. ACUA, NCWC papers, 10/86/5.

185. Egidio Vagnozzi to Most Rev. Patrick A. O'Boyle, 27 June 1964. ACUA, NCWC papers, 10/86/5. O'Boyle, archbishop of Washington DC, was chairman of the Administrative Committee of the NCWC.

186. John C. Ford, S.J., "Fourth Question: What Would Be the Doctrinal and Pastoral Tendencies in This Country?" typescript, undated but ca. March 1964, 1–3. ACUA, NCWC papers, 10/86/5.

187. Ibid., 12, 15, 7.

188. Ibid., 5–6, 9–10, 22, 23–24.

189. Ibid., 13, 15.

190. "Fifth Question: What Would Be the Viewpoint of the Bishops on This Whole Question?" typescript with penciled date 13 May 1964, 1–6, no author given. ACUA, NCWC papers, 10/86/5. Few of the quotes that appear in this document are identified as to author. For the views of Chicago's Cardinal Albert Meyer (yes to a statement, preferably by the Council), see Meyer to Archbishop Patrick O'Boyle, 16 April 1964. AAC. Albert Meyer papers, box 43827.01. For Baltimore's Lawrence Shehan (a statement now would be inopportune), see Shehan to O'Boyle, 28 April 1964. AAB. Lawrence Shehan papers, uncatalogued.

191. Author interview with Fr. Thomas McDevitt, 14 Dec. 1998, in East Lansing MI.

192. John C. Ford, S.J., ms. diary, spring/early summer 1964, entry for 29 May. NESJ. John C. Ford, S.J. papers, box 10 (preliminary cataloguing).

193. John C. Ford, S.J., ms. notes on "Interview with Card. Ottaviani, 3 June 1964." NESJ. John C. Ford, S.J. papers, box 10 (preliminary cataloguing).

194. Ford diary, entry for 6 June 1964.

195. Quoted in John C. Ford, S.J., "First Draft: Proposed Statement on Birth Control," typescript with penciled date 24 Aug. 1965, 6–7. ACUA, NCWC papers, 10/86/8.

196. John C. Ford, "Memorandum for Archbishop [Leo] Binz, 28 March 1965. NESJ. John C. Ford, S.J. papers, box 7 (preliminary cataloguing).

197. Ford, "First Draft: Proposed Statement on Birth Control," 1.

198. Archbishop Patrick O'Boyle to Egidio Vagnozzi, 18 April 1965. ACUA, NCWC papers, 10/86/9.

199. Cardinal John Dearden to Patrick O'Boyle, 27 Aug. 1965. ACUA, NCWC papers, 10/86/8.

200. Telegram, Bp. John Wright to Msgr. Paul Tanner, 31 Aug. 1965. ACUA, NCWC papers, 10/86/8.

201. John R. Sullivan, S.S. to Msgr. Paul Tanner, undated but Aug. 1965. ACUA, NCWC papers, 10/86/8.

202. Bp. Ernest Primeau to Archbishop Patrick O'Boyle, 1 Sept. 1965. ACUA, NCWC papers, 10/86/9.

203. John C. Ford, S.J. to Cardinal Amleto Cicognani, 2 Oct. 1965. NESJ. John C. Ford, S.J. papers, box 8 (preliminary cataloguing).

204. John C. Ford, S.J., "Excerpts from a letter written by Arthur W. Kane, S.J.," typescript dated 24 Aug. 1964. Kane is quoting Paul Quay, S.J., who was relaying gossip met with in France,

though the comments on Janssens are Kane's own. Ford subsequently sent the document to Archbishop John Dearden. AUND. John Dearden papers—CDRD, 6/14.

205. Unsigned carbon, probably from Msgr. Paul Tanner to Archbishop Patrick O'Boyle, 8 Sept. 1964 See also memo, Msgr. John Knott to Paul Tanner, 9 Sept. 1964. Both in ACUA, NCWC papers, 10/86/6.

206. John C. Ford, S.J. to Egidio Vagnozzi, 6 Nov. 1965. NESJ. John C. Ford, S.J. papers, box 8 (preliminary cataloguing).

207. John C. Ford, S.J., "First Audience with Pope, Monday Nov. 22," undated typescript. NESJ. John C. Ford, S.J. papers, box 9 (preliminary cataloguing).

208. Ford diary, entry for Friday, 26 Nov. 1965.

209. John C. Ford, S.J., "Notes on conversation with Pope Paul VI, " 22 Nov. 1965. NESJ. John C. Ford, S.J. papers, box 9 (preliminary cataloguing).

210. Ford, "First Audience with Pope."

211. Rynne, *Vatican Council II,* 554–555. Quote from 554.

212. Kaiser, *Politics of Sex and Religion,* 114–122.

213. Ford, "First Audience with Pope."

214. Rynne, *Vatican Council II,* 558.

215. Ibid., 563.

216. Ford diary, entry for Friday, 26 Nov. 1965.

217. Bernard Häring, *Free and Faithful: My Life in the Catholic Church* (Liguori, MO: Liguori/Triumph, 1998), 102.

218. Ford diary, entry for Friday, 26 Nov. 1965.

219. Germain Grisez (signed carbon copy) to Fr. Stanislaus de Lestapis, 21 Dec. 1965. NESJ. John C. Ford, S.J. papers, box 8 (preliminary cataloguing).

220. John C. Ford, "Memo to Bishop Tanner re Misleading press reports on Council's statements about birth control," 17 Dec. 1965. NESJ. John C. Ford, S.J. papers, box 7 (preliminary cataloguing).

221. Ford, "Memorandum for Archbishop Binz."

222. John C. Ford, S.J. to Archbishop Leo Binz, 11 Feb. 1966. See also, John C. Ford, "Interim Statement" of the same date. Both in NESJ. John C. Ford, S.J. papers, the letter in box 8, the statement in box 7 (preliminary cataloguing).

223. Author interview with Msgr. George Higgins, 9 April 1999, in Washington DC.

224. Quote from author interview with Fr. Ferdinand De Cneudt, 19 Oct. 1998, in Roseville MI.

225. Msgr. George A. Kelly, "A Summary of One Man's Opinion for the Pontifical Commission on Population and Birth Control," undated typescript, but ca. March 1965. NESJ. John C. Ford, S.J. papers, box 7 (preliminary cataloguing).

226. Sherzer to Valade, 21 Jan. 1967.

227. Donald T. Critchlow, *Intended Consequences: Birth Control, Abortion, and the Federal Government in Modern America* (New York: Oxford University Press, 1999), 53, 74–75, 77, 78.

228. Archbp. William Cousins to "Dear Monsignor/Father," 29 Nov. 1968. AAM. Chancery records—circular letters file.

229. Msgr. Paul Tanner to Msgr. Frank J. Rodimer, 10 March 1965. ACUA, NCWC papers, 10/86/7.

230. Memo, Msgr. Paul Tanner to Fr. John F. Cronin, 8 July 1965. ACUA, NCWC papers, 10/86/7.

231. Egidio Vagnozzi to Patrick O'Boyle, 9 Aug. 1965. ACUA, NCWC papers, 10/86/8. See also Vagnozzi to Msgr. Paul Tanner, 12 March 1964. ACUA, NCWC papers, 10/86/5.

232. Msgr. Francis Hurley to Msgr. Paul Tanner, 13 Aug. 1965. ACUA, NCWC papers, 10/86/8.

233. NCWC Administrative Board, minutes for the meeting of 12 Nov. 1966. ACUA. *Minutes of the Administrative Board, NCWC,* 27 April 1965–12 Nov. 1966.

234. Bp. Martin D. McNamara to Cardinal Albert Meyer, 5 Jan. 1965. AAC. Albert Meyer papers, box 43785.02, folder "CBC General Correspondence: Birth Control."

235. See, for example, Barrett, ed., *Problem of Population.*

236. Press release, Catholic Committee on Population and Government Policy [Notre Dame, IN], 10 May 1966.

237. Msgr. George A. Kelly to John C. Ford, S.J., undated but April 1965. NESJ. John C. Ford, S.J. papers, box 8 (preliminary cataloguing).

238. All quotes from "On the Government and Birth Control: Statement of the Administrative Board of the National Catholic Welfare Conference," 14 Nov. 1966. Copy in ACUA, NCWC papers, 10/86/10.

239. Quoted in Critchlow, *Intended Consequences,* 76.

240. NCWC Administrative Board, minutes for the meeting of 13 Nov. 1965. ACUA. *Minutes of the Administrative Board, NCWC,* 27 April 1965–12 Nov. 1966.

241. Ibid., 88.

242. Scripts for the four-part series are in ACUA. National Council of Catholic Men papers, 10/17.

243. "Cancel 'Church & Marriage' TV Series; May Run Later," *National Catholic Reporter,* 3 Jan. 1965, 1:3–6. The *NCR* named Spellman as the prime mover in the cancellation; Binz's involvement was necessitated by his being the bishop directly responsible for the work of the NCCM. Martin Work, the NCCM's executive director, noted in a private letter "that the National Catholic Reporter had pretty close to the full story." Work to Rev. William Nerin, 13 Jan. 1965. ACUA. National Council of Catholic Men papers, 10/18, folder "Letters re: 'The Church & Marriage' (TV), 1965."

244. Patrick O'Boyle to Egidio Vagnozzi, 4 Sept. 1965. ACUA, NCWC papers, 10/86/9.

245. Archbishop Patrick O'Boyle, "Birth Control and Public Policy," 29 August 1965. Copy in ACUA, NCWC papers, 10/86/7. The sermon was apparently drafted by the NCWC's Msgr. John Knott. It was subsequently published as a pamphlet.

246. Bp. John Wright to Bp. Alexander Zaleski, 27 July 1967. ADL. Alexander Zaleski papers, folder "Correspondence re Fr. Curran's Book."

247. Richard McCormick, S.J. to Bp. Alexander Zaleski, 27 July 1967. ADL. Alexander Zaleski papers, folder "Correspondence re Fr. Curran's Book."

248. C. Joseph Nuesse, *The Catholic University of America: A Centennial History* (Washington, DC: Catholic University of America Press, 1990), 399–401.

249. John C. Ford, S.J. to Bp. Alexander Zaleski, 27 Sept. 1967. ADL. Alexander Zaleski papers, folder "Correspondence re Fr. Curran's Book."

250. Kelly, "A Summary of One Man's Opinion," 8.

251. Greeley, "Is Catholic Sexual Teaching Coming Apart?," 35.

252. Bp. Kenneth Untener, "*Humanae Vitae:* What Has It Done to Us?" *Commonweal* 120 (18 June 1993), 13.

Epilogue

1. *Humanae Vitae: Encyclical Letter of His Holiness Pope Paul VI on the Regulation of Births.* I have used a translation from the original Italian by Marc Caligari, S.J., done in 1978. Found at http://www.cin.org/docs/humanvt.htm.

2. Ibid.

3. "Meeting with Chancellor of Catholic University and a Number of Members of the Faculty of the School of Sacred Theology, the Department of Religious Education and the School of Philosophy, 20 Aug. 1968." These minutes are a complete stenographic record. ADL. Alexander Zaleski papers, folders "CU Board of Trustees: Humanae Vitae Crisis; Meeting of Faculty & Chancellor."

4. Bernard Häring, "The Encyclical Crisis," in Daniel Callahan, ed., *The Catholic Case for*

Contraception (New York: Macmillan, 1969), 77. This is an abridged version of an essay that initially appeared in *Commonweal,* 6 Sept. 1968.

5. Avery Dulles, S.J., *"Humanae Vitae* and the Crisis of Dissent," *Origins* 22, no. 45 (April 1993): 775.

6. Joseph A. Komonchak, *"Humanae Vitae* and Its Reception: Ecclesiological Reflections," *Theological Studies* 39, no. 2 (June 1973): 224.

7. Bp. Alexander Zaleski to Fr. John H. Wright, S.J., 10 Oct. 1968. ADL. Alexander Zaleski papers, folder "NCCB Committee on Doctrine: General Correspondence, Nov. 1968–Dec. 1969."

8. Richard A. McCormick, S.J., "Moral Theology 1940–1989: An Overview," *Theological Studies* 50, no. 1 (March 1989): 12.

9. Robert Blair Kaiser, *The Politics of Sex and Religion: A Case History in the Development of Doctrine, 1962–1984* (Kansas City, MO: Leaven Press, 1985), 207.

10. Mrs. Richard T. Walter to Cardinal Shehan, 10 Sept. 1968. AAB. Shehan papers, uncatalogued.

11. Undated, but Nov. 1968, clipping from the *Washington Post.* GULSC. Joseph E. Jeffs Collection about 'Humanae Vitae,' uncatalogued. CUF was founded in Sept. 1968.

12. Figures quoted in Maurice J. Moore, "Death of a Dogma? The American Catholic Clergy's Views of Contraception" (Ph.D. dissertation, Department of Sociology, University of Chicago, 1972), 19.

13. Wilfrid Scanlon, "Orthodoxy? Anomie? Or Pluralism? An Empirical Sociological Analysis of Attitudes of the Catholic Laity in the Archdiocese of Boston toward Contraception" (Ph.D. dissertation, Boston University, 1975), 217.

14. Charles F. Westoff and Larry Bumpass, "The Revolution in Birth Control Practices of U.S. Roman Catholics," *Science* 179 (5 Jan. 1973): 41, 42.

15. "The Birth Control Encyclical," *Commonweal* 88, no. 18 (9 Aug. 1968), 515.

16. Charles and Jane Smith to Pat and Patty Crowley, 8 Oct. 1968. AUND. Crowley papers—SPCBPC, box 11, folder 10.

17. Cronan Regan, C.P., "Signpost," *Sign,* 48, no. 3 (Oct. 1968), 22.

18. Mr. and Mrs. N.N. to Cardinal Lawrence Shehan, 2 July 1971. AAB. Lawrence Shehan papers, uncatalogued.

19. "Catholic Parish Priests and Birth Control: A Comparative Study of Opinion in Columbia, the United States, and the Netherlands," *Studies in Family Planning* (New York: Population Council, June 1971), 132. No author given, although the various research collaborators are named in the introduction.

20. Author interview with Fr. Louis Grandpre, 27 April 1999, in Clinton Township MI.

21. Michael Novak, "Frequent, Even Daily, Communion" in Daniel Callahan, ed., *Catholic Case for Contraception,* 93.

22. A study done in 1969–70 found that 32 percent of diocesan priests regarded contraception as a matter best left to individual consciences; another 13 percent thought that the teaching was dubious and hence not binding on the faithful; an additional 4 percent thought that the use of some contraceptives was morally acceptable. The figures for priests in religious orders were similar. Andrew M. Greeley, *The Catholic Priest in the United States: Sociological Investigations* (Washington, DC: United States Catholic Conference, 1972)106.

23. Author interview with Fr. Andrew Nelson, 19 Nov. 1998, at St. Francis Seminary, Milwaukee.

24. Rev. Thomas F. Maher to Pat and Patty Crowley, 15 Oct. 1968. AUND. Crowley papers—SPCBPC, box 11, folder 12.

25. Greeley, *Catholic Priest in the United States,* 106.

26. Author interview with Fr. William Keveney, 3 Oct. 1998, in Eastpointe MI. Keveney was ordained in 1956.

27. Fr. James A. O'Donahue, who worked closely with Cushing with regard to the 1966 amendment of the Massachusetts anti-contraception law, was especially emphatic in this regard.

28. Author interview with Fr. Lawrence Jackson, 15 Oct. 1998, in Sterling Heights MI.

29. Author interview with Fr. John Blaska, 6 Nov. 1998, in Troy MI.

30. Bp. John Wright, untitled statement on *Humanae Vitae,* for release on 2 Aug. 1968. ADL. Alexander Zaleski papers, folder "NCCB Committee on Doctrine, Correspondence on H[umanae] V[itae]."

31. Kevin and Mary Catherine [no surname given] to Pat and Patty Crowley, 20 Oct. 1968. AUND. Crowley papers—SPCBPC, box 11, folder 12.

32. Bp. John Fearns to Bp. Alexander Zaleski, 7 Aug. 1968. ADL. Alexander Zaleski papers, folder "NCCB Committee on Doctrine, Correspondence on H[umanae] V[itae]."

33. "Statement of Bishop Robert E. Tracy of Baton Rouge on Pope Paul's Encyclical of Human Life," undated but ca. August 1968. AAB. Lawrence Shehan papers, uncatalogued. Cardinal Patrick O'Boyle to "Reverend and dear Father," 1 Aug. 1968 and "Pastoral Instruction to the Priests of the Archdiocese of Washington," 31 Aug. 1968. Both in AUND. John Dearden papers—CDRD, 34/12.

34. Cardinal Patrick O'Boyle, "The Catholic Conscience: An Instruction," 9 Oct. 1968. AUND. John Dearden papers—CDRD, 34/12.

35. Charles and Jane Smith to Pat and Patty Crowley.

36. Author interview with Fr. Philip Keane, 2 Feb. 1999, in Baltimore.

37. Joseph Gallagher, *The Pain and the Privilege: Diary of a City Priest* (Garden City, NY: Doubleday/Image, 1983), 241–243.

38. See his quite irenic letter to "My brother priests," 31 July 1968. AUND. Association of Chicago Priests' papers—CACP, 6/3.

39. Author interview with Fr. Thomas Ventura, 17 Nov. 1998, in Winnetka IL.

40. Bud and Mary Brennan to Pat and Patty Crowley, 26 Oct. 1968. AUND. Crowley papers—SPCBPC, box 11, folder 8.

41. W. Barry Smith, "*Humanae Vitae* in a Local Context: Events at a Diocesan Seminary," unpublished paper dated 27 March 1998.

42. Cardinal Patrick O'Boyle to "Dear friends in Christ," 2 Aug. 1968. AUND. John Dearden papers—CDRD, 34/12.

43. Michael J. O'Connor to Cardinal John Dearden, 1 April 1970. AUND. Association of Chicago Priests papers—CACP 9/64.

44. James Patrick Shannon, *Reluctant Dissenter: An Autobiography* (New York: Crossroad, 1998), 154. Shannon submitted his resignation to Archbishop Leo Binz in Nov. 1968, a fact that became public in June 1969. The proffered resignation languished at higher levels—neither accepted nor rejected—until Shannon married in August 1969 and ipso facto left the active priesthood. He died on 27 Aug. 2003, at the age of 82.

45. Msgr. Henry G. Burke to Cardinal John Dearden, 18 July 1969. AUND. John Dearden papers—CDRD, 35/13.

46. Rev. John Reidy, C.S.C. to Cardinal John Dearden, 17 June 1969. AUND. Dearden papers—CDRD, 35/13.

47. Richard A. McCormick, S.J., "Flaws Mar Pastoral Comments on Contraception, Dissent According to Jesuit Theologian," undated clipping from the *New World,* the newspaper of the Archdiocese of Chicago. ADL. Alexander Zaleski papers, folder "NCCB Committee on Doctrine: General Correspondence, Nov. 1968–Dec. 1969."

48. Richard McCormick, S.J. to Bp. Alexander Zaleski, 22 March 1969. ADL. Alexander Zaleski papers, folder "NCCB Committee on Doctrine: General Correspondence, Nov. 1968–Nov. 1969."

49. Author interview with Fr. Anthony Kosnik, 27 May 1998, in Detroit.

50. Msgr. Dennis Harrity (Detroit), Fr. Leo Mahan (Chicago), and Bp. Kenneth Untener (Saginaw) all mentioned the form, which they had seen, in my interviews with them. See also Richard A. McCormick, S.J., "'Humanae Vitae' 25 Years Later," *America* 169, no. 2 (17 July 1993), 8 and Dulles, "'Humanae Vitae' and the Crisis of Dissent," 776.

51. Greeley, *Catholic Priest in the United States,* 110, 111.

52. Rev. Joseph Byron to His Holiness, Pope Paul VI, 11 Feb. 1970. Copy in AUND. Association of Chicago Priests' papers—CACP, 8/30.

53. "Vatican Findings on Washington '19'," *Catholic Mind* 69 (Dec. 1971): 5–9.

54. Quoted in Francis E. Brown, *Priests in Council: A History of the National Federation of Priests' Councils* (Kansas City, MO: Andrews and McMeel, 1979), 31.

55. John Dedek, *Contemporary Sexual Morality* (New York: Sheed and Ward, 1971), 92.

56. Rev. Joseph Byron to Rev. Raymond Goedert, 9 Feb. 1970. AUND. Association of Chicago Priests' papers—CACP, 8/30.

57. "Confidential Memorandum re Meeting of Bishops and Theologians," unsigned (but by Bp. Joseph Bernardin) and undated, but ca. Aug. 1968. ADL. Alexander Zaleski papers, folder "NCCB Committee on Doctrine, Correspondence on H[umanae] V[itae]." Emphasis in original.

58. Richard A. McCormick, "The Silence Since 'Humanae Vitae'," *America* 129, no. 2 (21 July 1973), 32. Emphasis in original.

59. Dean R. Hoge et al., *Young Adult Catholics: Religion in the Culture of Choice* (Notre Dame, IN: University of Notre Dame Press, 2001), 36–37.

60. William V. D'Antonio et al., *American Catholics: Gender, Generation, and Commitment* (Walnut Creek, CA: AltaMira Press, 2001), 76, 78–79, 80, 82.

61. Ibid., 52–53. The decline has been steady since the Council.

62. Andrew Greeley, "Is Catholic Sexual Teaching Coming Apart?" *Critic* 30, no. 4 (March–April 1972): 33.

63. Jackson interview.

64. Author interview with Fr. Thomas McDevitt, 14 Dec. 1998, in East Lansing MI.

65. Keane interview.

66. Author interview with Msgr. William Sherzer, 18 October 1998, in Ann Arbor MI.

67. McCormick, "The Silence Since 'Humanae Vitae'," 32.

68. Dulles, "'Humanae Vitae' and the Crisis of Dissent," 776.

69. (Rev.) Gerard S. Sloyan, *Catholic Morality Revisited: Origins and Contemporary Challenges* (Mystic, CT: Twenty-Third Publications, 1990), 100.

70. Bp. Kenneth Untener, "*Humanae Vitae:* What Has It Done to Us?" *Commonweal* 120 (18 June 1993), 13.

71. Quoted in McCormick, "'Humanae Vitae' 25 Years Later," 8.

Index